AN EXEGETICAL SUMMARY OF
1, 2, and 3 JOHN

AN EXEGETICAL SUMMARY OF
1, 2, and 3 JOHN

Second Edition

John L. Anderson

SIL International

Second Edition
© 1992, 2008 by SIL International

Library of Congress Catalog Card Number: 2008923523
ISBN: 978-155671-197-8

Printed in the United States of America

All Rights Reserved
No part of this publication may be reproduced, stored in a retrieval system, or transmitted in any form or by any means without the express permission of SIL International. However, brief excerpts, generally understood to be within the limits of fair use, may be quoted without written permission.

Copies of this and other publications
of SIL International may be obtained from

International Academic Bookstore
SIL International
7500 West Camp Wisdom Road
Dallas, TX 75236-5699, USA

Voice: 972-708-7404
Fax: 972-708-7363
academic_books@sil.org
www.ethnologue.com

PREFACE

Exegesis is concerned with the interpretation of a text. Exegesis of the New Testament involves determining the meaning of the Greek text. Translators must be especially careful and thorough in their exegesis of the New Testament in order to accurately communicate its message in the vocabulary, grammar, and literary devices of another language. Questions occurring to translators as they study the Greek text are answered by summarizing how scholars have interpreted the text. This is information that should be considered by translators as they make their own exegetical decisions regarding the message they will communicate in their translations.

The Semi-Literal Translation

As a basis for discussion, a semi-literal translation of the Greek text is given so that the reasons for different interpretations can best be seen. When one Greek word is translated into English by several words, these words are joined by hyphens. There are a few times when clarity requires that a string of words joined by hyphens have a separate word, such as "not" (μή), inserted in their midst. In this case, the separate word is surrounded by spaces between the hyphens. When alternate translations of a Greek word are given, these are separated by slashes.

The Text

Variations in the Greek text are noted under the heading TEXT. The base text for the summary is the text of the fourth revised edition of *The Greek New Testament,* published by the United Bible Societies, which has the same text as the twenty-sixth edition of the *Novum Testamentum Graece* (Nestle-Aland). The versions that follow different variations are listed without evaluating their choices.

The Lexicon

The meaning of a key word in context is the first question to be answered. Words marked with a raised letter in the semi-literal translation are treated separately under the heading LEXICON. First, the lexicon form of the Greek word is given. Within the parentheses following the Greek word is the location number where, in the author's judgment, this word is defined in the *Greek-English Lexicon of the New Testament Based on Semantic Domains* (Louw and Nida 1988). When a semantic domain includes a translation of the particular verse being treated, **LN** in bold type indicates that specific translation. If the specific reference for the verse is listed in *A Greek-English Lexicon of the New Testament and Other Early Christian Literature* (Bauer, Arndt, Gingrich, and Danker 1979), the outline location and page number is given. Then English equivalents of the Greek word are given to show how it is translated by commentators who offer their own translations of the whole text and, after a semicolon, all the versions in the list of abbreviations for translations. When reference is made to "all versions," it refers to only the versions in the list of translations. Sometimes further comments are made about the meaning of the word or the significance of a verb's tense, voice, or mood.

The Questions

Under the heading QUESTION, a question is asked that comes from examining the Greek text under consideration. Typical questions concern the identity of an implied actor or object of an event word, the antecedent of a pronominal reference, the connection indicated by a relational word, the meaning of a genitive construction, the meaning of figurative language, the function of a rhetorical question, the identification of an ambiguity, and the presence of implied information that is needed to understand the passage correctly. Background information is also considered for a proper understanding of a passage. Although not all implied information and background information is made explicit in a translation, it is important to consider it so that the translation will not be stated in such a way that prevents a reader from arriving at the proper interpretation. The question is answered with a summary of what commentators have said. If there are contrasting differences of opinion, the different interpretations are numbered and the commentaries that support each are listed. Differences that are not treated by many of the commentaries often are not numbered, but are introduced with a contrastive 'Or' at the beginning of the sentence. No attempt has been made to select which interpretation is best.

In listing support for various statements of interpretation, the author is often faced with the difficult task of matching the different terminologies used in commentaries with the terminology he has adopted. Sometimes he can only infer the position of a commentary from incidental remarks. This book, then, includes the author's interpretation of the views taken in the various commentaries. General statements are followed by specific statements, which indicate the author's understanding of the pertinent relationships, actors, events, and objects implied by that interpretation.

The Use of This Book

This book does not replace the commentaries that it summarizes. Commentaries contain much more information about the meaning of words and passages. They often contain arguments for the interpretations that are taken and they may have important discussions about the discourse features of the text. In addition, they have information about the historical, geographical, and cultural setting. Translators will want to refer to at least four commentaries as they exegete a passage. However, since no one commentary contains all the answers translators need, this book will be a valuable supplement. It makes more sources of exegetical help available than most translators have access to. Even if they had all the books available, few would have the time to search through all of them for the answers.

When many commentaries are studied, it soon becomes apparent that they frequently disagree in their interpretations. That is the reason why so many answers in this book are divided into two or more interpretations. The reader's initial reaction may be that all of these different interpretations complicate exegesis rather than help it. However, before translating a passage, a translator needs to know exactly where there is a problem of interpretation and what the exegetical options are.

Acknowledgments

This volume has been thoroughly reviewed by Richard C. Blight. He has studied the questions and answers and has made a significant contribution in determining their final forms. James Mignard and Gerald E. Montgomery have reviewed and commented on the manuscript.

ABBREVIATIONS

COMMENTARIES AND REFERENCE BOOKS

AB   Brown, Raymond E. *The Epistles of John*. The Anchor Bible, edited by W. F. Albright and D. N. Freedman. Garden City: Doubleday, 1982.

Alf   Alford, Henry. *Alford's Greek Testament*. Vol. 4. 1857. Reprint. Grand Rapids: Baker, 1980.

BAGD   Bauer, Walter. *A Greek-English Lexicon of the New Testament and Other Early Christian Literature*. Translated and adapted from the 5th ed., 1958 by William F. Arndt and F. Wilbur Gingrich. 2d English ed. revised and augmented by F. Wilbur Gingrich and Frederick W. Danker. Chicago: University of Chicago Press, 1979.

Br   Bruce, F. F. *The Epistles of John*. Grand Rapids: Eerdmans, 1970.

Brd   Burdick, Donald W. *The Letters of John the Apostle*. Chicago: Moody, 1985.

EBC   Barker, Glenn W. *1, 2, 3 John*. In *The Expositor's Bible Commentary*, edited by Frank E. Gaebelein, vol. 12. Grand Rapids: Zondervan, 1981.

EGT   Smith, David. *The Epistles of John*. In *The Expositor's Greek Testament*, edited by W. Robertson Nicoll, vol. 5. London: Hodder and Stoughton, n.d.

Herm   Bultmann, Rudolf. *The Johannine Epistles*. 2nd ed., 1967. Translated by R. Philip O'Hara, Lane C. McGaughy and Robert W. Funk. Hermeneia—A Critical and Historical Commentary on the Bible, edited by Robert W. Funk. Philadelphia: Fortress Press, 1973.

HNTC   Houlden, J. L. *A Commentary on the Johannine Epistles*. Harper's New Testament Commentaries, edited by Henry Chadwick. New York: Harper & Row, 1973.

ICC   Brooke, A. E. *A Critical and Exegetical Commentary on the Johannine Epistles*. The International Critical Commentary, edited by S. R. Driver, A. Plummer, and C. A. Briggs. Edinburgh: T. & T. Clark, 1912.

LN   Louw, Johannes P. and Eugene A. Nida. *Greek-English Lexicon of the New Testament Based on Semantic Domains*. New York: United Bible Societies, 1988.

Lns   Lenski, R. C. H. *The Interpretation of the Epistles of St. Peter, St. John and St. Jude*. Minneapolis: Augsburg, 1966.

My   Huther, Joh. Ed. *Critical and Exegetical Handbook to the General Epistles of James, Peter, John, and Jude*. Translated from the 3rd. ed. by Paton J. Gloag, D. B. Croom, and Clarke H. Irwin. Meyer's Commentary on the New Testament. New York: Funk & Wagnalls, 1887.

NCBC	Grayston, Kenneth. *The Johannine Epistles*. New Century Bible Commentary, edited by M. Black. Grand Rapids: Eerdmans, 1984.
NIC	Marshall, I. Howard. *The Epistles of John*. The New International Commentary on the New Testament, edited by F. F. Bruce. Grand Rapids: Eerdmans, 1978.
NTC	Kistemaker, Simon J. *Exposition of the Epistle of James and the Epistles of John*. New Testament Commentary. Grand Rapids: Baker, 1986.
TH	Haas, C., M. de Jonge, and J. L. Swellengrebel. *A Translator's Handbook on the Letters of John*. New York: United Bible Societies, 1972.
TNTC	Stott, J. R. W. *The Epistles of John*. The Tyndale New Testament Commentaries, edited by R. V. G. Tasker. Grand Rapids: Eerdmans, 1964.
WBC	Smalley, Stephen S. *1, 2, 3 John*. Word Biblical Commentary, edited by R. P. Martin, vol. 51. Waco, Texas: Word, 1984.
Ws	Westcott, Brooke Foss. *The Epistles of John*. 1966. Reprint. Grand Rapids: Eerdmans, 1971.

GREEK TEXT AND TRANSLATIONS

GNT	Aland, Kurt, Matthew Black, Carlos Martini, Bruce Metzger, and Allen Wikgren. *The Greek New Testament*. 3d ed. (corrected). London, New York: United Bible Societies, 1983.
KJV	*The Holy Bible*. Authorized (or King James) Version. 1611.
NAB	*The New American Bible*. Camden, New Jersey: Thomas Nelson, 1971.
NASB	*The New American Standard Bible*. 1977. Nashville, Tennessee: Holman.
NIV	*The Holy Bible: New International Version*. Grand Rapids: Zondervan, 1978.
NJB	*The New Jerusalem Bible*. Garden City, New York: Doubleday, 1985.
NRSV	*The Holy Bible: New Revised Standard Version*. New York: Oxford University Press, 1989.
REB	*The Revised English Bible*. Oxford: Oxford University Press and Cambridge University Press, 1989.
TEV	*Holy Bible: Today's English Version*. New York: American Bible Society, 1976.
TNT	*The Translator's New Testament*. London: British and Foreign Bible Society, 1973.

GRAMMATICAL TERMS

act.	active
fut.	future
impera.	imperative
indic.	indicative
infin.	infinitive
mid.	middle
opt.	optative
pass.	passive
perf.	perfect
pres.	present
subj.	subjunctive

EXEGETICAL SUMMARY OF 1 JOHN

Title: The First of John
TEXT—The original letter did not have a title, but all copies of the Greek text do now [Herm]. Instead of Ἰωάννου α 'the first of John' [GNT], some manuscripts have Ἰωάννου ἐπιστολή α 'the first epistle of John.'
QUESTION—Who wrote this letter?
The text itself does not state the writer's name. Many commentators note the similarities of structures, word choices, and topics between the Gospel of John, 1 John, 2 John, and 3 John. Some think that the writer of 1 John is the same person who wrote 2 John, and 3 John [Alf, Br, Brd, EGT, ICC, Lns, NIC, TNTC] and was known as ὁ πρεσβύτερος 'the Elder' (2 John 1 and 3 John 1). Others think that the same person was not the author of all these writings [AB, Herm, HNTC, My, NCBC]. Most think that the writer was the Apostle John, who was also known as 'the Elder' [Alf, Br, Brd, EBC, EGT, Lns, My, TNTC, Ws]. Some think that the writer was not the Apostle John [AB, Herm, HNTC, ICC, NCBC, WBC], but may have been a follower of the Apostle [AB, WBC], or someone influenced by the Gospel of John [Herm].

DISCOURSE UNIT: 1:1–4 [AB, Alf, Br, Brd, EBC, EGT, Herm, HNTC, ICC, Lns, My, NIC, NTC, TH, TNTC, WBC, Ws; NAB, NASB, NIV, NJB, TEV]. The topic is the preface [EGT, TH, TNTC, WBC], prologue [AB, Br, HNTC, NIC; NAB], introduction [Alf, Brd, Herm, HNTC, ICC, My, TH, Ws], theme [Lns], the word of life [NIC, NTC, TH, WBC; NIV, TEV], the reality of the incarnation [Brd], the incarnate word [NJB], life in the Son [NCBC], the incarnate Word and sharing with the Father and Son [NJB], the fellowship which brings joy [Ws]. 1:1–4 constitutes one long sentence in Greek. Because of the parenthetical remark in 1:2, the first main verb is ἀπαγγέλλομεν 'we announce' in 1:3. Some translate 1:1 as a complete sentence by supplying the main verb from 1:3 [AB; NAB, NIV, NRSV, TNT]: we announce what was from the beginning, etc. Another translation supplies the verb γράφομεν 'we write' from 1:4 [TEV]: we write about the Word of life, which is from the beginning, etc. Another method is to make the verse complete by supplying a copulative verb [REB]: it was there from the beginning; we have heard it, etc.

1:1 What[a] was[b] from[c] (the) beginning,[d]
LEXICON—a. ὅ (neuter) (LN 92.27): 'what' [AB, WBC; NAB, NASB, NRSV, TNT], 'that which' [HNTC, Lns; KJV, NIV], 'it' [REB], 'something which' [NJB], 'which' [TEV].
  b. imperf. act. indic. of εἰμί (LN 13.69): 'to be' [AB, HNTC, LN, Lns; all versions except NJB, REB, TEV], 'to be there' [WBC; REB], 'to exist' [HNTC, LN; NJB, TEV].
  c. ἀπό with genitive object (LN 67.131): 'from' [AB, HNTC, LN, Lns, WBC; all versions except NJB], 'since' [LN; NJB].

d. ἀρχή (LN 67.65) (BAGD 1.c. p. 112): 'the beginning' [AB, BAGD, HNTC, LN, Lns, WBC; all versions except TEV], 'the very beginning' [TEV].

QUESTION—What do the four occurrences of the neuter relative pronoun ὅ 'what' in this verse and the one occurrence of this pronoun in 1:3 refer to?

In 1:3, ὅ 'what' seems to simply refer to the content of the message the writer announces, that is, 'we announce what we have seen and heard' [Brd, WBC, Ws]. However, in addition to talking about what they have seen and heard, the writer talks about 'what' was from the beginning and 'what' they touched. All these pronouns are concerned with the 'word of life' (the last phrase in 1:1), and this 'word' may refer to the 'message' about Jesus or to Jesus himself as the personal 'Word' of God (as in John 1:1). In 1:5 the writer talks about ἡ ἀγγελία 'the message' he heard from Christ and announces to the readers. Since ὅ 'what' is neuter, it does not appear to merely refer to the person of the Son of God (who is masculine), nor to either λόγου 'word' (a masculine noun), or ζωῆς 'life' (a feminine noun) at the end of 1:1, nor to ἀγγελία 'message' (a feminine noun) in 1:5.

Most commentators think that instead of ὅ 'what' referring to any specific noun, it has a more complex reference. It does not refer to Jesus directly, but to that which the writer declares about Jesus [Brd]. It refers to the person, words, and acts of Jesus [AB, Brd, ICC], to both the gospel message and the person of Jesus [Herm, NIC, NTC], to the gospel message about Jesus [WBC, Ws], to the content of ἡ ἀγγελία 'the message' (1:5) which is identical with the person of Jesus [Herm], to Jesus and all that he is and does for us [Lns], to Jesus as the Word and the life he manifested [EGT], the content of the Christian doctrine [HNTC]. Another thinks that it refers specifically to the Word, but the neuter form suggests that the Word cannot be adequately described in human language [TH].

QUESTION—To what does ἀρχῆς 'beginning' refer?
1. It is used in an absolute sense of eternity past [Alf, Brd, EBC, NIC, NTC, WBC, Ws]: what/who always existed. When this is taken to refer primarily to the person of Jesus, it suggests his eternal preexistent nature [Alf, Brd, NTC]. When it is taken to refer primarily to the gospel message, it refers to the fact that the message has its source in God and therefore precedes creation [EBC], it was the eternal purpose of God [Ws], and that it was true from eternity and was disclosed and experienced in history [WBC].
2. It refers to the creation of the world [EGT, ICC, Lns, TH, TNTC]: what/who was from the beginning of the world. When this is taken to refer primarily to the person of Jesus, it means that the Word already existed when time began [EGT, Lns]. When it is taken to refer primarily to the gospel message, it means that the revelation about life began at the time of creation [ICC].
3. It refers to Christ's earthly ministry [AB, Br, Herm, My]: what/who was from the beginning of Christ's ministry. When this is taken to refer

primarily to the person of Jesus, it refers to Jesus' public ministry when he revealed himself to his disciples after his baptism [AB]. When it is taken to refer primarily to the gospel message, it refers to the saving events witnessed by the disciples [Br].
4. It refers to the original message of the gospel [HNTC, NCBC]: what has been proclaimed from the beginning. This is the message Christians have had from the start [NCBC].

what we-have-heard,[a] what we-have-seen[b] with-our eyes,
LEXICON—a. perf. act. indic. of ἀκούω (LN 24.52) (BAGD 1.b.α. p. 32): 'to hear' [AB, BAGD, HNTC, LN, Lns, WBC; all versions]. The perfect tense here and in the following verb indicate that the effects and memory of the hearing and seeing continue on to the time of the writing [Alf, Brd, ICC, Lns, TH, TNTC, WBC].
   b. perf. act. indic. of ὁράω (LN 24.1) (BAGD 1.a.β. p. 578): 'to see' [AB, BAGD, HNTC, LN, Lns, WBC; all versions].
QUESTION—To whom do the references to the first person plural form ('we') of the verbs in 1:1–3 refer?
'We' refers to the writer and other eye witnesses of Jesus' ministry [Br, Brd, EBC, HNTC, ICC, Lns, My, TH, TNTC, Ws]: what we (exclusive) have heard, etc., we announce to you. Some include all the disciples who personally heard and saw Jesus [Br, ICC, TH]. Some think it refers specifically to the apostles [Brd, Lns, My, Ws].
QUESTION—Why is the phrase τοῖς ὀφθαλμοῖς ἡμῶν 'with our eyes' included?
'With our eyes' is added to 'we have seen' for emphasis [ICC, NTC, TH] and makes clear the literalness of the seeing [Brd, Herm, ICC]. Some translations emphasize this personal witness [AB, HNTC; NAB, NJB, TNT]: what we have seen with our *own* eyes.

what we-looked-at[a] and our hands touched,[b]
LEXICON—a. aorist mid. (deponent = act.) indic. of θεάομαι (LN 24.14) (BAGD 1.a. p. 353): 'to look at' [AB, BAGD, LN; NIV, NRSV, TNT], 'to observe' [LN, WBC], 'to look upon' [KJV, NAB, REB], 'to watch' [NJB], 'to behold' [BAGD, Lns; NASB], 'to gaze upon' [HNTC], 'to see' [BAGD; TEV].
   b. aorist act. indic. of ψηλαφάω (LN **24.76**) (BAGD p. 892): 'to touch' [BAGD, LN; NAB, NIV, NJB, NRSV, TEV], 'to feel' [AB, BAGD, HNTC, LN, WBC; REB, TNT], 'to handle' [BAGD, **LN**, Lns; KJV, NASB].

QUESTION—What is indicated by the change from the perfect tense in the preceding verbs ἀκηκόαμεν…ἑωράκαμεν 'we have heard…we have seen' to the aorist tense of the verbs ἐθεασάμεθα…ἐψηλάφησαν 'we looked at…(our hands) touched'?

1. A change from the perfect tense to the aorist tense marks a change of focus from the continuing effect to the historical event [Alf, Brd, ICC, Lns, TNTC, Ws].
2. The change from the perfect tense to the aorist tense is stylistic and carries no significant meaning [AB, Herm, TH, WBC].

QUESTION—How does ἐθεασάμεθα 'we looked at' differ from the preceding verb ἑωράκαμεν 'we have seen'?

1. There is a difference in meaning [Br, Brd, ICC, LN, Lns, TNTC; probably all versions except TEV]. This verb refers to seeing with attention and careful examination [LN, Lns]. It implies that there is something unusual in what is seen [LN]. The preceding verb refers to physical sight, while this verb refers to understanding the significance of what was seen [Br, Brd, ICC, Lns, TNTC]. Christ's inward glory was discerned [Br].
2. There is no significant difference; this is a repetition of synonymous verbs for stylistic, not semantic reasons [AB, TH, WBC; TEV]: what we have seen.

QUESTION—Why are the hands mentioned?

The reference to feeling with their hands is used here to stress the physical reality of Christ's body [AB, Alf, Br, Brd, Herm, HNTC, ICC, NCBC, TH, Ws]. Some commentators see in it a reference to Jesus' post-resurrection invitation to touch his resurrected body [AB, Br, HNTC, NTC, TH, Ws].

concerning[a] the word[b] of-life[c]

LEXICON—a. περί with genitive object (LN 89.6): 'concerning' [HNTC, LN, Lns; NASB, NIV, NRSV], 'of' [KJV]. This preposition is also translated as a phrase: 'our concern is' [AB], 'our theme is' [NJB, REB, TNT], 'our subject is' [WBC], 'we speak of' [NAB], 'we write about' [TEV].

b. λόγος (LN 33.98, 33.260, 33.100) (BAGD 3. p. 479): 'word' [AB, HNTC, WBC; NAB, NRSV, TNT], 'Word' [BAGD; KJV, NASB, NIV, NJB, REB, TEV], 'Logos' [Lns].

c. ζωή (LN 23.88) (BAGD 2.a.β. p. 340): 'life' [AB, BAGD, HNTC, LN, WBC; all versions except NASB], 'Life' [Lns; NASB].

QUESTION—What relationship is indicated by περί 'concerning'?

This indicates a clarification or identification of the topic of the preceding four 'what' clauses [AB, Br, Herm, HNTC, ICC, Lns, My, WBC, Ws]: what was from the beginning, what we have heard, what we have seen, what we looked at and touched, i.e., the things that concern the word of life.

1 JOHN 1:1

QUESTION—What is the meaning of τοῦ λόγου 'the word' and how is it related to life in the genitive construction τοῦ λόγου τῆς ζωῆς 'the word of life'?

1. 'Word' is a title that refers to Jesus [Alf, BAGD, Brd, EGT, Lns, My, NTC, TH; probably KJV, NASB, NIV, NJB, REB, TEV]: it concerns him who is the Word of life. 'Word' has the same meaning as 'Word' in the Gospel of John (John 1:1) [Brd, Herm, NTC, TH].
    1.1 'Life' is in apposition to 'Word' and both are titles of Jesus [Alf, Brd, Lns, TH]: it concerns the Word, who is Life.
    1.2 The 'Word' produces life [EGT, My, NTC, TH; REB]: it concerns the Word who gives life. The Word has life in himself and is the source of life [My, NTC].
2. 'Word' is impersonal and means 'a message' [AB, Br, EBC, HNTC, ICC, NCBC, NIC, TNTC, Ws]: it concerns the message of life.
    2.1 'Life' is a title for Jesus [Br; NASB]: it concerns the message about him who is Life.
    2.2 The message is about life [AB, HNTC, TNTC, WBC; NAB, NRSV, TNT]: it concerns the message about spiritual life. It tells about and offers life [TNTC].
    2.3 The message produces life [NCBC]: it concerns the message which imparts life.

1:2 —and

LEXICON—καί (LN 89.93): 'and' [HNTC, Lns; NASB], 'for' [AB; KJV], parentheses [AB; KJV, NAB], not explicit [WBC; NIV, NJB, NRSV, REB, TEV, TNT].

QUESTION—How is this verse related to its context?

This verse is a parenthetical comment [AB, Alf, Brd, EBC, EGT, Herm, ICC, Lns, My, NCBC, NIC, NTC, TH, TNTC, WBC, Ws; KJV, NAB, NASB, NRSV]. It is an extended comment about the immediately preceding word ζωῆς 'life' [AB, My, NCBC, NTC, TH, Ws]. The article in ἡ ζωή 'the life' refers to the previously mentioned noun τῆς ζωῆς 'the life' (1:1) [AB, Lns]. This explains more fully what had been witnessed in 1:1 and how it had been witnessed [Brd].

the life[a] was-made-visible,[b]

LEXICON—a. ζωή: 'life'. See this word at 1:1.
   b. aorist pass. indic. of φανερόω (LN 24.19) (BAGD 2.b.β. p. 853): 'to be made visible' [LN; NJB, REB], 'to be revealed' [AB, BAGD, HNTC, WBC; NRSV, TNT], 'to be manifested' [Lns; KJV, NASB], 'to become visible' [NAB, TEV], 'to appear' [BAGD; NIV]. The aorist tense views the action as a whole and covers all of Christ's life on earth [Brd, Lns].

QUESTION—In what way was the life made visible?

Some consider 'life' to be a title for Jesus, who became visible at his incarnation and remained so during his ministry [Alf, Brd, Herm, Lns, TH, TNTC]. He was specifically manifested to the disciples from the time he was baptized to the time he ascended to heaven [Lns]. Others who take 'life' to be the spiritual life possessed by Jesus and imparted by him think that this life became known in the person of Jesus when he was on earth [EBC, ICC, NIC, WBC, Ws]. Life is one aspect of Jesus' being, and by looking at him one sees the embodied ideal of life [Ws]. He made the concept of spiritual life understandable [ICC].

and we-have-seen[a] and we-testify[b] and we-announce[c] to-you (plural) the eternal[d] life,[e]

LEXICON—a. perf. act. indic. of ὁράω: 'to see'. See this word at 1:1.
- b. pres. act. indic. of μαρτυρέω (LN 33.262) (BAGD 1.b. p. 493): 'to testify' [AB, HNTC; NIV, NRSV], 'to witness' [LN], 'to bear witness' [BAGD, WBC; KJV, NAB, NASB, TNT], 'to bear testimony' [Lns], 'to give one's testimony' [NJB, REB], 'to speak of' [TEV]. The present tense is used here and with the following verb because the author is still testifying and announcing [Brd, TH]. Even though the other apostles had died, their testimony continued on [Lns]. This is the result of having seen the life [TH; TEV]: we have seen the eternal life and therefore we testify about it and announce it to you. These actions are not limited to this letter, but they refer to a general declaration in speech and writing [Alf, Brd, Lns], to the whole apostolic ministry [Ws].
- c. pres. act. indic. of ἀπαγγέλλω (LN 33.198) (BAGD 2. p. 79): 'to announce' [HNTC], 'to proclaim' [AB, BAGD, WBC; NAB, NASB, NIV], 'to declare' [Lns; NJB, NRSV, REB, TNT], 'to show' [KJV], 'to tell about' [LN; TEV], 'to proclaim' [AB].
- d. αἰώνιος (LN 67.96) (BAGD 3. p. 28): 'eternal' [AB, BAGD, HNTC, LN, Lns, WBC; all versions].
- e. ζωή (LN 23.88) (BAGD 2.b.α. p. 341): 'life' [AB, BAGD, HNTC, LN, Lns, WBC; all versions].

QUESTION—How does μαρτυροῦμεν 'we testify' differ from ἀπαγγέλομεν 'we announce'?
1. The two verbs are semantically equivalent and refer to the same act [Lns, TH]: we proclaim to you.
2. Μαρτυροῦμεν 'we are testifying' is the means by which ἀπαγγέλλομεν 'we are announcing' is accomplished [NIC]: by testifying, we announce to you.
3. Μαρτυροῦμεν 'we are testifying' refers to personal witness, while ἀπαγγέλλομεν 'we are announcing' refers to public proclamation [EBC, TNTC, WBC]: what we privately testify and what we publicly announce.

which was[a] with[b] the Father and was-made-visible[c] to-us—

LEXICON—a. imperf. act. indic. of εἰμί (LN 13.69): 'to be' [AB, HNTC, LN, Lns; all versions], 'to exist' [LN, WBC]. The imperfect tense indicates continuous existence [Ws].

b. πρός with accusative object (LN 89.112) (BAGD III.7. p. 711): 'with' [HNTC, LN, Lns, WBC; all versions except NAB, NJB], 'near' [BAGD], '(was) present to' [NAB, NJB], 'in the presence of' [AB].
c. aorist. pass. indic. of φανερόω: 'to be made visible'. See this word in the first phrase of this verse.

QUESTION—In what way was the life with the Father?
1. When 'Life' is considered to be a title of Christ, this refers to the pre-incarnation existence of Christ with God the Father [AB, Brd, Lns, NTC, TNTC, WBC]: he who is Life was with the Father. 'With' indicates fellowship and oneness with the Father [Alf, Brd, ICC, Lns, My, TH]. Life is personified in the Son [NTC].
2. When 'life' is considered to be spiritual life, 'with' refers to close association [ICC, TH]: life is associated with God. 'With' indicates that God is the ultimate source of life [WBC]. The Son's true life was realized in union and communion with the Father [ICC].

QUESTION—Does 'Father' refer to God's relationship to believers or to the special relationship with God's Son in the Trinity?
The term 'Father' is being used here for God since He is Father of all believers [TH]: the life was with our (inclusive) Father.

QUESTION—Why is ἐφανερώθη 'was made visible' repeated from the first clause of this verse?
The repetition makes this fact prominent [Brd], and expands on the first statement by adding that it was made visible *to us*, stressing the personal involvement of the witnesses [WBC].

1:3 what^a we-have-seen^b and have-heard,^c
LEXICON—a. ὅ (neuter): 'what'. See this word at 1:1.
b. perf. act. indic. of ὁράω: 'to see'. See this word at 1:1.
c. perf. act. indic. of ἀκούω: 'to hear'. See this word at 1:1.

QUESTION—How is this clause related to the context?
Since the sentence began in 1:1 but was interrupted by the parenthetical comment in 1:2, this clause repeats two of the verbs used in 1:1 and leads to the conclusion of this long sentence [AB, Alf, Brd, EGT, ICC, My, NIC, NTC, WBC, Ws]. It ties the direct object clauses in 1:1 to the main verb ἀπαγγέλλομεν 'we announce' [Brd].

QUESTION—What is the significance of the change of order of the verbs ἑωράκαμεν 'we have seen' and ἀκηκόαμεν 'we have heard' from the reverse order in the first verse?
Some commentators think that the change of order is for stylistic reasons and does not indicate a change of meaning or emphasis [AB, Lns, My, TH]. Some think that the order was changed because ἑωράκαμεν 'we have seen' is semantically closer to ἐφανερώθη 'was manifest' (1:2) than is ἀκηκόαμεν 'we have heard' [Lns, My, TH]. Others think that the change of order occurs because in 1:1 the author is working up to the incarnation while in 1:3 he is working away from the incarnation [Ws]. Still another view is

that the order is changed to tie τοῦ λόγου τῆς ζωῆς 'the word of Life' more closely to the verb ἀπαγγέλλομεν 'we announce' by forming a chiasm [AB, Brd]. Another view is that the change of order puts emphasis on ἑωράκαμεν 'we have seen' in order to make prominent the earthly ministry of Christ [ICC].

we-announce[a] also[b] to you,
TEXT—Some manuscripts omit καί 'also'. It is included in GNT without comment. It is omitted or not explicitly translated by KJV, NAB, NIV, and NJB.
LEXICON—a. pres act indic. of ἀπαγγέλλω (LN 33.198) (BAGD 2. p. 79): 'to announce' [HNTC; TEV], 'to proclaim' [AB, BAGD; NAB, NASB, NIV], 'to declare' [Lns, WBC; KJV, NJB, NRSV, REB, TEV, TNT], 'to tell' [LN]. See this word at 1:2.
  b. καί (LN 89.93): 'also' [LN, Lns; NASB, REB, TEV, TNT], 'in turn' [AB; NAB], 'as well' [WBC], 'yes, to you' [HNTC], not explicit [KJV, NIV, NJB, NRSV].
QUESTION—What relationship is indicated by the word καί 'also'?
  1. It links the readers with the writer and other eye witnesses [AB, Brd, EGT, ICC, Lns, TH, WBC, Ws]: what has come to us, we also pass on to you. The message was not only for those who saw and heard, but also for the readers who had not seen [Ws].
  2. The word καί 'also' links the readers to other hearers [Alf, My]: we announce to you as well as to others. It includes the readers of this letter with those who were addressed in the Gospel (John 20:31) [Alf].
QUESTION—In what way do they announce this?
  They do this whenever they proclaim the gospel, including the present letter [Herm, Lns, NIC, WBC].

in-order-that[a] also[b] you may-have fellowship[c] with[d] us.
LEXICON—a. ἵνα (LN 89.59) (BAGD I.1.a. p. 376): 'in order that' [BAGD, LN, Lns; REB], 'so that' [AB, HNTC, LN, WBC; NAB, NIV, NJB, NRSV, TEV], 'that' [KJV, NASB, TNT].
  b. καί (LN 89.93): 'also' [LN, WBC; KJV, NASB, NIV, NRSV], 'too' [HNTC, LN; NJB], not explicit [AB; NAB, REB, TEV, TNT].
  c. κοινωνία (LN **34.5**) (BAGD 1. p. 439): 'fellowship' [BAGD, LN, Lns; KJV, NASB, NIV, NRSV, TNT]. The phrase κοινωίαν ἔχω 'to have fellowship' is translated 'to share life' [NAB, NJB], 'to share fellowship' [HNTC, WBC], 'to join' [TEV], 'to join in communion' [AB], 'to have in common' [AB], 'unity of faith' [Herm, HNTC, WBC], 'to share in a common life' [REB].
  d. μετά with genitive object (LN 89.108) (BAGD A.II.3.b. p. 509): 'with' [AB, BAGD, LN, Lns; all versions except NJB]. The phrase μεθ' ἡμῶν 'with us' is translated by the possessive pronoun 'our' modifying 'fellowship' [WBC; NJB].

QUESTION—What relationship is indicated by ἵνα 'in order that'?
It indicates their purpose in proclaiming this message [BAGD, Br, Brd, EBC, Herm, Lns, NIC, NTC, TH, TNTC, WBC; all versions]: we announce it to you in order that you may have fellowship with us.

QUESTION—In what way are they to fellowship with the apostles *also*?
1. They, in addition to others, are to fellowship with the apostles [My]: in order that you also (as well as others) may fellowship with us.
2. They, in addition to the apostles, are to fellowship with the Father and his Son [NCBC, TH; REB, TEV]: in order that you also (as well as we) may fellowship with whom we fellowship with, specifically with the Father and his Son.
3. They also are to share in the fellowship that the apostles are already sharing [Alf, Br, Brd, EBC, ICC, Lns, NIC, TNTC, WBC, Ws]: in order that you also may share in the fellowship we share with each other. The fellowship is an interpersonal relationship they have in common with one another [Brd]. It is a reciprocal spiritual relationship [WBC]. By their acceptance of the message, they will be joined together in Christian love with the writer [NIC].

QUESTION—Does this purpose imply that the recipients of the letter were not yet Christians?
In 5:13 it states that they are believers. Some of the members of the congregation had left and so the writer feared that there might be others who did not truly believe or that there might be some who might be misled to accept another teaching. Here he states the Christian message that must be the basis for fellowship with him and thus with God [NIC, WBC]. He writes to make sure that the readers would continue in fellowship with him and this teaching provides the basis for it [Brd]. The fellowship already experienced by the readers can be realized to a greater degree [ICC].

And indeed[a] the fellowship[b] of-ours[c] (is) with[d] the Father and with his son Jesus Christ.

LEXICON—a. καί (LN 91.12): 'indeed' [NASB], 'truly' [KJV, NRSV], 'yes' [AB]. The words καὶ δέ 'and indeed' are translated 'and' [Lns; NIV], not explicit [HNTC, WBC; NAB, NJB, REB, TEV, TNT].
  b. κοινωνία (LN 34.5) (BAGD 1. p. 439): 'fellowship' [BAGD, HNTC, LN, Lns, WBC; all versions except NJB, REB], 'communion' [AB, BAGD]. This noun is also translated as a verb phrase: 'to share life' [NJB, REB].
  c. ἡμέτερος (LN 92.5) (BAGD p. 347): 'ours' (emphatic), 'of ours' [HNTC, Lns; NAB, TNT], 'our' [BAGD, LN; KJV, NASB, NIV, NJB, NRSV]. This is also translated as subject of a verb: 'we' [AB, WBC; REB, TEV].
  d. μετά with genitive object (LN 89.108) (BAGD A.II.3.b. p. 509): 'with' [AB, BAGD, HNTC, LN, Lns, WBC; all versions].

QUESTION— What relationship is indicated by καὶ δέ 'and indeed'?

The καί 'indeed' develops and intensifies the thought [Brd, ICC, NCBC, NIC, NTC]. The fellowship the writer is involved in includes the Father and the Son [NIC]. Some commentators think that δέ connects this clause with the preceding one and καί emphasizes the noun 'fellowship' [AB, TH, Ws]. Another view is that καί adds this clause to the preceding one while δέ indicates that it is another point [Lns]. Another thinks that καί connects the clauses and δέ means 'but', contrasting the greater fellowship with the Father and Son with the fellowship between Christians [Alf].

QUESTION—Does 'Father' refer to God's relationship to believers or to the special relationship with God the Son in the Trinity?

The relationship in focus in the term 'Father' is the special relationship God bears to the Son Jesus Christ [My, WBC]: the Son's Father.

QUESTION—What is the significance of the repetition of the preposition μετά 'with'?

It marks the Father and the Son as distinct but equal [AB, Alf, Brd, TNTC, WBC, Ws].

1:4 And[a] these (things) we write[b]

TEXT—Instead of ἡμεῖς 'we', some manuscripts have ὑμῖν 'to you (plural)'. GNT selects ἡμεῖς 'we' with a C rating, indicating a considerable degree of doubt. The reading 'to you' is selected only by KJV and NJB.

LEXICON—a. καί (LN 89.92): 'and' [Lns, WBC; KJV, NASB, TNT], 'indeed' [AB; NAB], not explicit [HNTC; NIV, NJB, NRSV, REB, TEV].

b. pres. act. indic. of γράφω (LN 33.61): 'to write' [AB, HNTC, LN, Lns, WBC; all versions].

QUESTION—What relationship is indicated by καί 'and'?

It adds one last thought to the introduction [Lns]. It adds a further purpose to the one stated in 1:3 [NIC, WBC]. It functions to introduce the result of the preceding verse [TH].

QUESTION—To what does ταῦτα 'these things' refer?

1. It refers to the whole letter [AB, Alf, Herm, My, NIC, TH, WBC, Ws]: we write this letter to you.
2. It refers to the preceding statements (1:1–3) [Brd, TNTC]: we write these aforementioned things to you.
3. It refers to what follows [ICC]: we write the following things to you. The preceding material is a reference to the writer's general proclamation of the gospel, while 1:4 introduces the message of the letter [ICC].
4. It refers to all the writings of all the apostles [Lns]: whatever things we write.

QUESTION—How does the word γράφομεν 'we write' relate to ἀπαγγέλλομεν 'we announce' of verses 2 and 3?

1. The focus of γράφομεν 'we write' is to tell or communicate and so functions as a synonym, not a contrast, to ἀπαγγέλλομεν 'we announce' [My, TH]: we are telling you.

2. The contrast is between the general announcement that has gone out to all and the writing of this letter to specific recipients [Brd, ICC, Ws]: to you, our readers, we write.

QUESTION—To whom does ἡμεῖς 'we' refer?

1. It is a plural form meaning the same as the 'we' in 1:1–3 [AB, Alf, Brd, ICC, Lns, My, NIC, NTC, TH, WBC]. It refers to the writer as a representative of the group of eye witnesses of Jesus' ministry [Alf, Brd, ICC, My, NIC, TH]. He is conscious of representing the orthodox members of the church [WBC].

2. It is an epistolary plural referring only to the writer [EGT]: and these things I write to you. It is equivalent to the singular form γράφω 'I write' in 2:1.

in-order-that[a] the joy[b] of-us may-be made-complete.[c]

TEXT—Instead of ἡμῶν 'of us', some manuscripts have ὑμῶν 'of you (plural)'. GNT selects ἡμῶν 'of us' with a B rating, indicating some degree of doubt. The reading 'your joy' is selected only by KJV.

LEXICON—a. ἵνα (LN 89.59): 'in order that' [Lns, WBC; REB, TEV], 'so that' [AB; NASB, NJB, NRSV], 'that' [KJV, TNT]. This is also translated with an infinitive: 'to make' [HNTC; NIV], and as a clause: 'our purpose is' [NAB].

b. χαρά (LN 25.123) (BAGD 1. p. 875): 'joy' [AB, BAGD, HNTC, LN, Lns, WBC; all versions].

c. perf. pass. participle of πληρόω (LN 59.33) (BAGD 3. p. 671): 'to be made complete' [LN; NASB], 'to complete' [HNTC, WBC; NAB, NJB, NRSV, REB, TEV, TNT], 'to make complete' [NIV], 'to bring something to completion' [BAGD], 'to be full' [KJV], 'to be fulfilled' [AB], 'to be filled full' [Lns]. The perfect tense indicates a state of being full of joy [AB, Alf, Brd].

QUESTION—What relationship is indicated by ἵνα 'in order that'?

It indicates the purpose of writing [Brd, EBC, Herm, Lns, My, NIC, TH, TNTC, WBC; all versions]: we write in order that our joy will be complete. Because of the purpose clause in 1:3, some commentators consider this to be a further purpose [WBC], a subsidiary purpose [NIC], or an ultimate purpose [TNTC]. This is but one aspect of his purpose for writing; other purposes are in 1:3–4, 2:1, and 5:13 [Brd].

QUESTION—To whom does ἡμῶν 'of us' refer and how would writing this make their joy complete?

1. 'Us' is exclusive, and does not include the hearers [AB, Brd, Lns, My, NIC, NTC, TH]. The writer cannot be completely joyful until all those he feels responsible for experience the full blessings of the gospel [NIC]. He will become joyful if the hearers respond to the message [Brd] and are saved [Herm], and share in the fellowship [AB, NIC]. The writer's joy of fellowship with God can obtain its highest degree only when other

Christians share that fellowship [TH]. The apostles would rejoice that their word had produced fruit in the hearers [My].
2. 'Us' includes the readers [Br, Herm, ICC, TNTC, WBC]. The writer wanted his readers to experience joy, and their joy would be his [Br, ICC]. Joy is complete when mutual fellowship is restored [TNT, WBC].

DISCOURSE UNIT: 1:5–3:10 [AB]. The topic is the obligation of walking in the light.

DISCOURSE UNIT: 1:5–2:29 [WBC]. The topic is living in the light.

DISCOURSE UNIT: 1:5–2:28 [Alf, Brd, EBC; NJB]. The topic is walking in the light [NJB], fellowship with the Father and the Son [Brd, EBC], requirements for fellowship with God [Alf].

DISCOURSE UNIT: 1:5–2:27 [ICC]. The topic is the two signs of fellowship with God.

DISCOURSE UNIT: 1:5–2:17 [ICC, NTC, Ws]. The topic is walking in the light as a sign of fellowship with God [ICC, NTC], the problem of life [Ws].

DISCOURSE UNIT: 1:5–2:14 [NIV]. The topic is walking in the light.

DISCOURSE UNIT: 1:5–2:11 [Brd, HNTC, NCBC]. The topic is testing fellowship on ethical grounds [Brd, NCBC], the two ways [HNTC].

DISCOURSE UNIT: 1:5–2:2 [AB, Br, EBC, Herm, Lns, NIC, TNTC]. The topic is exclusions from fellowship because of sin [TH], the moral implications of the message [TNTC], fellowship with God [Herm, Lns], God's being light [AB], walking in the light [Br, EBC, Herm, NIC].

DISCOURSE UNIT: 1:5–1:10 [EGT, ICC, NTC, Ws; NASB, TEV]. The topic is the nature of God and fellowship with him [ICC, Ws], fellowship and forgiveness [NTC], God's being light [NASB, TEV], the message of the incarnation and the duties the message brings [EGT], the relation of man to God [ICC].

DISCOURSE UNIT: 1:5–7 [Brd, TNTC, WBC; NJB]. The topic is God's being light [WBC], walking in the light [NJB], fellowship demanding moral likeness [Brd], the denial that sin breaks fellowship [TNTC].

DISCOURSE UNIT: 1:5 [Br; NAB]. The topic is God's being light [NAB], God's character [Br].

1:5 And
LEXICON—καί (LN 89.93): 'and' [HNTC, Lns; NASB], 'then' [KJV, NAB], 'now' [AB, WBC; TEV], not explicit [NIV, NJB, NRSV, REB, TNT].
QUESTION—What relationship is indicated by this word?
It marks the beginning of a new discourse unit [AB, Alf, My, WBC]. It also links the previous paragraph with this paragraph as carrying on the idea of proclaiming a message [Brd, Herm, ICC, Lns, TNTC, WBC, Ws]. It is a part

of the formula 'and this is' which occurs also at 2:25; 3:25; 5:4, 11, 14 [AB]. In order to have fellowship with God, they must know God's character [EBC, Ws].

this is the message[a] that we-have-heard[b] from him and we-announce[c] to-you,

LEXICON—a. ἀγγελία (LN **33.193**) (BAGD 1. p. 7): 'message' [BAGD, HNTC, LN; all versions except NJB], 'news' [WBC], 'gospel' [AB], 'report' [Lns], 'what' [NJB].
  b. perf. act. indic. of ἀκούω (LN 24.52) (BAGD 1.b.β. p. 32): 'to hear' [AB, BAGD, HNTC, LN, Lns, WBC; all versions]. The perfect tense is used to show that the action in the past still has effects in the present [Brd, Lns, TH]. What they had heard is still vivid in their memory [Brd]. See this word at 1:1, 3.
  c. pres. act. indic. of ἀναγγέλλω (LN 33.197) (BAGD 2. p. 51): 'to announce' [BAGD, HNTC, LN; NAB, NASB, TEV], 'to declare' [AB; KJV, NIV, NJB], 'to proclaim' [BAGD, WBC; NRSV], 'to tell' [LN; TNT], 'to pass on' [REB], 'to report back' [Lns], 'to inform' [LN], 'to disclose' [BAGD].

QUESTION—What does the pronoun αὕτη 'this' refer to?
  It refers to the following ὅτι 'that' clause [AB, Alf, Herm, HNTC, Lns, My, NIC, TH, WBC; all versions]: the following is the message: God is light and there is no darkness in him at all.

QUESTION—To whom does αὐτοῦ 'him' refer?
  1. It refers to God's Son, Jesus Christ [AB, Alf, Brd, EBC, Herm, Lns, My, NCBC, NIC, NTC, TH, TNTC, WBC, Ws]. This is implied by the reference to 'hearing' and by God being the subject of the message [NIC, WBC].
  2. It refers to God [ICC]. This message is from God and is to be delivered to the people [ICC].

QUESTION—Since this particular statement is not recorded in the Gospels, in what sense did they hear this from Jesus?
  It is possible that Jesus had said this without its being recorded in the Gospels [Brd, Ws]. Even if Jesus had not said these particular words, it sums up the whole of Christ's teaching about God [Alf, Brd, EBC, NIC, TNTC, WBC]. It is also taught through the example of Christ, who is light [Alf, Brd, EBC, NIC, WBC, Ws].

QUESTION—How does this verb ἀναγγέλλομεν 'we announce' differ from ἀπαγγέλλομεν 'we announce' in 1:2 and 1:3?
  1. There is no significant difference of meaning between them [AB, Brd, Herm, HNTC; NJB, NRSV]. The two verbs can be used interchangeably [Brd].
  2. There is a meaningful difference between them. Ἀπαγγέλλομεν 'we announce' (1:2, 3) with the prefix ἀπό 'from' stresses the source of the message [EGT, ICC, LN, Lns, NTC, Ws]. The source is God [ICC] or the

eye witnesses [Lns]. Ἀναγγέλλομεν 'we announce' with the prefix ἀνά 'back' stresses the receptor to whom they pass the report on to [EGT, ICC, Lns, NTC, Ws], or it implies a detailed report [LN]. For the three verbs ἀπαγγέλομεν (1:2), ἀπαγγέλομεν (1:3), and ἀναγγέλλομεν (1:5), most translations do not have the same translation for each: 'we proclaim, proclaim, announce' [NAB, NASB], 'we proclaim, proclaim, declare' [AB; NIV], 'we proclaim, declare, proclaim' [WBC], 'we declare, declare, pass on' [NAB], 'we declare, declare, report back' [Lns], 'we show, declare, declare' [KJV], 'we tell, announce, announce' [TEV], 'we declare, declare, tell' [TNT].

that[a] God is light[b]
LEXICON—a. ὅτι (LN 90.21) (BAGD 1.a. p. 588): 'that' [BAGD, LN, Lns; KJV, NAB, NASB, NRSV]. This is also translated as direct discourse [AB, HNTC, WBC; NIV, NJB, REB, TEV, TNT].
  b. φῶς (LN 14.36) (BAGD 2. p. 872): 'light' [AB, BAGD, HNTC, LN, Lns, WBC; all versions].
QUESTION—What relationship is indicated by ὅτι 'that'?
  1. It introduces direct discourse [HNTC, WBC; NIV, NJB, REB, TEV, TNT]: this is the message: God is light and there is no darkness in him at all.
  2. It introduces indirect discourse [AB, Herm, Lns; KJV, NAB, NASB, NRSV]: this is the message, namely, that God is light and there is no darkness in him at all.
QUESTION—What is the significance of the lack of the article with φῶς 'light'?
  It indicates that 'light' is a quality possessed by God [Brd, ICC, Lns, My, NTC, TH, TNTC]: God is by nature light. God is the source and essence of this quality [Br]. 'Light' is an attribute of God [Lns], it refers to his being and nature [WBC, Ws].
QUESTION—What is meant by φῶς 'light'?
  'Light' is a symbol. It symbolizes all the ethically good qualities of God: goodness [Br, TH; NIV], holiness [Br, Brd, ICC, Lns, My, NIC, NTC, WBC], purity [Alf, EBC, ICC, TNTC, Ws], righteousness [Br, Brd, ICC, Lns, My, NIC, TH, WBC], truth [Br, Brd, EBC, Lns, My, NTC, WBC], glory [Alf, EBC, EGT, NTC, WBC, Ws], love [Brd, TH], and life [Br, EGT, Herm]. Some commentators also speak of 'light' as a metaphor and mention grounds of comparison: light and God both illuminate [Br, Herm, ICC, NCBC, NIC, TH], reveal [TNTC], diffuse everywhere [Ws].

and (there) is no darkness[a] in[b] him, none.[c]
LEXICON—a. σκοτία (LN 14.53, 88.125) (BAGD 2. p. 757): 'darkness' [AB, BAGD, HNTC, LN, Lns, WBC; all versions].
  b. ἐν with dative object (LN 89.119): 'in' [AB, HNTC, Lns, WBC; all versions].

c. οὐδείς (LN 92.23): 'none' [LN]. The words οὐκ...οὐδεμία 'no...none' is translated 'no...at all' [AB; all versions except NAB], 'no...whatsoever' [HNTC], 'not a single bit' [Lns], 'no...any kind' [WBC], 'no' [NAB]. This word strengthens the negative, making it very emphatic [AB, Alf, Brd, EGT, ICC, Lns, My, TH, WBC].

QUESTION—What is meant by σκοτία 'darkness'?
It is the opposite of light [Alf, Brd, HNTC]. It is a symbol for evil [Br, Brd, NIC, WBC], sin [EGT, My], unrighteousness [Br], falsehood [Alf, Br, Brd, My], and error [WBC].

QUESTION—What relationship is indicated by ἐν 'in'?
The statement that there is no darkness 'in' God means that there is no imperfection in God's nature [Brd], there is no imperfection 'in his case' [NCBC], he has nothing in common with darkness [TH]. There is nothing to dim God's truth, righteousness, and holiness [Lns].

DISCOURSE UNIT: 1:6–2:2 [Br; NAB]. The topic is the three tests of life [Br], the claims of false teachers [NAB].

1:6 **QUESTION—How is this verse related to its context?**
Verse 1:5 gives the general principle and the following verses 1:6–10 give the implications of that principle [Herm, ICC, Lns, My, NCBC, NIC, WBC; TEV]. This verse begins a series of six conditional sentences in three pairs of negative falsehoods (1:6, 8, 10), each followed by positive truths (1:7, 9; 2:1) [AB, Alf, Br, Brd, EBC, ICC, Lns, NCBC, NIC, NTC, TH, TNTC, WBC]. The falsehoods are all introduced by the phrase 'if we say' [Lns, NCBC, TNTC, WBC], and are followed by the consequence 'we lie' or its equivalent [TNTC, WBC]. Then follows a positive contrast ('but if') related to the error [TH, TNTC, WBC]. The author makes use of parallel couplets (two lines that are paraphrases or near paraphrases of each other) that are reminiscent of Hebrew poetry [WBC]. There is a heavy repetition of thought and words that lead to tight cohesion for the passage [NCBC]. At least some of the falsehoods represent the teachings of the false teachers [AB, Alf, Br, Brd, EBC, ICC, Lns, NCBC, NIC, TNTC, WBC]. Then 2:3 contains one more similar conditional [My]. The author is dealing with the problem of sin in the Christian's life [Br, HNTC, Ws], particularly the error of those who thought sinning was irrelevant to the Christian life [EBC, HNTC, ICC, WBC]. The implicit claim of the false teachers was that they had fellowship with God quite apart from ethical considerations and the author is refuting this error [Brd, EBC, EGT, Herm, HNTC, Lns, NIC, TH, TNTC, WBC].

If[a] we-say[b] that[c] we-have fellowship[d] with[e] him
LEXICON—a. ἐάν (LN 89.67): 'if' [AB, HNTC, Lns, WBC; all versions].
b. aorist act. subj. of λέγω (LN 33.69): 'to say' [HNTC, LN, Lns; all versions except NIV, REB], 'to claim' [WBC; NIV, REB], 'to boast' [AB]. The subjunctive mood indicates a hypothetical condition [Alf, Brd,

EGT, My]. However, there is a real possibility that some did meet this condition [Brd, ICC, NIC].
  c. ὅτι (LN 90.21): 'that' [HNTC, LN, Lns; KJV, NASB, NJB, NRSV, TEV, TNT], not explicit [NIV, REB]. This is also translated as direct discourse [AB, WBC; NAB].
  d. κοινωνία (LN 34.5) (BAGD 1. p. 439): 'fellowship' [BAGD, HNTC, LN, Lns; all versions except NAB, NJB], 'communion' [BAGD], 'association' [BAGD]. The phrase κοινωίαν ἔχω 'to have fellowship' is translated 'to be in communion' [AB], 'to share life' [NJB, REB], 'to share fellowship' [WBC]. The use of the verb ἔχω 'to have' plus the nominalization of the verb emphasizes the nominalized verb [AB, ICC], and thereby the realization of the fellowship [Ws]. The present tense of the verb indicates continuing fellowship [Brd]. See this word at 1:3.
  e. μετά with genitive object (LN 89.108) 'with' [AB, HNTC, Lns, WBC; all versions except NAB, NJB].
QUESTION—What relationship is implied by ἐάν 'if'?
  It sets up a hypothetical but possible condition and it reflects the author's concern that the readers remain in the faith [AB, Brd, ICC, Lns, NTC, Ws]. Some commentators think it indicates that the author assumes that some of his readers have fallen into this error [NIC, TH].
QUESTION—Who is the semantic subject of εἴπωμεν 'we say'?
  'We' means the writer and those to whom he is writing [AB, Brd, ICC, Lns, NCBC, TH, Ws]. It may also include all other Christians [AB, Lns, Ws]. It is a literary device meaning 'whoever might say this' [Alf, Herm, My, TNTC]: if anyone says that he has fellowship with God. He is not implying that he has ever said the things that he is rebutting [TNTC]. The false teachers and those following them are probably in the forefront of the author's mind [AB, WBC].
QUESTION—To whom does αὐτοῦ 'him' refer?
  This pronoun refers to God the Father [AB, Brd, EGT, Herm, ICC, Lns, NIC, TH, TNTC, WBC, Ws].

and[a] in[b] the darkness[c] we-walk,[d]
LEXICON—a. καί (LN 91.12): 'and' [Lns; KJV, TNT], 'and yet' [NASB], 'yet' [HNTC; NIV], 'yet at the same time' [TEV], 'while' [AB, WBC; NAB, NJB, NRSV, REB].
  b. ἐν with dative object: 'in' [AB, HNTC, Lns, WBC; all versions].
  c. σκότος (LN 14.53, 88.125) (BAGD 2.b. p. 758): 'darkness' [AB, BAGD, HNTC, LN, Lns, WBC; all versions except NAB], 'dark' [NAB]. There is no difference in meaning from σκοτία 'darkness' (1:5) [AB, BAGD, Herm, ICC, LN; all versions]. The article with this word points out the contrast with τῷ φωτί 'the light' (1:7) [Brd].
  d. pres. act. subj. of περιπατέω (LN 41.11) (BAGD 1.d. p. 649): 'to walk' [AB, BAGD, HNTC, Lns; all versions except NJB, REB, TEV], 'to go about' [BAGD, LN], 'to live' [LN, TNTC, WBC; NJB, REB, TEV], 'to

conduct one's life' [NCBC]. The present tense indicates habitual action [AB, Brd, TNTC, WBC]. The habitual action expressed in living and lifestyle are in focus [EBC, Herm, NCBC, TNTC]. Both attitudes and actions are included [WBC, Ws].

QUESTION—What relationship is indicated by καί 'and'?

It indicates a contrast between what is professed and what is done [AB, Brd, HNTC, TH, WBC; NAB, NASB, NIV, NJB, NRSV, TEV]: if we say we have fellowship, and yet we are living in darkness.

QUESTION—What is meant by σκότει 'darkness'?

'Darkness' is a symbol of untruthfulness [Ws], sin [Br, My, NIC, TNTC], evil deeds [ICC, TH], error [Brd, TNTC], and an evil way of life [AB]. It is the antithesis of all that God is [Brd, HNTC]. Wrong doctrine is included [TNTC]. To walk in darkness is to live in the sphere of sin and error [Brd], to have an evil way of life [AB], to do evil [TH], to allow darkness to define a person's life [EBC].

we-lie[a] and we-do-not-practice[b] the truth;[c]

LEXICON—a. pres. mid. (deponent = act.) indic. of ψεύδομαι (LN 33.253) (BAGD 1. p. 891): 'to lie' [BAGD, LN, Lns, WBC; all versions except NAB, REB], 'to be liars' [AB, HNTC; NAB]. This compound clause is also translated 'our words and our lives are a lie' [REB].

b. pres. act. indic. of ποιέω (LN **41.7**) (BAGD I.1.c.β. p. 682): 'to practice' [BAGD, WBC; NASB, TNT], 'to do' [BAGD, Lns; KJV, NRSV], 'to act in' [AB; NAB], 'to act according to' [HNTC], 'to act in accordance with' [LN], 'to live' [NJB], 'to live by' [NIV]. This verb is also translated with a compound noun phrase 'our words and our lives' [REB], 'in our words and actions' [TEV]. The present tense indicates continuing action [Brd].

c. ἀλήθεια (LN 72.2) (BAGD 2.β. p. 36): 'truth' [AB, BAGD, HNTC, Lns, WBC; all versions except NRSV, REB, TEV], 'what is true' [NRSV], not explicit [REB, TEV].

QUESTION—How is the clause ψευδόμεθα 'we lie' different from the clause οὐ ποιοῦμεν τὴν ἀλήθειαν 'we do not practice the truth'?

Some commentators identify ψευδόμεθα 'we lie' with spoken falsehood and οὐ ποιοῦμεν τὴν ἀλήθειαν 'we are not practicing the truth' with false actions [Alf, Brd, EBC, My, NCBC, Ws]. Some take this to mean deliberate falseness, both in word and in deed [AB, ICC, TH, TNTC, Ws]. Others hold that these people may be self-deceived [EBC, EGT, NIC]. These people would not agree that they were not in fellowship with God and were walking in darkness [EBC].

QUESTION—What is meant by not 'doing the truth'?

'Truth' is Christian doctrine [BAGD, Brd, Lns], reality [Herm], that which corresponds to God's nature [My] and will [My, NIC, TH]. Not doing the truth means not putting the truth into practice, i.e., not living in accordance with the true standard God has revealed [NIC, Ws] and not being in accord with the moral ideal taught by Jesus [ICC].

1:7 but[a] if[b] in[c] the light[d] we-walk[e] as[f] he is in the light,

LEXICON—a. δέ (LN 89.124): 'but' [AB, HNTC, Lns, WBC; all versions except TNT], not explicit [TNT].
- b. ἐάν (LN 89.67): 'if' [AB, HNTC, Lns, WBC; all versions].
- c. ἐν with dative object: 'in' [AB, HNTC, Lns, WBC; all versions].
- d. φῶς (LN 14.36) (BAGD 3.a. p. 872): 'light' [AB, BAGD, HNTC, LN, Lns, WBC; all versions].
- e. pres. act. subj. of περιπατέω (LN 41.11) (BAGD 1.d. p. 649): 'to walk' [AB, BAGD, HNTC, LN, Lns; all versions except NJB, REB, TEV], 'to live' [LN, WBC; NJB, REB, TEV]. The present tense indicates a habitual practice [Brd, ICC, Lns, NTC, WBC]. See this word at 1:6.
- f. ὡς (LN 64.12): 'as' [AB, HNTC, Lns, WBC; all versions except TEV], 'just as' [TEV].

QUESTION—What relationship is indicated by δέ 'but'?

It indicates contrast [AB, Alf, Br, HNTC, Lns, My, NIC, WBC, Ws; all versions except TNT]: but. It contrasts living in the light with living in the darkness [AB, Br, NIC, TH, TNTC, WBC], or it contrasts the action of living in the light with a false claim to have fellowship with God (1:6) [Alf, Ws].

QUESTION—What relationship is indicated by ἐάν 'if'?

It indicates the condition for the following two consequences [EBC, EGT, ICC, TNTC, WBC, Ws]: if we live in the light, then we have fellowship with each other and Jesus' blood purifies us from all sin.

QUESTION—What is meant by 'walking in the light'?

Truth and holiness are in focus here [Brd, TNTC, WBC] and it means living in the sphere of truth and holiness [Brd]. It means living in openness before God without concealing anything [TNTC]. It means to respond to God's revelation of the truth which shows us how to live [NIC], to endeavor to live in accordance with what God has revealed [ICC, WBC]. It is believing and practicing the gospel truth [Lns].

QUESTION—To whom does αὐτός 'he' refer?

It refers to God the Father [AB, Alf, Brd, ICC, Lns, My, NIC, NTC, TNTC, Ws].

QUESTION—In what way is our living in the light compared with God's being in the light?

We are identified with the nature of God [My, Ws]. But our living in the light is temporary and marred, while God's being is eternal and unmarred in the light [My, Ws]. The same element in which we walk is the element in God's eternal being [Alf]. God exists in the sphere of truth and holiness, and we are to live in that same sphere [Brd]. We live the same way God does [NIC]. One commentary says that this word focuses on the degree in which we walk in the light [TH]: if we live in the light as fully and completely as God exists in the light.

QUESTION—How does αὐτός ἐστιν ἐν τῷ φωτί 'he is in the light' differ from θεὸς φῶς ἐστιν 'God is light' in 1:5?
1. There is a difference of meaning. God is in the light because he is light [Brd, Lns, TNTC, WBC, Ws]. 'God is light' speaks of his nature while 'he is in the light' speaks of his deeds [AB]. One who is light is therefore in that light [Lns]. This statement is another aspect of truth and the metaphors concerning being light and being in light do not harmonize [TH].
2. There is no distinction of meaning [Alf, EBC, Herm, NIC]. The ἐν 'in' is inserted for parallelism with 'walking in the light' [Alf, EBC, Herm, NIC].

we-have fellowship[a] with each-other[b]

LEXICON—a. κοινωνία (LN 34.5) (BAGD 1. p. 439): 'fellowship' [BAGD, HNTC, LN, Lns; all versions except NJB, REB], 'communion' [BAGD]. The phrase κοινωνίαν ἔχω 'to have fellowship' is translated 'to join in communion' [AB], 'to share fellowship' [WBC], 'to share a (common) life' [REB], '(to have) a share in (each other's life)' [NJB]. The use of the verb ἔχω 'to have' plus the nominalization of the verb emphasizes the nominalized verb [AB, ICC]. Assuming that the condition is met, the present tense indicates that this is in effect at the time of writing [TH] and is a continuing experience [Brd].
b. ἀλλήλων (LN 92.26): 'each other' [HNTC, LN, WBC; NJB], 'one another' [AB, LN, Lns; all versions except NJB, REB], 'common' [REB].

QUESTION—To whom does ἀλλήλων 'each other' refer?
It refers to those who believe [AB, Alf, Brd, EBC, Herm, ICC, Lns, My, NIC, TH, TNTC, WBC, Ws]: we believers fellowship with one another.

QUESTION—Why isn't the expected consequence 'we have fellowship with God' given instead of 'we have fellowship with each other'?
The consequence, 'we have fellowship with God', is assumed in the statement that we walk in the light as God is in light [Alf, Br, Brd, Herm, Lns, NIC]. Fellowship among Christians is a sign that they have fellowship with God [Brd, EGT, ICC, WBC, Ws]. The writer goes back to the purpose of his message (1:3), that the reader might have fellowship with them [Alf, Lns, NIC, TNTC, WBC]. John has in view a splinter group which boasted that it had fellowship with God while separating from the rest of the believers [AB, EBC, NIC, TNTC, WBC].

and the blood[a] of-Jesus his Son purifies[b] us from[c] all[d] sin.[e]

TEXT—Some manuscripts include χριστοῦ 'Christ' after Ἰησοῦ 'Jesus'. GNT does not mention this alternative. It is included only by KJV.
LEXICON—a. αἷμα (LN 23.107) (BAGD 2.b. p. 23): 'blood' [AB, BAGD, HNTC, LN, Lns, WBC; all versions], 'sacrificial death' [LN].
b. pres. act. indic. of καθαρίζω (LN 53.28) (BAGD 2.b.α. p. 387): 'to purify' [BAGD, LN, WBC; NIV, TEV], 'to cleanse' [AB, BAGD, HNTC, LN, Lns; all versions except NIV, TEV]. The present tense denotes

continuous purification [Brd, EBC, Lns, My, TH, TNTC, WBC, Ws] and parallels the continual walk in the light [Brd].
  c. ἀπό with genitive object (LN 89.122): 'from' [AB, HNTC, Lns, WBC; all versions].
  d. πᾶς (LN 59.23): 'all' [AB, HNTC, Lns; all versions except TEV], 'every' [WBC; TEV].
  e. ἁμαρτία (LN **88.310**): 'sin' [AB, HNTC, LN, Lns, WBC; all versions], 'guilt' [LN].

QUESTION—What is meant by αἷμα 'blood'?

'Blood' is a metonymy for Jesus' death on the cross [NIC, TH, WBC], but it means more than just death, it means a sacrificial death [AB, Alf, EBC, EGT, HNTC, ICC, LN, Lns, My, TNTC, WBC]. This has reference to the sacrificial system in the Old Testament [EBC, HNTC, NIC, TH, WBC].

QUESTION—Why is the phrase τοῦ υἱοῦ αὐτοῦ 'his Son' mentioned when Jesus has already been identified by name?

The combined name 'Jesus, his Son' is used to combat the heresy that made a distinction between the human Jesus and the divine Son [Brd, ICC, Lns, TNTC, WBC, Ws]. This shows that Jesus and God are together in this plan of sacrifice [My]. Jesus is the intermediate cause of purification but God the original cause [TH].

QUESTION—In what way does Jesus' blood purify us from all sin?

1. This refers to the removal of sin from a believer's life [Alf, Brd, EBC, EGT, ICC, My, TH, WBC, Ws]. It means a gradual removal of sin from one's life as that person grows in holiness [Alf, Brd, ICC, My]. 'All sin' means all sinful deeds [TH], not every last sin, but any sin that may occur [Brd]. Some take the singular form to refer to the sin principle [EBC, EGT, ICC, Ws]. Then 'all sin' is explained to be sin in all its forms and manifestations [ICC], or every outbreak of the sin principle [EGT]. Another view is that this looks to the consummation of Christ's work towards which the believer is continually moving, the final removal of the sin principle itself [Ws].
2. This refers to the forgiveness of sin, the removing of the guilt which our sins incur [AB, Lns, NIC]. When they try to walk in the light, they may yet sin, but the blood of Jesus provides forgiveness for all these sins [AB]. While walking in the light, the believer still falls into sin and Jesus' blood provides constant justification so that our sins are daily forgiven [Lns]. As we walk in the light we become conscious of our sins, but its defiling effects no longer condemn us in God's sight [NIC].

DISCOURSE UNIT: 1:8–2:2 [Alf, Brd, WBC; NJB]. The topic is the confession of sins for fellowship [Brd], renouncing sins in order to live in the light [WBC], the break with sin [NJB], purification from sin [Alf].

DISCOURSE UNIT: 1:8–9 [NTC, TNTC]. The topic is the denial that sin exists in one's nature [TNTC], deception and confession [NTC].

1:8 If^a we-say^b that^c (we) do-not have sin^d

LEXICON—a. ἐάν (LN 89.67): 'if' [AB, HNTC, Lns, WBC; all versions except TEV], 'if then' [TEV], 'whenever' [TH]. See this word at 1:6.
  b. aorist act. subj. of λέγω (LN 33.69): 'to say' [HNTC, LN, Lns; all versions except NIV, REB], 'to claim' [WBC; NIV, REB], 'to boast' [AB]. See this word at 1:6.
  c. ὅτι (LN 90.21): 'that' [HNTC, LN, Lns; KJV, NASB, NRSV, TEV, TNT], not explicit [NIV, REB]. This is also translated as direct discourse [AB, WBC; NAB, NJB].
  d. ἁμαρτία (LN 88.289; 88.310) (BAGD 2. p. 43): 'sin' [BAGD, HNTC, LN, Lns; all versions except NAB, REB, TNT], 'sinfulness' [BAGD]. The clause ἁμαρτίαν οὐκ ἔχω 'to have no sin' is translated 'to be without sin' [NIV], 'to be free from the guilt of sin' [AB; NAB], 'to be sinless' [WBC; REB, TNT]. It speaks of something that continually influences a person [TH, WBC]. The present tense of the verb indicates the present condition of the believer after conversion [Alf, Brd]. See this word at 1:7.

QUESTION—How is this verse related to its context?
  This picks up the word 'sin' from the previous verse [Alf, WBC, Ws]. The opponents would claim that they did not need to be purified of sin because they were without sin [WBC]. Those who boasted that they lived in the light while walking in darkness were, in effect, committing sin without acknowledging it [WBC]. The conditional structure parallels 1:6 [Herm].

QUESTION—What is meant by the statement ἁμαρτίαν οὐκ ἔχομεν 'we have no sin'?
  1. It means to have no sin principle in one's nature [Alf, Brd, EBC, EGT, ICC, My, NTC, TH, TNTC, WBC, Ws]: if we say that we do not have an inward disposition to sin. 'Sin' is the disposition or principle of which sinful actions are individual manifestations [WBC]. The present tense in ἁμαρτίαν οὐκ ἔχομεν 'sin (singular) we do not have' describes a present state and is in contrast with the individual sins produced in the past in the phrase οὐχ ἡμαρτήκαμεν 'we have not sinned' (1:10) [Brd]. Most commentators think this is a claim for present perfection [Alf, Brd, EGT, My, NTC, TH, TNTC, WBC], but another thinks that it refers to a claim for freedom from the power of the principle of sin even though unimportant sins are still being committed [ICC].
  2. It means not to commit sin and is equivalent to the expression οὐχ ἡμαρτήκαμεν 'we have not sinned' (1:10) [Lns, NIC]: if we say that we have not sinned. The writer seems to interpret this phrase in terms of the need for forgiveness of individual sins (1:9) [NIC]. Actions which the writer regarded as sinful did not appear sinful to them [NIC].
  3. It means not to be guilty of sin [AB, Br, Herm, NCBC; NAB]: if we say that we are not guilty in regard to sin. It is possible that this means that the person is not guilty because he has not committed sin [NCBC]. However, it might not be a denial of doing wrong, rather that there is no guilt

attached to sinful acts or that the particular sins are not important enough to affect one's relationship with God [AB].

we-deceive[a] ourselves and the truth[b] is[c] not in[d] us.
LEXICON—a. pres. act. indic. of πλανάω (LN 31.8) (BAGD 1.b. p. 665): 'to deceive' [AB, BAGD, HNTC, LN, Lns, WBC; all versions], 'to mislead' [BAGD, LN].
    b. ἀλήθεια: 'truth'. See this word at 1:6.
    c. pres. act. indic. of εἰμί (LN 13.1): 'to be' [AB, HNTC, Lns; all versions except NJB], 'to have a place' [WBC; NJB], 'to be found' [NAB]. The present tense here has a durative force to indicate that this condition will continue [TH].
    d. ἐν with dative object: 'in' [AB, HNTC, Lns, WBC; all versions except NAB]. The phrase is translated 'we are strangers to the truth' [NAB].
QUESTION—In what way did they deceive themselves?
This refers to a deliberate error, a choice being made to ignore the evidence of sin in one's life [EBC, Herm, ICC, My, WBC], for which he is wholly responsible [TH]. It is willful blindness to the truth [Brd, EBC, ICC]. It is a refusal to face the facts of the sinfulness of human nature [WBC]. It means to persuade oneself to accept what is known to be false [Ws]. They are self-deceived, not deliberate liars [TNTC].
QUESTION—What is meant by the statement that truth is not in them?
They do not accept the truth concerning human sinfulness and God's holiness [Alf]. They do not accept the true doctrine revealed by God [Brd]. Truth is not controlling them as an effective principle in their lives [AB, EBC, ICC].

1:9 If[a] we-confess[b] our sins,[c]
LEXICON—a. ἐάν (LN 89.67): 'if' [AB, HNTC, Lns, WBC; all versions].
    b. pres. act. subj. of ὁμολογέω (LN **33.275**) (BAGD 3.b. p. 568): 'to confess' [AB, BAGD, HNTC, **LN**, Lns; all versions except NAB, NJB], 'to acknowledge' [WBC; NAB, NJB], 'to admit' [LN]. The present tense indicates repeated action [Brd, Lns, NTC], that is, confession is made after each sin occurs [Brd].
    c. ἁμαρτία (LN 88.310) (BAGD 1. p. 43): 'sin'. See this word at 1:8.
QUESTION—How is this clause related to its context?
It relates back to ἐν τῷ φωτί περιπατῶμεν 'walking in the light' as the second of three tests of our walk [EBC, WBC]. Each test is expressed by a pair of contrasts. Consequently, it contrasts with the verse before it ('but if') [AB, EBC, My, NIC, TH, WBC; NAB], as the answer to the false claim [Br, TH]. The contrast is not as sharp as the contrast between verses 6 and 7 [WBC, Ws] because of a continuation of the motif of not considering yourself sinless [Herm, My]. Sin is a fact of life, but this does not prevent fellowship with God if it is confessed [ICC, WBC, Ws]. Confession is the natural response to recognition of sin [Br, EBC, TH, TNTC].

QUESTION—What is implied by the conditional clause?

It has the force of an implied command [Herm, NIC, TH, WBC]: we should confess our sins, and when we do so, God is faithful and righteous to forgive us. It expresses a general truth [AB].

QUESTION—What is meant by confessing one's sins?

It means to admit one's sins [Brd, Lns, TH, TNTC, WBC] with real contrition and seeking forgiveness [Alf, My, NIC].

QUESTION—To whom is this confession made?

Confession is made to God [AB, Alf, Brd, EBC, Lns, NIC, TH, TNTC, WBC, Ws; TEV]: if we confess our sins to God. Some of these commentators think that this confession to God is to be made openly before the congregation [AB, Alf, EBC, WBC, Ws]. One commentator goes no further than stating that the confession is an admission to one's self [My].

QUESTION—What is the significance of the change to the plural form, ἁμαρτίας 'sins' here from the singular form ἁμαρτίαν 'sin' in 1:8?

The plural form ἁμαρτίας 'sins' refers to a confession of specific acts of sin rather than to sin as a general disposition [Brd, EGT, Herm, Lns, My, TH, TNTC, WBC, Ws]. The plural shows that we have many sins to confess [EBC, Lns, NTC].

he-is faithful[a] and righteous,[b] that[c] he-may-forgive[d] us the sins[e]

LEXICON—a. πιστός (LN 31.87) (BAGD 1.a.β. p. 664): 'faithful' [BAGD, HNTC, LN, Lns, WBC; KJV, NASB, NIV, NRSV, TNT], 'reliable' [AB, LN], 'trustworthy' [BAGD, LN; NJB], 'dependable' [BAGD, LN]. The clause πιστός ἐστιν 'he is faithful' is translated 'he will keep his promise' [TEV], 'he can be trusted' [NAB, REB].

b. δίκαιος (LN 88.12) (BAGD 2. p. 196): 'righteous' [BAGD, HNTC, LN, Lns, WBC; NASB, TNT], 'upright' [NJB], 'just' [AB, BAGD, LN; KJV, NAB, NIV, NRSV, REB]. The clause ἐστιν δίκαιος 'he is righteous' is translated 'he will do what is right' [TEV].

c. ἵνα (LN 91.15) (BAGD II.2. p. 378): 'that', 'so that' [WBC; NJB], 'which means that' [HNTC], 'and' [NIV], not explicit [AB; NRSV, TEV, TNT]. The phrase 'that he may forgive' is translated 'to forgive' [Lns; KJV, NAB, NASB, REB].

d. aorist act. subj. of ἀφίημι (LN 40.8) (BAGD 2. p. 126): 'to forgive' [AB, BAGD, HNTC, WBC; all versions], 'to remit' [BAGD, Lns], 'to pardon' [BAGD]. The aorist puts the focus on the completion of the act, not the result [TH, Ws].

e. ἁμαρτία (LN 88.310) (BAGD 1. p. 43): 'sin' [AB, BAGD, HNTC, Lns, WBC; all versions]. See this word at 1:7.

QUESTION—How is the statement 'he is faithful and righteous' related to its context?

Some commentators point out that it cannot mean that only if we confess our sins does God become faithful and righteous [Alf, My].

1. This clause is the consequence of the preceding condition. It implies that this is how God will act [Alf, ICC, Lns, My, NTC, TH, WBC; all versions except NRSV, TNT]: if we confess our sins, God will show/exercise his faithfulness and righteousness. The following ἵνα 'that' clause is explained in two ways.
    1.1 The following clause indicates the result of God's acting with faithfulness and righteousness [Alf, NTC, WBC; NJB]: if we confess our sins, God will show his faithfulness and righteousness with the result that he will forgive us and purify our unrighteousness. Another commentator calls this God's purpose in showing the two qualities [My].
    1.2 The following clause indicates the sphere in which God will act with faithfulness and righteousness [ICC, Lns, NIC, TH; KJV, NAB, NASB, REB, TEV]: if we confess our sins, God will show his faithfulness and righteousness to forgive us and to purify our unrighteousness.
2. This clause is the grounds of the following ἵνα 'that' clause, which, in turn, is the consequence of the preceding conditional clause [AB, Brd, NIC, TNTC; NRSV, TNT]: if we confess our sins, since God is faithful and righteous, he therefore will forgive us and purify our unrighteousness.

QUESTION—Who is the implied subject of the verb ἐστιν 'he is'?
    1. God is the implied subject [AB, Alf, EBC, Herm, Lns, My, NCBC, TH, WBC, Ws; TEV].
    2. Jesus Christ is the implied subject [Br].

QUESTION—What is meant by the statement that he is faithful?
    He is faithful to his promises [Alf, Br, Brd, EBC, EGT, ICC, Lns, My, NCBC, NIC, NTC, TH, TNTC, WBC, Ws; TEV]: he does what he had promised to do. His promise concerning forgiveness is recorded in Jer. 31:34 [Brd, EBC, TNTC, WBC] and Micah 7:18–20 [EBC, NIC, WBC].

QUESTION—What is meant by the statement that he is righteous?
    This refers to a quality of God [Lns, NIC, TH]: God does what is right. God's righteousness requires that he keep his promise to forgive all who repent and confess their sins [Brd, EGT, ICC, NIC]. In forgiving sinners God is acting righteously because Christ's death has atoned for sin and made forgiveness possible [Brd, Lns, TNTC, WBC].

and he-may-purify[a] us from[b] all[c] unrighteousness.[d]
LEXICON—a. aorist act. subj. of καθαρίζω (LN 53.28) (BAGD 2.b.α. p. 387): 'to purify' [BAGD, HNTC, LN, WBC; NIV, TEV], 'to cleanse' [AB, BAGD, LN, Lns; all versions except NIV, TEV]. See this word at 1:7.
    b. ἀπό with genitive object (LN 89.122): 'from' [AB, HNTC, Lns, WBC; all versions].
    c. πᾶς (LN 58.28, 59.23): 'all' [AB, HNTC, Lns; all versions except NAB, REB], 'every' [NAB], 'every kind of' [WBC; REB].

d. ἀδικία (LN 88.21) (BAGD 2. p. 18): 'unrighteousness' [BAGD, LN, Lns, WBC; KJV, NASB, NIV, TNT], 'sin' [HNTC], 'wrong' [NAB], 'wrongdoing' [AB; REB, TEV], 'evil' [NJB], 'wickedness' [BAGD].

QUESTION—What is the relationship between καθαρίσῃ 'he purifies' used here and ἀφῇ 'he forgives' in the preceding clause?

The two clauses are parallel and some commentators think that there is no difference of meaning [AB, Br, NIC]: he forgives/purifies our sins/wrongdoings. Some make distinctions between the two words. He forgives our sins and purifies our characters [Alf, Brd, NIC, NTC, WBC, Ws].

QUESTION—What is the difference between ἀδικίας 'unrighteousness' used here and ἁμαρτίας 'sin' used in 1:7 and earlier in this verse?

There is no significant difference [AB, Alf, Br, Brd, Herm, My, NIC, TH, WBC, Ws]. The choice of ἀδικίας 'unrighteousness' was made to contrast with the word δίκαιος 'righteous' earlier in the verse [Alf, WBC]. Some commentators take unrighteousness to be a type of sin, 'injustice' [EBC, ICC], or to be a description of all sin [Lns].

DISCOURSE UNIT: 1:10–2:2 [TNTC]. The topic is denial of sinful conduct.

1:10 If[a] we-say[b] that[c] we-have-not-sinned,[d]

LEXICON—a. ἐάν (LN 89.67): 'if' [AB, HNTC, Lns, WBC; all versions].

b. aorist act subj. of λέγω (LN 33.69): 'to say' [BAGD, HNTC, LN, Lns; all versions except NIV], 'to claim' [WBC; NIV], 'to boast' [AB]. See this word at 1:6 and 1:8.

c. ὅτι (LN 90.21): 'that' [HNTC, LN, Lns; KJV, NASB, NRSV, TEV, TNT], not explicit [NIV, REB]. This is also translated as direct discourse [AB, WBC; NAB, NJB].

d. perf. act. indic. of ἁμαρτάνω (LN 88.289): 'to sin' [AB, HNTC, LN, Lns, WBC; all versions except REB], 'to commit a sin' [REB]. The perfect tense speaks of past action with its consequences continuing to the present [ICC, TH, Ws], or of past actions which includes all the past time up to the present [Brd, Lns, My, NTC].

QUESTION—How is this verse related to its context?

This lists the third heretical claim about the unimportance of sin [Br, EBC, ICC, TH, TNTC, WBC, Ws] The mention of the confession of sin in 1:9 may have suggested this further claim of not needing to confess because of not having sinned [WBC].

QUESTION—How is the claim ἁμαρτίαν οὐκ ἔχομεν 'we have no sin' (1:8) different from the claim in this verse οὐχ ἡμαρτήκαμεν 'we have not sinned'?

1. The claim in 1:8 denies having a sin nature, while the claim here denies having committed sinful acts [Alf, Brd, EBC, EGT, ICC, My, TH, TNTC, WBC, Ws]. Some commentators point to the change in tense of the verbs in support of this: 'we do not have sin (present tense)' (1:8) and 'we have not sinned (perfect tense)' [Brd, WBC]. Some think that the claim in this

verse is only for the time since conversion [Alf, EBC, My]. Others think that this is an absolute claim of never having sinned [Brd, ICC, TH, Ws].
2. The claim in 1:8 and the claim here are the same: they claim to have never sinned [Herm, Lns, NIC; NAB, NJB]. The difference in wording is that in 1:8 'to have sin' refers to sin as an entity and here 'to have sinned' refers to the many acts of sin that have been committed [Lns]. This adds a new point; they not only deceive themselves, but they even imply that God is a liar [NIC].
3. The claim in 1:8 denies that a person is guilty for committing sin, while here the claim is that no sin has been committed [AB]. This refers to the time since conversion.

a-liar[a] we-make[b] him

LEXICON—a. ψεύστης (LN 33.255) (BAGD p. 892): 'liar' [AB, BAGD, HNTC, LN, Lns, WBC; all versions]. This initial position makes the word emphatic to highlight how terrible the accusation is [Brd, Lns].
  b. pres. act. indic. of ποιέω (LN 13.9) (BAGD I.1.b.ι. p. 682): 'to make' [AB, HNTC, Lns; all versions except NIV, REB, TEV], 'to make someone out to be' [WBC; NIV, REB], 'to make (a liar) out of someone' [TEV].
QUESTION—To whom does αὐτόν 'him' refer?
  It refers to God the Father [AB, Alf, Brd, EBC, Lns, My, NIC, TH, WBC, Ws; TEV].
QUESTION—In what sense does such a person make God a liar?
  The claim to be without sin implies that God has lied when he attributed sin to everyone [Brd, EBC, My, TH, TNTC, WBC, Ws]. Scripture states that all are sinners [Alf, ICC, Lns, TNTC, WBC]. Throughout the Old and New Testaments it is implied that all have sinned [Brd, ICC, NIC, TNTC, Ws]. It must mean that God has declared that even Christians sin and God's promise of forgiveness and purification in 1:9 assumes this [My]. This means more than saying that God has lied; it implies that he has the character of a liar [Brd].

and his word[a] is not in[b] us.

LEXICON—a. λόγος (LN 33.260) (BAGD 1.b.β. p. 478): 'word' [AB, BAGD, HNTC, LN, Lns, WBC; all versions].
  b. ἐν with dative object (LN 89.119) (BAGD I.5.a. p. 259): 'in' [AB, HNTC, Lns; KJV, NASB, NRSV, TEV, TNT]. This preposition is also translated by a clause 'to have no place in' [WBC; NAB, NIV, NJB], 'to find no place in' [NAB].
QUESTION—What is meant by ὁ λόγος αὐτοῦ 'his word'?
  'His word' means, in general, the revelation God has made of himself [Alf, EBC, My]. It refers to the scriptures [EGT, Lns] and specifically to the gospel [My, TH, Ws] or God's message spoken by Jesus [AB]. The word is the truth (1:8) that has been spoken or revealed [Brd]. One commentator

thinks that it is ambivalent between meaning the personal Word, Christ, or the message about him [WBC].

QUESTION—What is meant by saying that God's word is not in a person?
God's word has not been accepted by the person [Brd, Lns]. It has not affected the person's belief or conduct [NIC]. It is not in his thoughts as a rule of life [Alf]. It is not believed nor obeyed [Lns]. This phrase is virtually synonymous with 'the truth' in 1:8 [AB, Br, Herm, WBC].

DISCOURSE UNIT: 2:1–14 [NASB]. The topic is Christ our advocate.

DISCOURSE UNIT: 2:1–6 [ICC, NTC, Ws; TEV]. The topic is knowledge and obedience as conditions for fellowship [ICC, NTC], Christ our helper [TEV], the remedy for sin and the sign of its effectiveness [Ws].

DISCOURSE UNIT: 2:1–2 [EGT]. The topic is the remedy for the sins of believers.

2:1 My children,[a] these (things) I write[b] to-you in-order-that[c] you-may-not-sin.[d]

LEXICON—a. τεκνίον (LN 9.46) (BAGD p. 808): 'child' [BAGD, HNTC, LN; NJB, REB, TEV, TNT], 'little child' [AB, BAGD, Lns; KJV, NASB, NRSV], 'little one' [NAB], 'dear child' [WBC; NIV], 'dear friend' [LN]. The use of the diminutive here shows an affectionate relationship [AB, Alf, Brd, EBC, EGT, ICC, Lns, My, NCBC, NIC, NTC, TH, TNTC, WBC, Ws], from an old man [Alf, Brd, EGT, ICC, Lns, NTC, TNTC], to those he sees in a disciple-teacher relationship to himself [AB, EGT, NTC, TH].

b. pres. act. indic. of γράφω (LN 33.61): 'to write'. See this word at 1:4.

c. ἵνα (LN 89.59): 'in order that' [WBC], 'so that' [HNTC, Lns; NIV, NRSV, REB, TEV], 'that' [KJV, NASB, TNT], not explicit [NAB]. This conjunction is also translated 'to keep from' [AB; NAB], 'to prevent from' [NJB].

d. aorist act. subj. of ἁμαρτάνω (LN 88.289): 'to sin'. See this word at 1:10. The aorist is used to refer to a specific act of sin [AB, Alf, Brd, ICC, TH, TNTC, WBC, Ws]. It is ingressive, indicating that the readers should not commit even one sin [Brd].

QUESTION—How is this verse related to its context?
It answers the third heretical claim given in 1:10 [WBC]. However, the 'if' clause is held up while a parenthetical remark [AB, NIC, TH, WBC, Ws] is added to correct possible misunderstandings of the previous verses [AB, Brd, EBC, EGT, Herm, ICC, Lns, NIC, TNTC, WBC, Ws]. The possible misunderstandings are that sin is to be accepted as an inevitable part of the normal Christian life [AB, Br, Brd, EBC, EGT, Herm, ICC, Lns, NIC, TH, Ws], or that it is inconsequential since God will cleanse sin [AB, Brd, EBC, EGT, Herm, ICC, Lns, NIC, TNTC, Ws].

QUESTION—What is the significance of the change from the plural γράφομεν 'we write' in 1:4 to the singular γράφω 'I write' here?

This singular form naturally follows from the address 'my children' [Ws]. It makes the letter more personal [AB, EGT, TH, WBC, Ws]. Some who take the 'we' of 1:1–5 to refer to the author as a representative of the Apostles or of another group, think that the change to singular is a sign that the author is writing this section on his own behalf and not as the representative of a group as before [Herm, NTC, TH, WBC].

QUESTION—What does the pronoun ταῦτα 'these things' refer to?
1. It refers to the preceding section [AB, Alf, Brd, Herm, Lns, My, TH, WBC]. It refers to 1:5–10 [Brd, TH], or to 1:6–10 [My], or to 1:8–10 [AB, Alf, Herm], and especially to 1:10 [TH].
2. It refers to the whole letter [ICC, Ws]. The whole letter is already present in his mind as he writes this [ICC, Ws].

But/And[a] if[b] anyone sins,[c]

LEXICON—a. καί (LN 91.12): 'but' [AB, HNTC, WBC; all versions except KJV, NASB, TNT], 'yet' [LN; TNT], 'and' [Lns; KJV, NASB].

b. ἐάν (LN 89.67): 'if' [AB, HNTC, Lns, WBC; all versions].

c. aorist act. subj. of ἁμαρτάνω (LN 88.289): 'to sin'. The aorist tense shows it is talking about a specific act of sin [Alf, Brd, ICC, Lns, TNTC, WBC, Ws] and not the state of sin [WBC].

QUESTION—What relationship is indicated by καί 'but/and'?
1. It indicates a contrast with the preceding clause [AB, Brd, HNTC, TH, WBC; all versions except KJV, NASB]: but. The goal is perfection; however, the writer recognizes the weakness of human beings [Brd].
2. It is shows continuity with the preceding clause [ICC; KJV, NASB]: and.

QUESTION—What is implied by the change from the first person plural 'we' in 1:6–10 to the indefinite τις 'anyone'?
1. The change is for stylistic reasons and carries no difference in meaning [AB, Alf, My].
2. The indefinite reference makes the possibility of sinning a little more removed from the people being addressed [Brd].
3. The change is made to achieve a singular reference [Lns, TH, WBC, Ws]. A singular is needed here since an individual commits specific sins [Lns, WBC, Ws]. He is speaking only of individual sins [WBC, Ws]. However, the difference should not be pressed since the next clause again uses 'we' [TH].

we-have[a] an-advocate[b] with[c] the Father, Jesus Christ (the) righteous;[d]

LEXICON—a. pres. act. indic. of ἔχω (LN 90.65) (BAGD I.2.d. p. 332): 'to have' [AB, HNTC, Lns, WBC; all versions]. The present tense is used here to show that we have such an advocate as an abiding possession [TH].

b. παράκλητος (LN **35.16**) (BAGD p. 618): 'advocate' [KJV, NASB, NJB, NRSV], 'intercessor' [BAGD, WBC; NAB], 'helper' [BAGD, LN],

'mediator' [BAGD], 'Paraclete' [AB, Lns] 'someone to speak on our behalf' [HNTC], 'one who speaks in our defense' [NIV], 'someone who pleads on our behalf' [TEV], 'one to plead for us' [TNT], 'one who will plead our cause' [REB].
  c. πρός with accusative object (LN 89.7) (BAGD III.7. p. 711): 'with' [LN, Lns, WBC; all versions except NAB, NIV], 'in the presence of' [AB; NAB], '(speaks) to' [HNTC; NIV].
  d. δίκαιος (LN 88.12) (BAGD 3. p. 196): 'righteous' [LN, Lns; KJV, NASB, NRSV], 'upright' [NJB], 'just' [LN], 'the righteous one' [HNTC; NIV, TEV]. This adjective is also translated by a relative clause: 'who is righteous' [WBC; TNT], 'who is just' [AB; NAB], 'who is acceptable to God' [REB].

QUESTION—What is meant by παράκλητος 'advocate'?
This word basically means 'helper' and the help that is given varies according to the context [Brd, WBC].
  1. This is a metaphor concerning a trial. Some commentators take the comparison to be that Christ pleads our case before God as a lawyer pleads a case before a judge [AB, Br, EBC, NIC, TNTC, WBC, Ws]. A couple of commentators speak of Satan as our accuser [TNTC, Ws]. Others take the comparison to be that Christ intercedes on our behalf to God as someone appears in court to speak on behalf of the defendant [Brd, EGT, ICC, Lns, My, NCBC, TH] or as someone appears before a king to plead the cause of a friend [HNTC].
  2. The metaphor is religious. Christ intercedes for us as a priest intercedes for the people [My].

QUESTION—What relationship is indicated by πρός 'with'?
Although there are several interpretations, they amount to much the same thing, since being in the presence of the Father implies that Jesus is there to address the Father on behalf of his people [Br, Lns, NTC, TH, WBC].
  1. It indicates the location where Jesus is [AB, Lns, TH, WBC; NAB]: we have an advocate who is in the presence of the Father.
  2. It indicates who is addressed by the advocate [Alf, HNTC, TNTC; NIV]: we have an advocate who pleads on our behalf to the Father.

QUESTION—What is implied by mentioning that Jesus is δίκαιον 'righteous'?
  1. It means he is spotless, unblemished and free from sin [AB, Alf, EGT, HNTC, ICC, Lns, My, TNTC; REB]. Being free from sin uniquely qualifies him [NIC, TH], and gives him free access to the presence of God, before whom all sin is excluded [AB, Alf, EGT, ICC, NCBC]. Jesus, as spotless, is an acceptable sacrifice [HNTC, Lns].
  2. It means that he has accomplished the righteous act of dying on the cross. Jesus can ask for our forgiveness on the basis of his one righteous act at the cross [Lns, NIC, WBC, Ws].
  3. It implies that Jesus acts in a righteous and forthright manner in securing our acquittal [Br].

2:2 and[a] he is[b] an-expiation/propitiation[c] for[d] our sins,[e]

LEXICON—a. καί (LN 89.93): 'and' [AB, HNTC, Lns, WBC; KJV, NASB, NRSV, TEV], not explicit [NAB, NIV, NJB, REB, TNT].

b. pres. act. indic of εἰμί (LN 13.1): 'to be' [AB, HNTC, Lns, WBC; all versions]. The present tense indicates a continuous state [TNTC, Ws]. This does not mean that he continues to offer the sacrifice of himself, but that his one sacrifice continues to be effective [TNTC].

c. ἱλασμός (LN **40.12**) (BAGD 1., 2. p. 375): 'expiation' [BAGD, LN, Lns], 'propitiation' [BAGD; KJV, NASB], 'atonement' [AB], 'offering' [NAB], 'sin offering' [BAGD], 'the means of forgiveness' [LN], 'the atoning sacrifice' [WBC; NIV, NRSV], 'the sacrificial offering' [HNTC]. The noun phrase ἱλασμός...περὶ τῶν ἁμαρτιῶν ἡμῶν 'expiation/propitiation for our sins' is translated 'a sacrifice to atone for our sins' [REB], 'the sacrifice to expiate our sins' [NJB], 'the means of taking away our sin' [TNT], 'the means by which our sins are forgiven' [TEV].

d. περί with genitive object (LN 90.39; 89.7): 'for' [AB, HNTC, WBC; KJV, NAB, NASB, NIV, NRSV], 'with regard to' [LN], 'regarding' [Lns]. See above for NJB, REB, TEV, TNT.

e. ἁμαρτία (LN 88.289): 'sin' [AB, HNTC, LN, Lns, WBC; all versions].

QUESTION—What relationship is indicated by καί 'and'?

It adds to the description of Jesus Christ [My, WBC]: he is righteous and he is an expiation/propitiation. It also provides a second reason why he is able to intercede for the sinner [TNTC, WBC, Ws]. It indicates the grounds on which the Advocate rests his case [EGT, NIC].

QUESTION—What is the significance of the use of the overt subject pronoun αὐτός 'he'?

It emphasizes that it is Jesus who is the expiation/propitiation [Brd, ICC, TH, Ws]. He who is our advocate is himself the propitiation [Brd]. Some translations show this by adding 'himself' [WBC; NASB, REB, TEV]: he himself is the expiation/propitiation.

QUESTION—What is meant by ἱλασμός 'expiation/propitiation'?

1. It means 'expiation' and the emphasis is on the effect Christ's sacrifice had on our sin [AB, EBC, Herm, HNTC, ICC, Lns, My, TH, WBC, Ws; NIV, NJB, NRSV, TEV, TNT]. It means that he cleanses us from sin [AB, ICC, My, TH]. God is not against men since he is the one who loved us and sent his Son; it is the sin that must be atoned for [EBC, Lns].

2. It means 'propitiation' and the emphasis is on the effect Christ's sacrifice had on God the Father [Alf, Brd, TNTC, WBC; KJV, NASB]. It satisfied God's justice [Alf, NIC, TNTC, WBC], and reconciled us with God through Christ. The propitiation appeases God's wrath [TNTC].

3. It means both of the above [NIC, NTC, WBC]. Jesus is the offering for our sins and on this basis God forgives us [WBC]. Jesus is the 'atoning sacrifice' [WBC; NIV, NRSV]. He propitiates God, not asking him to declare us innocent of having committed sin, but to grant us pardon for

the sins we have committed. This, in effect, cancels out our sins and so it both expiates sin and propitiates God [NIC].

QUESTION—What metaphoric picture is the author intending with the use of ἱλασμός 'expiation/propitiation'?

It is a picture of a sacrifice [AB, Alf, Brd, EBC, Herm, HNTC, ICC, My, NIC, TH, TNTC, WBC, Ws]. Christ is the offering, offered to God [Alf, Herm, HNTC, My, NIC, TNTC, WBC, Ws]. Christ is also the priest whose offering covers our sin [AB, Brd, ICC, TH, Ws].

and not concerning ours only[a] but[b] also[c] concerning the whole[d] world.[e]

LEXICON—a. μόνος (LN 58.50): 'only' [AB, HNTC, Lns; all versions], 'alone' [WBC].
- b. ἀλλά (LN 89.125): 'but' [AB, HNTC, Lns, WBC; all versions].
- c. καί (LN 89.93): 'also' [AB, Lns, WBC; all versions except NAB, REB], not explicit [HNTC; NAB, REB].
- d. ὅλος (LN 63.1): 'whole' [AB, HNTC, LN, Lns, WBC; all versions except TEV]. For TEV see below.
- e. κόσμος (LN 9.23) (BAGD 5.A. p. 446): 'world' [AB, BAGD, HNTC, Lns, WBC; all versions except TEV], 'mankind' [BAGD]. The noun phrase 'the whole world' is translated 'everyone' [TEV]. See this word at 4:14.

QUESTION—What is implied by the genitives τῶν ἡμετέρων 'of ours' and τοῦ κόσμου 'of the world'?

1. There is an ellipsis of 'sins' [AB, Alf, Brd, EGT, NTC, TH, TNTC, WBC; all versions]: not concerning our sins only, but also concerning the sins of the whole world.
2. There is an advance from the thought of our sins to all sinners [Lns, Ws]: he is an expiation/propitiation, not concerning our sins only, but concerning all the people of the world. The propitiation is valid for all people [Ws].

QUESTION—What is meant by the phrase ὅλου τοῦ κόσμου 'the whole world'?

'World' is a metonymy for all the human beings who live in the world [AB, Br, Brd, Lns, My, NCBC, NIC, TH, TNTC] and this means that the atonement is for people of all kindreds, tribes, and nations [NTC].

QUESTION—In what sense is Christ the expiation concerning the whole world?

Christ has made salvation available to all people [Br, Brd, NIC, TNTC]. It is sufficient for all [EBC]. This is in contrast to the false teachers who taught that only they, the enlightened ones, were included in the atonement [Brd]. It is strongly implied that all people have a desperate need for Christ's atoning work [EBC, NIC].

DISCOURSE UNIT: 2:3–27 [TNTC]. The topic is the application of tests.

DISCOURSE UNIT: 2:3–17 [Br, Lns]. The topic is the new commandment [Br, Lns].

DISCOURSE UNIT: 2:3–11 [AB, Alf, EBC, Herm, NIC, TH, WBC; NAB, NJB]. The topic is obeying God's commands [AB, Alf, EBC, NIC, TH, WBC; NAB, NJB], the knowledge of God and keeping his commands [Herm].

DISCOURSE UNIT: 2:3–6 [Br, Brd, EGT, TNTC]. The topic is the test of obedience [Br, TNTC], the proof of our interest in Christ's propitiation and advocacy [EGT], the need of obedience for fellowship [Brd].

2:3 And[a]

LEXICON—a. καί (LN 89.93): 'and' [HNTC, Lns, WBC; KJV, NASB], 'now' [AB; NRSV], not explicit [NAB, NIV, NJB, REB, TEV, TNT].
QUESTION—What relationship is indicated by this conjunction?
It begins a new section [AB, Alf, EBC, Lns, NCBC, NIC, TH, TNTC, WBC, Ws]. It elaborates on 'walking in the light' [My, WBC], with the first verse being the theme [AB, TH]. This is followed by three statements (2:4, 6 and 9 that parallel 1:6, 8 and 10 of the first section) [AB, TH], and they deal with the claims made by the false teachers [AB, EBC, Herm, NIC, TH, TNTC, WBC, Ws]. But the emphasis is switched from 'fellowship' to 'knowledge' [Herm, HNTC, NIC, TH, WBC, Ws], and from 'confession of sins' to 'obeying the commandments' [Alf, Herm, WBC, Ws] as the test. Now the participles 'the one saying' (2:4, 6 and 9) [EBC, Herm, TH, TNTC] replace the conditional clause 'if we say' [TH, TNTC] in introducing the false teaching which then is refuted. Finally, this section closes with the idea of darkness, begun in verse 1:5. This verse also begins the first of nine (with some minor variations) 'by this we know' *that* [HNTC, WBC], three in this section (2:3, 5 and 9) [TH, TNTC]; each followed by an application in the third person [TNTC]. The verb γινώσκω 'to know' occurs twenty-five times in this short epistle [HNTC].

by[a] this we-know[b] that we-have-known[c] him,

LEXICON—a. ἐν with dative object (LN 89.26; 89.76): 'by' [NASB, NRSV, REB], not explicit [NIV, TEV, TNT]. The prepositional phrase ἐν τούτῳ 'by this' is translated 'this is how' [AB, HNTC, WBC], 'hereby' [KJV], 'in connection with' [Lns], 'the way' [NAB], 'in this way' [NJB].
  b. pres. act. indic. of γινώσκω (LN 28.1) (BAGD 1.c. p. 160): 'to know' [BAGD, HNTC, Lns; KJV, NASB, NIV, NJB], 'to be sure' [AB, WBC; NAB, NRSV, REB, TEV, TNT], 'to come to understand' [LN]. The present tense indicates a state of understanding [Ws], or knowing from day to day [Alf] or coming to know [ICC, TNTC].
  c. perf. act. indic. of γινώσκω (LN 27.18) (BAGD 1.b. p. 161): 'to know' [AB, BAGD, LN, Lns, WBC; all versions except NASB, NIV, NJB], 'to come to know' [BAGD, HNTC; NASB, NIV, NJB]. The clause is translated by a noun phrase: 'our knowledge of' [NAB]. The perfect tense indicates a knowledge acquired in the past with effects continuing into the present [Alf, Brd, ICC, Lns, NIC, NTC, WBC]. One commentator says

that it has the force of a present tense and the variety of tenses are a stylistic device [AB].

QUESTION—What relationship is indicated by the preposition ἐν 'by'?

It indicates the means by which they know that they know God [AB, Brd, NTC]: by means of this we know that we have known him.

QUESTION—What does the pronoun τούτῳ 'this' refer to?

It refers forward to 'if we keep his commandments' [AB, Alf, BAGD, Brd, Herm, ICC, Lns, My, NCBC, NIC, NTC, TH, WBC, Ws; NAB, NIV, REB, TEV, TNT]: by keeping his commandments, we know that we have known him.

QUESTION—What is meant by ἐγνώκαμεν αὐτόν 'we have known him'?

It means to be personally acquainted with God [AB, ICC, NTC, TH, TNTC, Ws]. It is experiential knowledge [AB, HNTC, ICC, WBC, Ws], a personal relationship [AB, Brd, ICC, WBC, Ws]. It is another way of saying that we have fellowship with God (1:6) [Herm, NIC].

QUESTION—To whom does αὐτόν 'him' and αὐτοῦ 'his' refer?

1. The pronouns refer to God [AB, Alf, Br, EBC, Herm, ICC, Lns, My, NCBC, NIC, NTC, TH, TNTC, WBC; REB, TEV]. The distinction between God and Christ is not in focus, since knowing one necessarily implies knowing the other [TH].
2. The pronouns refer to Christ [Brd, EGT].

if[a] we-keep[b] his commandments.[c]

LEXICON—a. ἐάν (LN 89.67): 'if' [HNTC, Lns, WBC; all versions except NAB, REB], 'by' [AB], not explicit [NAB, REB].

b. pres. act. subj. of τηρέω (LN 36.19) (BAGD 5. p. 815): 'to keep' [AB, BAGD, HNTC, LN, Lns; all versions except NIV, NRSV, TEV], 'to obey' [LN, WBC; NIV, NRSV, TEV], 'to observe' [BAGD], 'to pay attention to' [BAGD]. The present tense indicates a habitual practice [AB, Alf, Brd, WBC].

c. ἐντολή (LN 33.330): 'commandment' [AB, HNTC, LN, Lns; all versions except TEV], 'command' [TEV], 'order' [LN, WBC].

QUESTION—How is this clause related to the context?

The keeping of his commandments is the proof of knowing God; not the means of knowing God [AB, Brd, EBC, Herm, ICC, Lns, My, NCBC, NIC, TH, WBC].

QUESTION—What is meant by keeping his commandments?

It refers to actual obedience [My], being careful not to break the commandments [Brd, TNTC]. It is to realize in one's life what the commandments require [AB]. Sympathetic obedience to the spirit of the commandments is in focus [ICC]. Obedience is never perfect, but the desire to obey is what is vital [NIC, TNTC, WBC].

2:4 The-(one) saying[a] that[b] I-have-known[c] him, but[d] not keeping[e] his commandments,

LEXICON—a. pres. act. participle of λέγω (LN 33.69) (BAGD II.1.e. p. 469): 'to say' [HNTC, LN, Lns, WBC; all versions except NAB], 'to claim' [AB; NAB], 'to maintain' [BAGD], 'to declare' [BAGD]. The present tense marks a continued claim of knowing him [Brd, Lns].

b. ὅτι (LN 90.21): 'that' [TEV]. This is translated as direct discourse [AB, Brd, HNTC, Lns, TH, WBC; all versions except TEV]: the one saying, 'I have known him'.

c. perf. act. indic. of γινώσκω: 'to know'. See this word at 2:3. The perfect tense shows that the knowing began in the past but its effects are still active in the present [Lns, WBC].

d. καί (LN 91.12): 'but' [WBC; NIV, NRSV, REB, TEV], 'and' [HNTC, Lns; KJV, NASB, TNT], not explicit [AB; NAB, NJB].

e. pres. act. participle of τηρέω: 'to keep'. See this word at 2:3. The present tense indicates habitual action [Brd, WBC].

QUESTION—How is this verse related to its context?

It has the first of three masculine singular present participles of the verb 'to say' (2:4, 6, 9) [AB, Br, Brd, Lns, NCBC, WBC]. They are reminiscent of the three conditionals in the preceding chapter (1:6, 8, 10) [AB, Alf, Br, ICC, Lns, My, NIC, WBC], and have a conditional force [AB, My, TH]. These claims could be made by any Christian [WBC], but some commentators think that they represent the words of the false teachers [AB, Brd, EGT, ICC, NCBC, NIC, TH]. This verse parallels 1:8 closely [Alf, Br, NIC] with 'if we say' paralleling 'the one who says', 'we lie' paralleling 'is a liar', and 'the truth is not in us' paralleling 'the truth is not in him' [Alf, NIC]. By restating the ideas of 2:3 in a contra-positive manner [Br, My, NIC, TNTC, WBC, Ws], it increases the prominence of that verse [Br, TNTC], and gives a negative example of the principle given there [TNTC].

is a-liar,[a] and the truth[b] is not in[c] this-(one);

LEXICON—a. ψεύστης (LN 33.255) (BAGD p. 892): 'liar' [AB, BAGD, HNTC, LN, Lns, WBC; all versions]. See this word at 1:10.

b. ἀλήθεια: 'truth'. See this word at 1:6, 8.

c. ἐν with dative object: 'in'. See this word at 1:8.

QUESTION—What is meant by calling such a person a ψεύστης 'liar'?

The person's claim to know God is false [NIC]. This noun refers to the character of a deceiver [Brd, ICC, NTC, Ws]. Some commentators see the use of the noun form to be only a stylistic variation of using the verb 'to lie' (1:6) [AB, My]. It means to act dishonestly [HNTC], to deliberately lie [Lns], or to state a falsehood which one believes to be true [NCBC].

QUESTION—What is meant by saying that the truth is not in him?

It refers to a willful exclusion of God's truth [Ws] and not having God's truth in control of his life [NIC, Ws]. The truth is what God has revealed

[Brd]. Truth is reality [Herm] and genuineness [HNTC]. Truth as an active principle does not regulate his thoughts [ICC, WBC, Ws].

2:5 but[a] whoever keeps[b] his word,[c]

LEXICON—a. δέ (LN 89.124): 'but' [AB, HNTC, Lns, WBC; all versions].
- b. pres. act. subj. of τηρέω: 'to keep'. See this word in 2:3, 4.
- c. λόγος (LN 33.98) (BAGD 1.b.β. p. 478): 'word' [AB, BAGD, HNTC, LN, Lns, WBC; all versions].

QUESTION—What relationship is indicated by δέ 'but'?

It indicates a contrast with the person who does not keep God's commandments (2:4) [Lns, My, NTC, WBC]. It restates the positive theme [NIC, TH, WBC].

QUESTION—What is the difference between keeping his λόγος 'word' here and keeping his ἐντολάς 'commandments' in 2:3, 4?

Λόγος 'word' refers to all that God has revealed [Brd, TNTC] and, as such, is a generic term which includes ἐντολάς 'commandments' [Brd, EBC, Herm, ICC, NIC, NTC, TNTC, WBC, Ws]. Many commentators think that the meaning of 'word' here is virtually synonymous with 'commandments' in 2:3, 4 [AB, Alf, HNTC, My, NCBC, TH] since the part of the word one keeps is the commandments [Brd, Ws].

truly[a] in this-(one) the love[b] of-God has-been-perfected.[c]

LEXICON—a. ἀληθῶς (LN 70.3) (BAGD 1. p. 37): 'truly' [AB, BAGD, LN, Lns; all versions except KJV, TEV], 'really' [BAGD, LN, WBC; TEV], 'verily' [KJV], 'actually' [BAGD], not explicit [HNTC].
- b. ἀγάπη (LN 25.43) (BAGD I.1.b.γ. p. 5): 'love' [AB, BAGD, HNTC, LN, Lns, WBC; all versions].
- c. perf. pass. indic. of τελειόω (LN **73.7, 88.38**) (BAGD 2.e.β. p. 810): 'to be perfected' [BAGD, HNTC; KJV, NASB], 'to be made genuine' [LN], 'to be made complete' [NIV], 'to be made perfect' [BAGD, LN; NAB, REB, TEV, TNT], 'to reach perfection' [AB; NJB, NRSV], 'to reach fulfillment' [WBC], 'to be brought to its goal' [Lns]. The perfect tense indicates that the perfecting is timeless and means that the love of God is customarily perfected in such a one [NTC]. It has the force of a present tense [AB, TH, WBC].

QUESTION—How are the two nouns related in the genitive construction ἡ ἀγάπη τοῦ θεοῦ 'the love of God'? What is meant by τετελείωται 'it has been perfected'?

1. 'Love of God' means God's love for people [EGT, Herm, HNTC, Lns, NTC, TH]. Τετελείωται here means 'attained its purpose' [EGT, Herm, HNTC, Lns]: God's love for him has attained its purpose when that person keeps God's word.
2. 'Love of God' means a person's love for God [Alf, BAGD, Br, Brd, ICC, My, NIC, TNTC, WBC; TEV, TNT].
   2.1 Τετελείωται here means 'to be completed'. Only when it has produced obedience is love complete [Alf, Br, Brd, ICC, My, TNTC]: his love for

God has been completed. This sets forth the ideal—whoever perfectly obeys God's word has come to perfectly love him [Alf, ICC, My].
   2.2 Τετελείωται here means 'matured' [EBC, NIC, WBC] and is speaking of a continual growth in our love [EBC]: then his love for God has matured.
3. 'Love of God' means the love God produces in a person for others [EBC, Ws]. Τετελείωται here means 'matured' [Ws]: then the love which God produces has matured in him. There is a continual growth implied in this word [EBC, Ws].

By^a this we-know^b that we-are^c in^d him.
LEXICON—a. ἐν with dative object: 'by'. See this word at 2:3.
   b. pres. act. indic. of γινώκσω: 'to know'. See this word at 2:3.
   c. pres. act. indic. of εἰμί (LN 13.1) (BAGD III.4 p. 225): 'to be' [AB, Lns; all versions except TNT], 'to exist' [HNTC, WBC].
   d. ἐν with dative object (LN 89.119): 'in' [AB, HNTC, LN, Lns, WBC; all versions except NAB, TEV, TNT], 'in union with' [LN; NAB, TEV], 'joined closely to' [LN]. The phrase 'to be in' is translated 'to belong to' [TNT].
QUESTION—What does the pronoun τούτῳ 'this' refer to?
   1. It refers forward to 2:6 [Br, EGT, HNTC, ICC, NIC, NTC, TNTC, WBC, Ws; NAB, NASB, NIV, NRSV, REB, TEV]: by the following we know that we are in him, namely, by walking in the same way he walked.
   2. It refers back to the first clause of this verse [AB, Alf, Brd, EBC, Herm, Lns, NCBC, TH; KJV]: by keeping his word, we know that we are in him. It also includes 2:3 [EBC, Herm]: by obeying the commandments and keeping his word, we know that we are in him.
QUESTION—What relationship is indicated by the preposition ἐν 'in'?
   It refers to intimate fellowship [Alf, Br, Brd, EGT, Lns, NIC], close communion [NIC], a mystic unity [Brd, Lns], and an enduring interrelationship [AB].
QUESTION—To whom does αὐτῷ 'him' refer?
   1. It refers to God, the Father [AB, Alf, Br, Herm, ICC, Lns, My, NCBC, NTC, TH, TNTC, WBC, Ws; NJB, TEV, TNT].
   2. It refers to Jesus [Brd, TNTC].

2:6 The-(one) saying^a (he) remains^b in^c him
LEXICON—a. pres. act. participle of λέγω: 'to say'. See this word at 2:4.
   b. pres. act. infin. of μένω (LN 68.11) (BAGD 1.a.β. p. 504): 'to remain' [BAGD, LN, Lns; NJB, TEV], 'to continue' [BAGD, LN], 'to abide' [AB, BAGD, WBC; KJV, NAB, NASB, NRSV], 'to live' [NIV], 'to dwell' [HNTC; REB]. The phrase 'to remain in' is translated 'to belong to' [TNT].
   c. ἐν with dative object (LN 89.119): 'in' [AB, HNTC, Lns, WBC; all versions except TEV, TNT], 'in union with' [TEV]. For TNT see above.

1 JOHN 2:6

QUESTION—How is this verse related to its context?
　It is transitional [TH], linking the section before it to the following section by repeating the idea of 'in him' and implying the commandment of the next section [AB, TH]. It is parallel with 2:4 and 9 because they all begin with 'the one saying' [Brd, NCBC, TNTC]. It takes up the idea of not sinning from 2:1 [Lns].

QUESTION—What is the difference between ἐν αὐτῷ μένειν 'to remain in him' here and ἐν αὐτῷ ἐσμεν 'to be in him' in 2:5?
　There is no basic difference in meaning [AB, Herm, ICC, My, NIC, TNTC, WBC; TEV, TNT]. There is an added component of meaning of permanency [AB, Brd, Herm, ICC, My, NCBC, NIC, TH, WBC]. Μένειν 'to remain' implies personal determination and action [NIC, Ws].

QUESTION—To whom does αὐτῷ 'him' refer?
　1. It refers to God, the Father [AB, Alf, EBC, ICC, Lns, My, NCBC, NTC, TH, WBC, Ws; TEV, TNT].
　2. It refers to Jesus [Brd, EGT, TNTC].

ought^a as^b that-(one) walked^c so^d also^e himself to-walk^f.

LEXICON—a. pres. act. indic. of ὀφείλω (LN 71.25) (BAGD 2.a.β. p. 599): 'to be obligated' [BAGD], 'to be under obligation' [LN, Lns], not explicit [NAB]. This verb is translated 'ought' [AB, BAGD, HNTC; KJV, NASB, NRSV, TNT], 'must' [BAGD, WBC; NIV, NJB, REB], 'should' [TEV]. The present tense marks continual obligation [Brd].
　b. καθώς (LN 78.53) (BAGD 1. p. 391): 'as' [HNTC, WBC; NASB, NIV, NJB, REB, TNT], 'just as' [AB, BAGD, LN; NAB, NRSV, TEV], 'even as' [Lns; KJV], 'in the same manner as' [NASB].
　c. aorist act. indic. of περιπατέω (LN 41.11) (BAGD 2.a.γ. p. 649): 'to walk' [AB, BAGD, HNTC, Lns; KJV, NASB, NIV, NRSV], 'to live' [BAGD, LN, WBC; REB, TEV, TNT], 'to conduct oneself' [BAGD; NAB], 'to behave' [LN], 'to act' [NJB]. The aorist shows that the action is past and completed [TH] and that the author is thinking of Christ's life as a whole [Brd, My]. See this word at 1:6.
　d. οὕτως: 'so' [HNTC; KJV], 'in the same manner' [NASB], not explicit [AB, Lns, WBC; all versions except KJV].
　e. καί (LN 89.93): 'also' [Lns; KJV], not explicit [AB, HNTC, WBC; all versions except KJV].
　f. pres. act. infin. of περιπατέω (LN 41.11): 'to walk' [AB, HNTC, Lns; KJV, NASB, NIV, NRSV], 'to live' [WBC; REB, TEV, TNT], 'to conduct oneself' [NAB], 'to behave' [LN], 'to act' [NJB]. The present tense marks habitual or continuous action [Brd, TH, WBC].

QUESTION—To whom does ἐκεῖνος 'that one' refer?
　It refers to Jesus [AB, Alf, Br, Brd, EBC, EGT, Herm, HNTC, ICC, Lns, NCBC, NIC, NTC, TH, TNTC, Ws; NIV, REB, TEV, TNT].

QUESTION—Why should a person walk as Jesus walked?
> Consistency with one's profession obliges one to 'walk as he walked' [Alf, My, WBC]. Relationship with God requires moral living [EBC, Lns].

QUESTION—What is meant by the word περιεπάτησεν 'he walked (aorist tense)'?
> It refers to Christ's manner of life on earth [AB, Alf, Br, Brd, EBC, HNTC, Lns, My, NIC, NTC, WBC].

DISCOURSE UNIT: 2:7–17 [ICC; TEV]. The topic is the new command [ICC; TEV].

DISCOURSE UNIT: 2:7–11 [Alf, Br, Brd, EGT, ICC, NTC, TNTC, Ws]. The topic is the love of fellow believers [Brd, ICC, NTC], a test for love [Br, TNTC], the new commandment [EGT; TEV], the command to love [Alf], obedience in love [Ws], love and light [NTC].

2:7 Beloved,ᵃ not a-newᵇ commandmentᶜ I-am-writingᵈ to-you, butᵉ an-oldᶠ commandment

TEXT—Instead of ἀγαπητοί 'beloved', some manuscripts have ἀδελφοί 'brothers'. GNT does not mention this reading. The reading ἀδελφοί 'brothers' is selected only by KJV.

LEXICON—a. ἀγαπητός (LN 25.45) (BAGD 2. p. 6): 'beloved' [AB, BAGD, LN, Lns, WBC; NASB, NRSV], 'dearly beloved' [NAB], 'my dear ones' [HNTC], 'dear friends' [BAGD; NIV, REB, TNT], 'my dear friends' [NJB, TEV].
> b. καινός (LN 28.33) (BAGD 2. p. 394): 'new' [AB, BAGD, HNTC, LN, Lns, WBC; all versions].
> c. ἐντολή (LN 33.330): 'commandment' [AB, HNTC, LN, Lns; all versions], 'order' [LN], 'law' [WBC].
> d. pres. act. indic. of γράφω: 'to write'. See this word at 1:4; 2:1.
> e. ἀλλά (LN 89.125): 'but' [AB, HNTC, Lns, WBC; all versions except TEV], not explicit [TEV]. It shows emphatic contrast between the 'new' and the 'old' [Brd, TH].
> f. παλαιός (LN 67.97) (BAGD 1. p. 605): 'old' [AB, BAGD, HNTC, LN, Lns, WBC; all versions].

QUESTION—How is this verse related to its context?
> It is transitional [NIC, NTC]. It ties back to 2:3–6 by further developing the idea of commandments [Herm, Lns, TH, WBC] and leads into a discussion of love, thereby preparing for 2:9–11 [Herm, Lns, NTC]. It introduces another test for walking in the light: love for the brethren [EBC, TNTC].

QUESTION—Why does the vocative 'beloved' occur at this point?
> It indicates the beginning of a new subsection [NIC, Ws]. It is a term of endearment [AB, Brd, EGT, Lns, NCBC, TNTC, WBC, Ws] used to make the following clause prominent [My] and to make an appeal for love between Christians [AB, ICC]. 'Beloved' is used here in preference to the vocative

'children' (2:1, 12) because love is one of the themes of this section [AB, Brd, EGT, NCBC, NIC, TNTC, WBC, Ws].

QUESTION—Who is the implied actor in the event word 'beloved'?
1. They are loved by John [Brd, HNTC, Lns, TNTC, Ws; NIV, NJB, REB, TEV, TNT]: you whom I love.
2. They are loved by God [AB, NTC]: you whom God loves.

QUESTION—To what commandment does he refer in this verse?

He refers to Jesus' well known commandment to love one another (John 13:34) [AB, Brd, EBC, ICC, NIC, NTC, TNTC, WBC, Ws]. This commandment has already been alluded to in 2:3–6 as Christ's commandments, the change from the plural form to singular here not being significant [Herm, NCBC]. It is also alluded to as 'walking as Christ walked' (2:6), since Christ walked in love [Alf, EBC, My].

QUESTION—In what sense is the commandment not καινός 'new'?

It is not new in the sense of 'a novel kind of commandment' [AB, Br, Brd, EGT, NCBC, NIC, TNTC]. If the focus was on not being new in respect to time, the word would have been νέος 'new' [Brd]. The reason it is not novel or strange is given in the rest of the verse [Brd]. Continuity with Christ's message is an important theme of this whole passage [AB, EBC, Herm, HNTC]. Perhaps the false teachers might charge the author with unauthorized additions to the message [AB, EBC, NIC]. Yet, time is involved. Although it was new when Jesus gave it, it has now been a long time since Jesus commanded it [NIC]. It was a time-honored commandment, not a recent innovation [TH].

QUESTION—In what sense was the commandment old?
1. It was old because it dates back to Christ's teaching [AB, HNTC, WBC]. The readers were already the second generation of Christians [WBC].
2. It was old because it dates back to the time the readers received the gospel [AB, Alf, Brd, My, NIC, TNTC]. Taking the following phrase 'from the beginning' to be the beginning of their Christian lives determines this interpretation [Brd, My].
3. It was old because it dates back to the Jewish teachings on the duties to love [Br, ICC, WBC]. The command to love was in the Jewish Torah (Lev. 19:18) [WBC]. All of God's commandments are summed up in the law of love [Br].

which you-had[a] from[b] (the) beginning;[c]

LEXICON—a. imperf. act. indic. of ἔχω (LN 90.65) (BAGD I.2.i. p. 333): 'to have' [AB, BAGD, HNTC, LN, Lns, WBC; all versions], 'to have over one' [BAGD]. The imperfect tense shows duration in past time [AB, Brd, My, TH].
b. ἀπό with genitive object (LN 67.131): 'from' [AB, HNTC, LN, Lns, WBC; all versions except NIV], 'since' [LN; NIV].

c. ἀρχή (LN 67.65) (BAGD 1.b. p. 112): 'the beginning' [AB, BAGD, HNTC, LN, Lns, WBC; all versions except NAB, TEV], 'the very beginning' [TEV], 'the start' [NAB].

QUESTION—To what does ἀπ' ἀρχῆς 'from the beginning' refer?
1. It refers to the beginning of their Christian lives [Alf, Brd, EGT, Herm, Lns, My, NCBC, NIC, NTC, TH, TNTC, WBC, Ws]: which you had from the time you began to believe in Christ.
2. It refers to the time the gospel began to be proclaimed [AB, Br, Herm, HNTC, NCBC]: which you had since the beginning of the gospel. This is the beginning of the Christian era, either with the teaching of Christ or the preaching of the gospel [AB].
3. Long continuity rather then a starting point is in focus [ICC, WBC]: that you have had for a long time. Mankind has always recognized the social need for love [WBC]. It is a reference to the teaching of Judaism [ICC].

the old commandment is the word[a] which you-heard.[b]

TEXT—Some manuscripts have ἀπ' ἀρχῆς 'from the beginning' at the end of this verse. GNT does not mention this reading. It is included only by KJV.

LEXICON—a. λόγος (LN 33.260) (BAGD 1.b.β. p. 478): 'word' [AB, BAGD, Lns; KJV, NAB, NASB, NRSV], 'message' [HNTC, WBC; NIV, NJB, TEV, TNT], 'instruction' [REB].
b. aorist act. indic. of ἀκούω (LN 24.52): 'to hear' [AB, HNTC, LN, Lns, WBC; all versions except REB], 'to receive' [REB]. The use of the aorist tense is a stylistic variant of the perfect tense and carries the idea of continued effect of the action on the present [AB]. It indicates that the action is viewed as a completed whole [TH, WBC].

QUESTION—To what does λόγος 'the word' refer?
It refers specifically to the commandment they had from the beginning [AB]. It is the gospel message that had been taught them [Alf, Brd, EGT, TH, WBC]. This message contained Jesus' command to love [AB, Brd, Herm, Lns, TNTC]. The essence of the gospel is love [Alf, WBC].

QUESTION—Who told them the word they had heard?
They had heard it when they first became Christians from their teachers [ICC, Lns, NIC, NTC, WBC]. They had heard it from 'us (exclusive)' [TH]: what you heard us tell you.

2:8 On-the-other-hand[a] a-new[b] commandment[c] I-am-writing to-you,

LEXICON—a. πάλιν (LN 89.129) (BAGD 4. p. 607): 'on the other hand' [BAGD, LN, WBC; NASB], 'on second thought' [AB; NAB], 'yet in another way' [NJB], 'again' [Lns; KJV], 'however' [LN; TEV], 'yet' [NIV, NRSV, REB, TNT], 'but again' [HNTC], 'but in turn' [LN].
b. καινός (LN 28.33): 'new' [AB, HNTC, LN, Lns, WBC; all versions].
c. ἐντολή (LN 33.330): 'commandment' [AB, HNTC, LN, Lns; all versions], 'law' [WBC].

QUESTION—What relationship is indicated by πάλιν 'on the other hand'?
It indicates that the 'new commandment' and the 'old commandment' are two ways of talking about the same commandment [AB, Alf, Br, Brd, EBC, EGT, Herm, HNTC, ICC, Lns, My, NIC, TNTC, WBC, Ws]: in one way it is not new but old; in another way it is new. This is a paradox: 'old yet new' [Brd, EGT, Herm]. It comes at it from a different aspect [Alf, NCBC, TH]. It modifies the whole previous idea [Brd, EGT, ICC, Lns].

QUESTION—In what way is the commandment new?
Christ gave new meaning to the OT command [NTC, TH, TNTC]. It is new because it is being fulfilled in a way not previously done [Brd, EBC, NIC, WBC]. It has more depth of meaning than ever before [Br, ICC, TNTC, WBC, Ws] or it had a higher ideal than ever before because they were to love as Christ loved [Br, Brd, TNTC]. The idea is not new, but it is 'new' because it is for the 'new' age [AB, Br, Herm]. The commandment to love is called 'new' by Christ, so the author also calls it 'new' [AB, Br, Brd, EBC, HNTC, TH, TNTC, WBC, Ws]. It is 'new' because the author has written it down afresh [My].

which is true[a] in[b] him and in you,

LEXICON—a. ἀληθής (LN 72.1) (BAGD 2. p. 36): 'true' [AB, BAGD, HNTC, LN, Lns; KJV, NASB, NJB, NRSV, REB]. This adjective is also translated with a verb: 'to be realized' [WBC; NAB]; and as a noun: 'truth' [NIV, TEV, TNT].
  b. ἐν with dative object (LN 89.5, 90.56): 'in' [AB, Lns, WBC; all versions except NJB], 'in relation to' [HNTC], 'for' [NJB].

QUESTION—To whom does αὐτῷ 'him' refer?
It refers to Christ [AB, Alf, Br, Brd, EGT, Herm, ICC, Lns, NIC, TH, TNTC, WBC; REB].

QUESTION—Since ὅ 'which' is a neuter pronoun and does not refer directly to ἐντολή 'commandment', a feminine noun, what does 'which' refer to and how is it true in him and in Christians?
  1. It refers to the newness of the commandment [AB, Alf, Brd, EBC, ICC, Lns, NIC, TH, TNTC, WBC; NAB]: the newness of the commandment to love is true in him and in you. This newness is true in the case of Christ because he taught it, and in the case of Christians because they have newly passed from darkness to light [Alf]. The newness was true in Christ in that his death was a new demonstration of love, and was true in Christians in that they are to love as Christ loved [Brd]. The reality of a new kind of love was shown by its fulfillment by Christ and by his disciples who followed his example [NIC]. Its newness was realized or demonstrated in Christ and in Christians [WBC]. The newness was shown to be true by Christ's life and actions and by Christians [TH].
  2. It refers to the commandment [Br, EGT, Ws; probably all versions except NAB]: the commandment is true in him and in you. The neuter refers to the content of the commandment [Br]. The substance of the

commandment has come true perfectly in Christ and in a measure in Christians [Br]. It corresponds with the facts of Christ's life and with the facts of the Christian life [Ws]. This truth is contained in the revelation of Christ and proved in the experience of the Christians [EGT].

QUESTION—What is meant by the word ἀληθής 'true'?
1. Verification is in focus [AB, TH]. The commandment was verified in the lives of Christ and the believers to whom this epistle is written [AB, TH].
2. Genuineness and reality are in focus [Lns, TH]: which is genuine in him and in you.
3. Demonstration is in focus [WBC; NAB]: which is shown in him and in you.

QUESTION—What is the significance of the repetition of the preposition ἐν 'in' before 'him' and before 'you'?
The repetition shows that the relationships shown are not the same [Br, Brd]. Christ's example is perfect, the Christian's marred [Br].

because[a] the darkness[b] is-passing-away[c] and the true[d] light[e] already[f] is-shining.[g]

LEXICON—a. ὅτι (LN 89.33): 'because' [HNTC, Lns, WBC; KJV, NASB, NIV, NRSV, REB], 'since' [AB], 'for' [NAB, NJB, TEV, TNT].
b. σκοτία (LN 88.125) (BAGD 2. p. 757): 'darkness' [AB, BAGD, HNTC, LN, Lns, WBC; all versions]. It has a figurative reference to everything that is at enmity with God [BAGD].
c. pres. pass. indic. of παράγω (LN 13.93): 'to pass away' [AB, HNTC, Lns; NASB, NJB, NRSV, TEV, TNT], 'to be past' [KJV, NIV, REB], 'to be fading' [WBC], 'to cease' [LN], 'to be over' [NAB]. The present tense marks the action as a process [Br, Brd, ICC, TH].
d. ἀληθινός (LN 70.3) (BAGD 3. p. 37): 'true' [AB, HNTC, LN; all versions except NAB, TEV], 'genuine' [BAGD, Lns], 'real' [BAGD, LN, WBC; NAB, TEV].
e. φῶς (LN 14.36) (BAGD 3.a. p. 872): 'light' [AB, BAGD, HNTC, LN, Lns, WBC].
f. ἤδη (LN 67.20): 'already' [AB, HNTC, LN, Lns, WBC; all versions except KJV, NAB], 'now' [KJV], not explicit [NAB].
g. pres. act. indic. of φαίνω (LN 14.37) (BAGD 1. p. 851): 'to shine' [AB, BAGD, HNTC, LN, Lns, WBC; all versions], 'to give light' [BAGD, LN]. The present tense marks the action as a process [Brd, ICC, TH].

QUESTION—What relationship is indicated by ὅτι 'because'?
1. It indicates the grounds for saying that the commandment is new [NIC, TH; TNT]. That it is new is shown by the fact that darkness is passing away and the light is getting stronger [TH]. The lack of love in the darkness of the old age is being replaced by the light of the new age in which Christian love is shown [NIC]. It was a new teaching for a new age which came with the true light, Jesus [TNTC].

2. It indicates the grounds for saying that the new command is true in Christ and in Christians [EGT, WBC]. The reason the writer knows this is that this truth was first hidden from him and now he sees it in the light of the revelation of the gospel [EGT].
3. It indicates the grounds for saying that the newness of the command is true in the Christians [Brd, NTC]. It is true because as a believer experiences the newness of the command to love, love influences more of his being so that the darkness of wickedness and error is replaced by truth and holiness. This refers only to Christians since Christ does not have any darkness to be replaced [Brd]. It is true that the readers are obeying the new command because the darkness in their lives is being replaced by the light of the gospel [NTC].
4. It indicates the grounds for saying that the new commandment is true in Christ and in the Christians [AB]. The lives of both Christ and Christians cause the light of salvation to gradually overcome darkness [AB].

QUESTION—To what do σκοτία 'darkness' and φῶς 'light' refer?
1. 'Darkness' refers to the old pre-Christian way of life [Br, Lns, Ws]. Then 'light' refers to believing the gospel [Lns, NTC, Ws].
2. 'Darkness' refers to the epoch of history before the last time [Br, Herm, NCBC, TNTC]. 'Light' then refers to the end times [Br, Herm, NCBC].
3. The 'darkness' is lack of love [EBC, ICC, NIC]. 'Light' then refers to 'loving one's brother' [EBC, ICC, NIC].
4. The 'darkness' is sin and error [Brd, My, WBC]. 'Light' then refers to truth and holiness [Brd, My, WBC].

2:9 The-(one) saying^a to-be in the light but^b hating^c his brother^d

LEXICON—a. pres. act. participle of λέγω: 'to say'. See this word at 2:4, 6.
    b. καί (LN 91.12): 'but' [WBC; NIV, NJB, REB], 'and' [HNTC Lns; KJV, TNT], 'yet' [LN; TEV], 'and yet' [NASB], 'while' [NRSV], 'all the while' [AB; NAB].
    c. pres. act. participle of μισέω (LN 88.198) (BAGD 1. p. 522): 'to hate' [AB, BAGD, HNTC, LN, Lns, WBC; all versions], 'to detest' [BAGD, LN], 'to abhor' [BAGD]. The present tense marks a continuing attitude of hatred [Brd, WBC].
    d. ἀδελφός (LN 11.23): 'brother' [AB, HNTC, LN, Lns, WBC; all versions except NRSV, REB], 'brother and sister' [NRSV], 'fellow Christian' [LN; REB].

QUESTION—How is this verse related to its context?
It is the third (2:4, 6, 9) false claim marked by a participle of λέγω 'to say' [AB, Br, Brd, EBC, NCBC, NTC, WBC], each one giving the negative first, followed by the positive [Brd] and marking a new sub-section [AB]. The other two gave the general principle first, followed by an illustration, but this one reverses that order [TNTC, WBC, Ws]. Because the main commandment is love [Alf, Br], therefore, loving is obeying the commandments [Br]. It parallels 1:6, 8, and 2:3 as an additional character

test [Brd, Lns]. It ties into the previous verse by developing the idea of light [Brd, WBC, Ws], and the verse before that with walking in the light [Brd]. The writer assumes that the reader knows that the new commandment is about loving one's brother [NIC].

QUESTION—What is meant by μισῶν 'hating'?

The author is speaking in black and white terms; one either loves or hates [AB, Alf, Br, EBC, Herm, ICC, My, NCBC, NIC, TNTC]. Hate is a lack of love [AB, Br, EBC, Herm, NCBC, NIC] or a lack of sympathy [Ws]. Some commentators focus on actions, not feelings [Br, EBC, NIC, TH]: it is a lack of benevolent deeds [EBC, EGT, NIC], a lack of self-sacrifice [EBC, NIC, TH]. The absence of deeds of love is hate [EBC, NIC]. However, some commentators take it to be a strong feeling of hate against someone, not just a mild dislike or lack of love [AB, Brd, NTC].

QUESTION—To whom does ἀδελφόν 'brother' refer?

1. It refers to fellow Christians [AB, Brd, EBC, EGT, ICC, LN, Lns, My, NIC, TH, WBC, Ws]. Though grammatically singular it is semantically indefinite plural [Brd, TH]. It is a test for family membership [Brd]. John is writing about a specific situation in the congregation [NIC, WBC], but there is no implication that it does not apply to people outside the congregation as well [WBC]. 'Brother' refers to female Christians as well [AB; NRSV].

2. It refers to others whether or not they are Christians [Herm, NCBC]: but hates another person.

is in[a] the darkness[b] until[c] now.[d]

LEXICON—a. ἐν with dative object: 'in' [AB, HNTC, Lns, WBC; all versions].

b. σκοτία (LN 88.125): 'darkness' [AB, HNTC, LN, Lns, WBC; all versions].

c. ἕως (LN 67.119) (BAGD II.1.c. p. 335): 'until' [BAGD, LN; NASB], 'even until' [KJV], 'still . . . even' [AB], 'even' [NAB]. The phrase ἕως ἄρτι 'until now' is translated 'still' [Lns, WBC; NIV, NJB, NRSV, REB, TNT], 'still very much' [HNTC], 'to this very hour' [TEV].

d. ἄρτι (LN 67.38) (BAGD 3. p. 110): 'now' [AB, BAGD, LN; KJV, NAB, NASB].

QUESTION—What is being implied by the phrase ἕως ἄρτι 'until now'?

He has always been and still is in darkness [Brd, Ws] even though he thinks and claims to be in the light [EGT, Ws]. The writer hopes that he will leave his darkness [Lns, NTC]. It means 'just as he was before' [TH] or 'even now' [NIC], in spite of apparent changes when he joined the congregation [Alf].

2:10 The-(one) loving[a] his brother remains[b] in the light,

LEXICON—a. pres. act. participle of ἀγαπάω (LN 25.43) (BAGD 1.a.α. p. 4): 'to love' [AB, BAGD, HNTC, LN, Lns, WBC; all versions]. The present tense indicates the continuing reality of that love [Alf, Brd].

b. pres. act. indic. of μένω (**LN 68.11**) (BAGD 1.a.β. p. 504): 'to remain' [BAGD, LN, Lns, WBC; NJB], 'to abide' [AB, BAGD; KJV, NASB], 'to dwell' [HNTC; REB], 'to live' [NIV, NRSV, TEV], 'to continue' [BAGD, LN; NAB], 'to be' [TNT].

QUESTION—How is this verse related to its context?

It is the positive parallel to 2:9, the test of love [EBC, Lns, NIC]. It is also in positive-negative contrast with 2:11 [NIC, TH, TNTC, WBC].

QUESTION—What is the difference between ἐν τῷ φωτὶ μένει 'remains in the light' here and ἐν τῷ φωτὶ εἶναι 'to be in the light' in 2:9?

They are similar but ἐν τῷ φωτὶ μένει 'remains in the light' stresses duration of the state of being in the light [AB, ICC]. 'To remain' means maintaining a constant, habitual, permanent relationship with the light [Brd, NIC, TH, WBC, Ws].

and[a] there-is no cause-for-stumbling[b] in[c] him/it;

LEXICON—a. καί (LN 89.92): 'and' [AB, HNTC, Lns, WBC; all versions except NAB, REB, TEV], 'and so' [TEV], not explicit [NAB, REB].

b. σκάνδαλον (LN 25.181, 88.306) (BAGD 3. p. 753): 'cause for stumbling' [NASB, NRSV, REB], 'occasion of stumbling' [KJV], 'stumbling' [AB], 'something to trip someone up' [WBC], 'something to make one stumble' [HNTC; NIV], 'something to cause one to fall' [NAB, TNT], 'something to make one fall away' [NJB], 'something to make one sin' [LN; TEV], 'entrapment' [Lns], 'offence' [BAGD, LN], 'object of disapproval' [BAGD], 'stain, fault' [BAGD].

c. ἐν with dative object (LN 89.119): 'in' [AB, Lns, WBC; all versions except NIV]. For HNTC, NIV see above.

QUESTION—Σκάνδαλον can mean 'a cause of sin' or 'a cause for offence' and αὐτῷ can mean either 'him' or 'it'. What does this clause mean?

1. There is nothing in him that would cause the person himself to sin [AB, Alf, Brd, EGT, ICC, My, NIC, NTC, TH, Ws; NIV, NJB].
2. There is nothing in him that would cause someone else to sin [Lns; TEV].
3. There is no fault in him [BAGD].
4. There is nothing in him that would cause others to be offended by him [EBC]. He will never cause the offense that his opponents cause [EBC].
5. There is nothing in it, the light, that would cause him to sin [WBC; TNT].

2:11 **but[a] the-(one) hating[b] his brother is in the darkness[c] and walks[d] in the darkness,**

LEXICON—a. δέ (LN 89.124): 'but' [AB, HNTC, WBC; all versions], 'now' [Lns].

b. pres. act. participle of μισέω (LN 88.198) (BAGD 1. p. 522): 'to hate' [AB, BAGD, HNTC, LN, Lns, WBC; all versions], 'to detest' [BAGD], 'to abhor' [BAGD]. The present tense is used here to show a continuous state [TH, WBC]. See this word at 2:9.

c. σκοτία (**LN 88.125**) (BAGD 2. p. 757): 'darkness' [AB, BAGD, HNTC, LN, Lns, WBC; all versions]. This is a figurative use of darkness for everything that is at enmity with God [BAGD], 'the realm of evil' [LN]. See this word at 2:9.

d. pres. act. indic. of περιπατέω (LN 41.11) (BAGD 1.d. p. 649): 'to walk' [AB, HNTC, Lns; all versions except NIV, NJB], 'to walk around' [WBC; NIV], 'to walk about' [NJB], 'to go about' [BAGD], 'to live' [LN], 'to behave' [LN]. The present tense indicates continuous action [TH]. See this word at 1:6.

QUESTION—What relationship is indicated by δέ 'but'?

It shows contrast between verse 2:10 and 2:11 [AB, Brd, NIC, TH, WBC]. It adds a fuller explanation of 2:10 [Lns].

QUESTION—What is the relationship between 'being in darkness' and 'walking in darkness'?

'Being in darkness' refers to his state and 'walking in darkness' to his deeds [Alf].

and (does) not know[a] where[b] he-is-going,[c] because[d] the darkness has-blinded[e] his eyes.

LEXICON—a. perf. (with present meaning) act. indic. of οἶδα (LN 28.1): 'to know' [HNTC, LN, Lns, WBC; all versions except REB]. The phrase οὐκ οἶδεν 'does not know' is translated 'has no idea' [AB; REB]

b. ποῦ (LN 83.6) (BAGD 2.b. p. 696): 'where' [AB, HNTC, Lns, WBC; all versions except KJV, NRSV], 'whither' [KJV], 'where' [NRSV].

c. pres. act. indic. of ὑπάγω (LN 15.15): 'to go' [AB, HNTC, Lns, WBC; all versions], 'to go along' [LN]. The present tense indicates continuous action [TH].

d. ὅτι (LN 89.33): 'because' [HNTC, Lns, WBC; all versions except NAB], 'for' [AB], 'since' [NAB].

e. aorist act. indic. of τυφλόω (LN **32.25**) (BAGD p. 831): 'to blind' [AB, BAGD, Lns; all versions except NRSV, REB, TEV], 'to make blind' [HNTC, WBC; REB, TEV], 'to bring on blindness' [NRSV], 'to deprive of sight' [BAGD]. It is an idiom for 'to cause to not understand' or 'to make unable to comprehend' [LN]. The aorist indicative shows a definite past action [Alf, Brd, TH].

QUESTION—What is meant by the word τυφλόω 'to blind'?

Failure to believe is in focus [AB]. Some commentators say that he is unaware that he is going into complete darkness [Brd], that is, hell [Lns]. Others suggest that he is acting selfishly without the goal of loving his brother [My].

QUESTION—What is being pictured in the metaphor?

1. It pictures a person wandering in the dark for so long that the darkness has caused sight to atrophy [AB, EGT, My, NIC, NTC, TH, WBC, Ws]. His eyes can no longer see the light [NIC]. Living in darkness causes spiritual blindness [WBC].

2. It pictures a person wandering in the dark as if he were blind [ICC]. He cannot see because of the dark [ICC].

DISCOURSE UNIT: 2:12–17 [AB, Brd, EBC, EGT, Herm, HNTC, ICC, NIC, TH, WBC, Ws; NJB]. The topic is resisting the world [AB, WBC], not loving the world [TH], detachment from the world [NJB], relationship to the world [NIC], a warning against the world [ICC; NJB], knowing God and abiding in him [EBC], the appeal of experience [EGT], the Christian cause [HNTC], the status of believers and their relation to the world [NIC], things temporal and eternal [Ws], two digressions [Brd].

DISCOURSE UNIT: 2:12–14 [Alf, Br, Brd, NCBC, NTC, TNTC; NAB]. The topic is the encouragement to three age groups [Br], a threefold reason for writing [Alf], two appeals [NTC], assumptions concerning readers [Brd], the members of the community [NAB], digression about the church [TNTC].

2:12 **I-write[a] to-you, children,[b]**
LEXICON—a. pres. act. indic. of γράφω: 'to write'. See this word at 1:4; 2:1, 7. The present tense indicates that he is in the process of writing this letter [Brd, ICC].
  b. τεκνίον: 'child'. See this word at 2:1.
QUESTION—How does 2:12–14 relate to the context?
  This is the first half [Herm, Ws] of a digression [Brd, HNTC] which extends through 2:17. It is self-contained [WBC] and difficult to relate to the context either before or after [Herm, HNTC, NIC, TNTC, WBC]. The author turns from refuting the false teachers to addressing his followers affectionately [AB, TH, TNTC, Ws]. The author wishes to assure the readers [Brd, EBC, EGT, ICC, My, NCBC, NIC, TNTC] of their Christian experience [ICC, NIC, TNTC] and to give them strength to help them withstand the false teachers [Herm]. It may be the grounds for the appeal in 2:15 [EGT, ICC, NIC, Ws]; or it may describe the Christian 'walking in the light' while 2:15–17 describe the false teachers [Herm, TH].
QUESTION—How are these three verses organized?
  There are two sets of three exhortations each [Alf, EBC, Herm, My, NCBC, NIC, TH, TNTC, WBC], arranged rhythmically [Herm, TH, WBC], each addressed to a slightly different audience [EBC, Herm]. The first three begin with 'I am writing to you' in the present tense and are followed by three occurrences of 'I wrote to you' in the aorist [Herm, NCBC, NIC, TNTC]. These are followed by six subordinate clauses, each begun by the conjunction ὅτι 'that' [NIC, WBC].
QUESTION—How are the 'children', 'fathers', and 'young men' related to each other?
  1. They comprise only two groups of readers. 'Children' is a general term for the whole group, and this group is then divided into 'fathers' and 'young men' [AB, Alf, Brd, EGT, Herm, ICC, Lns, My, NCBC, NTC, TH, WBC, Ws].
    1.1 These two groups differ primarily in chronological age [Herm, ICC, Lns, My, TH]. Length of years give opportunities for Christian maturity [ICC].

1.2 These two groups differ primarily in spiritual maturity [EGT, Ws].
2. They comprise three distinct groups [Br, EBC, HNTC, TNTC].
2.1 They are ranked by spiritual maturity. 'Children' are the new believers, young men are the more experienced believers, and fathers are the mature believers. [Br, TNTC].
2.2 The 'children' are the congregation as a whole, the 'fathers' are the presiding leaders, and the 'young men' are their assistants [HNTC].
3. There is only one group, the whole Christian community [NIC]. All Christians should have the innocence of children, the strength of youth, and the mature knowledge of older people [NIC].

because/that[a] (your) sins[b] have-been-forgiven[c] you

LEXICON—a. ὅτι (LN 89.33, 90.21) (BAGD 1.b.α., 3.a. p. 588, 589): 'because' [BAGD, HNTC, Lns, WBC; all versions except NAB], 'since' [BAGD], 'for' [NAB], 'that' [BAGD], not explicit [AB].

b. ἁμαρτία (LN 88.289; 88.310): 'sin'. See this word at 1:8; 2:2.

c. perf. passive indic. of ἀφίημι (LN 40.8) (BAGD 2. p. 126): 'to be forgiven' [AB, BAGD, LN, WBC; all versions], 'to be remitted' [BAGD, Lns], 'to be pardoned' [BAGD, LN], 'to be removed' [HNTC]. The perfect tense shows that the forgiveness was in the past but is still in effect [AB, EBC, ICC, Lns, NIC, TH, TNTC, Ws].

QUESTION—What relationship is indicated by the conjunction ὅτι 'because/that'?

1. It indicates the reason for writing to them [Alf, Brd, Herm, HNTC, ICC, Lns, My, NCBC, NIC, WBC, Ws; all versions]: I am writing to you, children, because God has forgiven your sins. The author writes to enforce the duties growing out of their privileges as believers [Ws]. The Christian experience of the readers forms the presuppositions used in the letter [My]. He writes because they are spiritually capable of responding [ICC, WBC]. Because certain things are true of the readers, he writes further instructions [NIC]. Since they are God's children, they need instruction about doctrinal error [Brd].

2. It means 'that' and gives the content of what he is writing [AB, EBC, TH]: I am writing to you, children, that God has forgiven your sins. This gives reassurance to the unsure Christians [AB, EBC]. The writer is stressing vital truths [TH].

because-of[a] his name.[b]

LEXICON—a. διά with genitive object (LN 90.44) (BAGD A.IV. p. 181): 'because of' [AB, BAGD, LN], 'for the sake of' [Lns; KJV, NASB, REB, TEV, TNT], 'on account of' [HNTC, WBC; NIV, NRSV], 'through' [NAB, NJB].

b. ὄνομα (LN 9.19) (BAGD I.4.c.α. p. 572): 'name' [AB, BAGD, HNTC, Lns, WBC; all versions except TEV], 'Christ' [TEV].

QUESTION—What relationship is indicated by διά 'because'?
It indicates the reason God forgave their sins [AB, Alf, Brd, ICC, Lns, My, NIC, NTC, TH, TNTC, WBC]: your sins have been forgiven because of Christ. It was because of what he has done [Alf, NTC, TH]. It was because of who Christ is and what he has done [ICC]. It was because of his sacrificial death and his role as an advocate [NIC, TNTC]. It was because they bear his name and believe in him [Herm, My].

QUESTION—To whom does ὄνομα αὐτοῦ 'his name' refer?
It refers to Christ [AB, Alf, Brd, Herm, ICC, Lns, My, NTC, TH, TNTC, WBC, Ws; TEV].

QUESTION—How does ὄνομα αὐτοῦ 'his name' here differ from αὐτός 'him'?
There is no difference in meaning [AB, Herm, My, TH; TEV]. 'Name' expresses the nature and character of the person [Brd] and his saving work [TNTC].

2:13 I-write[a] to-you, fathers,[b] because/that[c] you-have-known[d] the-(one) from[e] (the) beginning.[f]

LEXICON—a. pres. act. indic. of γράφω: 'to write'. See this word at 2:12.
    b. πατήρ (LN 11.26) (BAGD 2.c. p. 635): 'father' [AB, BAGD, HNTC, LN, Lns, WBC; all versions]. It is a title of respect for the older generation [NIC].
    c. ὅτι (LN 89.33, 90.21) (BAGD 1.b.α., 3.a. p. 588, 589): 'because' [BAGD, HNTC, Lns, WBC; all versions except NAB], 'since' [BAGD], 'for' [NAB], 'that' [BAGD], not explicit [AB]. See 2:12 for interpretations of this word.
    d. perf. act. indic. of γινώσκω: 'to know'. See this word at 2:3b, 4. The perfect tense indicates a past action with effects in the present [AB, Brd, EBC, WBC, Ws].
    e. ἀπό with genitive object (LN 67.131): 'from' [AB, HNTC, LN, Lns, WBC; all versions except NJB], 'since' [LN; NJB].
    f. ἀρχή (LN 67.65) (BAGD 1.c. p. 112): 'beginning' [AB, BAGD, HNTC, LN, Lns, WBC; all versions].

QUESTION—To whom does 'the one from the beginning' refer?
    1. It refers to Christ [AB, Alf, Brd, EBC, Herm, HNTC, ICC, Lns, My, NCBC, NIC, TH, WBC, Ws].
    2. It refers to God [Br, TNTC].

QUESTION—In what sense did they know him?
All Christians know Christ and God the Father, but here a depth of spiritual relationship is the special mark of mature believers [WBC]. They had looked deep into the eternal nature of Christ [My]. It refers to fellowship with him [Herm]. Their knowledge makes them spiritually capable of responding to what is written [WBC] and of explaining it to younger believers [Lns].

QUESTION—What is meant by ἀρχῆς 'the beginning'?
1. It refers to Christ's pre-existence [HNTC, ICC, Lns, My, NIC, WBC, Ws; TEV]: you have known the one who existed from the beginning.
2. It refers to the beginning of Christ's ministry here on earth [AB, NCBC]: you have known the one who appeared when he began his ministry.

I-write[a] to-you, young-men,[b] because/that[c] you-have-overcome[d] the evil-one.[e]

LEXICON—a. pres. act. indic. of γράφω: 'to write'.
    b. νεανίσκος (LN 9.32) (BAGD 1. p. 534): 'young man' [BAGD, HNTC, LN, WBC; all versions except NJB, NRSV], 'youth' [BAGD, Lns], 'young people' [AB; NJB, NRSV].
    c. ὅτι (LN 89.33, 90.21) (BAGD 2.d. p. 167): 'because' [BAGD, HNTC, Lns, WBC; all versions except NAB], 'since' [BAGD], 'for' [NAB], 'that' [BAGD], not explicit [AB]. See 2:12 for interpretations of this word.
    d. perf. act. indic of νικάω (LN 39.57) (BAGD 2.a. p. 539): 'to overcome' [BAGD, HNTC; KJV, NASB, NIV, NJB], 'to conquer' [AB, BAGD, LN, Lns, WBC; NAB, NRSV, REB, TNT], 'to defeat' [TEV], 'to be victorious over' [LN], 'to vanquish' [BAGD]. The perfect tense indicates that the action was in the past and its effects remain in the present [AB, Brd, EBC, Lns, TH, TNTC, WBC, Ws]. This shows that the victory was already won at conversion, although fighting must still persist for the Christian [NIC, TH].
    e. πονηρός (LN 12.35) (BAGD 2.b. p. 691): 'evil one' [AB, BAGD, HNTC, LN, WBC; all versions except KJV], 'wicked one' [Lns; KJV].

QUESTION—How did they overcome the evil one?
They overcame him by being converted [Alf, NIC]. They resisted false teaching [Brd, WBC]. They overcame evil by exposing the false teachers [ICC, TNTC]. They are using Christ's power to defeat the devil [EBC, NCBC]. They overcame by obedience to the word of God [TNTC]. They were conforming ethically to the gospel demands on their life [TNTC]. They shared in the victory won by Jesus in his life and death [AB].

QUESTION—To whom does τὸν πονηρόν 'the evil (masculine form)' refer?
1. It refers to the devil [AB, Alf, Brd, EBC, HNTC, ICC, Lns, My, NCBC, NIC, TH, WBC, Ws; TEV]: you have overcome the devil.
2. It refers to evil and is a personification [ICC, TNTC]: you have overcome evil. This means deliverance from sin's power [TNTC].

2:14 I-wrote[a] to-you, children,[b] because/that you-have-known[c] the Father.

TEXT—Some manuscripts include this sentence in 2:13. GNT, AB, EGT, HNTC, Lns, WBC, NAB, NJB, NRSV, TEV and TNT begin verse 14 here. EBC, TNTC, KJV, NASB, NIV and REB begin it after this sentence.

TEXT—Instead of ἔγραψα 'I wrote' (aorist tense), some manuscripts have γράφω 'I write' (present tense). GNT does not mention this alternative. The present tense is selected only by KJV.

1 JOHN 2:14

LEXICON—a. aorist act. indic. of γράφω: 'to write'. See this word at 2:13.
  b. παιδίον (LN 9.46) (BAGD 2.a. p. 604): 'child' [AB, BAGD, LN; NAB, NASB, NJB, NRSV, REB, TNT], 'little one' [HNTC], 'lad' [Lns], 'little child' [WBC; KJV], 'dear child' [NIV], 'my child' [TEV].
  c. perf. act. indic. of γινώσκω: 'to know'. See this word at 2:3b, 4, 13. The perfect tense is used here to show a past action with effects in the present [EBC].

QUESTION—What is the significance of the change in tense from the present tense γράφω 'I write' in 2:12–13 to the aorist tense ἔγραψα 'I wrote' in this verse?
  1. There is no significant difference [AB, Alf, Br, Brd, HNTC, Lns, NIC, TH, TNTC, WBC, Ws]. The two tenses are translated in the same way [KJV, NIV, NJB, REB, TEV, TNT]. This whole epistle is being referred to as written [AB, Alf, Brd, EBC] and the aorists are epistolary aorists used for rhetorical repetition [Lns]. The present tense refers to the time of the writer's act of writing the letter and the past tense refers to the time of the reader's act of reading it [Alf, Lns]. At this point John looks back as this statement of purpose: 'I write, yes, I have written, because you have all had experience in the Faith' [Ws].
  2. The change to the aorist tense marks a change in reference as to what he wrote [EGT, ICC, My].
  2.1 In 2:12–13 he is speaking of the whole letter; but in 2:14 he is referring only to the part already written [ICC, My].
  2.2 In 2:12–13 he is speaking of this letter; but in 2:14 he is referring to the Gospel of John [EGT].
  3. The present tense is used to introduce the three summary statements of orthodox belief (2:12–13), while the aorist tenses introduce a discussion of those statements which is carried on in the teaching which follows [WBC].
  4. The change to the aorist tense marks a change in authority. The author has been speaking as a representative of the apostles. He now speaks for himself alone [NCBC].

QUESTION—How does παιδία 'children' used here differ from τεκνία 'children' used in 2:12?
  1. There is no significant difference [AB, Alf, Br, Brd, EBC, EGT, HNTC, Lns, My, NCBC, TH, WBC].
  2. In 2:12 τεκνία 'children' refers affectionately to them and emphasizes their relationship, but here παιδία 'children' stresses immaturity and the need for discipline [EBC, ICC, TNTC, Ws].

I-wrote[a] to-you, fathers, because/that you-have-known the-one from (the) beginning.

LEXICON—a. aorist act. indic. of γράφω: 'to write'.

QUESTION—Why is this clause repeated from 2:13?
 It is repeated for emphasis [Lns, NIC]. It indicates the seriousness of the appeal; they cannot relax the process of their spiritual growth [NTC]. There can be no greater reason [EGT] and this includes all that we can know [Ws].

I-wrote[a] to-you, young-men, because/that you-are strong[b]
LEXICON—a. aorist act. indic. of γράφω: 'to write'.
 b. ἰσχυρός (LN 79.63) (BAGD 1.b. p. 383): 'strong' [AB, BAGD, HNTC, LN, Lns, WBC; all versions], 'mighty' [BAGD], 'powerful' [BAGD], 'vigorous' [LN].
QUESTION—What is meant by the word ἰσχυρός 'strong'?
 It refers to spiritual strength [AB, Br, Brd, Herm, Lns, NTC, TH, WBC], strength for fighting against attacks against the church [Alf], courage [TH], steadfastness [TH]. They are strong because God's word is in them [Brd, EBC, Herm Lns, My, NIC, NTC, TNTC]. Because they are strong, they have overcome the evil one [Brd, EGT, Lns, NTC].

and the word[a] of-God remains[b] in[c] you and you-have-overcome the evil one.
LEXICON—a. λόγος (LN 33.260) (BAGD 1.b.β. p. 478): 'word' [AB, BAGD, HNTC, LN, Lns, WBC; all versions], 'Divine revelation' [BAGD].
 b. pres. act. indic of μένω (LN 68.11) (BAGD 1.a.β. p. 504): 'to remain' [BAGD, LN, Lns; NAB, NJB, REB], 'to continue' [BAGD, LN], 'to abide' [AB, BAGD; KJV, NASB, NRSV], 'to dwell' [HNTC, WBC], 'to live' [NIV, TEV], 'to be' [TNT]. The present tense indicates a constant abiding [Brd].
 c. ἐν (LN 89.119): 'in' [AB, HNTC, Lns, WBC; all versions].
QUESTION—How are the two nouns related in the genitive construction ὁ λόγος τοῦ θεοῦ 'the word of God'?
 It means the 'word which God spoke' [Brd, TH], the message from God [Brd] revealed by and in Jesus [AB].
QUESTION—What is meant by 'the word of God'?
 1. It refers to the command to love one's brother [AB]. This is what is stressed in 2:5–11 [AB].
 2. It refers to the gospel [Alf, Br, Brd, ICC, My].

DISCOURSE UNIT: 2:15–3:10 [NCBC]. The topic is dealing with the end of the world.

DISCOURSE UNIT: 2:15–24 [NASB]. The topic is not loving the world.

DISCOURSE UNIT: 2:15–17 [Alf, Br, Brd, Herm, ICC, My, NCBC, NTC, TNTC, Ws; NAB, NIV]. The topic is a digression about the world [TNTC], the world and the will of God [NTC], the attraction of the world [NCBC], a warning against loving the world [Alf, Br, Brd; NAB, NIV].

1 JOHN 2:15

2:15 (Do) not love[a] the world[b] nor the (things) in[c] the world.

LEXICON—a. pres. act. impera. of ἀγαπάω (LN 25.104) (BAGD 2. p. 5): 'to love' [AB, BAGD, HNTC, LN, Lns, WBC; all versions except NAB, REB], 'to have love for' [NAB], 'to set one's heart on' [REB], 'to take pleasure in' [LN]. It means to have a high esteem for something [BAGD].
  b. κόσμος (LN 41.38; 1.39) (BAGD 6. p. 446): 'world' [AB, BAGD, HNTC, LN, Lns; all versions]. The phrase 'the things in the world' is translated 'worldly things' [WBC].
  c. ἐν with dative object (LN 89.5): 'in' [AB, HNTC, Lns; all versions except NAB, TEV], not explicit [WBC]. This preposition is also translated 'to afford' [NAB], 'to belong to' [TEV].

QUESTION—How is this verse related to its context?
  The author turns from describing the church to describing the world and the church's attitude towards it [TNTC, Ws]. He appeals to the readers on the basis of their Christian standing just affirmed in verses 2:12–14 [ICC, Ws]. It is yet another test for walking in the light [EBC, ICC, WBC] and gives another difference between believers and the false teachers [EBC].

QUESTION—What does the use of the present tense of the verb indicate?
  1. The present imperative with the negative μή implies that they are already engaged in loving the world [Brd, NTC]: stop loving the world. This either implies that to some extent all of the believers love the world [Brd] or that only some of the believers love the world [NTC].
  2. The present imperative forbids a course of action but without any implication as to whether or not they are now loving the world [Lns]: do not be in the state of loving the world.

QUESTION—What is meant by τὸν κόσμον 'the world'?
  The 'world' is the system of all that is opposed to God [Brd, EBC, Lns, TH, TNTC]. It is human society controlled by evil [Alf, NIC, WBC, Ws]. It is fallen mankind and all that it lives for [My]. It includes all unregenerate people and their attitudes [Brd]. It is all human concerns apart from God [Herm]. It is dominated by Satan [Brd, EBC, Lns, My, TH, TNTC]. Another view takes the world to be all that God made. Although not evil in itself, it is transitory and not the supreme end for Christians [EGT].

QUESTION—What is meant by loving the world?
  The 'love' mentioned here is selfish desire [Alf, TNTC] and avarice [Alf]. It is an attitude of esteeming the world to be of utmost value [Brd]. It is the attraction to what a person thinks he will enjoy [NIC]. It means striving after or coveting things [TH]. It means depending or relying on the world [EGT, Herm].

QUESTION—What is meant by τὰ ἐν τῷ κόσμῳ 'the things in the world'?
  It is whatever the world offers [TH]. It refers to the objects that are desired by people [ICC]. Some take it to be all the material things that are transient, even good things [EGT]. Others take it to be just those objects that are desired by ungodly people [Alf]. They are the individual things, pleasures, and honors in the world that are hostile to God [Lns, My].

If^a anyone loves the world, the love^b of-the father is not in^c him;

LEXICON—a. ἐάν (LN 89.67): 'if' [AB, HNTC, Lns, WBC; all versions except REB], not explicit [REB]. This introduces a hypothetical statement to support the preceding prohibition [Brd]. It gives the first reason why one should not love the world [EBC].
  b. ἀγάπη: 'love'. This noun is also translated by a verb: 'to love' [REB, TEV]. See this word at 2:5.
  c. ἐν with dative object (LN 89.119): 'in' [AB, HNTC, Lns, WBC; all versions except REB, TEV], not explicit [REB, TEV].

QUESTION—How are the two nouns related in the genitive construction ἡ ἀγάπη τοῦ πατρός 'the love of the Father'?
  1. It means a person's love for the Father [Alf, Brd, EBC, My, NIC, NTC, TNTC, Ws; NRSV, REB, TEV, TNT]: if anyone loves the world, then he does not love the Father. By stating that this love is not 'in him', he means that it is not a continuing principle [Brd]. The two loves are incompatible [NIC, TNTC].
  2. It means the Father's love for the person [HNTC, Lns; NAB]: if anyone loves the world, then the Father does not love him. Such a person prevents the Father from loving him and coming into his heart to dwell [Lns].
  3. It means both the Father's love for the person and the person's love for the Father [TH, WBC]: if anyone loves the world, then he does not love the Father and the Father does not love him. Love for the world works against love for the Father, a love that both answers and derives from the Father's love for him [WBC]. Other commentators mention this connection and do not decide on the first two possibilities [EGT, Herm].

2:16 because^a all (that is) in^b the world,^c

LEXICON—a. ὅτι (LN 89.33): 'because' [LN, Lns; NJB], 'for' [AB, HNTC, WBC; all versions except NJB, REB, TEV], 'since' [LN], not explicit [REB, TEV].
  b. ἐν with dative object (LN 89.5): 'in' [AB, HNTC, Lns, WBC; all versions except NAB, TEV]. This preposition is also translated by a verb: 'to belong to' [TEV], '(that the world) affords' [NAB].
  c. κόσμος: 'world'. See this word at 2:15.

QUESTION—What relationship is indicated by ὅτι 'because'?
  1. It indicates the grounds for saying that love for God and love for the world and the things in it are incompatible [Alf, Brd, Herm, Lns, My, NIC, TH, WBC].
  2. It indicates the grounds for saying that God's love for him is not in him [Lns].

the desire^a of-the flesh^b

LEXICON—a. ἐπιθυμία (LN 25.20) (BAGD 3. p. 293): 'desire' [AB, BAGD, HNTC, LN, WBC; NRSV], 'lust' [LN, Lns; KJV, NASB, TNT], 'allurements' [NAB], 'cravings' [NIV], 'all that panders to' [REB], 'disordered desires' [NJB], 'what is desired' [TEV].

b. σάρξ (LN 26.7) (BAGD 7. p. 744): 'flesh' [BAGD, HNTC, Lns; KJV, NASB, NRSV], 'appetites' [REB], 'human nature' [AB], 'sinful man' [NIV], 'sinful self' [TEV]. This noun is also translated as an adjective: 'sinful' [WBC], 'carnal' [NAB], 'bodily' [NJB], 'the world's (lusts)' [TNT].

QUESTION—How are this and the following two clauses connected with 'the things of the world' in the preceding clause?

They are examples of what is meant by 'all that is in the world' [AB, Alf, Brd, Herm, ICC, Lns, My, NIC, NTC, TH, TNTC, WBC]. They explain that what is meant is attitudes and not material things [Brd]. They represent the three kinds of temptations [EGT, NIC, Ws].

QUESTION—How are the two nouns related in the genitive construction ἡ ἐπιθυμία τῆς σαρκός 'the desire of the flesh'?

The desires are caused by the flesh [AB, Alf, Brd, EGT, ICC, Lns, My, NCBC, NIC, TH, TNTC, WBC, Ws]. These are the desires which appeal to a person to gratify his human nature as corrupted by sin [ICC, Lns]. Although 'desire' is a morally neutral word [NIC, TH, WBC], in this context, the desires are evil and sinful [Brd, Lns, NCBC, NIC, NTC, TH, WBC]. 'Flesh' means the unrenewed human nature [AB, Alf, NCBC], which is fallen [TNTC, WBC], depraved [Lns], sinful [NTC, TNTC], and corrupted [My]. It is the sinful tendency in human nature [Brd], a disposition of hostility toward God [NIC, WBC].

and the desire[a] of-the eyes[b]

LEXICON—a. ἐπιθυμία (LN 25.20) (BAGD 3. p. 293): 'desire' [BAGD, HNTC, LN; NRSV], 'lust' [Lns; KJV, NASB, NIV], 'hungry for all they see' [AB], 'craving for' [WBC], 'desire for something forbidden' [BAGD], 'enticements' [NAB], 'covetousness' [TNT], 'disordered desire' [NJB], 'all that entices' [REB], 'what people want' [TEV].

b. ὀφθαλμός (LN 8.23, 24.16) (BAGD 1. p. 599): 'eye' [AB, BAGD, HNTC, LN, Lns; all versions except TEV, TNT], 'what is seen' [WBC], 'what people see' [TEV], not explicit [TNT].

QUESTION—How are the two nouns related in the genitive construction ἡ ἐπιθυμία τῶν ὀφθαλμῶν 'the desire of the eyes'?

The desire is caused by what people see [AB, Alf, EBC, Herm, HNTC, Lns, NCBC, NIC, NTC, TH, TNTC, WBC; TEV, TNT]. They desire what they see. The basic attitude is greed [EBC, HNTC, NIC] and lust [HNTC]. A person's sinful desires are aroused chiefly by what he sees [TH], whether objects or people are viewed [NCBC]. Some think that it is a desire that is satisfied by looking at some object [Brd, ICC, My]. This is the type of desire that takes pleasure in viewing sinful things [My].

QUESTION—What is the relationship between ἐπιθυμία τῆς σαρκός 'lust/desire of the flesh' and ἐπιθυμία τῆς ὀφθαλμῶν 'lust/desire of the eyes'?

1. The desire of the flesh is all wrong desire and is a generic term that includes the more specific desire of the eyes [ICC, NIC, WBC]. The sinful

desires of the flesh are further defined by describing two possible aspects of it [WBC]. The desires of the sinful nature are stimulated by what the eyes see and expresses itself in outward show [NIC].
2. The desire of the flesh refers to the temptations within one's grasp to enjoy, while the desire of the eyes is generic and includes all you can imagine as well [Lns].
3. They are separate evils. They are two types of temptations. The desire of the flesh is speaking of internally inspired temptation from our human nature and the desire of the eyes is the external temptations from things and people [AB, My, NCBC, TNTC, Ws].

and the pride[a] of-life,[b]
LEXICON—a. ἀλαζονεία (LN 88.219) (BAGD p. 34): 'pride' [HNTC, WBC; KJV, NJB, NRSV], 'boastful pride' [NASB], 'pretentious pride' [LN], 'boasting' [NIV], 'boastful haughtiness' [LN], 'empty pride' [TNT], 'pretensions' [BAGD, Lns], 'arrogance' [BAGD; REB], 'false arrogance' [LN], 'inflated self-assurance' [AB], 'empty show' [NAB], 'everything that people are proud of' [TEV].
b. βίος (LN **57.18**) (BAGD 3. p. 142): 'life' [KJV, NAB, NASB], 'life style' [WBC], 'possessions' [HNTC, LN; NJB, TNT], 'worldly possessions' [**LN**], 'riches' [NRSV], 'wealth' [REB], 'means of subsistence' [BAGD], 'livelihood' [LN], 'property' [BAGD, LN], 'material life' [AB], 'course of life' [Lns], 'what he has and does' [NIV], '(everything) in this world' [TEV].
QUESTION—How are the two nouns related in the genitive construction ἡ ἀλαζονεία τοῦ βίου 'the pride of life'?
The object of one's pride is life [Alf, Brd, EBC, HNTC, ICC, Lns, NCBC, NIC, NTC, TNTC, WBC]. Some commentators take 'life' to mean what sustains life: one's livelihood, wealth, and possessions [AB, Brd, HNTC, ICC, LN, NCBC, NIC, TH; NJB, NRSV, REB, TNT]. Others take it to mean one's life style and social status [Lns, WBC]. Others think that it means both the means of life, such as possessions and income, and the manner of life, such as one's self, status, and deeds [Alf, EBC, NTC, TNTC]. Pride is derived from one's life [AB, Herm, My, NCBC, TH]. It is an arrogance that comes from having possessions or power [NCBC].

is[a] not from[b] the father, but[c] is from the world.
LEXICON—a. pres. act. indic. of εἰμί (LN 13.1): 'to be' [HNTC, Lns; KJV, NASB, NJB], 'to derive' [WBC], 'to come' [NAB, NIV, NRSV, TEV, TNT], 'to spring' [REB], 'to belong to' [AB].
b. ἐκ with genitive object (LN 89.3) (BAGD 3.b p. 235): 'from' [HNTC, LN, WBC; all versions except KJV], 'origin' [BAGD], 'of' [KJV], 'out of' [Lns], not explicit [AB].
c. ἀλλά (LN 89.125): 'but' [HNTC, Lns, WBC; all versions except NAB, TEV], 'all that' [AB], not explicit [NAB, TEV].

QUESTION—What relationship is indicated by ἐκ 'from'?
1. It refers to the source of something [Alf, BAGD, Brd, ICC, Lns, NTC, WBC]: God doesn't cause these, the world does. These desires are not what God endowed humanity with [ICC].
2. It is showing close identification with [AB, My, TH]: these things aren't godly, but worldly. Anything in the 'world' belongs to the world, not to God [AB].

2:17 And the world^a is-passing-away^b and the desire^c of-it;

LEXICON—a. κόσμος: 'world'. See this word at 2:15, 16.
b. pres. pass. indic. of παράγω (LN **13.93**) (BAGD 1.b. p. 613): 'to pass away' [AB, BAGD, LN, Lns, WBC; all versions], 'to disappear' [BAGD], 'to be transient' [HNTC]. See this word at 2:8.
c. ἐπιθυμία (LN 25.20) (BAGD 3. p. 293): 'desire' [AB, BAGD, HNTC, LN, WBC; NIV, NRSV], 'lust' [LN, Lns; KJV, NASB], 'seductions' [NAB], 'allurement' [REB], 'disordered desire' [NJB], 'everything that people desire' [TEV], 'all (the world) offers to satisfy men's desires' [TNT].

QUESTION—How is this verse related to its context?
It is the second grounds for giving the exhortation 'do not love the world' (2:15) [EBC, My, NIC, TH, TNTC, WBC, Ws]: do not love the world because (1) love for the world and love for God are mutually exclusive and (2) the world is coming to an end.

QUESTION—What is meant by the passing away of the world?
The present tense indicates that it is now in the process of passing away [Alf, Brd, Lns, TH, TNTC, WBC; NAB, NASB, NJB, NRSV, REB] and this continuous process will eventually be completed [TH, WBC]. One commentator takes the view that this is middle voice instead of passive, with the reflexive meaning that the world's attitudes and practices cause its own destruction [Brd]. This 'world' is not the created world as such, but the external system of worldly things and desires [AB, WBC, Ws]. It includes ungodly men [Alf]. It is described in 2:8 as the passing away of the darkness [AB, Brd, My, NCBC, NIC, TNTC, WBC]. It is in the process of being purified [EBC]. It is also possible that there is a reference to the created world which is even now in the process of coming to an end [AB, My, WBC]. A few commentators think that instead of meaning that the world is now in the process of passing away, the expression means that the world is transitory in nature [Herm, HNTC, ICC].

QUESTION—How are the event noun and pronoun related in the genitive construction ἡ ἐπιθυμία αὐτοῦ 'the desire of it'?
1. 'It' refers to the agent of the desire [AB, Alf, Brd, EGT, HNTC, ICC, My, TH]. It means that what the world lusts after will pass away [TH]. It means that the sinful desires which belong to the world system will pass away [AB, WBC, Ws]. It means that the desires aroused by the world will

pass away [ICC, TH, Ws]. It is also true that these desires are directed toward the things in the world [WBC, Ws].
2. 'It' refers to the goal of the desire [Br, Lns, NIC; TEV]: all the worldly things that people lust for will pass away. When the world passes away, so will the desire for it [Br]. Those who lust for the world will find that all they take pleasure in will be gone, leaving them in endless remorse [Lns]. It is possible that 'desire' is a metonymy standing for the person who desires the things in the world. Such a desire will cause the person to pass away along with the world [NIC].

but[a] the-(one) doing[b] the will[c] of-God remains[d] forever.
LEXICON—a. δέ (LN 89.124): 'but' [AB, HNTC, Lns, WBC; all versions].
   b. pres. act. participle of ποιέω (LN 90.45) (BAGD I.1.c.α. p. 682): 'to do' [AB, BAGD, HNTC, LN, Lns, WBC; all versions], 'to keep the will obediently' [BAGD]. The present tense indicates that the doing of the will of God is a continuing practice [Brd].
   c. θέλημα (LN 25.2, 30.59) (BAGD 1.c.γ. p. 354): 'will' [AB, BAGD, HNTC, Lns, WBC; all versions].
   d. pres. act. indic. of μένω (LN 13.89) (BAGD 1.c.α. p. 504): 'to remain' [AB, BAGD, LN, Lns, WBC; NJB, REB, TNT], 'to abide' [HNTC; KJV, NASB], 'to last' [BAGD], 'to persist' [BAGD], 'to continue' [LN], 'to live' [BAGD; NIV, NRSV, TEV], 'to endure' [NAB].
QUESTION—What relationship is indicated by δέ 'but'?
   It indicates a contrast with the preceding clause [Lns, My, TH, WBC, Ws]: the world is passing away, but these men will exist forever.
QUESTION—How are the two nouns related in the genitive construction τὸ θέλημα τοῦ θεοῦ 'the will of God'?
   It means that God performs the action of willing [Lns, Ws; NAB, REB]: the one who does what God wills for him to do.
QUESTION—In what way do they remain forever?
   They will continue to exist forever [Brd]. They are imperishable [Herm]. They will remain alive [TH]. They will be saved [Lns].

DISCOURSE UNIT: 2:18–4:6 [Ws]. The topic is truth and falsehood.

DISCOURSE UNIT: 2:18–3:24 [NTC, TH]. The topic is the presence of the antichrist [TH], believing in Jesus [NTC].

DISCOURSE UNIT: 2:18–29 [EGT, WBC, Ws; REB, TEV]. The topic is a warning against heretical teaching [EGT; REB], the revelation of falsehood and truth [Ws], the enemy of Christ [TEV], the coming of the antichrist [TH], keeping the faith [WBC].

DISCOURSE UNIT: 2:18–28 [Alf, Brd, EBC, Lns; NJB]. The topic is a warning against false teachers [Alf, EBC], being on guard against antichrists [NJB], antichrists [Lns], Christological tests of fellowship [Brd].

DISCOURSE UNIT: 2:18–27 [AB, Br, Herm, HNTC, ICC, My, NIC, TNTC; NIV]. The topic is a warning against antichrists [AB, Herm, My, NIC; NIV], the teaching of antichrist [Br], Christ or antichrist [HNTC], faith in Christ as a test of fellowship [ICC, TNTC].

DISCOURSE UNIT: 2:18–25 [NCBC]. The topic is the final hour [NCBC], the denial of the Son [NCBC].

DISCOURSE UNIT: 2:18–23 [NAB]. The topic is antichrists.

DISCOURSE UNIT: 2:18–21 [Brd, ICC, TNTC, Ws]. The topic is the contrast between heretics and believers [Brd, TNTC, Ws], the end of the world [ICC].

DISCOURSE UNIT: 2:18–19 [NTC]. The topic is a warning against the antichrist.

2:18 Children,[a] it-is (the) last[b] hour,[c]
LEXICON—a. παιδίον: 'child'. See this word at 2:14.
    b. ἔσχατος (LN 61.13) (BAGD 3.b. p. 314): 'last' [AB, BAGD, HNTC, LN; all versions except NAB, NJB, TEV], 'final' [LN, Lns, WBC; NAB, NJB]. Ἐσχάτη ὥρα 'the last hour' is translated 'the end is near' [TEV].
    c. ὥρα (LN 67.1) (BAGD 3. p. 896): 'hour' [AB, HNTC, Lns, WBC; all versions except KJV, TEV], 'time' [BAGD, LN; KJV]. For TEV see above.
QUESTION—How is this verse related to its context?
    This is the beginning of a new section [Brd, Herm, NIC, WBC]. It ties into the previous earlier section by taking up the idea of the end of the world [EBC, ICC, My, NIC, TH, WBC, Ws]. The author has presented ethical tests for being a Christian and now he presents a doctrinal test [Brd, ICC, TNTC, WBC].
QUESTION—Why does he call them παιδία 'children' at this point?
    This marks the beginning of a new section [Herm, NIC]. The author is addressing all his readers [Alf, Br, Brd, Lns, My, NIC, Ws], expressing endearment [Brd, WBC], and indicating their subordination [Brd], dependence [Brd], and need of instruction [ICC, NIC, WBC]. It expresses the writer's authority [Brd, NIC, NTC, Ws], based on age [Brd, NTC, Ws] and experience [Brd, Ws].
QUESTION—What is meant by ἐσχάτη ὥρα 'the last hour'?
    1. It means 'the last hour' and is the final time before Christ's return and the end of the world [AB, Alf, Br, Brd, EBC, EGT, Herm, HNTC, ICC, Lns, My, NIC, NTC, TH, TNTC, WBC]. Some take it to be equivalent to the term 'the last days', that period between Christ's first advent and his second advent [NTC]. Others take it to refer to the final phase of the last days [Br, ICC, My, TNTC]. It is the time period within the last days that began with the appearance of many antichrists and ends when Christ returns [Lns]. There are various times during the last days when the sense of being at the last hour is especially acute [Br].

2. It means 'a last hour' and refers to a period of hardship not necessarily related to the end of the world or the return of Christ [Ws].
3. It means the final moment for deciding the future of the church [NCBC].

and as[a] you heard[b] that antichrist[c] is-coming,[d]

LEXICON—a. καθώς (LN 64.14) (BAGD 1. p. 391): 'as' [WBC; KJV, NIV, NRSV], 'even as' [Lns], 'just as' [BAGD, LN; NAB, NASB], not explicit [AB, HNTC; NJB, REB, TEV, TNT].
  b. aorist act. indic. of ἀκούω (LN 33.212): 'to hear' [AB, HNTC, LN, Lns, WBC; all versions except REB, TEV], 'to be told' [REB, TEV]. The aorist tense refers to the time when they were taught the Christian doctrines [ICC].
  c. ἀντίχριστος (LN **53.83**) (BAGD p. 76): 'antichrist' [AB, HNTC, LN, Lns, WBC; all versions except TEV], 'the Enemy of Christ' [TEV].
  d. pres. mid. (deponent = act.) indic. of ἔρχομαι (LN 15.81) (BAGD I.1.a.θ. p. 311): 'to come' [AB, HNTC, LN, Lns, WBC; all versions], 'to appear' [BAGD]. The present tense is used with a future meaning [AB, Alf, Brd, TH; KJV, TEV] and assumes that the future coming is as certain as a present reality [Brd]. It indicates that this is a common teaching [ICC].

QUESTION—How had they heard this?
  This was included in Jesus' teachings [AB, NIC, NTC], carried on by the apostles [ICC, My, TNTC, Ws], added to by apostolic prophecy [Lns, My], and taught to the readers when they heard the gospel [Alf, Br, ICC, My, NCBC, NTC, Ws].

QUESTION—To whom does ἀντίχριστος 'antichrist' refer?
  1. It refers to the one evil person expected and foreshadowed in many of the apocalyptic writings [AB, Alf, Br, Brd, Herm, NIC, NTC, TH, TNTC]. It should be capitalized to indicate a specific expectation: the Antichrist [AB; NJB, TEV, TNT]. The many antichrists are advance copies of the final antichrist [Brd]. These false teachers are possessed by the spirit of the one antichrist [NIC].
  2. It refers to a principle of being against Christ [Lns, Ws]. 'Antichrist' is not a single individual, but is a single opposition that has a succession of occurrences until Christ comes [Lns]. It is the personification of a principle shown in various antichrists. [Ws]. The many antichrists are varied oppositions, each started by some person who had a following [Lns].

QUESTION—What is meant by the word ἀντίχριστος 'antichrist'?
  1. It means one who opposes Christ [AB, Alf, Lns, My, NIC, TH, TNTC, WBC; TEV]: you have heard that Christ's enemy will come. He is the enemy of Christ who seeks to destroy Christ's works [My].
  2. It means one who takes the place of Christ [Br, HNTC]: you have heard that the false Christ will come. He will claim the honor that rightfully belongs to Christ [Br].

3. It means both of the above [EGT, ICC, NTC, Ws]: you have heard that Christ's enemy will come pretending to be Christ. Although he pretends to be Christ, he opposes Christ and his works [ICC]. A substitute Messiah is, by the nature of the case, opposed to the true Messiah [Brd].

so^a now^b many antichrists^c have-appeared;^d

LEXICON—a. καί: 'so' [NAB, NRSV], 'and' [NJB, TEV], 'even' [KJV, NASB, NIV], 'and in fact' [TNT], 'well' [REB].

b. νῦν (LN 67.38) (BAGD 1.a.β. p. 545): 'now' [AB, BAGD, HNTC, LN, Lns; all versions except REB, TNT], 'already' [REB, TNT].

c. ἀντίχριστος (LN **53.83**): 'antichrist' [AB, HNTC, LN, Lns, WBC; all versions except TEV], 'enemies of Christ' [TEV], 'ones opposed to Christ' [BAGD, LN].

d. perfect act. indic. of γίνομαι (LN 85.7, **68.1 fn2**) (BAGD II.5. p. 160): 'to appear' [BAGD, HNTC, LN, WBC; NAB, REB, TEV], 'to arise' [NASB], 'to begin' [**LN**], 'to be' [KJV], 'to come to be' [LN, Lns], 'to come' [NIV, NJB, NRSV, TNT], 'to exist' [BAGD]. This verb is also translated with a verb phrase 'to make an appearance' [AB]. The perfect tense shows that many Antichrists have already come and are presently exerting their influence [Brd, Ws].

QUESTION—To whom does ἀντίχριστοι πολλοί 'many antichrists' refer?

It refers to the many people in the secessionist party [AB, EGT, TNTC, WBC], false teachers [Brd, Herm], everyone who denies that Jesus is the Christ (2:22) [Herm], the deceivers (2:26) [Herm].

QUESTION—What is the relationship between the prophecy of the coming of the ἀντίχριστος 'Antichrist' and the presence of ἀντίχριστοι πολλοί 'many antichrists'?

1. The coming of many antichrists is a sign that the Antichrist will soon come [Alf, Br, Brd, Lns, NIC, NTC, TH, TNTC, WBC]. The spirit of the Antichrist who is still to come is already at work in the world [My, NIC, TH, WBC]. These individuals prefigure the Antichrist's coming [Alf]. They are the forerunners of Antichrist [Br, NTC, TNTC] and his agents [Br].

2. The prophecy is now being fulfilled in the coming of the many antichrists [AB, ICC, NCBC, Ws]. The writer reinterprets tradition to associate the false teachers with ultimate evil [AB]. The many false teachers are actual manifestations of the Antichrist [ICC].

from-this^a we-know^b that it-is (the) last^c hour^d.

LEXICON—a. ὅθεν (LN 89.25) (BAGD 2. p. 555): 'from this' [NASB, NJB, NRSV, TNT], 'from which' [BAGD, WBC], 'whence' [Lns], 'this is how' [HNTC; NIV], 'this (makes us certain)' [NAB], 'and this' [AB], 'whereby' [KJV], 'for which reason' [BAGD], 'and so' [TEV], 'therefore' [BAGD], not explicit [REB].

b. pres. act. indic. of γινώσκω: 'to know'. See this word at 2:3a, 5. This verb is also translated by a noun: 'proof' [REB].

c. ἔσχατος (LN 61.13) (BAGD 3.b. p. 314): 'last' [AB, BAGD, HNTC, LN; all versions except NAB, NJB, TEV], 'final' [LN, Lns, WBC; NAB, NJB]. ἐσχάτη ὥρα 'the last hour' is translated 'the end is near' [TEV].
d. ὥρα (LN 67.1) (BAGD 3. p. 896): 'hour' [AB, HNTC, Lns, WBC; all versions except KJV], 'time' [BAGD, LN; KJV]. For TEV see above.

QUESTION—What relationship is indicated by ὅθεν 'from this'?
   It indicates a conclusion drawn from the fact that many Antichrists have arisen [ICC, NIC, TH, TNTC].
QUESTION—To whom does the implied subject of γινώσκομεν 'we know' refer?
   It is 'we inclusive' and means all believers, thus including both the writer and his readers [TH, WBC]. The evidence can be known to every believer [WBC].

DISCOURSE UNIT: 2:19–21 [ICC]. The topic is relationship to community.

2:19 They-went-out[a] from[b] us,
LEXICON—a. aorist act. indic. of ἐξέρχομαι (LN 15.40) (BAGD 1.b.α. p. 275): 'to go out' [AB, BAGD, HNTC, LN, Lns; KJV, NASB, NIV, NRSV, TNT], 'to go' [NJB], 'to withdraw' [WBC], 'to leave' [BAGD; REB, TEV], 'to take one's leave' [NAB]. The aorist tense shows that a definite event is being referred to [TH, WBC], a major rift rather than constant leakage [AB].
   b. ἐκ with genitive object (LN 89.121): 'from' [AB, HNTC, Lns, WBC; all versions except NJB, REB, TEV], 'from among' [NJB], not explicit [REB, TEV].

QUESTION—Who are these people and in what way did they go out from the believers?
   'They' refers to the many antichrists mentioned in 2:18 [Lns, NIC, TH, TNTC, WBC]. These are the false teachers [Brd, Herm ICC, TNTC], or they may be not only the false teachers, but also ordinary members who agreed with them [WBC].
   1. A schism had occurred in the church and a group had left voluntarily [AB, Alf, EBC, HNTC, ICC, Lns, NIC, NTC, TH, TNTC, WBC]. These people no longer considered themselves a part of the church [AB]. Their departure was not caused by expulsion or excommunication [EBC, ICC]. They could no longer tolerate fellowship with the orthodox believers [HNTC] or win the church leaders over to their views [TNTC].
   2. False teachers who still claimed to be Christians and still remained a part of the congregation had left the true faith theologically and sought to take others with them [Herm].
QUESTION—To whom does ἡμῶν 'from us' refer?
   It is 'we inclusive' and refers to the author and all those belonging to the church to whom this is written [AB, EBC, NCBC, TNTC, WBC], or it refers to the worldwide church [My, NIC, Ws].

1 JOHN 2:19

but^a they-were^b not from^c us;

LEXICON—a. ἀλλά (LN 89.125): 'but' [HNTC, WBC; all versions except NAB, TEV], 'not that' [AB; NAB], 'yea' [Lns], not explicit [TEV].

b. imperf. act. indic. of εἰμί (LN 58.67): 'to be' [Lns; KJV], 'to be really' [NASB, TEV]. The expression ἦσαν ἐκ 'were from' is translated 'to belong to' [HNTC, WBC; NRSV, TNT], 'to really belong to' [AB; NAB, NIV, NJB, REB, TEV]. The imperfect tense refers to the whole previous time these people were connected with the congregation [My].

c. ἐκ with genitive object (LN 63.20, 89.3): 'from' [LN], 'of' [Lns; KJV, NASB], 'a part of' [LN]. The phrase ἐξ ἡμῶν 'from us' is translated 'belong to our fellowship' [TEV]. For AB, HNTC, WBC; all versions except KJV, NASB, TEV see above.

QUESTION—What relationship is indicated by ἀλλά 'but'?

1. It indicates contrast [AB, Brd, HNTC, My, WBC; all versions except TEV]: but. It is a strong contrast between hypothetically remaining with the congregation and actually departing from it [WBC]. In spite of their nominal membership, they were not true members of the Christian fellowship [ICC]. Although they went out from the church (and thus were connected with it), yet they were not really part of it [My].
2. Some translate this to indicate result [Lns; TEV]: they were not from us, so they left us.

QUESTION—What is the difference between ἐξ ἡμῶν 'from us' used here and ἐξ ἡμῶν 'from us' used earlier in this verse?

The author is using a play on the ambiguity of the word ἐξ 'from' [Brd, My, TH, WBC]. The first occurrence speaks of leaving the fellowship of the church [AB, Alf, Brd, Lns, My, TH, WBC], the second speaks of not being essentially the same kind as the true members of the church [Brd, Lns, My, TH, WBC], never having truly shared the fellowship [ICC, WBC], never inwardly belonging [AB, Br, Herm, ICC, NIC, TH].

for^a if^b they-were from us they would have-remained^c with^d us;

LEXICON—a. γάρ (LN 89.23): 'for' [AB, HNTC, Lns, WBC; KJV, NAB, NASB, NIV, NRSV], not explicit [NJB, REB, TEV, TNT].

b. εἰ (LN 89.65): 'if' [AB, HNTC, Lns, WBC; all versions]. It marks a contrary-to-fact condition [AB, Brd, NCBC, NIC, TH].

c. pluperf. act. indic. of μένω (LN 68.11) (BAGD 1.b. p. 504): 'to remain' [AB, BAGD, LN, Lns; NASB, NIV, NRSV, TNT], 'to stay' [HNTC, WBC; NAB, NJB, REB, TEV], 'to continue' [BAGD, LN; KJV].

d. μετά with genitive object (LN 89.108) (BAGD A.II.1.a. p. 508): 'with' [AB, HNTC, Lns, WBC; all versions].

QUESTION—What relationship is indicated by γάρ 'for'?

It indicates the grounds for saying that they were 'not of us'. It implies that if they had really belonged to the church, they would have remained with it [Alf, Br, Brd, EBC, HNTC, ICC, My, NIC, NTC, TNTC, Ws]. If they were

74   1 JOHN 2:19

inwardly with the true believers, they would have remained outwardly with them [Lns, WBC].

but[a] in-order-that[b] it-might-be-revealed[c] that they-are all not from[d] us.
LEXICON—a. ἀλλά (LN 89.125): 'but' [Lns, WBC; all versions except NAB, REB, TNT], 'rather' [AB], not explicit [NAB, REB, TNT].
    b. ἵνα (LN 89.59): 'in order that' [NASB], 'so that' [REB, TEV], 'that' [Lns; KJV, TNT], not explicit [HNTC, WBC; NAB, NIV, NJB, NRSV]. This conjunction is also translated 'this helped' [AB], 'this was' [NJB], 'it only served' [NAB].
    c. aorist pass. subj. of φανερόω (LN 28.36) (BAGD 2.b.α. p. 853): 'to be revealed' [AB, LN], 'to be made known' [BAGD, LN], 'to be made manifest' [Lns; KJV], 'to be made clear' [WBC], 'to be clear' [REB, TEV], 'to make plain' [LN; NRSV], 'to be made plain' [TNT], 'to be shown' [BAGD, HNTC; NASB], 'to show' [NAB, NIV], 'to prove' [NJB].
    d. ἐκ with genitive object (LN 63.20, 89.3): 'of' [Lns; KJV, NASB]. The phrase ἐξ ἡμῶν is translated with a pronoun 'ours' [NAB], or a verb phrase 'to belong to us' [AB, HNTC, WBC; all versions except KJV, NAB, NASB].
QUESTION—How is this clause related to the context?
    There is an ellipsis with the implicit statement 'but they went out from us' [Brd, EGT, ICC, Lns, My, NCBC, NIC, TH, WBC, Ws; all versions except NAB], 'but this happened' [AB, EGT, NIC, TH], 'but they have not remained' [My].
QUESTION—What relationship is indicated by ἵνα 'in order that'?
    1. It indicates God's purpose to make clear the distinction between the truth and error [Alf, Brd, HNTC, ICC, My, TH, TNTC, WBC]: they went out in order that God might reveal that not all belong to us. God willed that they be manifest so that true believers would not be led astray [TNTC]. God separated the chaff from the wheat [HNTC].
    2. No personal agent is implied. It means that it was inevitable that it should show up because judgment is inevitable [AB]: but this helped to reveal them.
QUESTION—What is being negated?
    1. The whole phrase 'to be from us' is negated and 'all' refers to the antichrists [AB, Brd, ICC, NIC, NTC, TH, WBC, Ws; NAB, NIV, NJB, NRSV, REB, TEV, TNT]: none of the antichrists are of us.
    2. The word 'all' is negated, and 'all' refers to the true church [Alf, Br, Herm, HNTC, Lns, My; REB]: not all of our company really belong to us. Not all who claim to belong to us actually do [Herm].

DISCOURSE UNIT: 2:20–27 [Br, NTC]. The topic is the anointing from the Holy One [NTC], distinguishing truth and error [Br].

2:20 But/And[a] you have[b] an-anointing[c] from[d] the Holy[e] (One),
LEXICON—a. καί (LN 91.12): 'but' [all versions except REB] 'too' [HNTC], 'as for' [AB], 'and on your part' [Lns], 'moreover' [WBC], 'what is more' [REB].
  b. pres. act. indic. of ἔχω (LN 57.1): 'to have' [HNTC, Lns; KJV, NAB, NASB, NIV], 'to be' [AB], 'to possess' [WBC], 'to have poured out' [TEV]. For NJB, NRSV, REB, TNT see below.
  c. χρῖσμα (LN **37.107**) (BAGD p. 886): 'anointing' [AB, BAGD, HNTC; NAB, NASB, NIV], 'anointment' [Lns], 'consecration' [WBC], 'unction' [KJV], 'the Holy Spirit' [TEV]. The phrase χρῖσμα ἔχετε ἀπό 'to have an anointing from' is translated 'to be anointed by' [LN; NJB, NRSV, REB, TNT], 'you have had (the Holy Spirit) poured out on you' [TEV].
  d. ἀπό with genitive object (LN 90.15) (BAGD V.4. p. 88): 'from' [AB, BAGD, HNTC, Lns, WBC; KJV, NASB], 'by' [NJB, NRSV, REB, TEV, TNT], 'that comes from' [NAB].
  e. ἅγιος (LN 88.24) (BAGD 2.c.α. p. 10): 'holy' [LN]. With the article the phrase is translated 'the Holy One' [AB, BAGD, HNTC, Lns, WBC; all versions except TEV], 'Christ' [TEV].
QUESTION—What relationship is indicated by the conjunction καί 'but/and'?
  1. It indicates contrast [AB, Brd, EBC, Herm, NTC, TH, WBC; all versions except REB]: but as for you. The pronoun 'you' is placed in an emphatic position [Brd, NCBC, NTC, WBC, Ws] and marks a shift from speaking about the antichrists to speaking to John's readers [AB, Brd, NCBC, TH]. The secessionists claim special knowledge [EBC, WBC], which they claim for only the chosen 'anointed ones' [EBC, NCBC]. The author is showing that true knowledge is really with all the faithful who do not deny the Son [Br, WBC], and is open to all believers [EBC, ICC, NCBC].
  2. It is used to conjoin this clause with the preceding verse as continuing the idea of the falseness being manifest [Alf, Lns, My, NIC, Ws; REB]: and you. In 2:19 they recognize the falsity of the heretics, and in addition they should know that what the heretics taught was untrue [NIC].
QUESTION—What is the metaphor here?
  The metaphor is based on the appointment to office of king, priest, or prophet by pouring oil on the head of the appointee [ICC, My, WBC]. Those so anointed were endued with God's Spirit [ICC]. Some understand χρῖσμα 'anointing' to mean the act of anointing [AB, ICC], in which case this is a metonymy for what was received at the anointing [Lns]; others understand it as the oil used in anointing [NIC, TNTC, WBC, Ws], in which case it is a symbol for what was received [NIC, TH, WBC, Ws].
QUESTION—To whom or what does χρῖσμα 'anointing' refer?
  1. It refers to the Holy Spirit [AB, Alf, Brd, EBC, EGT, Herm, ICC, Lns, My, NCBC, NTC, TNTC, Ws; TEV]. The anointing with the Holy Spirit constituted a person a Christian [AB]. The Spirit enables a Christian to understand the truth of God [Brd].

2. It refers to the teachings of the gospel [HNTC, NCBC]. A person is anointed when he has received a doctrine [HNTC]. To be anointed is to receive a doctrine [HNTC]. Although the Gnostics claim to have a secret teaching, believers have all the information required [NCBC].
3. It refers to both the Holy Spirit and the teachings of the gospel [NIC, TH, WBC]. The anointing is God's Word apprehended through the work of the Holy Spirit in their hearts [NIC].

QUESTION—To whom or what does ἅγιος 'holy' refer?
1. It refers to Christ [AB, Alf, EBC, Herm, ICC, Lns, My, NIC, NTC, TH, WBC, Ws; TEV].
2. It refers to God, the Father [BAGD, Brd, EGT, HNTC]. It is the Father who sends the Spirit at the request of the Son (John 14:16, 26) [Brd, EGT].
3. It refers to the Holy Place, the spiritual world [NCBC].

QUESTION—How is this clause related to the context?
It is a play on words [Brd, EGT, ICC, My, NCBC, NIC, TNTC, WBC]. The author is saying that his followers have a χρῖσμα 'anointing' in contrast to the secessionists who are the ἀντίχριστοι 'the ones against the anointed one' [Alf, Brd, EGT, Lns, TNTC, WBC].

and you-know[a] all.

TEXT—Instead of πάντες 'all' (masculine nominative), meaning 'all of you know', many manuscripts have πάντα 'all things' (neuter accusative), meaning 'you know all things'. GNT selects the nominative form 'all' with a D rating, indicating a very high degree of doubt. The reading with πάντα 'all things' is selected by Alf, My, KJV, and NAB.

LEXICON—a. perf. (with pres. sense) act. indic. of οἶδα (LN 28.1; 32.16): 'to know' [LN; KJV, NASB, NIV, TEV], 'to have knowledge' [AB, HNTC, Lns, WBC; NAB, NRSV, REB], 'to receive knowledge' [NJB], 'to possess knowledge' [TNT]. The perfect tense indicates that the knowledge is already acquired [Brd].

QUESTION—What relationship is indicated by καί 'and'?
It implies that the result of their being anointed is that they all have received knowledge [AB, Herm, Lns, My]. Knowledge is not confined to a special group [Br] and they need not feel deprived when the antichrists claim special knowledge [AB, Brd, ICC].

QUESTION—What do they know?
They know the truth (from 2:21) [EBC, EGT, Herm, My, NIC, NTC, TH, Ws; NASB, TEV]. They know the difference between truth and falsehood [Br]. They know God [WBC], that Jesus is the Christ (2:22) [AB], what is necessary for the Christian life [Alf], and how to recognize false teaching [Lns]. They have enough knowledge for what John is writing about [Lns].

2:21 (I-did) not write[a] to-you because/that[b] (you-did) not know[c] the truth,[d] but[e] because/that you-knew it,

LEXICON—a. aorist act. indic. of γράφω (LN 33.61): 'to write' [AB, HNTC, LN, Lns, WBC; all versions].
  b. ὅτι (LN 89.33, 90.21): 'because' [Lns, WBC; all versions except NAB] 'my reason is that' [NAB]. This conjunction is also translated 'to tell you that' [AB].
  c. perf. (= pres.) act. indic. of οἶδα (LN 28.1; 32.4): 'to know' [AB, HNTC, LN, Lns, WBC; all versions except NJB, REB]. The phrase οὐκ οἴδατε 'not know' is translated 'to be ignorant of' [NJB, REB].
  d. ἀλήθεια (LN 72.2) (BAGD 2.b. p. 36): 'truth' [AB, BAGD, HNTC, LN, Lns, WBC; all versions].
  e. ἀλλά (LN 89.125): 'but' [AB, Lns, WBC; all versions except TEV], 'but precisely' [HNTC], 'instead' [TEV].

QUESTION—How is this verse related to its context?
  This is written in order to reassure John's readers that he does not doubt their orthodoxy [EBC, EGT, Herm, ICC, NCBC, NIC, TH, TNTC, WBC] and to get them to act on the knowledge they already have [Alf, EBC, TNTC, Ws] by rejecting the false claims of the false teachers, whom he will identify in the next verse [Alf].

QUESTION—What written material is he referring to?
  1. He uses an epistolary aorist 'I wrote' to refer to the whole letter [AB, Brd, Lns].
  2. He refers to the immediately preceding passage [Alf, EGT, ICC, My, WBC]. Having just spoken about the antichrists, he hastens to assert his confidence in the readers [EGT].

QUESTION—What relationship is indicated by ὅτι 'because/that'?
  1. It indicates the reason he is writing [Alf, Brd, EBC, Herm, HNTC, ICC, Lns, My, NIC, NTC, WBC, Ws; KJV, NAB, NASB, NIV, NJB, NRSV, REB, TEV, TNT]: I write to you, not because you do not know the truth, but because you do know it. Because they know the truth, he can instruct them further about the gospel [WBC]. Based on their knowledge, he can appeal to them to use their power of discernment [ICC, NIC]. He writes to urge them to apply the truth they already know [Brd].
  2. It means 'that' and indicates the content of what he is writing. [AB, EGT, NCBC, TH]: I write to tell you, not that you do not know the truth, but that you do know it. He does this so that they will not want the "deeper" knowledge the false teachers are offering [NCBC].

QUESTION—To what does τὴν ἀλήθειαν 'the truth' refer?
  'The truth' refers to the body of Christian doctrine [Brd, WBC], and especially here to the truth about Christ [Brd, TH]. The Christian doctrine of the incarnation is directly opposed to the lie of the antichrists [Brd].

and because/that[a] **every**[b] **lie**[c] **is**[d] **not from**[e] **the truth.**[f]

LEXICON—a. ὅτι (LN 89.33/90.21): 'because' [HNTC, Lns; NASB, NIV, NJB, REB], 'that' [AB, WBC; KJV, NAB, NRSV, TEV, TNT].

b. πᾶς (LN 59.23) (BAGD 1.a.α. p. 631): 'every' [AB, BAGD, Lns]. The phrase πᾶν...οὐκ 'all not' is translated 'no' [HNTC, WBC; all versions except REB], 'never' [REB]. The universal negation here means 'no lie is of the truth' [Brd].

c. ψεῦδος (LN **33.254**) (BAGD p. 892): 'lie' [AB, BAGD, HNTC, **LN**, Lns; all versions], 'falsehood' [BAGD, LN, WBC].

d. pres. act. indic. of εἰμί (LN 13.4, 58.67) (BAGD III.3. p. 225): 'to be' [Lns; KJV, NASB], 'to come' [NIV, NRSV, REB, TEV, TNT], 'to be able to come' [NJB], 'to be alien to' [AB]. The phrase 'is from' is translated by a clause 'to have a part with' [HNTC], 'to have anything in common with' [NAB], 'to have a share in' [WBC], 'to belong to' [BAGD, LN].

e. ἐκ with genitive object (LN 63.20, 89.142) (BAGD 3.c. p. 235): 'from' [NIV, NJB, NRSV, REB, TEV, TNT], 'of' [Lns; KJV, NASB]. For AB, HNTC, WBC; NAB see above.

f. ἀλήθεια (LN 72.2) (BAGD 2.b. p. 36): 'truth' [AB, BAGD, HNTC, Lns, WBC; all versions].

QUESTION—What relationship is indicated by ὅτι 'because/that'?

1. It means 'because' and gives the second reason why he wrote to them [Alf, HNTC, ICC, Lns, NTC, Ws; NAB, NASB, NIV, NJB, REB]: I write because you know the truth and because no lie is from the truth. He writes so that they may recognize the proper reaction to the lie [Alf]. Their knowledge of the truth will enable them to detect the true character of the lies that he informs them about [ICC].
2. It means 'that' and gives an additional content of what they know [Brd, EBC, Herm, My, NIC, WBC; KJV, NRSV, REB, TEV, TNT]: I write because you know the truth and you know that no lie is from the truth.
3. It means 'that' and gives another thing that he writes to them about [AB, TH]: I write to you that you do know the truth and to tell you that no lie is from the truth.

QUESTION—What is meant by ψεῦδος 'lie'?

It is refers to anything that the author thinks is untrue whether or not the speaker believes it to be true [ICC, NCBC].

QUESTION—To what does ἀλήθειαν 'truth' refer?

Some commentators keep the same meaning as the previous reference to 'truth' [Brd]: no lie comes from true Christian teaching. Others think that the word goes beyond the meaning of 'truth' in the previous clause to refer to God, because God is truth [EGT, TH]: no lie comes from God. Or the meaning of 'truth' passes from its content to its character [WBC].

DISCOURSE UNIT: 2:22–25 [ICC, Ws]. The topic is the content and significance of false teaching [ICC], the essence and power of the truth [Ws].

1 JOHN 2:22

DISCOURSE UNIT: 2:22-23 [Brd, TNTC]. The topic is the Christological tests [Brd], the nature and effect of the heresy [TNTC].

2:22 Who is the liar[a] except[b] the-(one) denying[c] that Jesus is the Christ?

LEXICON—a. ψεύστης (LN 33.255) (BAGD p. 892): 'liar' [AB, BAGD, HNTC, LN, Lns, WBC; all versions].

b. εἰ μή (LN 89.131): 'if not' [Lns, WBC; NJB], 'but' [KJV, NASB, NRSV, TNT], 'none other than' [AB], 'it is the man who' [HNTC; NIV], 'anyone' [REB], not explicit [NAB, TEV].

c. pres. mid. (deponent = act.) participle of ἀρνέομαι (LN 33.277) (BAGD 2. p. 107): 'to deny' [AB, BAGD, HNTC, LN, Lns, WBC; all versions except NJB, TEV], 'to claim (that he is not)' [NJB], 'to say (that Jesus is not)' [TEV]. The present tense indicates a continuing practice [Brd]. The negative following the verb is redundant in English [BAGD, EGT, WBC], or it is part of direct speech being referred to: the one denying, saying "Jesus is not the Christ" [Brd, Lns, WBC].

QUESTION—How is this verse related to its context?

The mention of 'lies' in 2:21 leads to a discussion of the character of the person who lies [Alf, Ws]. This reveals the false teaching of those who left the congregation [TNTC, WBC]. The rhetorical question is used to identify the antichrists spoken of in 2:18-19 as those who deny that Jesus is the Christ [Brd, Herm, My].

QUESTION—To whom does 'the liar' refer?

It refers to the false teachers [Br, Brd, EBC, My] and to all who hold this false doctrine [Lns]. 'The Liar' was also a current title for the Antichrist [AB]. The article with the noun singles out the characteristic representative of this class of liars [TH] and means the liar *par excellence* [Br, Brd, ICC, NIC, WBC]. It shows that no ordinary lie is intended but the ultimately evil lie [Alf, Br, Brd, ICC, My, NIC, WBC]. It is a lie that strikes at the core of the gospel [Brd].

QUESTION—What is meant by ἀρνούμενος 'denying' that Jesus was the Christ?

Denial has both the component of rejecting a fact and the component of refusing to commit to the relationship and obedience that fact entails [HNTC]. Some take it to refer to a public utterance [TH]. The liar denies that the human Jesus is identical to the divine Christ [AB, Alf, Br, Brd, EBC, Herm, HNTC, Lns, My, TH, TNTC, Ws], thereby denying his incarnation [Brd, EBC, EGT, Herm, ICC, NIC, TNTC, WBC], his sonship [Br, NCBC, NIC], and the efficacy of his death [Br, EBC, Lns]. Many commentators mention a Gnostic teaching that Jesus was only a human being while the Christ was a divine being who came upon Jesus at his baptism and left him at the crucifixion [Brd, EGT, Herm, Lns, My, NIC, NTC, TNTC, Ws]. Another view was that the true Christ merely appeared to be in human form and the actions done by a human Jesus were of little significance [EBC]. The word χριστός 'Christ' means more than just that Jesus is the Jewish Messiah

[AB, Brd, ICC, My, NIC, TNTC, Ws]. It had come to stand for a special relationship to God as Son of God [AB, Brd, ICC, NIC, TH, TNTC].

This-(one) is the antichrist,[a] the-(one) denying[b] the Father and the Son.
LEXICON—a. ἀντίχριστος: 'antichrist'. See this word at 2:18.
    b. pres. mid. (deponent = act.) participle of ἀρνέομαι (LN 33.277; 34.48; 36.43) (BAGD 3.b. p. 108): 'to deny' [AB, BAGD, HNTC, LN, Lns; all versions except TEV], 'to reject' [TEV], 'to disown' [BAGD, WBC], 'repudiate' [BAGD].
QUESTION—To whom or what does ἀντίχριστος 'antichrist' refer?
    It refers to the spirit of antichrist displayed in anyone who denies that Jesus is the Christ [AB, Alf, Brd, HNTC, ICC, My, NIC, TNTC, WBC, Ws]. Anyone who has the attitude of the antichrist can be said to be antichrist [NIC]. This word refers to the embodiment of a principle and does not refer to any one person.
QUESTION—What is being implied by this clause?
    Although probably the false teachers did not consciously deny the Father and probably thought of themselves as having the Father [Br, HNTC, NIC, WBC, Ws], nevertheless 'denying that Jesus is the Christ' is equivalent to 'denying both the Father and the Son' [Alf, Br, Brd, EBC, HNTC, ICC, My, NIC, WBC, Ws]. To deny the agent of the Father is to deny the Father [HNTC]. Without the Son, there is no Father of the Son [Lns, NTC]. God has revealed himself through the incarnation of the Son [EGT, ICC, NIC, TH, Ws] and his atoning death [EBC]. Because of the unity of the Father and the Son [Herm, My, WBC], a wrong relationship to one means a wrong relationship to both [EBC, Herm, ICC, My].
QUESTION—What is the relationship between ὁ ἀρνούμενος 'the one denying' used here and ὁ ἀρνούμενος 'the one denying' used earlier in the verse?
    'Denial' is used in two different senses. The first reference is to the denial of the truth of a fact [TH]. The second reference is the rejection of allegiance to a person [Brd, HNTC, TH] expressed publicly [TNTC].
QUESTION—What is the significance of the change from 'Christ' to 'the Son'?
    The term 'Christ' had come to mean more than the Jewish Messiah and had come to include a special relationship to God [ICC]. Here 'Christ' is used to refer to Jesus' deity [Brd]. To deny that Jesus is the Christ is to deny that he is the Son of God [Br]. 'Christ' and 'Son of God' are virtually equivalent [AB, Brd, NIC, TH] and 'the Son' is used here to parallel 'the Father' [AB, My].
QUESTION—What is the significance of the order in which 'Father' and 'Son' are introduced?
    To deny the Son results in denying the Father. The result is placed first in order to show the heinousness of the crime of denying that 'Jesus is the Christ' [AB, TH, WBC] because it entails complete loss of fellowship with God the Father [TH].

2:23 **Everyone denying[a] the Son neither has[b] the Father;**
LEXICON—a. pres. mid. (deponent = act.) participle of ἀρνέομαι (LN 33.277; 34.48; 36.43) (BAGD 3.a. p. 108): 'to deny' [AB, BAGD, HNTC, LN, Lns; all versions except TEV], 'to reject' [TEV], 'to disown' [BAGD, WBC], 'to repudiate' [BAGD]. See this word at 2:22.
    b. pres. act. indic. of ἔχω (LN 90.65) (BAGD I.2.b.β. p. 332): 'to have' [BAGD, LN, Lns; KJV, NASB, NIV, NJB, NRSV], 'to possess' [AB, WBC], 'to have a claim on' [NAB], 'to have a hold on' [HNTC], 'to be without' [REB]. The verb and negative are translated 'to lose' [TNT], 'to reject' [TEV].
QUESTION—What is the relationship between οὐδὲ ἔχει 'neither has' used here and ἀρνούμενος 'denying' used in the last clause?
    Both are talking about a relationship [Brd, EBC, Herm, WBC, Ws]. By denying ourselves a relationship to the Son we also deny ourselves a relationship to the Father [EGT, NIC]. To 'have' the Father means to have a spiritual relationship with him [NIC], to be in fellowship with him [Alf, Lns, TNTC], to have intimate communion with him [BAGD, TH], to have God as a father [Brd] and friend [ICC, Ws]. It is nearly equivalent to 'knowing' the Father [Herm].

the-(one) confessing[a] the Son also[b] has the Father.
LEXICON—a. pres. act. participle of ὁμολογέω (LN 33.274; 33.275) (BAGD 4. p. 568): 'to confess' [AB, BAGD, LN, Lns; NASB, NRSV], 'to acknowledge' [BAGD, HNTC, WBC; all versions except NASB, NRSV, TEV], 'to accept' [TEV], 'to declare publicly' [BAGD]. The present tense indicates a continuing practice [Brd].
    b. καί (LN 89.93): 'also' [Lns; all versions except NAB, NJB, REB], 'too' [HNTC; NJB, REB, TNT], 'as well' [AB, WBC; NAB].
QUESTION—What is meant by the word ὁμολογέω 'to confess'?
    It is a public proclamation of one's faith [Brd, Lns, TH, TNTC]. It refers to a verbal affirmation that Jesus is the Christ [Alf]. It is to openly acknowledge that Jesus is the Christ, the Son of God [TNTC, WBC, Ws].
QUESTION—What is the relationship between this clause and the first clause in the verse?
    They are parallel and express the same idea in the negative–positive contrast favored by the author [TH, TNTC, WBC].

DISCOURSE UNIT: 2:24–28 [Brd]. The topic is the key to continuing fellowship.

DISCOURSE UNIT: 2:24–27 [TNTC; NAB]. The topic is life for God's anointed [NAB], safeguards against heresy [TNTC].

2:24 **Let-remain[a] in you what you heard[b] from[c] (the) beginning.[d]**
TEXT—Some manuscripts have οὖν 'therefore' after ὑμεῖς 'you'. GNT does not mention this alternative. It is included in the translations of KJV, REB, and TEV.

LEXICON—a. pres. act. impera. of μένω (LN 68.11) (BAGD 1.a.β. p. 504): 'to remain' [BAGD, LN, Lns; NAB, NIV, NJB, TNT], 'to abide' [AB, BAGD; KJV, NASB, NRSV], 'to dwell' [HNTC, WBC], 'to continue' [BAGD, LN], 'to keep hold of' [REB], 'to keep in one's heart' [TEV]. The present tense marks the verb as durative: 'keep on remaining' [Brd].
  b. aorist act. indic. of ἀκούω (LN 33.212, 24.52): 'to hear' [AB, HNTC, LN, Lns, WBC; all versions]. The aorist tense indicates that the hearing was in the past and is viewed as a single continuing unit [Brd, TH] and has much the same meaning as a perfect form [AB, Brd].
  c. ἐκ with genitive object (LN 67.131): 'from' [AB, HNTC, Lns, WBC; all versions except REB], 'at' [REB].
  d. ἀρχή (LN 68.1) (BAGD 1.b. p. 112): 'beginning' [AB, BAGD, HNTC, LN, Lns, WBC; all versions].

QUESTION—What is the significance of the order in which 'you' appears first in the clause?

'You' is emphatic [AB, Brd, ICC, My, NCBC, NIC, NTC, TH; NAB, NASB, TNT]. It is emphasized by translating it 'as for you' [AB, Brd, NIC; NAB, NASB, TNT]. It marks the change of the main character from the false teachers to the readers, strongly contrasting the believers with the heretics mentioned in the verses before [Brd, EBC, ICC, My, NCBC, NIC, Ws]. There is also a change from giving information to exhortation [TH].

QUESTION—What had they heard?

They had heard the gospel [Herm, HNTC, My, NIC, NTC, TNTC, WBC, Ws], the truth about the Father and Son [Alf], the teaching that Jesus is the Christ [EBC, Herm, My, NIC, TH]. Another view is that it is the commandment they had from the beginning (2:7) [Lns].

QUESTION—What is meant by letting what they heard remain in them?

The preposition ἐν 'in' refers to interaction with the truth, not mere mental assent [Brd, EBC, WBC]. It means to accept and interact with the truth [Brd], to continually think about it and let it affect their lives [EBC], to control their thinking and actions [NIC], to continue believing it [Brd]. Every decision is to be guided by God's Word [NTC].

QUESTION—To what does ἀρχῆς 'the beginning' refer?

Most take it to refer to the first time they heard the gospel [Br, Brd, NIC, WBC, Ws], the beginning of their Christian experience [Brd, ICC]. Some extend the meaning to go back to Christ's teaching [AB].

If what you-have-heard from (the) beginning remains[a] in[b] you,

LEXICON—a. aorist act. subj. of μένω (LN 68.11) (BAGD 1.a.β. p. 504): 'to remain' [BAGD, LN, Lns; KJV, NAB, NJB, TNT], 'to abide' [AB, BAGD; NASB, NRSV], 'to dwell' [HNTC, WBC], 'to still dwell' [REB], 'to continue' [BAGD, LN], 'to keep' [TEV], not explicit [NIV].
  b. ἐν with dative object (LN 89.119): 'in' [AB, HNTC, LN, Lns, WBC; all versions except NIV], not explicit [NIV].

QUESTION—What is the significance of the change in order in which the phrases 'what you have heard from the beginning' and 'remain in you' occur in this verse?

The difference is stylistic [AB]. The order is changed to achieve a chiasmus in Greek [AB, TNTC, WBC]. One commentator sees a change in emphasis from receiving the message to describing the message as being from the beginning [Ws].

also[a] you will-remain[b] in[c] the Son and (in) the Father.
LEXICON—a. καί (LN 89.87, 89.93): 'also' [WBC; KJV, NASB, NIV, TNT], 'too' [Lns], 'in turn' [NAB], not explicit [AB, HNTC; NJB, NRSV, REB, TEV].
  b. fut. act. indic. of μένω (LN 68.11) (BAGD 1.a.β. p. 504): 'to remain' [BAGD, Lns; NAB, NIV, NJB, TNT], 'to live' [TEV], 'to abide' [AB, BAGD; NASB, NRSV], 'to dwell' [HNTC, WBC; REB], 'to continue' [BAGD; KJV]. The future tense strengthens the idea of continuity [Brd, Lns, WBC].
  c. ἐν with dative object (LN 89.119) (BAGD I.5.d. p. 259): 'in' [AB, HNTC, Lns, WBC; all versions except TEV, TNT], 'with' [TEV, TNT], 'in union with' [TEV, TNT], 'in close personal relationship' [BAGD].

QUESTION—What relationship is indicated by the conjunction καί 'and' at the beginning of this clause?

It means that they also will remain in the Son and the Father [Alf, Brd, Lns, WBC, Ws; KJV, NAB, NASB, NIV, TNT]. It does not mean 'they, along with others', but that in addition to allowing the truth to dwell in them, they will also dwell in the Son and the Father [Alf, Brd, WBC, Ws].

QUESTION—What is the significance of the order in which 'the Son' is mentioned before 'the Father'?

The Son is mentioned first because our relationship to the Father is dependent on our relationship to the Son [AB, Brd, EBC, My, TH, WBC, Ws].

DISCOURSE UNIT: 2:25–29 [NASB]. The topic is the promise of eternal life.

2:25 And this is the promise[a] which he promised[b] us, eternal[c] life.[d]
TEXT—Instead of ἡμῖν 'to us' some manuscripts have ὑμῖν 'to you (plural)'. GNT selects ἡμῖν 'to us' with a B rating, indicating some degree of uncertainty. The reading ὑμῖν 'to you' is selected only by NJB.
LEXICON—a. ἐπαγγελία (LN 33.288) (BAGD 2.b. p. 280): 'promise' [AB, BAGD, LN, Lns; all versions except NIV, NRSV, TEV], 'pledge' [BAGD, WBC], 'what' [HNTC; NIV, NRSV, TEV].
  b. aorist mid. (deponent = act.) indic. of ἐπαγγέλλομαι (LN 33.286) (BAGD 1.b. p. 281): 'to promise' [BAGD, HNTC, LN, Lns; KJV, NIV, NRSV], 'to promise to give' [TEV], 'to make' [AB; NAB, NASB, NJB, TNT], 'to give' [WBC; REB].
  c. αἰώνιος: 'eternal'. See this word at 1:2.

d. ζωή (LN 23.88) (BAGD 2.b.α. p. 341): 'life'. See this word at 1:1, 2.

QUESTION—What relationship is indicated by καί 'and'?

It indicates the continuation of the same subject [WBC] and equates remaining in the Father and Son with eternal life [Brd]. This is the result of faithfully remaining in the Father and Son [Alf, Herm, NTC, TNTC]. It is the reward for having God's Word remaining in them [NIC].

QUESTION—What does αὕτη 'this' refer to?

1. It refers forward to 'eternal life' [Br, Brd, Herm, ICC, Lns, My, NCBC, NIC, NTC, TH, WBC, Ws; all versions except TNT]: what he promised us is this: eternal life. The promise is recorded in John 3:15; 4:14; 6:40, 47, 57 [Alf]. Although there is no promise directly stated, there are many passages that imply a promise of eternal life [ICC].
2. It refers back to 'abiding in the Son and in the Father' [AB; TNT]. Abiding in the Father and the Son is what he promised them, and this abiding leads to, and is a form of, eternal life. Passages revealing this promise are John 15:4, 7 and 17:22–23 [AB].

QUESTION—To whom does αὐτός 'he' refer?

1. It refers to Christ [AB, Alf, Brd, ICC, Lns, My, NCBC, NIC, NTC, TH, WBC, Ws; TEV]. The pronoun is emphatic and it is Christ on whom the writer wants to focus [AB].
2. It refers to God [EGT].

QUESTION—When is this promise fulfilled?

1. The promise is partially fulfilled now and will be completely fulfilled in the future [Alf, Br, EBC, Herm, HNTC, NIC, WBC].
2. The promise has its fulfillment now in the present life of the believer [AB, Brd].

QUESTION—What is meant by the word αἰώνιος 'eternal'?

It refers to a quality of life that is experienced now [AB, Br, Brd, EBC, WBC] and will last eternally [Brd]. Or, it refers to the hope of future life in heaven [Alf, EGT, TH].

DISCOURSE UNIT: 2:26–27 [ICC, NCBC, NTC, Ws]. The topic is the assurance that readers have truth [ICC], teaching and anointing [NTC], the anointing of the community [NCBC], abiding in the truth [Ws].

2:26 These-things I-wrote[a] to-you concerning[b] the-(ones) deceiving[c] you.

LEXICON—a. aorist act. indic. of γράφω: 'to write'. See this word at 2:21.

b. περί with genitive object (LN 90.24; 89.36): 'concerning' [LN; KJV, NASB, NRSV], 'about' [AB, HNTC, LN, WBC; NAB, NIV, NJB, TEV, TNT], 'in regard to' [Lns], 'so much for those' [REB].

c. pres. act. participle of πλανάω (LN 31.8) (BAGD 1.b. p. 665): 'to deceive' [AB, BAGD, LN, Lns; NAB, NASB, NRSV, TEV], 'to lead astray' [HNTC, WBC; NIV, NJB, TNT], 'to mislead' [BAGD, LN; REB], 'to seduce' [KJV]. The present tense shows that the deception is still going on [Brd, TH, TNTC, WBC]. It is conative, in that they are trying to deceive them [Lns, NIC, NTC; NASB, NIV, NJB, TEV]. See this word at 1:8.

QUESTION—What does ταῦτα 'these things' refer to?
1. It refers to 2:18–25 [Alf, Brd, Herm, ICC, My, NIC, NTC, TH, WBC, Ws].
2. It refers to the whole letter [AB, Lns].

QUESTION—What is being implied by the phrase 'deceiving you'?
1. It refers to the intent and attempt of the false teachers to deceive them, not necessarily indicating how successful they were [Brd, EBC, EGT, ICC, Lns, My, TNTC; NASB, NIV, NJB, TEV]: these things I wrote to you concerning the ones who are trying to deceive you.
2. The false teachers were making headway and the author is seeking to meet an emergency that this has caused [AB, HNTC, NCBC, NIC, WBC, Ws]: these things I wrote to you concerning the ones who are deceiving (some of) you.

2:27 But[a] you, the anointing[b] which you-received[c] from[d] him remains[e] in[f] you,

LEXICON—a. καί (LN 91.12): 'but' [WBC; KJV, NJB, NRSV, REB, TEV], 'and' [Lns; NASB], 'and remember' [HNTC], not explicit [AB; NAB, NIV, TNT].
b. χρῖσμα (LN 37.107) (BAGD p. 886): 'anointing' [AB, BAGD, HNTC, Lns; all versions except TEV], 'consecration' [WBC]. The phrase 'the anointing you received' is translated 'Christ has poured out his Spirit on you' [TEV]. See this word at 2:20.
c. aorist act. indic. of λαμβάνω (LN 57.125) (BAGD 2. p. 465): 'to receive' [AB, BAGD, HNTC, LN, Lns, WBC; all versions except TEV], 'to get' [BAGD], 'to obtain' [BAGD]. The aorist tense points back to a specific time in the past [Brd, WBC]. It has the force of the perfect tense here [TH].
d. ἐκ with genitive object (LN 90.16): 'from' [AB, HNTC, Lns, WBC; all versions except KJV, TEV], 'of' [KJV], not explicit [TEV].
e. pres. act. indic. of μένω (LN 68.11) (BAGD 1.a.β. p. 504): 'to remain' [BAGD, LN, Lns; all versions except KJV, NASB, NRSV], 'to abide' [AB, BAGD; KJV, NASB, NRSV], 'to dwell' [HNTC, WBC], 'to continue' [BAGD, LN]. The present tense reinforces the idea of continuity in the verb [Brd, Lns]: keeps on remaining in you.
f. ἐν with dative object (LN 89.119): 'in' [AB, HNTC, Lns, WBC; all versions except REB], 'with' [REB].

QUESTION—What relationship is indicated by καί 'but'?
It indicates contrast with the preceding verse [Brd, WBC, Ws; KJV, NJB, NRSV, REB, TEV]: they are trying to deceive you, but as for you, you have been taught all things. The initial position of ὑμεῖς 'you' is emphatic [Brd, TH] and shows contrast between the false teachers and the faithful believers

[AB, Alf, Brd, ICC, TH, WBC, Ws]. Many translations indicate this emphasis by translating it 'as for you' [AB, WBC; all versions except KJV].
QUESTION—To whom does αὐτοῦ 'from him' refer?
It refers to the 'Holy One' (2:20) [AB, Alf, Lns, My, Ws]. Although Brd takes 'the Holy One' in 2:20 to refer to God, in this verse he takes 'him' to refer to Christ because the pronouns in 2:25 and 2:28 refer to Christ. Most commentators specify Christ [AB, Alf, EBC, Herm, ICC, Lns, My, NIC, NTC, TH, WBC, Ws; TEV].

and[a] you-have[b] no need[c] that[d] anyone should-teach[e] you;
LEXICON—a. καί: 'and' [HNTC, Lns, WBC; KJV, NASB, NIV, NJB, TNT], 'and so' [AB; NRSV], 'this means' [NAB], not explicit [REB, TEV].
b. pres. act. indic. of ἔχω (LN 90.65): 'to have' [AB, HNTC, Lns; NAB, NASB, NRSV], not explicit [WBC; all versions except NAB, NASB, NRSV].
c. χρεία (LN 57.40) (BAGD 1. p. 885): 'need' [AB, BAGD, HNTC, LN, Lns, WBC; NAB, NRSV]. This noun is also translated by a verb: 'to need' [WBC; all versions except NAB, NRSV].
d. ἵνα (LN 90.22) (BAGD II.1.c.α. p. 377): 'that' [KJV, NRSV], 'for' [AB, HNTC, Lns; NAB, NASB], not explicit [WBC; NIV, NJB, REB, TEV, TNT].
e. pres. act. subj. of διδάσκω (LN 33.224) (BAGD 2.c. p. 192): 'to teach' [AB, BAGD, LN, Lns, WBC; all versions except REB] 'to be one's teacher' [HNTC]. This verb is also translated by a noun: 'teacher' [REB].
QUESTION—What relationship is indicated by καί 'and'?
It indicates the result of the previous clause [AB, My, TH; NAB, NRSV]: the anointing remains in you and therefore you have no need for anyone to teach you.
QUESTION—To whom does τις 'anyone' refer?
1. It refers to additional teachers [Brd, EBC, Herm, NCBC, NTC], 'anyone' outside their fellowship group [Br, HNTC, TH]: you do not need any outsider to teach you. The Gnostics offered what they called advanced teaching [Brd]. This does not rule out the need for teaching by John in this letter and by church pastors and teachers [Brd].
2. It refers to all teachers because believers already have all the knowledge they need [Alf, ICC, My, WBC, Ws]. If that anointing was fully abiding in them, no human teacher would be needed [Alf].

but[a] since[b] the anointing of-him teaches[c] you concerning[d] all (things),
TEXT—Instead of αὐτοῦ 'of him', some manuscripts have αὐτό 'the same'. GNT selects the reading αὐτοῦ 'of him' and does not mention the other reading. The reading αὐτό 'the same' is selected only by KJV.
LEXICON—a. ἀλλά (LN 89.125): 'but' [HNTC; KJV, NASB, NIV, NRSV, REB], 'rather' [AB; NAB], 'on the contrary' [Lns], 'moreover' [WBC], not explicit [NJB, TEV, TNT].

b. ὡς (LN 64.12, 89.37): 'since' [WBC; NJB], 'inasmuch as' [AB], 'as' [Lns; KJV, NAB, NASB, NIV, NRSV], 'for', [TEV], not explicit [HNTC; REB, TNT].
c. pres. act. indic. of διδάσκω (LN 33.224): 'to teach' [AB, BAGD, HNTC, LN, Lns, WBC; all versions except REB]. The present tense marks continuing action [Brd, EGT, Lns, TH, Ws].
d. περί (LN 90.24): 'about' [AB, HNTC, WBC; all versions except KJV, REB], 'concerning' [Lns], 'of' [KJV], not explicit [NJB, REB].

QUESTION—What relationship is indicated by ἀλλά 'but'?
1. It indicates a strong contrast [Brd, EGT]: you have no need to be instructed; on the contrary, your anointing teaches you all things.
2. It indicates a transition [WBC]: moreover. This is a consecutive sentence, so ἀλλά acquires a transitional force [WBC].

QUESTION—What relationship is indicated by ὡς 'since'?
1. It indicates the grounds for the following exhortation 'remain in him' [Alf, Brd, EGT, NIC, WBC; NJB, TNT, and assuming that 'as' indicates grounds: NAB, NASB, NIV, NRSV]: since his anointing teaches you all things, remain in him.
2. It indicates the grounds for the following clause [AB, Lns, My, TH]: since his anointing teaches you all things, therefore it is true and not a lie.
3. It indicates the grounds for the preceding clause [TEV]: you do not need anyone to teach you, because his anointing teaches you all things.

QUESTION—To what does πάντων 'all things' refer?
It refers to everything they need to know [ICC, NIC, WBC], everything necessary and possible to know about the Word of life [EBC], to all truth [Alf, HNTC]. This is not referring to a new revelation of teaching beyond what they already had been given [EBC].

and is true[a] and is not a-lie,[b]

LEXICON—a. ἀληθής (LN 72.1) (BAGD 2. p. 36): 'true' [AB, BAGD, HNTC, LN, Lns; all versions except KJV], 'real' [WBC], 'truth' [KJV].
b. ψεῦδος (LN 33.254) (BAGD p. 892): 'lie' [AB, BAGD, LN, Lns; all versions except NIV, NJB, TEV], 'false' [HNTC; NJB, TEV], 'falsehood' [BAGD, LN], 'illusion' [WBC], 'counterfeit' [NIV].

QUESTION—How is this clause related to the context?
1. When the preceding clause is taken to be the grounds for the exhortation 'remain in him':
1.1 It is an additional grounds [NIC; NAB, NASB, NIV, NJB, NRSV]: since his anointing teaches you all things, and since it is true and no lie, remain in him.
1.2 It is a parenthetical comment about what the anointing teaches [Alf, WBC; TNT]: since his anointing teaches you all things (and it is true and not a lie), remain in him.

2. When the preceding clause is taken to be the grounds for this clause, this is the result of that clause [AB]: since his anointing teaches you all things, therefore it is true and not a lie.
3. When the preceding clause is taken to be the result of the clause before it, this is a comment [TEV].

QUESTION—What is the implied subject of the verb ἐστιν 'is'?
1. The anointing is true [AB, Alf, EBC, TNTC, WBC; NAB, NASB, NIV, NJB, NRSV]. It is real and not counterfeit or an illusion [EBC, WBC].
2. What the anointing teaches is true [Herm, ICC, Lns, My, TH, Ws; TEV, TNT]. It is completely trustworthy [Herm].

and as[a] it/he-taught[b] you,

LEXICON—a. καθώς (LN 64.14): 'as' [NAB, REB], 'as...so' [HNTC], 'just as...so' [AB], 'just as' [Lns; NASB, NIV, NJB, NRSV], 'even as' [KJV], 'even as...so' [TNT], 'as indeed' [WBC], not explicit [TEV].
b. aorist act. indic. of διδάσκω (LN 33.224) (BAGD 2.c. p. 192): 'to teach' [AB, HNTC, Lns; all versions except TEV], 'to instruct' [WBC]. This verb is also translated as a noun: '(obey the Spirit's) teaching' [TEV]. The aorist tense indicates a completed action in the past [Brd, Lns] and is used here to show that the teaching of the anointing now is the same as the teaching they received in the past [TH].

QUESTION—What relationship is indicated by καθώς 'as'?
It indicates comparison [AB, HNTC; NAB, NASB, NIV, NJB, NRSV, REB, TNT]: just as you were taught, so remain in him.

QUESTION—Who or what is the implied subject of the verb διδάσκω 'to teach'?
1. The anointing is the subject [AB, EGT, Herm, ICC, Lns, NTC, TH, TNTC, Ws; KJV, NAB, NASB, NIV, NJB, NRSV]: as it taught you.
2. Christ is the subject [Alf, Brd, HNTC, TH, WBC; TNT]: as he taught you.

QUESTION—What is the relationship between the aorist 'taught' used here and the present tense 'teaches' used earlier in the verse?
1. The teaching here refers to Christ's teachings while here on earth [Brd, WBC]: as the Spirit is now teaching you and as Christ taught you. The teaching earlier in the verse was referring to the ongoing teaching of the Spirit [Brd].
2. The teaching here refers to what they received at conversion [EGT, TH, Ws]: as the anointing of the Holy Spirit continues to teach you and as it taught you from the time of your conversion.
3. There is no significant difference [Herm].

remain[a] in[b] him/it.

TEXT—Instead of μένετε 'remain', some manuscripts have the future μενεῖτε 'will remain'. GNT does not mention this reading. Only KJV take the future reading.

LEXICON—a. pres. act. indic./impera. of μένω: 'to remain'. See this word at 2:6. The present tense indicates a continuous state of remaining in him [Lns].
b. ἐν with dative object: 'in'. See this word at 2:6.
QUESTION—What is the mode of this verb?
1. This verb is imperative [Alf, Brd, EBC, EGT, Herm, Lns, NIC, NTC, TH, WBC; all versions except KJV, NASB]: remain in him/it.
2. This verb is indicative [AB, ICC, My, Ws; KJV, NASB]: you are remaining in him/it.
QUESTION—To whom does αὐτῷ 'in him/it' refer?
1. It refers to Christ [AB, Alf, Brd, EBC, EGT, ICC, Lns, My, NIC, NTC, TH, WBC, Ws; all versions]: remain in him.
2. It refers to the teachings from the anointing [Herm]: remain in what the anointing teaches you.

DISCOURSE UNIT: 2:28–4:6 [ICC, TNTC]. The topic is the application of tests [TNTC], two theses [ICC].

DISCOURSE UNIT: 2:28–3:24 [Br, Herm, HNTC, ICC]. The topic is the children of God [Br], the two families [HNTC], the children of God and brotherly love [Herm].

DISCOURSE UNIT: 2:28–3:10 [AB, Br, NCBC, TNTC; NIV]. The topic is the children of God [NIV], the two families [Br], God's children against the devil's children [AB], claims to be God's children [NCBC], the test of righteousness [TNTC].

DISCOURSE UNIT: 2:28–3:3 [NIC, TNTC; NAB]. The topic is the children of God [NAB], the hope of God's children [NIC], Christ's appearing [TNTC].

DISCOURSE UNIT: 2:28–29 [NTC]. The topic is confidence before God.

2:28 **And now,**[a] **children,**[b] **remain**[c] **in**[d] **him,**
LEXICON—a. νῦν (LN 67.38) (BAGD 2. p. 546): 'now' [AB, HNTC, LN, Lns, WBC; all versions except TEV], not explicit [TEV].
b. τεκνίον: 'child'. See this word at 2:1, 12.
c. pres. act. impera. of μένω: 'to remain'. See this word at 2:6, 27. The present tense indicates a continuing state [Brd, Lns].
d. ἐν with dative object: 'in'. See this word at 2:6, 27.
QUESTION—How is this verse related to its context?
It is transitional, concluding the preceding section and introducing the following [AB, Alf, Brd, EBC, Herm, ICC, My, NTC, WBC, Ws]. It is a transition from false teachers to God's children [EBC]. It continues the idea of remaining in him and moves on to a new emphasis on being the children of God [Herm, Ws].

QUESTION—What relationship is indicated by the conjunctions καὶ νῦν 'and now'?

The phrase introduces a new thought [Br, Brd, NIC]. It introduces an exhortation based on the present circumstances [Alf, Brd, ICC, My, NTC, TH]. Some think it refers back to the 'last hour' (2:18) [AB, HNTC, ICC, WBC].

QUESTION—To whom does αὐτῷ 'him' refer?
1. It refers to Christ [AB, Alf, Br, Brd, HNTC, ICC, Lns, NIC, NTC, TH, TNTC, WBC, Ws; TNT].
2. It refers to God the Father [NCBC].

in-order-that[a] when[b] he-appears[c] we-may-have confidence[d]
LEXICON—a. ἵνα (LN 89.59): 'in order that' [Lns; TNT], 'so that' [AB, HNTC, WBC; all versions except KJV, TNT], 'that' [KJV].
b. ἐάν (LN 67.32) (BAGD I.1.d. p. 211): 'when' [AB, BAGD, HNTC, LN; all versions], 'whenever' [BAGD], 'if' [Lns], 'at (his appearance)' [WBC].
c. aorist pass. subj. of φανερόω (LN 24.19) (BAGD 2.b.β. p. 853): 'to appear' [BAGD, LN; all versions except NAB, TNT], 'to be revealed' [AB, BAGD, HNTC; TNT], 'to reveal oneself' [BAGD; NAB], 'to show oneself' [BAGD], 'to be made manifest' [Lns]. This verb is also translated by a noun 'appearance' [WBC]. The aorist tense indicates the suddenness of his coming [Brd, EGT, Lns]. See this word at 1:2.
d. παρρησία (LN 25.158) (BAGD 3.b. p. 631): 'confidence' [AB, BAGD, HNTC, WBC; KJV, NASB, NRSV, TNT], 'boldness' [BAGD, LN, Lns], 'courage' [BAGD, LN; TEV], 'joyousness' [BAGD]. This noun is also translated by an adjective 'confident' [NAB, NIV, REB], 'fearless' [NJB].

QUESTION—What relationship is indicated by the conjunction ἵνα 'so that'?
1. It indicates the purpose for remaining in him [Brd, ICC, Lns, TNTC, WBC; TNT]: remain in him so that we can have confidence when he appears.
2. It indicates the anticipated result [TH]: remain in him and then we may have confidence when he appears.

QUESTION—What relationship is indicated by the conjunction ἐάν 'when'?
1. It means 'when', taking it for granted that he will appear [HNTC, TH].
2. It means 'whenever' and indicates an uncertainty as to the time he will appear [AB, Brd, EGT, NIC, NTC, WBC]: whenever he appears.
3. It means 'if it occurs in our time' and indicates an uncertainty of who will participate [Alf, Ws].

QUESTION—What is meant by φανερωθῇ 'he appears'?
1. This refers to Christ's return [AB, Alf, Brd, EBC, ICC, My, NIC, NTC, TNTC].
2. It refers to seeing God at the resurrection [NCBC].

QUESTION—What is the significance of the change of person from 'you (plural)' to 'we'?

The 'we' is inclusive as both the author and his readers are included [AB, Alf, Br, Brd, My, TNTC, Ws]. The author wants to stress his unity with the readers [AB, Brd, Ws], indicating that he as well as the readers must remain in Christ [My] and will share equally in the return [Alf]. Another suggestion is that this marks a change of genre from hortatory to descriptive material [WBC].

QUESTION—What is meant by the word παρρησίαν 'confidence'?

The meaning in focus is boldness, freedom, a lack of fear or reserve in speaking to someone of higher status [AB, Br, Brd, EBC, EGT, HNTC, Lns, NIC, TH, WBC]. The word had acquired a more general meaning of 'confidence' [ICC]. It means the same as not being ashamed [HNTC]. We have this confidence since he will come as a friend [AB, ICC, Lns, WBC].

and not be-ashamed[a] before[b] him at[c] his coming.[d]

LEXICON—a. aorist pass./pass. (deponent = act.) subj. of αἰσχύνομαι (LN 25.190) (BAGD 2. p. 25): 'to be ashamed' [HNTC, LN; KJV], 'to be put to shame' [BAGD; NRSV], 'to be disgraced' [BAGD, WBC], 'to draw back in shame' [AB], 'to retreat in shame' [NAB], 'to turn away in shame' [TNT], 'to be shamed away' [Lns], 'to shrink in shame' [NJB], 'to shrink away in shame' [NASB], 'to hide in shame' [TEV]. The phrase μὴ αἰσχυθῶμεν 'not be ashamed' is translated 'to be unashamed' [NIV, REB].

b. ἀπό with genitive object (LN 89.122): 'before' [HNTC, WBC; KJV, NIV, REB], 'from' [AB, Lns; NASB, NJB, NRSV, TEV, TNT], not explicit [NAB].

c. ἐν with dative object (LN 67.33) (BAGD II.2. p. 260): 'at' [AB, HNTC, Lns, WBC; all versions except TEV], 'at the time of' [LN], 'on the day' [TEV].

d. παρουσία (LN 15.86) (BAGD 2.b.α. p. 630): 'coming' [AB, BAGD, LN; all versions except TEV], 'arrival' [WBC], 'appearing' [HNTC], 'Parousia' [Lns]. This gerund is also translated by a verb: 'to come' [TEV].

QUESTION—What is the voice of this verb?

1. It is middle or passive deponent and refers to the feeling the person has about himself [AB, Alf, Brd, ICC, My, NTC, TNTC, Ws; NAB, NASB, NJB, NRSV, TEV]: to be ashamed before him. We would be ashamed if we had fallen into apostasy [HNTC] or had a sense of guilt [ICC].
2. It is a passive and refers to what will happen to the person [BAGD, Lns, NIC, TH, WBC]: to be put to shame before him. They would be put to shame if they were rejected at the judgment [NIC].

QUESTION—To whom does αὐτοῦ 'of him' refer?

1. It refers to Christ [AB, Alf, Brd, EBC, ICC, Lns, NIC, TH, Ws].
2. It refers to God the Father [HNTC].

QUESTION—What is meant by παρουσία 'coming'?
It is a technical term for the coming of a ruler [AB, Brd, EBC, ICC, Lns, NIC, TH, TNTC, WBC] and refers to Christ's return [AB, EBC, HNTC, ICC, NIC, TH, TNTC].

QUESTION—What is the relationship between παρουσία 'his coming' used here and φανερωθῇ 'he appears' used earlier in the verse?
They both refer to the same event [Br, My, NIC, TH, TNTC].

QUESTION—To whom does αὐτῷ 'his' refer?
It refers to Christ [AB, Alf, Br, HNTC, ICC, Lns, NIC, TH, TNTC, WBC].

DISCOURSE UNIT: 2:29–4:6 [Brd, EBC; NJB]. The topic is the Christian life viewed as divine sonship [Brd], living as God's children [NJB] fellowship with God [EBC], requirements for fellowship with a righteous God [EBC].

DISCOURSE UNIT: 2:29–3:24 [Brd, Lns]. The topic is ethical tests of sonship [Brd], being born of God [Lns].

DISCOURSE UNIT: 2:29–3:10 [EBC]. The topic is doing what is right.

DISCOURSE UNIT: 2:29–3:10a [Lns]. The topic is the new birth and our relation to God.

DISCOURSE UNIT: 2:29–3:2 [NJB]. The topic is living as God's children.

2:29 **If[a] you-know[b] that he-is righteous,[c]**

LEXICON—a. ἐάν (LN 89.67): 'if' [HNTC, Lns, WBC; all versions except REB, TEV], 'once' [AB], not explicit [REB, TEV].
b. Perf. act. subj. of οἶδα: 'to know'. See this word at 2:11.
c. δίκαιος (LN 88.12): 'righteous' [HNTC, LN, Lns, WBC; all versions except NAB, NJB], 'just' [AB, LN], 'upright' [NJB]. This adjective is also translated by a noun: 'holiness' [NAB].

QUESTION—What relationship is indicated by ἐάν 'if'?
1. This sets down a condition for the realization of a general principle [Brd, ICC, NIC, WBC, Ws]: if you know that he is righteous. This does not indicate doubt about their knowing that he is, in fact, righteous [Brd, WBC, Ws].
2. It indicates an obvious fact that is the grounds for the following statement or exhortation [TH; REB]: since you know he is righteous.

QUESTION—Who is the implied subject of the verb ἐστιν 'is'?
1. Christ is the implied subject [AB, EGT, Herm, ICC, NIC, TH, WBC; TEV]: if you know that Christ is righteous.
2. God the Father is the implied subject [Alf, Br, Brd, EBC, Lns, My, NCBC, NTC, TNTC; REB]: if you know that God is righteous. Since the Father is righteous, his children will practice righteousness [Br].

QUESTION—What is meant by δίκαιος 'righteous'?
It is morally correct behavior that is acceptable to God [NIC]. It is righteous character and actions, all of which conform to God's revealed standard of right and wrong [Brd]. It is freedom from sin [NTC].

1 JOHN 2:29

you-know[a] **that also**[b] **everyone doing**[c] **righteousness**[d] **has-been-begotten**[e] **by**[f] **him.**

LEXICON—a. pres. act. indic./impera. of γινώσκω (LN 28.1, 32.16) (BAGD 6.c. p. 161): 'to know' [AB, BAGD, HNTC, LN, WBC; KJV, NASB, NIV, TEV, TNT], 'to come to know' [BAGD], 'to realize' [Lns], 'to be sure' [BAGD; NAB, NRSV], 'to recognize' [NJB, REB].

b. καί (LN 89.93): 'also' [Lns, WBC; NASB], 'as well' [AB], 'then' [HNTC; TEV], not explicit [all versions except NASB, TEV].

c. pres. act. participle of ποιέω (LN 42.7) (BAGD I.1.c.β. p. 682): 'to do' [BAGD, HNTC, LN, Lns; all versions except NAB, NASB, NJB], 'to act' [AB, WBC; NAB], 'to practice' [BAGD; NASB]. This verb is also translated by a relative clause: 'whose life is' [NJB]. The present tense indicates habitual practice [Brd].

d. δικαιοσύνη (LN 88.13) (BAGD 2.b. p. 196): 'righteousness' [BAGD, Lns; KJV, NASB], 'holiness' [NAB], 'uprightness' [BAGD], 'right' [NIV, NRSV, REB], 'what is right' [HNTC, TEV, TNT]. This noun is also translated as an adverb: 'justly' [AB], 'rightly' [WBC], and as an adjective: 'upright' [NJB].

e. perf. pass. indic. of γεννάω (LN 13.56; 23.58) (BAGD 1.b. p. 155): 'to be begotten' [AB, BAGD; NAB], 'to be born' [HNTC, LN, Lns, WBC; all versions except NAB, NJB, REB]. This phrase 'to be begotten by' is translated 'to be a child of' [NJB, REB, TEV, TNT]. The perfect tense indicates a past action with results continuing into the present [Brd, Lns, TH]

f. ἐκ with genitive object (LN 90.16): 'by' [AB, LN; NAB], 'of' [HNTC, WBC; KJV, NASB, NIV, NRSV], 'from' [LN, Lns]. For NJB, REB, TEV, TNT see above.

QUESTION—What is the mood of εἰδῆτε 'you know'?

1. It is in the indicative mood and makes a statement [AB, Alf, Brd, Herm, ICC, Lns, TH, WBC; all versions except REB, TEV]: if you know that he is righteous, then you also know, etc.

2. It is in the imperative mood and gives a command [EBC, EGT, My, Ws; REB]: if/since you know that he is righteous, then realize, etc.

QUESTION—What relationship is indicated by καί 'also'?

It adds another thing they know [TH, WBC]: if you know . . . , then you also know . . .

QUESTION—What is the relationship between δίκαιος 'righteous' used above and δικαιοσύνη 'righteousness' used here?

They are synonymous terms [TH]. The doing of righteousness demonstrates that the person is connected to the righteous one [AB, HNTC, ICC, Lns, NIC, Ws]; it does not cause one to be born of him [HNTC, ICC, Ws].

QUESTION—What are the grounds of comparison in the metaphor?

The metaphor is that of a male begetting a child [AB, Alf, NIC, TH, TNTC]. As begetting initiates physical life so God initiates spiritual life [AB, NIC, TH, TNTC]. Included is the similarity of natures: as genetic heritage transfers traits, so God/Christ has transferred traits to us [Alf, Brd]; bringing a family resemblance [Br, TNTC]. The trait he has transferred is righteousness [Alf, Br].

QUESTION—To whom does αὐτοῦ 'him' refer?

It refers to God [AB, Alf, Br, Brd, EBC, EGT, Herm, HNTC, Lns, My, NCBC, NIC, NTC, TH, TNTC, WBC, Ws; TEV, TNT].

DISCOURSE UNIT: 3:1–5:13 [WBC]. The topic is living as children of God.

DISCOURSE UNIT: 3:1–24 [NASB, REB]. The topic is the children of God [NASB], loving one another [NASB], living together as Christians [REB].

DISCOURSE UNIT: 3:1–12 [Ws]. The topic is the children of God and the children of the devil.

DISCOURSE UNIT: 3:1–10 [Alf; TEV]. The topic is the children of God [TEV], the distinguishing signs of God's children and the devil's children [Alf].

DISCOURSE UNIT: 3:1–3 [EGT, NTC, TH, WBC, Ws]. The topic is our present dignity [EGT], our future destiny [EGT], the children of God [NTC, TH], God as Father [WBC], the present and future positions of God's children [Ws].

3:1 See^a how-great^b a-love^c the Father has given^d to us

LEXICON—a. aorist act. impera. of ὁράω (LN 32.11): 'to see' [HNTC, LN, Lns; NAB, NASB, NJB, NRSV, TEV], 'to look at' [AB], 'to consider' [BAGD, WBC; REB], 'to behold' [KJV], 'to recognize' [LN], not explicit [NIV, TNT]. The aorist imperative calls for immediate action [Brd, Lns], calling the reader's attention to the following statement [TH].

b. ποταπός (LN 58.30) (BAGD p. 695): 'how great' [HNTC; NASB, NIV, REB], 'how much' [TEV], 'how wonderful' [TNT], 'how glorious' [BAGD], 'how lavish' [WBC], 'what' [AB; NAB, NRSV], 'what great' [Lns; NJB], 'what sort of' [BAGD, LN], 'what kind of' [BAGD, LN], 'what manner of' [KJV]. Wonder, admiration, and amazement are in focus [AB, Alf, Brd, EBC, ICC, Lns, My, NCBC, NIC, NTC, TH, TNTC, WBC]. It indicates a very high degree of that love [TH].

c. ἀγάπη: 'love'. See this word at 2:5, 15. It is made prominent by its forefronted position [Lns].

d. perfect act. indic. of δίδωμι (LN 57.71): 'to give' [HNTC, LN, Lns; NRSV], 'to bestow on' [AB; KJV, NAB, NASB, REB], 'to show to' [TNT], 'to shower on' [WBC], 'to lavish' [NIV, NJB]. The phrase 'to give love' is translated 'to love' [TEV]. The perfect tense indicates that the effects of giving the love remain [ICC, Lns, TH].

QUESTION—How is this verse related to its context?

It expands on the idea of being begotten by God (2:29) [Brd, EBC, Herm, ICC, Lns, My, TH, WBC; NIV], and the return of Christ [WBC].

1 JOHN 3:1

QUESTION—What is the significance of the use of 'Father' as a name of God?
It corresponds with 'children' in the next clause and refers to God's relationship to Christians [AB, ICC, Lns, WBC, Ws].

QUESTION—Who are the participants for the event word 'love'?
1. The Father has loved us [AB, Alf, Br, Brd, EBC, Herm, ICC, My, NCBC, NIC, TH, WBC; TEV]: see how greatly the Father has loved us.
2. The Father has caused us to love each other [Ws]: see how great a love the Father imparted to us to love as he does. It is because of our God-like love that we can claim to be God's children.

QUESTION—To whom does 'us' refer?
It is inclusive and refers to the writer and his readers [AB, Alf], and by extension to all Christians [Ws].

that^a we-should-be-called^b God's children,^{c}

LEXICON—a. ἵνα (LN 89.49; 91.15) (BAGD II.1.e. p. 378): 'that' [Lns, WBC; KJV, NASB, NIV, NRSV, TEV], 'so that' [HNTC], 'in enabling' [AB], 'by letting' [NJB], 'in letting' [NAB], 'in' [REB, TNT].
b. aorist pass. subj. of καλέω (LN 33.131) (BAGD 1.a.δ. p. 399): 'to be called' [AB, BAGD, HNTC, LN, Lns, WBC; all versions].
c. τέκνον (LN 10.36) (BAGD 2.e. p. 808): 'child' [AB, Lns, WBC; all versions except KJV], 'son' [KJV], 'offspring' [HNTC]. The designation 'child' indicates that God acts towards believers as a father does towards his children [NCBC, WBC], having an intimate relationship that is between a father and child [TH]. Being a child means that the person has a similar nature to his father [ICC, NIC, TNTC, WBC, Ws].

QUESTION—What relationship is indicated by ἵνα 'that'?
1. It indicates how that great love was expressed [AB, Br, Brd, EBC, Herm, ICC, Lns, NCBC, TH, WBC; NAB]: see how greatly God loves us, namely, that he calls us his children.
2. It indicates the purpose God had in loving us [Alf, EGT]: see how greatly God loves us, and he loved us in order to call us his children.

QUESTION—What is meant by κληθῶμεν 'we are called'?
1. It is essentially the same as 'to be' and indicates their identity [AB, BAGD, Herm]: that we are God's children. It also indicates that their status will be publicly known [AB].
2. It means 'to be acknowledged' as a child of God and refers to the title and possession of the believer before God [Alf, Brd, ICC, Lns, My, NCBC, NIC, TH, WBC, Ws]. God is the implied actor [Lns, NIC, TH]: that God acknowledges us to be his children. Although it includes the meaning of being God's child, it stresses the dignity of the title and the position one has as God's child [ICC]. When a father names a child as his son, he acknowledges that it is really his child [NIC].

and we-are.[a]

TEXT—Some manuscripts omit the words καὶ ἐσμέν 'and we are'. GNT includes these words with a B rating, indicating some degree of doubt in doing do. These words are omitted by only KJV.

LEXICON—a. pres. act. indic of εἰμί (LN 13.4) (BAGD II.1. p. 223): 'to be' [BAGD, HNTC, LN, Lns, WBC; all versions except KJV], 'to really be' [AB]. The use of the indicative indicates a sharp break with the preceding sentence to emphasize the fact that they are God's children [AB].

QUESTION—How is this clause related to its context?

It is a parenthetical comment [ICC, Ws]. It reinforces the reality of the statement needed in the face of the world's rejection of that truth [Alf, EGT, NIC]. The designation, 'children of God', is in accord with reality [EGT, ICC, TNTC].

Because-of[a] this the world[b] (does) not know[c] us, that/because[d] (it-did) not know[e] him.

LEXICON—a. διά with accusative object (LN 89.26; 89.33) (BAGD B.II.2. p. 181): 'because of' [LN]. The phrase διὰ τοῦτο 'because of this' is translated 'for this reason' [Lns; NASB], 'the reason is' [HNTC; NAB, NIV], 'the reason why' [NJB, NRSV, REB, TNT], 'this is why' [WBC; TEV], 'the reason that' [AB], 'therefore' [KJV].

b. κόσμος (LN 9.23) (BAGD 7. p. 447): 'world' [AB, BAGD, HNTC, Lns, WBC; all versions], 'people of the world' [LN]. It is that which is hostile to God [BAGD].

c. pres. act. indic. of γινώσκω (LN 31.27) (BAGD 1.b. p. 160): 'to know' [BAGD, Lns; KJV, NASB, NIV, NRSV, TEV], 'to recognize' [AB, HNTC, WBC; NAB, REB, TNT], 'to acknowledge' [NJB]. The present tense indicates continuing action [TH].

d. ὅτι (LN 89.33) (BAGD 3.a. p. 589): 'that' [AB, HNTC; all versions except KJV, NASB, TEV], 'because' [BAGD, Lns, WBC; KJV, NASB], 'since' [BAGD], not explicit [TEV].

e. aorist act. indic. of γινώσκω (LN 31.27) (BAGD 1.b. p. 160): 'to know' [BAGD, Lns; all versions except NAB, NJB, TNT], 'to recognize' [AB, HNTC, WBC; NAB, TNT], 'to acknowledge' [LN; NJB]. The aorist tense indicates that they never knew him [AB, Lns, TH]. It refers back to the historic manifestation of Jesus [Brd, EGT]. See this word at 2:3, 4, 13, 14.

QUESTION—What does the pronoun τοῦτο 'this' refer to?

1. It refers to the following statement [AB, HNTC, ICC, TNTC, WBC; NAB, NIV, NJB, NRSV, REB, TEV, TNT]: the world does not know us because of this reason, namely, because it did not know him. The ὅτι 'because' clause then specifies the reason indicated by 'this' [AB].

2. It refers to the preceding statement [Alf, Brd, EBC, EGT, Herm, Lns, My, NCBC, NIC, TH, Ws; KJV]: we are God's children and because of this fact, the world does not know us. The ὅτι 'because' clause then explains

why the world does not know God's children [Alf, Brd, EGT, Herm, Lns, NCBC] and gives a further explanation of the main clause [NIC, TH].

QUESTION—What is meant by κόσμος 'world'?

It is a metonymy for the godless people who live in the world [Brd, LN, Lns, TH, WBC].

QUESTION—What is meant by γινώσκει 'know'?

The world does not recognize believers to be God's children [ICC, NCBC]. It doesn't know what it is to be a child of God [Lns], and does not understand their true inner nature [My] or principles and character [Ws]. Understanding, appreciation, and friendly relationships are in focus [Brd, Ws].

QUESTION—To whom does αὐτόν 'him' refer?

1. It refers to God the Father [AB, Alf, Br, EBC, EGT, ICC, Lns, My, TH, WBC, Ws; TEV]: because the world did not know the Father. God is mentioned by name in both the preceding and following clauses [AB]. Because the world does not know the Father, they do not know the Father's children [Alf, WBC]. Some add that it means the Father as revealed in the Son [EGT], God in Christ [Ws].
2. It refers to Christ [Brd, Herm, TNTC; NAB]: because the world did not know Christ. The aorist tense points to Christ's first coming [Brd]. There is another reference to knowing Christ at 3:6 [TNTC].

3:2 **Beloved,[a] now[b] we-are children[c] of-God,**

LEXICON—a. ἀγαπητός: 'beloved'. See this word at 2:7.

b. νῦν (LN 67.38) (BAGD 1.a.α p. 545): 'now' [BAGD, HNTC, LN, Lns, WBC; all versions except NJB, TNT], 'right now' [AB], 'already' [NJB, TNT]. Its position at the front of the clause makes it emphatic [Brd, ICC], emphasizing the contrast between the present and future states of God's children [Brd, My, NIC, WBC].

c. τέκνον (LN 10.36): 'child' [AB, LN, Lns, WBC; all versions except KJV], 'son' [KJV], 'offspring' [HNTC].

QUESTION—How is this verse related to its context?

It gives a further clarification of being God's children [ICC, NCBC]. It develops the thought about the return of Christ (2:28) by telling what will happen to believers on that day (HNTC).

QUESTION—By whom are they loved?

They are loved by the writer [Lns, TNTC, WBC, Ws].

and/but[a] not-yet[b] it-was-revealed[c] what we-shall-be.

LEXICON—a. καί (LN 91.12): 'and' [AB, HNTC, Lns, WBC; KJV, NASB, NIV], 'but' [NJB, TEV, TNT], not explicit [NAB, NRSV, REB].

b. οὔπω (LN 67.129) (BAGD p. 593): 'not yet' [AB, BAGD, HNTC, LN, Lns, WBC; all versions except NASB], 'as yet' [NASB].

c. aorist pass. indic. of φανερόω (LN 28.36) (BAGD 1.b. p. 852): 'to be revealed' [AB, BAGD, HNTC; NJB, TNT], 'to become known' [BAGD], 'to be made known' [BAGD, LN; NIV], 'to be disclosed' [WBC; REB], 'to be made manifest' [Lns], 'to appear' [KJV, NASB, NRSV], 'to come to light' [NAB], 'to be clear' [TEV]. The aorist tense indicates that it never was manifested on any occasion [Alf, ICC, Ws]. This refers to being shown forth in reality rather than being shown to the understanding [Alf, My]. It refers to a public display of the Christian's future glory [Lns]. See this word at 2:19.

QUESTION—What relationship is indicated by καί 'and'?
1. It is coordinate [AB, Alf, HNTC, Lns, My, WBC; KJV, NASB, NIV]: we are God's children and it is not yet revealed what our future state will be. It is another aspect of our present state [Alf, My].
2. It is contrastive [Brd; NJB, TEV, TNT]: now we are God's children, but what we shall be has not yet been made manifest.

QUESTION—What is the subject of ἐφανερώθη 'it was revealed'?
1. The subject is τί ἐσόμεθα 'it', that is, 'what we shall be' [AB, EBC, EGT, HNTC, My, NIC, TH, TNTC, WBC; all versions]: we are now God's children, but what we shall be has not been revealed. All the future benefits of being God's children are not yet known, although one fact is known; that is, that we shall be like Christ. The manifestation of their real identity and nature is still in the future [EBC].
2. The implied subject is 'he', referring to God [NCBC]. This requires punctuating this sentence differently: we are now God's children, (although) he has not yet been revealed. What we shall be, we know, because when he is revealed we will be like him.

We know[a] that when/if[b] he/it is-revealed[c]

LEXICON—a. perfect act. indic. of οἶδα (LN 28.1): 'to know' [AB, BAGD, HNTC, LN, Lns; all versions except NJB], 'to be well aware' [NJB], to know only [WBC].
  b. ἐάν (LN 67.32): 'when' [HNTC, LN, WBC; all versions], 'if' [Lns], 'at' [AB]. The event is certain, but the time of the event is unknown [AB].
  c. aorist pass. subj. of φανερόω (LN 24.19, 28.36) (BAGD 2.b.β. p. 853): 'to be revealed' [BAGD, HNTC, LN; TNT] 'to show oneself' [BAGD], 'to appear' [BAGD, LN, WBC; all versions except NAB], 'to be made manifest' [Lns], 'to come to light' [NAB]. The phrase 'when it is revealed' is translated 'at this revelation' [AB]. See this word at 1:2; 2:28.

QUESTION—How is this clause connected with the preceding one?
Some manuscripts include δέ 'but', although GNT does not mention this alternative. The connection, whether or not the δέ is original, is in contrast with the preceding clause [Brd, EGT, TH, WBC; KJV, NIV, REB, TEV]: we do not know what we will be, but we do know that we will be like him. Although details have not yet been revealed about the future state of the believers, yet there is some knowledge, namely, that we will be like him [Brd]. Some commentators do not want to call this a contrast, but merely part of the present knowledge possessed by believers [Ws].

1 JOHN 3:2

QUESTION—What is the implied subject of φανερωθῇ 'he/it is revealed'?
1. The implied subject is 'he', referring to Christ when he comes in glory [Br, Brd, EBC, Herm, HNTC, ICC, Lns, NIC, NTC, TNTC, WBC, Ws; all versions except NAB]: it has not yet been revealed what we shall be, but we know that when Christ is revealed, we will be like him. One commentator takes 'he' to refer to God [NCBC].
2. The implied subject is 'it', referring to 'what we shall be' [AB, Alf, EGT, Lns, My, TH; NAB]: it has not yet been revealed what we will be, but we know that when it is revealed, we will be like him.

we-will-be[a] like[b] him, because[c] we-will-see[d] him as[e] he-is.
LEXICON—a. fut. mid. indic. of εἰμί (LN 13.1): 'to be' [AB, HNTC, LN, Lns, WBC; all versions].
b. ὅμοιος (LN **64.1**) (BAGD 1. p. 566): 'like' [AB, BAGD, HNTC, **LN**, WBC; all versions], 'similar' [BAGD, LN, Lns], 'of the same nature as' [BAGD].
c. ὅτι (LN 89.33): 'because' [HNTC, LN, Lns, WBC; NASB, NJB, REB, TEV], 'for' [AB, LN; KJV, NAB, NIV, NRSV, TNT].
d. fut. mid. (deponent = active) indic. of ὁράω (LN 24.1) (BAGD 1.a.γ. p. 578): 'to see' [AB, BAGD, HNTC, Lns, WBC; all versions].
e. καθώς (LN 64.14) (BAGD 1. p. 391): 'as' [AB, HNTC, Lns, WBC; all versions except NASB, NJB, TEV], 'just as' [BAGD, LN; NASB], 'as really' [NJB, TEV].

QUESTION—In what ways will we be like him?
We will be like him in character [Alf, EGT], righteousness [NCBC], purity [EBC, HNTC], holiness [Brd], immortality [NTC], and glory [Lns, NIC, Ws]. We too will be glorified in body and soul [NTC]. We will never be equal or identical to him, but there will be a similarity [NTC, TH, WBC].

QUESTION—To whom does αὐτόν 'him' refer?
1. The pronoun refers to Christ [Br, Brd, Herm, HNTC, ICC, Lns, NIC, NTC, TNTC, WBC]: when Christ is revealed, we will be like Christ, because we will see him as he is. This position follows from taking the previous pronoun to refer to Christ. Christ's full glory will then be seen [NIC], no longer veiled by the conditions of his earthly life [ICC].
2. The pronoun refers to God, the Father [AB, Alf, My, TH]: when it, our future state, is revealed, we will be like God, because we will see God as he is. Although we cannot see God now, in our glorified state this will be possible [Alf]. God's essential character will be seen [TH].

QUESTION—What relationship is indicated by ὅτι 'because'?
1. It indicates the reason we will be like him [Alf, Br, EGT, Herm, HNTC, ICC, NIC, TNTC, WBC]: we shall be like him because we shall see him as he is. The result of seeing him will be a transformation so that we will be like him [HNTC, ICC, TNTC, WBC]. The process of becoming like Christ has commenced in this present life, but it will be completed only when we see him as he is [Herm].

2. It indicates the grounds for saying that we will be like him [Brd, EGT, My, NCBC, TH, Ws]: we will be like him since we will see him as he is. Being like him is a condition for seeing him; if we were not like him, we would not be able to see him as he is [Brd, EGT].

DISCOURSE UNIT: 3:3–10 [NJB]. The topic is the break from sin.

3:3 And everyone having this hope^a in^b him purifies^c himself

LEXICON—a. ἐλπίς (LN 25.59) (BAGD 2.b. p. 253): 'hope' [AB, BAGD, HNTC, LN, Lns, WBC; all versions]. The phrase ἔχων τὴν ἐλπίδα 'having hope' is translated 'to hope' [NRSV]. Confident expectation is in focus [Brd, NCBC, TNTC]. The present tense of ἔχων 'having' indicates that this is a continuous hope [TH].
  b. ἐπί with dative object (LN 89.27; 90.23; 89.27) (BAGD II.1.b.γ. p. 287): 'in' [HNTC, WBC; KJV, NIV, NRSV, TEV, TNT], 'of' [NJB], 'set on' [Lns], 'based on' [AB; NAB], 'fixed on' [NASB], not explicit [REB].
  c. pres. act. indic. of ἁγνίζω (LN **88.30**) (BAGD 1.b. p. 11): 'to purify' [BAGD, HNTC, LN, Lns; all versions except NAB, REB, TEV], 'to make pure' [AB; REB], 'to cause to be pure' [LN], 'to keep pure' [WBC; NAB, TEV]. The present tense indicates a continuing process of purification [Brd, Lns, TH].

QUESTION—How is this verse related to its context?
  It is a parenthetical comment [Herm]. It specifies the practical outworking of the hope described in the preceding verses [EGT, NIC, TNTC, WBC, Ws]. It is an implied exhortation to purify oneself [Herm, NCBC, NIC, WBC]. It provides a transition from 2:28 to 3:4 [Herm, NCBC].

QUESTION—What is implied by the change from 'we' and 'us' in the previous verse to πᾶς 'everyone'?
  It implies that some of the readers would have excluded themselves from this rule [Brd, EBC, ICC, Ws]. It stresses the individual responsibility of each believer [WBC].

QUESTION—To what does 'this hope' refer?
  The hope is being like Christ [Brd, EBC] or like God [Alf, My, TH], seeing Christ as he really is [Brd, HNTC, ICC], the return of Christ and the glory to follow [TNTC], sharing God's eternal life [WBC].

QUESTION—What relationship is indicated by ἐπί 'in'?
  It means that the hope has him for its object [Br, Herm], it is based on him [AB, My, TH], founded on him [Brd], and rests on him [EGT, ICC, Lns, NIC, Ws]. It is grounded on his promises [Alf] and will be fulfilled by him [AB, TH].

QUESTION—To whom does αὐτῷ 'him' refer?
  1. It refers to Christ [Br, Brd, EBC, Herm, HNTC, ICC, Lns, NCBC, NIC, NTC, TNTC].
  2. It refers to God the Father [AB, Alf, EGT, My, TH, WBC, Ws].

QUESTION—What is the relationship between 'having this hope' and 'purifying oneself'?

The hope necessarily causes purity [ICC, WBC]. Hope stirs the desire to be pure [Alf]. To encounter Christ when he is revealed, believers must prepare now by purifying themselves [AB]. Present purity is required to be worthy of the call to be like Christ [Br].

as[a] that-one is pure.[b]

LEXICON—a. καθώς (LN 78.53, 64.14): 'as' [HNTC; NAB, NJB, NRSV, REB], 'even as' [AB, Lns; KJV], 'just as' [LN, WBC; NASB, NIV, TEV, TNT].

b. ἁγνός (LN 88.28) (BAGD 1. p. 12): 'pure' [AB, BAGD, HNTC, LN, Lns, WBC; all versions] 'innocent' [BAGD]. This refers to general moral purity [Brd, NIC, TNTC, WBC] and sinlessness [EBC, Herm, Lns, NCBC, NIC, NTC, TH, WBC]. It is equivalent to δίκαιος 'righteous' (2:29) [Herm].

QUESTION—To whom does ἐκεῖνος 'that one' refer?

1. It refers to Christ [AB, Br, Brd, EGT, Herm, ICC, Lns, My, NCBC, NIC, TH, TNTC, WBC; REB, TEV, TNT].
2. It refers to God the Father [Alf, Ws].

QUESTION—What relationship is indicated by καθώς 'as'?

It indicates comparison: believers become pure as that one is pure. The purity of 'that one' is to be the believer's example or norm [ICC, My, TH, WBC], his standard [NTC], or model [Lns]. Some include an additional relationship of reason: believers are to become pure because that one is pure.

DISCOURSE UNIT: 3:4–12 [EGT]. The topic is the children of God.

DISCOURSE UNIT: 3:4–10 [NCBC, NIC, TH, TNTC; NAB]. The topic is the sinlessness of the children of God [NIC, TH], the children of God and children of the devil [NCBC], avoiding sin [NAB], the past appearance of Christ [TNTC].

DISCOURSE UNIT: 3:4–9 [WBC, Ws]. The topic is renouncing sin [WBC], the character of God's children [Ws].

DISCOURSE UNIT: 3:4–8 [EGT]. The topic is the incompatibility of being God's child and continuing in sin.

3:4 Everyone doing[a] the sin[b] also[c] is-doing[d] the lawlessness,[e]

LEXICON—a. pres. act. participle of ποιέω (LN 90.45) (BAGD I.1.c.γ. p. 682): 'to do' [BAGD, LN, Lns], 'to commit' [HNTC, WBC; KJV, NRSV, REB], 'to practice' [NASB, TNT]. The phrase ποιῶν τὴν ἁμαρτίαν 'doing sin' is translated 'to sin' [NAB, NIV, NJB, TEV], 'to act sinfully' [AB]. The present tense indicates habitual sinning [Brd, Lns, My, NCBC, NTC].

b. ἁμαρτία (LN 88.289) (BAGD 1. p. 43): 'sin'. See this word at 1:8, 9; 2:2, 12.

c. καί (LN 89.93): 'also' [HNTC, Lns, WBC; KJV, NASB, TNT], 'really' [AB], not explicit [all versions except KJV, NASB, TNT].
d. pres. act. indic. of ποιέω (LN 90.45): 'to do' [AB, LN, Lns], 'to practice' [NASB, TNT], 'to act' [NAB, NJB], 'to be guilty of' [NRSV]. The phrase τὴν ἀνομίαν ποιεῖ 'to do lawlessness' is translated 'to transgress the law' [KJV], 'to break the law' [HNTC, WBC; NIV], 'to break God's law' [REB], 'to be guilty of breaking God's law' [TEV]. The present tense states a universal truth [TNTC].
e. ἀνομία (LN 88.139) (BAGD 2. p. 71): 'lawlessness' [BAGD, LN, Lns; NASB, NRSV, TNT], 'lawless deed' [BAGD], 'iniquity' [AB]. This noun is also translated as an adverb: 'lawlessly' [NAB], 'wickedly' [NJB].

QUESTION—How is this verse related to its context?

It expands the idea of the character of the children of God [Herm] and strengthens the idea of the previous verse [Herm, HNTC, ICC, Lns, My]. In contrast to those purifying themselves are those continuing to practice sin [HNTC, ICC, Lns, My]. They must purify themselves because the only alternative is lawlessness [My, Ws]. The positive side of 2:29 has been described and now the negative side is developed [Alf, Br, Brd, EGT, Lns, My, NIC]. It also contrasts man's sinfulness with Christ's sinlessness of the following verse [HNTC, WBC].

QUESTION—What is the difference between ποιέω τὴν ἁμαρτίαν 'to do sin' used here and ἁμαρτάνω 'to sin' used elsewhere?

The construction 'doing sin' indicates habitual practice of sin [Brd] and as such does not indicate any difference of meaning from the present tense usage [AB, My, TH], such as 3:6, 3:8 and 3:9. The difference is stylistic.

QUESTION—What is the significance of the article in the phrase τὴν ἁμαρτίαν '*the* sin'?

This is a reference to generic sin to indicate the complete extent of sin [My, WBC, Ws]. John discusses the concepts of sin and lawlessness rather than specific acts [Brd]. It is abstract sinfulness [Alf]. However, Lns takes the article to indicate that the abstract nouns are definite, so that 'the' sin is the one that misses the mark God has set and 'the' lawlessness is that which disregards God's law.

QUESTION—What is meant by ἀνομία 'lawlessness'?

1. It means breaking God's law [AB, Alf, Brd, EGT, ICC, Lns, My, NTC, TNTC, Ws; REB]. It is a deliberate disregard for the law [Brd, TNTC], particularly the law of love [HNTC, ICC]. It is willful sinning [NCBC, TNTC, Ws].
2. Rather than focusing on breaking God's law, it pertains to the attitude of rebellion against God [Herm, HNTC, NIC, TH, WBC]. Most see a connection with the 'man of lawlessness' in 2 Thess. 2:3 [AB, Herm, HNTC, NIC, TH, WBC]. It implies aligning oneself with the antichrist and Satan in direct rebellion against God [NIC, TH]. The article with 'lawlessness' indicates that it is a technical term for the rejection of God

that is inspired by Satan and will come to its climax just before the coming of Christ [TH, WBC].

and[a] sin is lawlessness.

LEXICON—a. (LN 89.92): 'and' [LN, Lns; NASB] 'for' [AB, WBC; KJV, NAB, REB], 'because' [HNTC; NJB, TEV], 'in fact' [NIV], not explicit [NRSV, TNT].

QUESTION—What relationship is indicated by καί 'and'?

    1. It indicates a restatement of the previous clause [Brd, ICC, My; NIV]: the one who sins is doing lawlessness, indeed, sin is lawlessness. Not only is sin a breaking of the law, its very nature is transgression of God's law [ICC].

    2. It indicates the grounds for the preceding statement [AB, HNTC, WBC; KJV, NAB, NJB, REB, TEV]: the one who sins is doing lawlessness because sin is lawlessness.

QUESTION—What is the relationship between ἀνομία 'lawlessness' and ἁμαρτία 'sin'?

Sin is defined as lawlessness [Alf, Br, Brd, EGT, HNTC, ICC, Lns, My, NCBC, NIC, NTC, TNTC, WBC]: sin is lawlessness. It isn't the only definition, but it indicates the nature of sin. Sin is anything against God's law [Alf, Br, Brd, EGT, ICC, Lns, My, TNTC, Ws], rebellion against God [EBC, TNTC]. Both terms mean sin in the nature of transgression of God's commandments [AB].

3:5 And[a] you-know[b] that that-one appeared/was revealed[c] in-order-to[d] take-away[e] sins,[f]

TEXT—Instead of ἁμαρτίας 'sins', some manuscripts have ἁμαρτίας ἡμῶν 'our sins'. GNT selects the reading ἁμαρτίας 'sins' with a C rating, indicating a considerable degree of doubt in doing so. The Textual choice does not affect the meaning because if the pronoun is not explicit, it is implied [AB, Br, Brd, ICC, My].

LEXICON—a. καί (LN 89.92): 'and' [AB, HNTC, Lns, WBC; KJV, NASB], 'but' [NIV], 'as' [REB], 'now' [NJB], not explicit [NAB, NRSV, TEV, TNT].

    b. perf. act. indic. of οἶδα: 'to know'. See this word at 3:2.

    c. aorist pass. indic. of φανερόω (LN 24.19) (BAGD 2.b.β. p. 853): 'to appear' [BAGD, LN, WBC; all versions except KJV, NAB], 'to be revealed' [AB, BAGD, HNTC; TNT], 'to reveal oneself' [NAB], 'to be manifested' [KJV], 'to be made manifest' [Lns]. The aorist is used to indicate that it is once and for all in history [Alf, TH, WBC]. See this word at 1:2; 2:28; 3:2.

    d. ἵνα (LN 89.59) (BAGD I.1.e. p. 377): 'in order to' [BAGD, HNTC, LN, Lns, WBC; NASB, NJB, REB, TEV, TNT], 'so that' [LN; NIV], 'to' [KJV, NRSV], not explicit [AB; NAB].

e. aorist act. subj. of αἴρω (LN 20.43) (BAGD 4. p. 24): 'to take away' [AB, BAGD, Lns; all versions], 'to remove' [BAGD, HNTC], 'to abolish' [WBC], 'to do away with' [LN].

f. ἁμαρτία (LN 88.289; 88.310) (BAGD 2. p. 43): 'sin' [AB, BAGD, HNTC, LN, Lns, WBC; all versions]. See this word at 1:8; 2:12; 3:4.

QUESTION—How do they know this?

They know because the anointing teaches them all things (2:27) [Alf, Brd]. They know because it is part of the apostolic teaching that they have heard [AB, Herm, NIC, WBC], and as such is universal knowledge [NIC].

QUESTION—To whom does ἐκεῖνος 'that one' refer?

It refers to Christ [AB, Alf, Brd, EBC, EGT, Herm, HNTC, ICC, Lns, My, NIC, NTC, TH, TNTC, WBC, Ws; REB, TEV].

QUESTION—When and how did he appear?

This refers to the incarnation [Alf, Br, Brd, EBC, EGT, ICC, Lns, WBC, Ws], his ministry [AB, Alf, ICC, Lns, NTC], or his earthly life [AB, Lns, WBC, Ws].

QUESTION—What relationship is indicated by ἵνα 'in order to'?

It shows the purpose for which Christ appeared [BAGD, Brd, Lns, My, WBC; NAB].

QUESTION—What is meant by 'taking away' sin?

1. It refers to taking away the penalty of sin and is expressed as expiation [AB, Lns], atonement [EGT, NIC, WBC], and blotting out sin [Alf].
2. It refers to sanctification and means taking away the practice of sin from the believers' lives [Brd, Herm, My, NCBC, TH]: he appeared in order to take away sin from our lives.

QUESTION—What is the significance of the use of the plural in ἁμαρτίας 'sins'?

The plural is used to indicate all the individual sins [AB, Alf, Br, Brd, ICC, Lns, TH, WBC, Ws]. The plural includes cleansing from sins committed in the past to those committed in the present [AB].

and^a sin in^b him is not.

LEXICON—a. καί (LN 89.92; 89.93): 'and' [AB, HNTC, Lns; all versions], 'moreover' [WBC].

b. ἐν with dative object (LN 89.119): 'in' [AB, HNTC, Lns, WBC; all versions].

QUESTION—What relationship is indicated by καί 'and'?

It explains how it is possible for him to take away sin—since he is sinless, he is able to take away our sins [Br, ICC, Lns, NTC, Ws]. It prepares for 3:6 [Herm, My]: because he is sinless, those who are his people should be sinless.

QUESTION—What is the significance of there being no sin in him?

It means he did not have a sin nature [Br, Brd, EBC] because his eternal nature is without sin [TNTC, WBC]. The absence of the article focuses on the sin principle rather than on acts of sin [Brd, TH]. The present tense emphasizes that this state is characteristic of his eternal nature [Brd, EBC, NIC, NTC, TH, TNTC, Ws].

3:6 Everyone remaining[a] in[b] him (does) not sin;[c]
LEXICON—a. pres. act. participle of μένω: 'to remain'. See this word at 2:6, 27, 28. The present tense indicates a continuous state [Brd, EGT, ICC, Ws].
  b. ἐν with dative object: 'in'. See this word at 2:6, 27, 28.
  c. pres. act. indic. of ἁμαρτάνω: 'to sin'. See this word at 1:10; 2:1.
QUESTION—How is this verse related to its context?
  It is the logical deduction from the verse before: since there is no sin in Christ, there should be no sin in those who remain in him [AB, Brd, EBC, Herm, NIC, TH, TNTC, WBC, Ws].
QUESTION—Is the author teaching sinless perfection? How is this verse related to verses 1:8-10 and 2:2 which teach that believers sin?
  1. The present tense indicates that continual life style is referred to [Br, Brd, EBC, EGT, Lns, NCBC, NTC, Ws; NIV, TEV]: everyone remaining in him does not habitually sin. This allows for single acts of sin [Brd]. The use of aorists in 2:1 concerns acts of sin, while the present tense here implies continuance in sin [EGT]. It describes the character of the believer [Brd, Ws].
  2. This is an absolute statement of the incompatibility of remaining in Christ and sinning [Alf, Herm, HNTC, ICC, My, NIC, TH, WBC]: everyone remaining in him does not sin. All who discuss it recognize the possibility of sin in a believer's life and explain this in various ways. The present tense presents a general truth [TH]. It is an ideal, and if the believer sins, it is an act against his nature [Alf]. It is what the believer's character ought to be [Alf]. To the degree that one abides in Christ, to that extent he does not sin [Herm, ICC, NIC]. This statement is made absolutely and does not describe the general character of the Christian [ICC]. Only in the eschatological consummation can this be fully realized [NIC, WBC]. There is an implied command to live without sin [NIC].
QUESTION—To whom does αὐτόν 'him' refer?
  It refers to Christ [AB, Brd, EBC, ICC, Lns, My, TH, TNTC, WBC, Ws; TEV].

everyone (who is) sinning[a] has-not-seen[b] him nor has-known[c] him.
LEXICON—a. pres. act. participle of ἁμαρτάνω (LN 88.289): 'to sin' [HNTC, LN, Lns, WBC; all versions except REB], 'to commit sin' [AB]. The phrase πᾶς ὁ ἁμαρτάνων 'everyone who sins' is translated 'the sinner' [REB]. The present tense means a continued life style [AB, Brd].
  b. perf. act. indic. of ὁράω (LN 24.1; 90.79) (BAGD 1.c.β. p. 578): 'to see' [AB, HNTC, LN, Lns, WBC; all versions], 'to mentally look at' [BAGD]. The perfect tense of this and the following verb indicate a past action with effects continuing into the present [Alf, Brd, EBC, Lns, NIC, TH, WBC].

The negated perfect tense carries the idea of never having done so [Brd, EBC, Lns].
  c. perf. act. indic. of γινώσκω: 'to know'. See this word at 3:1. It is ingressive, speaking of obtaining knowledge rather than possessing it [Brd].
QUESTION—How is this phrase related to remaining in him?
  They are parallel statements referring to the same condition; seeing and knowing God are the part and parcel of remaining in him [Brd, HNTC, Lns, TH, TNTC].
QUESTION—What is the difference between seeing him and knowing him?
  Some commentators take 'seeing him' to be equivalent to knowing him [Brd, HNTC]. Others make a difference between the verbs. To see him refers to spiritual vision and to know him is a subsequent subjective apprehension of what has been seen [ICC, My, Ws]. To see him is to discern his identity and to believe in him, while to know him is to have a personal relationship with him [WBC].

3:7 Children,[a] (let) no-one deceive[b] you;
LEXICON—a. τεκνίον: 'child'. See this word at 2:1, 12, 28.
  b. pres. act. impera. of πλανάω (LN 31.8) (BAGD 1.b. p. 665): 'to deceive' [AB, BAGD, LN, Lns, WBC; KJV, NAB, NASB, NRSV, TEV], 'to lead astray' [HNTC; NIV, NJB, TNT], 'to mislead' [BAGD, LN; REB]. The negative and present tense do not necessarily mean that some were already deceived, but that they are to continue not allowing anyone to deceive them [Brd]. They should not let anyone even try to do so [Lns].

the-(one) doing righteousness[a] is righteous,[b] as[c] that-one is righteous;
LEXICON—a. δικαιοσύνη (LN 88.13) (BAGD 2.b. p. 196): 'righteousness' [BAGD, LN, Lns; KJV, NASB, TNT], 'uprightness' [BAGD], 'right' [HNTC; NIV, NRSV, REB, TEV], 'holiness' [NAB]. This noun is also translated as an adverb: 'justly' [AB], 'righteously' [WBC], 'uprightly' [NJB]. See this word at 2:29.
  b. δίκαιος (LN 88.12) (BAGD 1.a., 3. p. 195, 196.): 'righteous' [BAGD, HNTC, LN, Lns, WBC; all versions except NAB, NJB], 'upright' [BAGD; NJB], 'just' [BAGD, LN], 'truly just' [AB], 'holy' [NAB]. With the present tense of εἰμί 'to be', this refers to continuing in righteousness [Brd]. See this word at 2:29.
  c. καθώς (LN 64.14): 'as' [HNTC; NRSV, REB], 'even as' [AB, Lns, WBC; KJV, NAB], 'just as' [LN; NASB, NIV, NJB, TEV, TNT].
QUESTION—What is the relationship between ποιῶν τὴν δικαιοσύνην 'doing righteousness' and δίκαιός ἐστιν 'being righteous'?
  The first word refers to the activity of living righteously, and the second word refers to the state or character of being righteous [My, TNTC, WBC, Ws]. Righteous character will necessarily show itself in righteous deeds [Alf, Br, Brd, EGT, ICC, Lns, TH, WBC, Ws]. Only those whose actions are

righteous can call themselves righteous [HNTC, ICC, My, NIC, TNTC, WBC].

QUESTION—To whom does ἐκεῖνος 'that one' refer?
1. It refers to Christ [AB, Br, Brd, EGT, Herm, Lns, My, NIC, NTC, TH, TNTC, WBC, Ws; NAB, REB, TEV, TNT].
2. It refers to God [Alf, ICC].

QUESTION—How is the believer's righteousness to be like Christ's righteousness?

It is the same manner, not extent, of righteousness [Brd]. Christ is the believer's pattern for righteousness [Lns, My, WBC, Ws], he is the source of the righteousness [Ws], he is both the motivation and means of righteousness [WBC].

3:8 the-(one) doing^a sin is from^b the devil,^c

LEXICON—a. ποιέω: See the phrase 'doing sin' at 3:4.
  b. ἐκ with genitive object (LN 90.16) (BAGD 3.a. p. 234): 'from' [BAGD, HNTC, LN, Lns], 'of' [KJV, NASB, NIV, NRSV]. The phrase ἐκ...ἐστίν 'is from' is translated 'belongs to' [AB, WBC; NAB, NJB, TEV, TNT], 'is a child of' [NRSV, REB].
  c. διάβολος (LN 12.34) (BAGD 2. p. 182): 'devil' [AB, BAGD, HNTC, LN, Lns, WBC; all versions], 'slanderer' [BAGD].

QUESTION—How is this verse related to its context?

This verse contrasts with the person who is doing righteousness in 3:7 [AB, Alf, Brd, ICC, My, NTC, TH, WBC, Ws] and with everyone begotten of God in 3:9 who cannot sin [AB, Brd, Herm, WBC].

QUESTION—What is meant by ποιῶν τὴν ἁμαρτίαν 'doing sin'?

It refers to a life pattern of sin [Alf, Brd, EGT, ICC, WBC], a complete rebellion against God [Br, NIC]. The use of the construction 'to do' plus the noun lends more prominence to the act of sinning than the simple verb would [EGT].

QUESTION—What is meant by being 'from the devil'?

This is a metaphor in which sinners are considered to be children of the devil [Br, EGT, Lns, NIC, TH, WBC]. As a father is the ultimate physical origin of the child so the devil is the ultimate spiritual source of the sinner [Brd, Lns], or at least of his sinfulness [WBC]. The devil is the source of the sin nature [AB, Brd, HNTC, Lns, My, TH, TNTC, WBC]. As a child resembles his father, the sinner resembles the devil by sinning [Br, NIC]. However, nowhere are children of the devil said to be begotten by him since people become his children not by the devil's action but by their own [AB, Alf]. The devil originates and instigates sin [NIC].

because^a from^b (the) beginning^c the devil sins.^d

LEXICON—a. ὅτι (LN 89.33): 'because' [AB, LN, Lns; NAB, NIV, TEV], 'for' [HNTC, WBC; KJV, NASB, NRSV, REB, TNT], 'since' [LN; NJB].
  b. ἀπό with genitive object (LN 67.131): 'from' [AB, HNTC, LN, Lns, WBC; all versions], 'since' [LN].

c. ἀρχή (LN 67.65) (BAGD 1.c. p. 112): 'beginning' [BAGD, HNTC, LN; all versions except REB], 'very beginning' [AB, Lns; TEV], 'start' [WBC], 'first' [REB]. This word is placed first in the clause to give it prominence [AB, My, WBC, Ws].

d. pres. act. indic. of ἁμαρτάνω (LN 88.289) (BAGD 1. p. 42): 'to sin'. See this word at 1:10; 2:1; 3:6. The present tense indicates that the devil has been sinning from the beginning and still continues to sin [AB, Alf, Br, Brd, ICC, Lns, My, NTC, TH, TNTC, WBC, Ws] and that sinning is his very nature [AB].

QUESTION—What relationship is indicated by ὅτι 'because'?

It indicates the grounds for saying the ones sinning are from the Devil [Brd, NIC]: we know the ones sinning are from the Devil because the Devil has kept on sinning from the beginning.

QUESTION—To what does ἀπ' ἀρχῆς 'from the beginning' refer?

1. It refers to the beginning of the world [TH], of time [WBC], of human history [AB, Ws], of the presence of sin in the world [WBC], and to the Devil's part in the temptation of Adam and Eve [EBC, WBC].
2. It refers to the beginning of the Devil's own apostasy [Alf, Brd, EGT, HNTC, ICC, My, NTC, TNTC].

For[a] this the Son of-God appeared,[b] in-order-that[c] he-might-destroy[d] the works[e] of-the devil.

LEXICON—a. εἰς with accusative object (LN 89.57) (BAGD 4.f. p. 229): 'for' [Lns], not explicit [NAB, REB]. The phrase εἰς τοῦτο 'for this' is translated 'the reason was' [AB; NIV], 'this was the purpose of' [NJB], 'this is why' [HNTC], 'for this purpose' [KJV, NASB, NRSV, TNT], 'for this very purpose' [WBC], 'for this very reason' [TEV].

b. aorist pass. indic. of φανερόω (LN 24.19; 28.36) (BAGD 2.b.β. p. 853): 'to appear' [BAGD, LN, WBC; all versions except KJV, NAB], 'to be revealed' [AB, BAGD, HNTC, LN; TNT], 'to reveal oneself' [BAGD; NAB], 'to be manifest' [Lns; KJV]. See this word at 1:2; 2:28; 3:2, 5.

c. ἵνα (LN 89.59) (BAGD I.5. p. 377): 'to' [AB, HNTC, Lns, WBC; all versions except KJV, NASB, REB], 'that' [KJV, NASB], 'for the purpose that' [BAGD], 'for the very purpose of' [REB].

d. aorist act. subj. of λύω (LN **13.100**) (BAGD 4. p. 483): 'to destroy' [AB, BAGD, Lns, WBC; all versions except NJB, REB], 'to bring to an end' [BAGD], 'to put an end to' [LN], 'to abolish' [BAGD, HNTC], 'to do away with' [BAGD], 'to undo' [NJB, REB].

e. ἔργον (LN 42.12) (BAGD 3. p. 308): 'work' [AB, BAGD, HNTC, Lns, WBC; all versions except TEV], 'what (the Devil) has done' [TEV].

QUESTION—What does the pronoun τοῦτο 'this' refer to?

It points forward to the ἵνα 'in order to' clause [AB, Brd, Lns, TH, WBC]: the Son of God appeared for this purpose, namely, in order that he might destroy the works of the devil.

QUESTION—To what does ἐφανερώθη 'appeared' refer?

It refers to Christ's incarnation [Alf, Brd, HNTC, ICC, Lns, NIC, WBC] including his ministry [AB] and death [Alf, HNTC, WBC]. The use of 'appeared' implies his pre-existence [WBC].

QUESTION—To what does τὰ ἔργα τοῦ διαβόλου 'the works of the devil' refer? How do these differ from ἁμαρτάνει 'sinning' attributed to the devil above?

The works of the devil are the sins he incites people to do and this refers to the sinning mentioned above [AB, Alf, Br, Brd, Herm, ICC, My, NCBC, TH, WBC, Ws]. It means all the activity of Satan including both sin and calamity such as sickness [Lns, TH, TNTC]. It means his work of tempting and enslaving people [NIC, TH, TNTC].

QUESTION—What is meant by λύσῃ 'he might destroy'?

It means that Christ takes away sin (3:5) [Brd]. Christ undoes what the devil has done and thwarts what the devil attempts [Brd, NIC]. He sets men free from Satan's bondage [NTC] and breaks Satan's power to bring about wrongdoing [WBC]. It refers to Christ's victory over the Devil at the cross [Brd, HNTC]. It is an ongoing destruction already begun but consummated at the second coming of Christ [Lns]. It means to undo the achievements of the Devil [Brd, EGT, ICC, NIC, TNTC, WBC, Ws; NJB, REB].

3:9 Everyone having-been-begotten[a] by[b] God (does) not do sin,

LEXICON—a. perf. pass. participle of γεννάω: 'to be begotten'. See this word at 2:29. The perfect tense indicates that the begetting continues to have effect in the present [Brd, ICC, NTC, WBC, Ws].

b. ἐκ with genitive object (LN 90.16) (BAGD 3.a. p. 234): 'by'. See this word at 2:29.

QUESTION—How is this verse related to its context?

The author takes up the idea of 3:6 that everyone who abides in him does not sin [Br, EBC, HNTC, My] but uses the metaphor of birth as in 3:8 [HNTC]. It contrasts with 3:8 by giving the positive presentation [Alf, My].

QUESTION—How absolute is the statement, 'he does not sin'?

See the discussion at 3:6.

because[a] the-seed[b] of-him remains[c] in[d] him;

LEXICON—a. ὅτι (LN 89.33): 'because' [AB, HNTC, Lns; all versions except KJV, NRSV, TEV], 'for' [WBC; KJV, NRSV, TEV].

b. σπέρμα (LN **58.13**) (BAGD 2.c. p. 762): 'seed' [AB, HNTC, Lns; KJV, NASB, NIV, NJB, REB], 'stock' [NAB], 'germ of new life' [BAGD], 'nature' [LN; NRSV, TNT], 'very nature' [WBC; TEV].

c. pres. act. indic. of μένω (LN 68.11) (BAGD 1.a.β. p. 504): 'to remain' [BAGD, LN, Lns, WBC; KJV, NAB, NIV, NJB, REB], 'to dwell' [HNTC], 'to continue' [BAGD, LN], 'to abide' [AB, BAGD; NASB, NRSV], 'to be' [TEV], 'to have' [TNT]. The present tense indicates a continuing state [Brd].

d. ἐν with dative object (LN 89.119): 'in' [AB, HNTC, Lns, WBC; all versions except NAB], not explicit [NAB].

QUESTION—What relationship is indicated by ὅτι 'because'?

It indicates the reason a person does not sin [Brd, Lns, TH, TNTC, Ws] or the grounds for making the preceding statement [My].

QUESTION—To whom does αὐτοῦ 'of him' refer in the phrase σπέρμα αὐτοῦ 'the seed of him'?

It refers to God [AB, Alf, BAGD, Br, Brd, Herm, ICC, Lns, My, NCBC, NIC, TH, TNTC, WBC, Ws; NIV, NJB, NRSV, REB, TEV, TNT]: God's seed remains in him.

QUESTION—What is meant by God's seed remaining in him?

'Seed' is used metaphorically for a 'seed' from God that remains in the believer [probably all commentators]. Some take the comparison to be with the human sperm [AB, Brd, Herm, My, TH] and the reference is to the new life that God imparts to a believer. Many do say that the 'seed' means God's nature [LN, NTC, TNTC, WBC; NRSV, TEV, TNT]. TH takes this reference to 'sperm' to mean the life that God gives. Others take the comparison to be with a plant seed [EGT, NCBC, NIC, NTC] and the reference is to something God puts in the heart of the believer that grows and keeps him from sinning. The views of what the seed means are varied: the life that God gives [TH], the Holy Spirit [AB, Brd, ICC, My, NIC], the Word of God [Alf, Lns, NCBC, NIC], or divine grace [BAGD, Herm].

and[a] (he is) not able[b] to sin,[c]

LEXICON—a. καί (LN 89.92): 'and' [HNTC, Lns, WBC; KJV, NASB, NRSV, TEV, TNT], 'and so' [AB], 'indeed' [REB], 'nor' [NJB], not explicit [NAB, NIV].

b. pres. pass. indic. of δύναμαι (LN 74.5): 'to be able' [AB, HNTC, LN, Lns, WBC; all versions].

c. pres. act. infin. of ἁμαρτάνω: 'to sin'. See this word at 2:1. The present tense indicates continuous or habitual action [Brd, EBC, EGT, TNTC, WBC; NASB, NIV, TEV, TNT].

QUESTION—What is being negated in the phrase οὐ δύναται ἁμαρτάνειν 'is not able to sin'?

The οὐ negates the verb δύναται 'can' and means he is unable to continue sinning [Alf, Brd, EBC, EGT, My, TH, WBC]. This is a moral impossibility [My, Ws].

because[a] by God he-has-been-begotten.

LEXICON—a. ὅτι (LN 89.33): 'because' [AB, HNTC, Lns, WBC; all versions].

QUESTION—What relationship is indicated by ὅτι 'because'?

It indicates the reason he cannot sin [Brd, NIC, TH, WBC] or the grounds for making the preceding statement [My]. Whatever is born of God shares God's nature and God's opposition to sinning [NIC]. A child produces the works of his father [ICC].

QUESTION—What is the significance of the order in which the phrase ἐκ θεοῦ 'by God' occurs?

It occurs before the verb to indicate prominence on it [Lns, My, WBC, Ws]: he cannot sin because it is from God himself that he has been born.

DISCOURSE UNIT: 3:10–24 [WBC]. The topic is obedience as a condition for living as God's children.

3:10a **By[a] this the children of-God are manifest[b] and the children of-the devil;**

LEXICON—a. ἐν with the dative object: 'by'. See this word at 2:3, 5.

 b. φανερός (LN 24.20) (BAGD 1. p. 852): 'manifest' [Lns], 'revealed' [AB, BAGD], 'clear' [BAGD, HNTC, LN], 'evident' [BAGD, LN]. This adjective is also translated as a verb: 'to see' [NAB], 'to be seen' [NRSV], 'to be seen plainly' [WBC], 'to be obvious' [NASB], 'to be manifested' [KJV], 'to know' [BAGD; NIV], 'to show' [BAGD; REB], 'to distinguish' [NJB], 'to be distinguished' [TNT]. The sentence is also restructured: 'here is the clear difference between' [TEV].

QUESTION—How is this verse related to its context?

This is a summary of this preceding section [Alf, Brd, EBC, NIC, TNTC] and a transition to the next section [AB, Alf, Brd, EBC, Herm, NIC, TNTC, WBC].

QUESTION—What relationship is indicated by ἐν 'by'?

It indicates the means by which one can determine who the children of God are [Brd, Herm, HNTC, NIC]: by this criterion we can determine who the children of God are and who the children of the devil are. Alf would rather use 'in this circumstance' since he thinks 'by' implies that there are no other means for distinguishing between them.

QUESTION—What does the pronoun τοῦτο 'this' refer to?

1. It refers to the following criterion that anyone who sins and does not love his brothers is not of God [Herm, HNTC, ICC, TH, Ws; all versions except NAB]: by the fact that people who sin and do not love their brothers are not begotten of God, it can be determined whose child a person is.
2. It refers to the preceding criterion that everyone who is begotten of God does not sin [AB, Lns, My; NAB]: by the fact that the people begotten by God do not continue in sin, it can be determined whose child a person is.
3. It refers both to the preceding and following criteria [Alf, Brd, NIC, WBC, Ws]. It not only refers to the remainder of the verse, but it is a summary of what precedes [Brd].

DISCOURSE UNIT: 3:10b–24 [Lns]. The topic is our relation to the brothers.

3:10b everyone not doing righteousness[a] is not by[b] God, and[c] the-(one) not loving[d] his brother.[e]

LEXICON—a. δικαιοσύνη: 'righteousness'. For the phrase 'doing righteousness', see 3:7. The present tense of ποιέω 'to do' indicates that the righteous deeds are habitual [Brd].

b. ἐκ with genitive object (LN 90.16): 'of' [KJV, NASB, NRSV], 'from' [Lns]. This pronoun is also translated as a verb: 'to belong to' [AB, WBC; NAB, TNT]. The phrase ἐκ θεοῦ 'from God' is translated 'to be God's child' [HNTC; NIV, REB, TEV]. It is equivalent to 'he is not a child of God' [Alf]. See this word at 3:9.

c. καί (LN 89.92): 'and' [Lns; NJB], 'or' [REB, TEV], 'nor' [AB; NAB, NASB, NIV, NRSV], 'neither' [KJV, TNT], 'that is' [WBC]. This conjunction is also translated 'the same goes for' [HNTC].

d. pres. act. participle of ἀγαπάω: 'to love'. See this word at 2:10. The present tense indicates a continuing action [Brd].

e. ἀδελφός (LN 11.23): 'brother' [AB, HNTC, LN, Lns, WBC; all versions except REB], 'fellow Christian' [REB], 'fellow believer' [LN].

QUESTION—What relationship is indicated by καί 'and'?

1. It indicates a specific example of the preceding generic criterion [AB, Alf, Brd, ICC, Lns, NIC, Ws]: anyone not doing righteousness, such as not loving his brother, is not begotten of God.
2. It defines the preceding criterion [EBC, EGT, Herm, My, TNTC, WBC]: anyone not doing righteousness, and by that I mean not loving his brother, is not begotten of God.
3. It adds a second criterion [Br, HNTC, Ws; NJB]: anyone not doing righteousness and not loving his brother is not begotten of God.

QUESTION—To whom does ἀδελφόν 'brother' refer?

1. It refers to a fellow Christian [AB, Alf, Brd, EBC, HNTC, ICC, Lns, My, WBC, Ws].
2. It refers to all people [Br, Herm]. 'Brother' is used in the same way as it was in 2:9–10 [Herm].

DISCOURSE UNIT: 3:11–24 [AB, EBC]. The topic is the message of loving one another.

DISCOURSE UNIT: 3:11–18 [Br, NCBC, NIC, TNTC]. The topic is the test of love [Br, TNTC], love being the mark of a Christian [NIC], the moral tradition [NCBC].

DISCOURSE UNIT: 3:11–15 [NTC]. The topic is the world's hatred.

3:11 For[a] this is the message[b] which you heard[c] from[d] (the) beginning,[e] that we-should-love[f] each other;

LEXICON—a. ὅτι (LN 90.21): 'for' [AB, HNTC, WBC; KJV, NASB, NRSV, TNT], 'because' [Lns], not explicit [NAB, NIV, NJB, REB, TEV].

b. ἀγγελία (LN 33.193) (BAGD 2. p. 7): 'message' [BAGD, HNTC, LN; all versions] 'command' [BAGD], 'report' [Lns], 'gospel' [AB], 'news' [WBC].
   c. aorist act. indic. of ἀκούω (LN 24.52): 'to hear' [AB, HNTC, LN, Lns, WBC; all versions]. The aorist tense indicates that the action of hearing is completed [TH, WBC].
   d. ἀπό with genitive object (LN 67.131): 'from' [AB, HNTC, LN, Lns, WBC; all versions].
   e. ἀρχή (LN 67.65) (BAGD 1.b. p. 112): 'beginning' [AB, HNTC, Lns; all versions except TEV], 'very beginning' [WBC; TEV], 'beginning of proclamation' [BAGD].
   f. pres. act. subj. of ἀγαπάω: 'to love'. See this word at 3:10. The present tense indicates continuous action [Lns, TH, WBC].

QUESTION—What relationship is indicated by ὅτι 'for'?
   It indicates the grounds for saying that loving one's brother is the sign that someone is a child of God (3:10) [Alf, Br, Brd, Herm, ICC, Lns, My, WBC].

QUESTION—To what does αὕτη 'this' refer?
   It refers to the following ὅτι 'that' clause [AB, Brd, EBC, EGT, Herm, ICC, Lns, My, NCBC, TH, TNTC, WBC, Ws; all versions]: this is the message that you have heard from the beginning, namely, that we should love each other. At the same time, the 'that' clause gives the aim of the message [EBC, Ws].

QUESTION—What is meant by ἀγγελία 'message'?
   It means the message of the gospel [AB, ICC, TH] of which the command to love is an important part [ICC, TH]. More specifically, it refers to Christ's command to love one another [Alf, BAGD, Brd, Herm, ICC, Lns, My, TH, TNTC, WBC].

QUESTION—To what time does ἀρχῆς 'the beginning' refer?
   It refers to the time they first heard the gospel [AB, Alf, Br, Brd, ICC, NIC, TNTC, WBC, Ws]. The writer is also thinking of the beginning of the preaching of the gospel [TH, WBC] or even the beginning of the history of the world [ICC, WBC].

QUESTION—What is the significance of the change from 'brother' used in 3:10, to 'each other' used here, and then to 'brothers' in 3:14?
   There is no meaning difference. The difference is stylistic [AB, Brd, EBC, Herm, NIC, WBC]. It refers to the brothers in 3:10 [AB, Brd, Lns, My, NIC, WBC].

3:12 not as[a] Cain (who) was from[b] the evil-one[c] and killed[d] his brother;

LEXICON—a. καθώς (LN 64.14): 'as' [Lns; KJV, NASB], 'like' [AB, HNTC, WBC; all versions except KJV, NAB, NASB], 'to follow the example of' [NAB].
   b. ἐκ with genitive object (LN 90.16): 'from' [Lns; NJB], 'of' [KJV, NASB, NRSV]. The phrase 'to be from' is translated 'to belong to' [AB, WBC; NAB, NIV, TEV, TNT], 'to be born of' [HNTC], 'to be a child of' [REB].

c. πονηρός (LN 12.35) (BAGD 2.b. p. 691): 'the evil one' [AB, BAGD, HNTC, LN, WBC; all versions except KJV], 'the wicked one' [Lns; KJV].

d. aorist act. indic. of σφάζω (LN 20.72) (BAGD p. 796): 'to kill' [AB, LN; NAB, TNT], 'to murder' [BAGD, HNTC; NIV, NJB, NRSV, REB, TEV], 'to butcher' [BAGD, WBC], 'to slaughter' [LN], 'to slay' [Lns; KJV, NASB].

QUESTION—How is this verse related to its context?

This presents a negative duty to follow the preceding positive one [TH, WBC, Ws] and this causes the positive duty to be emphasized [WBC]. It is an example of the lack of brotherly love [ICC]. The love for brothers in 3:11 suggests the opposite, namely, a brother's hatred [ICC, Lns, My, NIC, TNTC, WBC]. The epitome of failure to obey the command to love is Cain's hatred for Abel that led to murder [HNTC].

QUESTION—What is the point of comparison in the simile?

The sentence is elliptical and the implied construction is 'do not be like Cain' [WBC; NIV, REB], 'we must not be like Cain' [NRSV, TEV], 'we should not follow the example of Cain' [NAB]. Since the command to love other Christians is given in the preceding verse, most commentators talk about the underlying evil attitude of hatred in this example [Alf, EGT, Herm, HNTC, ICC, My, NIC, TNTC]: we should not hate our brothers as Cain did his. Another suggestion is that selfishness is the point of similarity [Ws]. This comparison is a litotes; the writer wants the readers not only to avoid Cain's attitude and deed, but to do just the opposite [AB].

QUESTION—What relationship is indicated by ἐκ 'from'?

It shows a spiritual or ethical relationship between Cain and the evil one [AB, Alf, Br, Brd, WBC], the ultimate spiritual source of his evil [ICC, TNTC, WBC].

QUESTION—What is the significance of the use of πονηρός 'evil one' here instead of διάβολος 'devil' used in 3:8?

It matches the use of the word as a description of Cain's deeds [AB, Alf, Brd, Lns, TNTC, WBC, Ws]: who was from the *evil* one . . . his deeds were *evil*. It connects Cain's evil deed with its spiritual source, the evil one [Ws].

QUESTION—What is meant by σφάζω 'to kill'?

It means to cause a violent death [AB, Brd, ICC, LN, My, NIC, NTC, TH, WBC], to slaughter [Brd, EBC, EGT, My, NCBC, TNTC], to butcher [BAGD, EBC, EGT, Herm, WBC], to murder [Alf, BAGD, Br, EBC, HNTC, Ws; NJB, NRSV, REB, TEV]. It is an act that is premeditated and done with malice [Br] and brutality [AB].

QUESTION—Who is the brother that Cain killed?

Cain murdered his younger brother, Abel [TH]. See Genesis 4:1–6.

QUESTION—Why is the murder mentioned?

It functions as the grounds for the assertion that Cain was from the evil one [Alf, Br, Brd, EBC, Herm, Lns, My, WBC]. Cain murdered because he was already evil [EBC, Lns, WBC].

and[a] because-of[b] what did-he-kill him?
LEXICON—a. καί (LN 89.93): 'and' [AB, HNTC, Lns, WBC; all versions except NAB, TEV, TNT], not explicit [NAB, TEV, TNT].
  b. χάριν (LN **89.29**) (BAGD 2. p. 877): 'because of' [LN]. The phrase χάριν τίνος 'because of what' is translated 'why' [AB, BAGD, HNTC, LN, Lns, WBC; all versions except KJV, NASB], 'for what reason' [BAGD, **LN**; NASB], 'wherefore' [KJV].
QUESTION—What is the function of this rhetorical question?
  It directs attention to the main point of the passage, not the slaying of Abel, but the reason behind the slaying [Lns], which is in contrast to the love commanded in the preceding verse.

Because[a] his deeds[b] were evil,[c] but[d] those of his brother righteous.[e]
LEXICON—a. ὅτι (LN 89.33) (BAGD 3.a. p. 589): 'because' [AB, BAGD, HNTC, Lns, WBC; all versions].
  b. ἔργον (LN 42.11) (BAGD 1.c.β. p. 308): 'deed' [AB, BAGD, HNTC, LN; NAB, NASB, NRSV, TNT], 'work' [Lns; KJV], 'actions' [WBC; NIV, NJB, REB], 'the things he himself did' [TEV].
  c. πονηρός (LN 88.110) (BAGD 1.b.β. p. 691): 'evil' [AB, BAGD, HNTC, LN, WBC; all versions except NAB, REB, TEV], 'wicked' [BAGD, LN, Lns; NAB], 'wrong' [REB, TEV].
  d. δέ (LN 89.124): 'but' [LN], 'while' [AB, Lns; NAB], 'whereas' [HNTC], 'and' [WBC; all versions except NAB].
  e. δίκαιος (LN 88.12) (BAGD 4. p. 196): 'righteous' [BAGD, HNTC, LN, Lns, WBC; KJV, NASB, NIV, NRSV, TNT], 'just' [AB, BAGD, LN; NAB], 'upright' [BAGD; NJB], 'right' [REB, TEV].
QUESTION—What relationship is indicated by ὅτι 'because'?
  It indicates the reason Cain murdered his brother, Abel [Brd, Lns, NCBC]. He murdered him not only because he was inherently evil [AB, WBC], but because he was jealous of his brother's righteousness [TNTC, WBC]. The two statements go together: it is the nature of the wicked to hate the righteous [Alf, Br, Brd, EBC, Herm, ICC, Lns, My, NCBC, NIC, TNTC, Ws]. Righteous people put the wicked in a bad light [Brd, EBC, Lns].
QUESTION—What relationship is indicated by δέ 'but'?
  It shows contrast [TH]. It gives the reason for Cain's hatred; Cain hated because Abel was righteous [Lns].

DISCOURSE UNIT: 3:13–24 [EGT, Ws]. The topic is assurance [EGT], brotherhood in Christ and the hatred of the world [Ws].

3:13 Therefore[a] (do) not be-surprised,[b] brothers,[c] if/that[d] the world[e] hates[f] you.
TEXT—Some manuscripts omit καί 'therefore/and'. GNT includes it with a D rating, indicating a very high degree of doubt in doing so. Several of the commentators are unsure about which is the best reading [AB, Brd, WBC].

LEXICON—a. καί: 'therefore', 'so' [WBC; TEV], 'then' [AB], not explicit or following the text which omits it [Herm, Lns; all versions except TEV].
   b. pres. act. impera. of θαυμάζω (LN 25.213) (BAGD 1.a.γ. p. 352): 'to be surprised' [AB, BAGD, HNTC, WBC; all versions except KJV, NASB, NRSV], 'to wonder' [BAGD, LN; NRSV], 'to marvel' [LN, Lns; KJV, NASB].
   c. ἀδελφός (LN 11.23): 'brother' [AB, HNTC, LN, Lns, WBC; all versions except REB], 'friend' [REB], 'fellow believer' [LN].
   d. εἰ (LN 89.65, 90.26) (BAGD II. p. 219): 'if' [Lns; all versions except NRSV], 'when' [AB], 'that' [BAGD, WBC; NRSV].
   e. κόσμος (LN 9.23) (BAGD 7. p. 446): 'world' [AB, HNTC, Lns, WBC; all versions except TEV], 'people of the world' [LN; TEV].
   f. pres. act. indic. of μισέω (LN 88.198) (BAGD 1. p. 522): 'to hate' [AB, BAGD, HNTC, LN, Lns, WBC; all versions], 'to detest' [BAGD, LN]. The present tense indicates a habitual state of hostility [ICC, Lns, WBC].

QUESTION—What relationship is indicated by καί 'therefore'?

It indicates a conclusion drawn from the preceding verse [AB, TH, TNTC, WBC; TEV]: Cain, a child of the evil one, hated and killed his brother because Cain was evil and his brother was righteous; therefore, do not be surprised that the evil people of the world hate you who are righteous. The world is Cain's posterity [TNTC]. Christians are to the world what Abel was to Cain [WBC].

QUESTION—What is the significance of the change in vocatives from ἀγαπητοί 'beloved' or τεκνία 'children' to ἀδελφοί 'brothers'?

The change is made because he is discussing brotherly love and the brothers Cain and Abel [AB, EGT, NIC, WBC]. The use of 'brother' indicates that the author is placing himself at the same level as his readers [Brd, EBC, HNTC, Lns, Ws].

QUESTION—Why should they not be surprised?

They should not be surprised because the previously mentioned principle that evil hates good should lead them to expect the world's hostility [AB, Herm, ICC, My, NIC, TNTC, WBC]. It is natural for the wicked people of the world to hate the righteous [Brd, HNTC] because the lives of the righteous contradict the maxims of the wicked and condemn their practices [AB].

QUESTION—What relationship is indicated by εἰ 'if/that'?

   1. It indicates a condition [Alf, Brd, Lns, My, Ws]: don't be surprised if the world hates you. It is viewed as an already existing condition [Alf, Lns, My, Ws]. However, although hatred is a fact, individual Christians do not always encounter it [AB].

   2. It introduces the object of surprise [AB, BAGD, NCBC, TH, WBC; NRSV]: do not be surprised that the world hates you.

QUESTION—What is meant by κόσμος 'world'?
It is a metonymy for the evil people in the world [Brd, TNTC], both those inside the church and outside [NIC]. They are the people who are enmeshed in the evil world system [Brd].

DISCOURSE UNIT: 3:14–18 [TNTC]. The topic is the love of Christ and of the church.

3:14 We know[a] that we-have-passed[b] from[c] death[d] into[e] life,[f]

LEXICON—a. perf. act. indic. of οἶδα (LN 28.1): 'to know' [AB, HNTC, LN, Lns, WBC; all versions except NJB], 'to be well aware' [NJB].
  b. perf. act. indic. of μεταβαίνω (LN 15.2) (BAGD 2.a. p. 510): 'to pass' [AB, BAGD, HNTC; KJV, NAB, NASB, NIV, NRSV], 'to pass over' [NJB, TNT], 'to move' [BAGD, LN], 'to step over' [Lns], 'to cross over' [WBC; REB]. The phrase μεταβαίνω ἐκ 'to pass from' is translated 'to leave' [TEV]. The perfect tense indicates that the action occurred in the past and its effects continue into the present [Brd, My, NTC, TH, WBC].
  c. ἐκ with genitive object (LN 89.121) (BAGD 1.c. p. 234): 'from' [AB, BAGD, WBC; all versions except NASB, NRSV, TEV], 'out of' [HNTC, Lns; NASB, NRSV]. For TEV see above.
  d. θάνατος (LN 23.99) (BAGD 2.a. p. 351): 'death' [AB, BAGD, HNTC, LN, Lns, WBC; all versions].
  e. εἰς with accusative object (LN 84.22): 'into' [HNTC, Lns, WBC; NASB, NRSV, TNT], 'to' [AB; NAB, NIV, NJB, REB], 'unto' [KJV], '(to come over) into' [TEV].
  f. ζωή: 'life'. See this word at 2:25.

QUESTION—How is this verse related to its context?
It is given as a comfort to those facing the hatred of the world [Alf]. In 3:13 it is implied that those who hate their brothers belong to the realm of death and this is the converse statement [NIC, WBC].

QUESTION—To whom does ἡμεῖς 'we' refer?
It is 'we inclusive' and refers to the whole congregation of true believers [Brd, Herm, ICC, My, TH, WBC, Ws]. The occurrence of the pronoun makes the subject prominent [AB, Alf, Br, Brd, EGT, Lns, My, TH, TNTC, WBC, Ws]. The emphasis on 'we' means that no matter what the world thinks, we know we have passed from death to life [AB, EGT], the world may hate but we love [TNTC], the world hates but we know we have passed from death [Brd, My].

QUESTION—What is meant by οἴδαμεν 'we know'?
Experiential knowledge is in focus [HNTC, ICC]. It draws a conclusion from the experiential fact that one loves the brothers [Brd]. The author is using a set phrase for common knowledge of those in his group [AB, Brd]. They have been taught this in the gospel [NTC].

QUESTION—What is meant by passing from death to life?
Life and death are alternative spiritual domains to which a person gives his allegiance [WBC]. 'Passing' is used metaphorically to indicate a change

from one spiritual sphere to another [Brd]. It means entering into the Kingdom of God here on earth through the new birth [AB, Br, HNTC, TNTC] with an emphasis on the change involved [Brd, EGT, WBC]. Because it refers to a change, it implies that they once were in the state of death [Lns, My, NIC] but are now in the state of life [My, NIC].

because[a] we-love[b] the brothers;[c]
LEXICON—a. ὅτι (LN 89.33) (BAGD 3.b. p. 589): 'because' [AB, HNTC, Lns, WBC; all versions].
  b. pres. act. indic. of ἀγαπάω: 'to love'. See this word at 2:10; 3:10, 11. The use of present tense indicates habitual practice [Brd, TH, WBC].
  c. ἀδελφός (LN 11.23): 'brother' [AB, HNTC, LN, Lns; all versions], 'brotherhood' [WBC] 'fellow believer', [LN].
QUESTION—What relationship is indicated by ὅτι 'because'?
  It indicates the grounds for knowing the preceding fact [Alf, Br, Brd, EBC, Herm, HNTC, Lns, My, NCBC, NIC, NTC, TH, TNTC, WBC, Ws]: we know that we have life because of the fact that we love our brothers. This implies that loving the brothers is the mark of being God's child (3:10) and God's child is the one who has been born into a new life (3:9). Many mention that it does not indicate the reason why they have passed from death to life but that it merely shows that it has happened [Br, Brd, EBC, HNTC, My, NCBC, NIC, NTC, TH, WBC, Ws].
QUESTION—Why is ἀδελφοί 'brothers' in the plural here, after the singular form in 2:9–11?
  The plural form refers to individuals, whereas a singular form would refer to the group as a whole [EBC, TH]. The plural form makes it clear that a spiritual relationship is meant rather than natural kinship [Brd]. The plural form is the common term for a group of Christians [Alf].

the-(one) not loving remains[a] in[b] death.
TEXT—Instead of ἀγαπῶν 'loving', some manuscripts have ἀγαπῶν τὸν ἀδελφόν 'loving the brother'. GNT selects the reading ἀγαπῶν 'loving' with a C rating, indicating a considerable degree of doubt in doing so. Only KJV includes 'the brother'.
LEXICON—a. pres. act. indic. of μένω (LN 68.11) (BAGD 1.a.β. p. 504): 'to remain' [AB, BAGD, LN, Lns, WBC; NIV, NJB, TNT], 'to continue' [BAGD, LN], 'to abide' [BAGD; KJV, NASB, NRSV], 'to dwell' [HNTC], 'to be' [NAB], 'to be still' [REB]. This verb is also translated 'to be still (under the power of)' [TEV]. The use of present tense indicates habitual continuing practice [TH, WBC].
  b. ἐν with dative object (LN 13.8) (BAGD I.4.d. p. 259): 'in' [HNTC, Lns, WBC; all versions except REB, TEV], 'among' [NAB], 'in the realm of' [REB], 'in the abode of' [AB], 'under the power of' [TEV].

1 JOHN 3:14

QUESTION—What is the relationship between 'not loving' and 'remaining in death'?

'Not loving' gives the grounds for knowing that one is 'remaining in death' and not the reason for remaining [Alf, Lns].

QUESTION—What is being implied by μένει 'he remains'?

It implies that the person has been spiritually dead since his birth and continues in that state of death [Brd, Lns, Ws].

3:15 **Everyone hating^a his brother is a-murderer,^b**

LEXICON—a. pres. act. participle of μισέω (LN 88.198) (BAGD 1. p. 522): 'to hate' [AB, BAGD, HNTC, LN, Lns, WBC; all versions], 'to detest' [BAGD, LN], 'to abhor' [BAGD]. The present tense indicates continuing action [Brd].

b. ἀνθρωποκτόνος (LN 20.85) (BAGD p. 68): 'murderer' [AB, BAGD, HNTC, LN, WBC; all versions], 'man-murderer' [Lns].

QUESTION—How is this verse related to its context?

It continues the contrast between those who love and live and those who hate and remain dead [Herm, Lns, NIC, TNTC, WBC]. If love is a proof of life then hate is a proof of death [NIC, TNTC].

QUESTION—In what respect is one who hates his brother a murderer?

Although AB thinks that classifying such a person as a murderer is hyperbole, with murder meaning maltreatment, most commentators take this to refer to actual murder. Many think this is drawn from Jesus' teaching in Matt. 5:21–22 where he equates anger with murder [Brd, EBC, EGT, ICC, Lns, NIC, TNTC]. Μισῶν τὸν ἀδελφὸν αὐτοῦ 'hating his brother' used here and ὁ μὴ ἀγαπῶν 'the one not loving' used in the previous verse mean the same thing [Alf, Brd, Herm, My, TH, WBC]. Hatred is an intense emotional feeling [NCBC], the desire to get rid of a person [Brd, NIC], and longing that he would die [NIC, TNTC]. Hate is the first step towards murder and belongs in the same moral category [TH]. In the heart there is no difference [EBC], a person who hates is no different from a murderer in his attitude [NIC]. The person who hates is potentially a murderer as shown by Cain [Alf, Br, EBC, HNTC, My, WBC] even if other things keep him back from fulfilling his wish [My].

and you-know^a that every murderer (does) not have^b eternal^c life^d remaining^e in him.

LEXICON—a. perf. act. indic of οἶδα: 'to know'. See this word at 3:2, 5.

b. pres. act. indic. of ἔχω (LN 90.65): 'to have' [AB, HNTC, LN, Lns, WBC; all versions except NAB], not explicit [NAB]. The present tense indicates a continuing state [TH, TNTC, WBC].

c. αἰώνιος: 'eternal'. See this word at 1:2, 2:25.

d. ζωή: 'life'. See this word at 2:25, 3:14.

e. pres. act. participle of μένω (LN 13.89) (BAGD 1.a.β. p. 504): 'to remain' [BAGD, LN, Lns; NJB], 'to abide' [AB, BAGD; KJV, NAB,

NASB, NRSV], 'to dwell' [HNTC, WBC; REB]. The phrase μένουσαν ἐν 'remaining in' is translated 'in' [NIV, TEV, TNT].

QUESTION—What is the source of their knowledge?

It is axiomatic, an appeal to their common sense and intuition [Alf, Br, Brd, ICC, My, TNTC, WBC]. They were also taught this from Genesis 9:6 [AB].

3:16 By[a] this we-have-known[b] the love,[c] that/because[d] that-one for[e] us laid-down[f] his life;[g]

TEXT—After ἀγάπην 'love', some manuscripts have τοῦ θεοῦ 'of God'. GNT makes no mention of the alternate reading. The reading ἀγάπην τοῦ θεοῦ 'love of God' is selected only by KJV.

LEXICON—a. ἐν with dative object: 'by'. See this word at 2:3, 5; 3:10.
- b. perf. act. indic. of γινώσκω: 'to know'. See this word at 2:3a, 5, 18, 29. The perfect tense indicates that the knowledge is based on an historical event: the crucifixion [AB, Brd, EBC, Herm, HNTC, Lns, WBC], or the time that the gospel message was heard [NTC]. It also points to an ongoing understanding of what love is [Brd].
- c. ἀγάπη: 'love'. See this word at 2:5, 15; 3:1. This noun is also translated 'what love means' [AB], 'what love is' [HNTC, WBC; NIV, REB, TEV].
- d. ὅτι (LN 89.33; 91.15) (BAGD 1.a. p. 588): 'that' [LN; NAB, NASB, NJB, NRSV], 'because' [LN; KJV, TNT], not explicit [NIV, REB, TEV].
- e. ὑπέρ with genitive object (LN 90.36) (BAGD 1.a.ε. p. 838): 'for' [AB, BAGD, HNTC, LN, WBC; all versions], 'in behalf of' [LN, Lns], 'for the sake of' [LN].
- f. aorist act. indic. of τίθημι (LN 23.113) (BAGD I.1.b.δ. p. 816): 'to lay down' [AB, BAGD, Lns; all versions except TEV], 'to give up' [BAGD], 'to give' [HNTC; TEV], 'to surrender' [WBC]. The phrase 'to lay down one's life' is translated 'to die voluntarily' [LN], 'to die willingly' [LN]. The aorist tense indicates a specific event, the death of Jesus [TH].
- g. ψυχή (LN 23.88) (BAGD 1.a.β. p. 893): 'life' [AB, HNTC, LN, Lns, WBC; all versions], 'earthly life' [BAGD].

QUESTION—How is this verse related to its context?

It explains what true love really is [ICC, My, NIC, TNTC] and gives a test for the genuineness of love about which he has been speaking [Brd, Herm, ICC]. It contrasts Cain's act of murder with the true love exemplified by Christ's dying for us [My, NIC, TNTC, Ws]. It develops the theme of obedience by considering the example of obedient love [WBC].

QUESTION—What does the pronoun τοῦτο 'this' refer to?

1. It refers to the following ὅτι 'that' clause [AB, Brd, ICC, Lns, My, TH; NAB, NIV, REB, TEV]: we have come to know love by this, namely, by the example that Christ gave in laying down his life for us.
2. It refers both to the preceding negative example of Cain and the following positive example of Christ [EBC, Ws].

1 JOHN 3:16

QUESTION—Who are the implied participants for the event word, 'love'?
1. There is no implied agent; it is the absolute quality of love [AB, Alf, EBC, EGT, Herm, ICC, Lns, My, NIC, TH, TNTC, WBC]: by this we know what it really means to love. The article indicates that it is 'love' in its essence [Lns, NIC]. From Christ's example we learn what true love is [Herm]. If it is necessary to indicate participants, it might be stated, 'by this we know how we should love our brothers' [TH].
2. The implied agent is God [Brd]: by this we know how God has loved us. The article indicates that the specific love of God is intended [Brd].

QUESTION—What relationship is indicated by the use of ὅτι 'that/because'?
1. It explains what is meant by the preceding 'this' [AB, Brd, ICC, Lns, My, NIC, TH, WBC; NAB, NIV, REB, TEV]: we have known love by this, namely, that Christ laid down his life for us.
2. It indicates the reason why they know [Ws; KJV, TNT]: we have known love because we have come to know the example of Christ's laying down his life for us.

QUESTION—To whom does ἐκεῖνος 'that one' refer?
It refers to Christ [AB, Alf, Br, Brd, EGT, Herm, HNTC, ICC, Lns, My, NCBC, NIC, NTC, TH, TNTC, WBC, Ws; NIV, REB, TEV, TNT].

QUESTION—What relationship is indicated by ὑπέρ 'for'?
It indicates that Christ laid down his life for our benefit [AB, Brd, Herm, My, NCBC, NIC, TH, TNTC, Ws]. His death saves us from destruction [My]. He died in order that we might not die [NIC]. It also implies substitution [Lns, NIC]: he died in our place.

QUESTION—What is meant by τὴν ψυχὴν αὐτοῦ ἔθηκεν 'he laid down his life'?
1. This is a metaphor with the comparison of a person taking off his garment [AB, ICC, TH, TNTC, WBC, Ws]: he put off his life as a person puts off a garment.
2. No metaphor is indicated. A voluntary self-sacrifice is in focus [Brd, Herm, LN, My, NCBC, NIC, NTC; all versions]: he let himself be killed.

QUESTION—What is the difference between ψυχήν 'life' used here and ζωήν 'life' used in the previous verse (3:15)?
Here the reference is to earthly life, in 3:15 the reference is to eternal life [AB, BAGD].

and we ought[a] to-lay-down (our) lives for the brothers.
LEXICON—a. pres. act. indic. of ὀφείλω: 'ought'. See this word at 2:6; 4:11. The present tense indicates a continuing obligation [AB, TH, WBC]. It is a general statement which is always true [Lns]. This refers to a moral obligation [Brd, My, NTC, Ws].

QUESTION—What relationship is indicated by καί 'and'?
1. It implies a conclusion to be drawn from the example of Christ in the preceding clause [AB, EBC, ICC, TH; TEV]: Christ laid down his life for us, therefore we ought to lay down our lives for our brothers. We should

follow Christ's example [AB, Brd, EBC, NCBC, NIC, TNTC, WBC, Ws] and be motivated by the same love he had [Alf, EBC, Lns, TNTC, WBC, Ws].

2. It indicates the duty included with the knowledge we have [Ws]: we know what love is by the example of Christ, and we know that we ought to lay down our lives for our brothers.

QUESTION—What is the significance of the occurrence of the pronoun ἡμεῖς 'we'?

It is emphatic to emphasize their responsibility [AB, Alf, EGT, ICC, Lns, TH, WBC; NAB, NJB, REB, TEV, TNT]: Christ laid down his life, and we, too, ought to lay down our lives. It is an inclusive 'we' and means all of Christ's followers [Brd, WBC].

QUESTION—What is meant by laying down one's life?

Some commentators think it refers to every self-denying sacrifice a person makes to meet the needs of his brother, even to loss of life [Brd, My, NIC]. Most think that it refers specifically to actual loss of life, some emphasizing the attitude of being willing to sacrifice one's life for another [AB, Br, TNTC], or the actual loss of life in saving a brother's life when the occasion arises [Alf, Herm, ICC, Lns, NTC, WBC].

3:17 But^a whoever has^b the possessions^c of-the world^d

LEXICON—a. δέ (LN 89.124): 'but' [KJV, NASB, NRSV, REB], 'indeed' [AB], 'on the other hand' [Lns], not explicit [HNTC, WBC; NAB, NIV, NJB, TEV, TNT].

b. pres. act. subj. of ἔχω (LN 57.1) (BAGD I.2.a. p. 332): 'to have' [AB, BAGD, LN, Lns, WBC; KJV, NAB, NASB, NIV, NRSV], 'to possess' [BAGD, LN; REB]. The phrase 'whoever has' is translated 'a man with' [TNT]. For HNTC, NJB and TEV, see below. The present tense indicates continuing action [Brd].

c. βίος (LN 57.18) (BAGD 3. p. 142): 'possessions' [BAGD, LN, WBC; NIV, TNT], 'means of subsistence' [BAGD], 'life sustenance' [Lns], 'good things' [REB], 'enough of goods' [NAB], 'livelihood' [LN], 'enough of livelihood' [AB], 'property' [BAGD, LN], 'goods' [BAGD; NASB, NRSV], 'good' [KJV]. The phrase 'to have possessions' is translated 'to be wealthy' [HNTC], 'to be well off with possessions' [NJB], 'a rich person' [TEV]. See this word at 2:16.

d. κόσμος (LN 41.38) (BAGD 6. p. 446): 'world' [AB, LN, Lns; KJV, NAB, NASB, NRSV, REB], not explicit [HNTC; TEV]. This noun is also translated as an adjective: 'worldly' [BAGD; NJB, TNT], 'material' [WBC; NIV].

QUESTION—How is this verse related to its context?

This is the second example of practical proofs of love [Br, EBC, Herm, ICC, Lns, My, TH, TNTC, WBC]. The occasions for this proof would be quite frequent in contrast with the rarer need of giving up one's life (3:16) [Br,

EBC, EGT, Herm, HNTC, NIC, TH, TNTC, WBC, Ws]. It further develops the theme that true belief causes ethical, loving actions [EBC, WBC].

QUESTION—What relationship is indicated by δέ 'but'?

It indicates a contrast with the previous verse by giving a negative example after a positive one [Brd, Lns], and going from the greater sacrifice to the lesser [Alf, My, TNTC].

QUESTION—How are the two nouns related in the genitive construction τὸν βίον τοῦ κόσμου 'the possessions of the world'?

It means the possessions located on this earth [Alf, BAGD, Brd, NIC, WBC, Ws], or the things needed to support life in this world [My, NCBC, NIC, WBC]. Βίος refers to that by which life is sustained [Alf, ICC, Lns, My, NIC, Ws], livelihood [AB, EGT], or material goods [Brd, EBC, HNTC, TH, WBC].

and sees[a] his brother having need[b] and closes[c] his heart[d] against him,

LEXICON—a. pres. act. subj. of θεωρέω (LN 32.11) (BAGD 1. p. 360): 'to see' [BAGD, HNTC, LN; all versions except NASB], 'to look at' [BAGD], 'to observe' [BAGD], 'to perceive' [AB, BAGD, LN], 'to notice' [WBC], 'to behold' [Lns; NASB]. Some commentators take this to be a generic term for seeing [TH], without any distinctions intended to contrast with other words referring to seeing [AB]. Others think it to be a distinctive kind of seeing, referring to both observing and thinking about the need [Alf, Brd, ICC, Lns, My, TNTC, WBC, Ws].

b. χρεία (LN 57.40) (BAGD 2. p. 885): 'need' [AB, BAGD, LN, Lns; KJV], 'lack' [BAGD, LN]. The participial phrase χρείαν ἔχοντα 'having need' is translated 'in need' [HNTC, WBC; all versions except KJV].

c. aorist act. subj. of κλείω (LN **25.55**) (BAGD 2. p. 434): 'to close' [BAGD, WBC; NAB, NASB, NJB, TEV], 'to shut' [TNT], 'to shut up' [KJV], 'to shut out' [AB], 'to lock out' [Lns]. The phrase 'to close one's heart' is translated 'to withhold compassion' [REB], 'to refuse to show compassion' [LN], 'to withhold kindness' [HNTC], 'to have no pity' [NIV], 'to refuse to help' [NRSV]. The aorist tense indicates a reaction to a specific case [Alf, Brd].

d. σπλάγχνον (LN 25.49) (BAGD 1.b. p. 763): 'heart' [WBC; all versions except NAB, NASB, NJB, TEV, TNT], 'pity' [NIV], 'compassion' [AB, BAGD, LN, Lns; REB], 'bowels of compassion' [KJV], 'kindness' [HNTC].

QUESTION—What is meant by closing one's heart?

Σπλάγχνον is generally the intestines, but includes the heart, lungs, small intestines, and liver [Brd, EGT, Lns, TH, WBC]. It was regarded by the Greeks to be the seat of the emotions [Brd, EGT, Lns, TH]. In English it is better translated as 'heart', and means compassion and pity [Br, Brd, EBC, EGT, HNTC, Lns, NCBC, NIC, TH, WBC]. To 'close one's heart' refers to a deliberate rejection of compassionate urges [AB, Alf, EBC, HNTC, ICC, Lns, My, NCBC, TH, WBC, Ws], a choice to withhold help [ICC, WBC].

how^a (does) the love^b of God remain^c in him?

LEXICON—a. πῶς (LN 92.16) (BAGD 1.d. p. 732): 'how' [AB, BAGD, HNTC, LN, Lns, WBC; all versions except REB, TEV], 'how can it be said that' [REB], 'how can he claim that' [TEV].

b. ἀγάπη : 'love'. See this word at 2:5, 15; 3:1, 16. This noun is also translated as a verb: 'to love' [TEV].

c. pres. act. indic. of μένω (LN 13.89) (BAGD 1.a.β. p. 504): 'to remain' [LN, Lns; NJB], 'to abide' [AB; NASB, NRSV], 'to dwell' [WBC; KJV, REB], 'to be' [NIV, TNT], 'to be present' [HNTC], 'to survive' [NAB].

QUESTION—What is meant by this question form?

It is a rhetorical question with an implied negative answer [AB, Alf, BAGD, NTC, TH, WBC]: the love of God certainly does not remain in him. The presence of love is shown by its actions [Lns]. This does not mean that such a person once had the love of God and has now lost it; rather it means that the love of God was never in him [My].

QUESTION—How are the two nouns related in the genitive construction ἡ ἀγάπη τοῦ θεοῦ 'the love of God'?

1. It means the person's love for God [Alf, EGT, ICC, Lns, My, NTC; TEV]: how could he be loving God? This is the same love for God mentioned in 2:5 [Alf].
2. It means the love that God gives the believer for others [AB, Brd, EBC, Herm, HNTC]: how could the love for others that God gives be abiding in him? This is the kind of love described in 3:11–16 [AB].
3. It refers to divine quality of love [NIC, TNTC, WBC]: how can he be loving others as God loves?
4. It refers to God's love for the person [TH]: how can God love him? This is the kind of love described in 3:1 [TH].
5. It refers to both the love for God and the divine quality of love [Ws]: how can he be loving God or have God-like love?

3:18 Children,^a (let-us) not love^b by-word^c nor by-tongue,^d

LEXICON—a. τεκνίον: 'child'. See this word at 2:1, 12, 28; 3:7.

b. pres. act. subj. of ἀγαπάω (LN **25.44**) (BAGD 1.c. p. 5): 'to love' [HNTC, Lns, WBC; KJV, NAB, NASB, NIV, NRSV], 'to show one's love' [LN]. This verb is also translated '(our) love (must be)' [AB; NJB, REB, TEV]. The present tense indicates continuing action [AB, Brd]. See this word at 2:10; 3:10, 11, 14.

c. λόγος (LN 33.99) (BAGD 1.a.α. p. 477): 'word' [AB, BAGD, HNTC, Lns, WBC; all versions except REB], 'theory' [REB], 'speech' [LN], 'speaking' [BAGD, LN]. The phrase is translated 'not merely by talking about it' [NAB].

d. γλῶσσα (LN **33.101**) (BAGD 1.a. p. 162): 'tongue' [BAGD, Lns; KJV, NASB, NIV], 'lip service' [AB], 'talk' [HNTC, LN; NJB, REB, TEV, TNT], 'speech' [WBC; NRSV], 'what is said' [LN].

QUESTION—What is the function of addressing the readers as 'children'?
   It functions to introduce an exhortation [Herm, My, WBC] on the grounds of their common spiritual heritage [Brd, ICC], and John's position as their spiritual father [EBC, WBC, Ws].
QUESTION—Who is the implied object of love?
   It is reciprocal [TH, WBC]: let us love one another. The word ἀλλήλους 'one another' is implied from 3:11 and 3:23 [WBC].
QUESTION—What is the relationship between λόγῳ 'word' and γλώσσῃ 'tongue'?
   1. The tongue is the source of the words [AB, Alf, Lns, My]: words produced by our tongues.
   2. Tongue and word are synonymous, both referring to merely saying as contrasted with doing [Alf, Brd, Lns, My, TH, WBC]. 'Tongue' is a metonymy for 'speech' and the two words reinforce each other [TH].
   3. This is a hendiadys and means spoken word [Herm].

but[a] in[b] deed[c] and truth.[d]
LEXICON—a. ἀλλά (LN 89.125): 'but' [AB, HNTC, Lns, WBC; KJV, NASB, NIV, NJB, NRSV], 'and' [NAB], not explicit [REB, TEV, TNT].
   b. ἐν with dative object (LN 90.10): 'in' [AB, HNTC, WBC; all versions except NIV, NJB, TNT], 'with' [NIV], 'in connection with' [Lns], not explicit [NJB, TNT].
   c. ἔργον (LN 42.11) (BAGD 1.a. p. 307): 'deed' [AB, BAGD, LN, Lns; KJV, NAB, NASB, NRSV], 'action' [BAGD, HNTC, WBC; NIV, REB, TEV, TNT], 'act' [LN]. This noun is also translated as an adjective: 'active' [NJB].
   d. ἀλήθεια (LN 70.4): 'truth' [AB, Lns; all versions except NJB, REB, TEV], 'genuineness' [WBC]. This noun is also translated as an adverb: 'genuinely' [HNTC] and by an adjective: 'genuine' [NJB], 'true' [REB, TEV]. The phrase ἐν ἀληθείᾳ 'in truth' is an idiom meaning 'actually, really' [LN].
QUESTION—What relationship is indicated by ἀλλά 'but'?
   It strongly contrasts mere words with actual deeds [Alf, Brd, EBC, EGT, Herm, HNTC, ICC, Lns, NCBC, NIC, TH, Ws]: not only with words but also with deeds and truth. It does not mean that love is never spoken about, but it means that love does not stop with mere speech [Lns, TH].
QUESTION—What is the relationship between ἔργῳ 'deed' and ἀληθείᾳ 'truth'?
   1. This is a hendiadys with truth being an attribute of deeds [Brd, Herm, HNTC, Lns, My, NCBC, TH, TNTC; NJB, REB, TEV]: let us love with genuine deeds.
   2. The deeds are produced by the truth [AB, NIC, WBC]: let us love with deeds produced by the truth. The truth is God's revelation [AB], especially that which was revealed in the love expressed by Jesus [NIC], or God's disclosure of himself as truth and love [WBC].

DISCOURSE UNIT: 3:19–24 [Br, NCBC, NIC, TH, TNTC, Ws; TEV]. The topic is Christian confidence [Br], the fruit of love [Ws], a digression about assurance and condemnation [NIC].

3:19 And by^a this we-will-know^b that we-are of^c the truth,^d

TEXT—Some manuscripts omit καί 'and'. GNT includes this word with a D rating, indicating a very great degree of uncertainty. It is included only by KJV.

LEXICON—a. ἐν with dative object: 'by'. See this word at 2:3, 5; 3:10, 16.
  b. fut. mid. (deponent = act.) indic. of γινώσκω: 'to know'. See this word at 3:16. The future tense is used to indicate that the fulfillment of the prerequisites will result in acquiring knowledge [Alf, Brd, My, TH, Ws], or it points to some coming crisis when reassurance is needed [WBC].
  c. ἐκ with genitive object (LN 89.142): 'of' [KJV, NASB, NRSV], 'from' [Lns]. The phrase 'to be of' is translated 'to belong to' [AB, HNTC, WBC; NIV, NJB, REB, TEV, TNT], 'to be committed to' [NAB].
  d. ἀλήθεια: 'truth'. See this word at 2:21.

QUESTION—How do 3:19 and 3:20 advance the writer's theme?
  1. The writer is reassuring the readers that when they are doing deeds of love, they can know that they are of the truth and, even if their overly sensitive consciences condemn them, they can comfort their hearts with the realization that God is greater than their consciences and knows everything about the matter and still forgives them [AB, Br, Brd, EBC, EGT, Herm, HNTC, ICC, Lns, My, NIC, NTC, TH, TNTC, WBC, Ws; probably all versions].
  2. The writer is giving them a way to know whether they are in the truth and warns them that if their consciences judge them guilty of wrongdoing, then God will do so even more, because he knows their every trespass and selfish thought [Alf, NCBC].

QUESTION—What relationship is indicated by ἐν 'by'?
  It indicates the means by which they know that they are of the truth [AB, HNTC, WBC; NAB, NIV, NJB, REB, TEV]: by means of this, we will know that we are of the truth.

QUESTION—What does the pronoun τοῦτο 'this' refer to?
  1. It refers to the preceding clause [AB, Alf, Brd, Herm, HNTC, ICC, My, NIC, NTC, TH, TNTC, WBC, Ws; NAB, NASB, NIV, NJB, NRSV, REB]: because we love others in deed and truth, we will know that we are of the truth.
  2. It refers to the following ὅτι 'that' clause (3:20) [Lns]: we will know that we are of the truth because of this, namely, that God is greater than our hearts and knows all things.

QUESTION—What is meant by being 'of the truth'?
  It means that they belong to the truth [NIV, NJB, REB, TEV, TNT], they are committed to the truth [NAB]. The truth is the gospel and people are of the truth when their spiritual experience comes from that source [Brd]. The

'truth' refers to God who is the ultimate truth [Alf, HNTC, ICC, Lns, NTC, TH, WBC, Ws]. It is another way of saying that they are of God or that they are children of God [HNTC, ICC, Lns, NTC, TH, WBC, Ws].

and^a before^b him we-will-reassure/convince^c our heart,^d

LEXICON—a. καί (LN 89.87) (BAGD I.2.f. p. 392): 'and' [HNTC, Lns, WBC; all versions], 'and then' [BAGD], 'and so' [BAGD], 'indeed' [AB], 'this is how' [TEV].

b. ἔμπροσθεν (LN 83.33) (BAGD 2.b. p. 257): 'before' [AB, Lns; KJV, NAB, NASB, NRSV, TNT], 'in the presence of' [BAGD, LN, WBC; NIV, NJB, TEV], 'in front of' [LN], 'in his sight' [HNTC; REB]. Being at the beginning of the clause, it is emphatic [Brd, Ws].

c. fut. act. indic. of πείθω (LN **25.166**) (BAGD 1.d. p. 639): 'to reassure' [WBC; NRSV, REB, TNT], 'to assure' [HNTC, LN; KJV, NASB], 'to conciliate' [BAGD], 'to pacify' [BAGD], 'to set at rest' [BAGD; NIV], 'to convince' [AB; NJB], 'to persuade' [Lns]. The phrase 'to persuade our hearts' is translated 'to be at peace' [NAB], 'to be confident' [LN; TEV].

d. καρδία (LN **25.166**): 'heart' [AB, Lns; KJV, NASB, NIV, NRSV], 'conscience' [BAGD, WBC], 'ourselves' [HNTC; REB, TNT], 'us' [NJB]. For LN, NAB, and TEV, see above.

QUESTION—What relationship is indicated by καί 'and'?

1. It adds a second conclusion [Brd, NTC, TH]: because of this, we will know that we are of the truth and we will reassure our hearts before God.
2. It implies the result of the preceding clause [AB, Herm, Ws]: we shall know that we are of the truth and as a result reassure/convince our hearts before God.

QUESTION—To whom does αὐτοῦ 'him' refer?

It refers to God [AB, Alf, Br, EGT, Herm, HNTC, WBC, Ws].

QUESTION—What is meant by ἔμπροσθεν αὐτοῦ 'before him' ?

It means to be in God's presence in some way [Herm, HNTC, Lns, NIC, TH, WBC, Ws]: we will assure our hearts when we are in God's presence. More specifically, it refers to God's presence when praying [Lns, My, NIC], at any time [Alf], at any time God judges us [Herm, WBC]. Since the assurance is experienced in the very presence of God, it is a valid assurance [Brd].

QUESTION—What is meant by πείσομεν 'we will reassure/convince' our hearts?

1. It means to reassure or calm our hearts when guilt or fear upsets them [BAGD, Brd, EGT, HNTC, ICC, LN, My, NCBC, NIC, NTC, TH, TNTC, WBC, Ws; all versions except NJB, REB]: and we will reassure our hearts before him. 'Heart' refers to the conscience [BAGD, Brd, EBC, ICC, NCBC, NIC, TH, TNTC, WBC].
2. It means to convince or persuade our hearts that God is greater than our hearts (3:20) [AB, Lns, My, NCBC; NJB, REB]: and we will convince our hearts that God is greater than our hearts.

128 1 JOHN 3:19

3. It means to convince or persuade our hearts that we are God's children [Alf]: and we will convince our hearts (that we are God's children).

3:20 **that[a] if (o r whenever or about whatever) our heart[b] condemns[c] us, because/that[d] God is greater[e] (than) our hearts and knows[f] all-things.**

LEXICON—a. ὅτι (LN 90.21; 89.33, 92.18): 'that', 'for' [KJV], not explicit [TEV]. The word ὅτι 'that' can also be interpreted to be two words ὅ τι 'what ever' and the phrase ὅ τι ἐάν 'whatever if' is translated 'whenever' [WBC; NIV, NRSV], 'where' [REB], 'in whatever' [NASB], 'no matter what' [NAB], 'even if' [AB, HNTC; NJB], 'where' [REB], 'in regard to anything' [TNT].

b. καρδία (LN 26.3) (BAGD 1.b.ε. p. 404): 'heart' [AB, Lns; KJV, NASB, NIV, NRSV], 'conscience' [BAGD, HNTC, WBC; NAB, REB, TEV, TNT], 'feelings' [NJB].

c. pres. act. subj. of καταγινώσκω (LN **30.118**) (BAGD p. 409): 'to condemn' [BAGD, HNTC, LN, Lns, WBC; all versions except NAB], 'to convict' [BAGD], 'to charge with' [NAB]. This verb is also translated 'to know something prejudicial to' [AB].

d. ὅτι (LN 89.33): 'because', 'for' [NAB, NASB, NIV, NRSV, REB, TNT], 'that' [NJB], not explicit [KJV, TEV].

e. μέγας (LN 78.2) (BAGD 2.b.α. p. 498): 'greater' [AB, BAGD, HNTC, Lns; all versions]. The phrase μείζων ἐστίν 'is greater than' is translated as a verb: 'to transcend' [WBC].

f. pres. act. indic. of γινώσκω (LN 28.1) (BAGD 6.a.α. p. 161): 'to know' [AB, BAGD, HNTC, LN, Lns, WBC; all versions]. See this word at 3:16, 19.

QUESTION—What relationships are indicated by the two ὅτι 'because/that' relational words?

1. The first ὅτι means 'because', indicating the grounds for the preceding reassurance, and there is an ellipsis before the second ὅτι which means 'that' [Brd, Herm]: we will reassure our hearts because (ὅτι), if our hearts condemn us, (it is evident [Brd]) / (we know [Herm]) that (ὅτι) God is greater than our hearts [Brd].

2. The initial phrase in 3:20, ὅτι ἐάν, is to be read ὅ τι ἐάν meaning 'whatever' [EGT, Ws; NAB, NASB, REB, TNT] or 'whenever' [TH, TNTC, WBC; NIV, NRSV] and the second ὅτι means 'because': we will reassure our hearts about whatever/whenever our hearts condemn us, because God is greater than our hearts. God is greater in that he is more merciful than our consciences [TH, TNTC], or he knows more than our consciences [TH]. The worst that is in us is known to God and still he cares for us; at the same time he knows our deepest motives and resolves that might fail to surface in our deeds [EGT].

3. Both occurrences of ὅτι mean 'that' and are the object of the preceding verb when the verb means 'convince'. Here the second 'that' is resumptive after the intervening conditional clause and one or the other is

not translated [AB, Herm; NJB]: if our hearts condemn us, we will convince our hearts that God is greater than our hearts.
4. When 3:19 and 3:20 are understood to be a warning, the relationships are ὅτι ἐάν 'if' ... ὅτι 'because' [Alf]: by the preceding we will convince our hearts (that we are God's children). (This is vital), because if our hearts condemn us, it is because God is greater than our hearts and will condemn us even more harshly. God is greater because our consciences are only a faint echo of God's voice, so if our consciences condemns us, God will condemn us even more [Alf].

QUESTION—What does that person's conscience condemn him about?
His conscience convicts him of having sinned [My, NIC, NTC] and of not loving his brothers [Lns, NIC].

QUESTION—In what way is God greater than our hearts?
1. God is more merciful than our hearts. Therefore his mercy overpowers the condemnation of our hearts [AB, BAGD, Br, Brd, Herm, HNTC, ICC, My, NIC, NTC, TH, TNTC].
2. God is greater in knowledge and knows our true spiritual state of being his children [Lns, Ws].
3. God's knowledge of all makes him more aware of all our sins, so if our hearts condemn us we know God will condemn us even more [Alf].

QUESTION—What relationship is indicated by the use of the conjunction καί?
1. It indicates a clarification of the preceding clause [Alf, Lns, NCBC, Ws]: God is greater in that he knows all things.
2. It conjoins two concepts about God [AB, BAGD, Br, Brd, Herm, HNTC, ICC, My, NTC, TNTC]: God is greater and he also knows all things.

QUESTION—To what does πάντα 'all' refer? What does God know?
1. God knows that our love is genuine even when, through weakness of the flesh, we do not meet our heart's standards [ICC, Lns, NIC, TNTC].
2. God knows that we are his [HNTC, Lns].
3. God knows that we have sinned [Alf].

3:21 Beloved,[a] if[b] our heart[c] (does) not condemn[d] (us), we-have confidence[e] before[f] God,

TEXT—Some manuscripts do not have ἡμῶν 'our'. GNT includes this word with a C rating, indicating a considerable degree of doubt. All translations include the possessive pronoun, possibly because it is implied, even if it is not explicit in the Greek text.

LEXICON—a. ἀγαπητός: 'beloved'. See this word at 2:7; 3:2; 4:1, 7, 11.
  b. ἐάν (LN 89.67): 'if' [AB, HNTC, Lns, WBC; all versions].
  c. καρδία (LN 26.3) (BAGD 1.b.ε. p. 404): 'heart' [AB, LN, Lns; KJV, NASB, NIV, NRSV], 'inner self' [LN], 'conscience' [BAGD, HNTC, WBC; NAB, REB, TEV, TNT], 'mind' [LN], 'feelings' [NJB]. See this word at 3:19.
  d. pres. act. subj. of καταγινώσκω (LN 30.118) (BAGD p. 409): 'to condemn' [BAGD, HNTC, LN, Lns, WBC; all versions except NAB], 'to

convict' [BAGD], 'to know something prejudicial' [AB], 'to have something to charge one with' [NAB]. See this word at 3:20.

e. παρρησία: 'confidence'. See this word at 2:28.

f. πρός with accusative object (LN **89.112**) (BAGD III.4.b. p. 710): 'before' [LN; NASB, NIV, NJB, NRSV], 'towards' [BAGD; KJV], 'in the presence of' [AB, WBC; TEV], 'as regards to' [Lns]. The phrase πρὸς τὸν θεόν 'before God' is translated 'we can approach God' [HNTC; REB], 'we can come to God' [TEV], 'God is with us' [NAB].

QUESTION—How is this verse related to its context?

1. Most commentators have taken 3:20 to mean that the heart's condemnation is put to rest because of God's greater authority and mercy. Some speak of this verse as a contrasting condition with 3:20 [AB, Brd, EBC, My, NTC, Ws]: if our hearts condemn us, we can put our hearts at rest by realizing that God will still accept us; but if our hearts do not condemn us, we can have even greater confidence in God's presence. This follows the pattern of negative and positive statements found throughout the letter [Brd]. Other commentators think that this verse can also include a result of putting our hearts at rest [Br, Herm, ICC, Lns, NIC, TH, TNTC, WBC]: even if our hearts condemn us, we can put our hearts at rest by realizing that God will still accept us; then, when our hearts no longer condemn us, we can have confidence in God's presence.

2. The commentators who take 3:20 to mean that the heart's condemnation is enforced by God's greater condemnation take this verse to indicate the opposite situation [Alf]: if our hearts condemn us, then God will condemn us even more; but if our hearts do not condemn us, then we can be confident in his presence.

QUESTION—What is meant by having confidence before God?

The confidence promised at the second coming of Christ in 2:28 is also a present possibility [Brd, Herm, HNTC, Lns, NIC, WBC]. This confidence means to have intimate fellowship with God [Brd, Lns, TH, TNTC, WBC]. It means to feel free to speak one's mind and express one's wants to God without fear or shame [EBC, Ws]. In the context of the following verse, it especially refers to prayer [Alf, Brd, EBC, Herm, HNTC, ICC, NIC, NTC, Ws].

3:22 **and whatever we-ask[a] we-receive[b] from him,**

LEXICON—a. pres. act. subj. of αἰτέω (LN 33.163) (BAGD p. 25): 'to ask' [AB, BAGD, Lns, WBC; all versions], 'to ask for' [HNTC, LN]. The present tense indicates habitual action [Lns, TNTC, WBC], or it indicates that the statement is part of a general rule, true at all times [Brd, NTC].

b. pres. act. indic. of λαμβάνω (LN 57.125) (BAGD 2. p. 465): 'to receive' [AB, BAGD, HNTC, LN, Lns, WBC; all versions except REB], 'to obtain' [REB]. The present tense indicates habitual action [Lns, My, TNTC, WBC], or a general rule [Brd, NTC].

QUESTION—What relationship is indicated by καί 'and'?
1. This gives an additional consequence of not having our heart accuse us [ICC, My, NIC, TH, TNTC, WBC]: if our hearts do not accuse us, then we have confidence before God and we receive what we ask for.
2. It explains in what respect we have confidence [AB, Alf, Brd]. This seems to require an intermediate step of logic: we have confidence before God, that is, we confidently go before him to ask for what we want, with the result that we receive it. AB takes this to be just one instance of the general state of being confident before God.

QUESTION—To whom does αὐτοῦ 'him' refer?
It refers to God [AB, Brd, EBC, ICC, Lns, NTC, TNTC, WBC].

because[a] we-keep[b] his commandments[c] and we-do[d] the-things pleasing[e] before[f] him.

LEXICON—a. ὅτι (LN 89.33): 'because' [AB, HNTC, Lns, WBC; all versions].
b. pres. act. indic. of τηρέω: 'to keep'. See this word at 2:3, 4, 5. The present tense indicates habitual action [Brd, TH, WBC].
c. ἐντολή: 'commandment'. See this word at 2:3, 7.
d. pres. act. indic. of ποιέω (LN 90.45) (BAGD I.1.b.ε. p. 681): 'to do' [AB, HNTC, LN, Lns, WBC; all versions]. The present tense indicates habitual action [Brd, TH, WBC].
e. ἀρεστός (LN 25.92) (BAGD p. 105): 'pleasing' [AB, BAGD, LN, Lns; KJV, NAB, NASB, TNT]. The phrase τὰ ἀρεστὰ ἐνώπιον αὐτοῦ 'the things pleasing before him' is translated 'what he approves' [HNTC; REB], 'what pleases him' [WBC; NIV, NRSV, TEV], 'what is acceptable to him' [NJB]. The present tense indicates habitual action [TH].
f. ἐνώπιον with accusative object (LN 90.20) (BAGD 3. p. 270): 'before', 'in one's sight' [AB, Lns; KJV, NAB, NASB], 'in the opinion of' [LN], not explicit [HNTC, WBC; all versions except KJV, NAB, NASB].

QUESTION—What relationship is indicated by ὅτι 'because'?
1. It indicates the reason we will receive what we ask for [Alf, Brd, My, NCBC, NIC, TNTC, WBC]: we receive whatever we ask because we keep his commandments and do what is pleasing before him. This does not indicate a meritorious reason, but the fulfillment of a condition [Brd, NCBC, TNTC, WBC].
3. It indicates the reason we have confidence before God (2:21) [Herm]: we have confidence before him because we keep his commandments and do what is pleasing before him.

QUESTION—What is the relationship between 'keeping his commandments' and 'doing what pleases him'?
1. They are two ways of saying the same thing [AB, Herm, Lns, My, NTC, WBC].
2. They are two conditions for receiving: obedience to the commandments and spontaneous obedience to God's will as discerned [Alf, Brd, ICC,

Ws]. The commandments are explicit statements to be obeyed; the things that please him are more than that, including any actions that please him [Brd]. That which pleases him is everything that is known to be in harmony with his will [ICC].

DISCOURSE UNIT: 3:23–24 [ICC]. The topic is belief and love [ICC].

3:23 And[a] this is his commandment,[b]

LEXICON—a. καί (LN 89.93): 'and' [Lns, WBC; KJV, NAB, NASB, NIV, NRSV], 'now' [AB], not explicit [HNTC; NJB, REB, TEV, TNT].

b. ἐντολή: 'commandment'. See this word at 3:22.

QUESTION—To what does the pronoun τοῦτο 'this' refer?

It points forward to the two-fold command to believe and love [Alf, Herm, ICC, My, TH, WBC; all versions].

QUESTION—To whom does αὐτοῦ 'his' refer?

It refers to God [AB, Br, Brd, ICC, TH, TNTC, WBC]. This is implied by the use of 'his Son' in the next clause [AB, Brd].

QUESTION—What is the significance of the change in number from the plural ἐντολάς 'commandments' in 3:22 to the singular ἐντολή 'commandment' here?

The singular form sums up all the individual commands and treats them as a unity [Alf, Brd, ICC, Lns, My, NIC, TH, TNTC, WBC, Ws]. According to the following clauses, this one command has two parts: to believe and to love [Brd, EGT, Herm, HNTC, ICC, NIC, NTC, TNTC, WBC, Ws] because the two are inseparably entwined [Brd, EGT, Herm, HNTC, Lns, My, NIC, NTC].

that we-should-believe[a] in-the name[b] of-his son Jesus Christ

LEXICON—a. aorist act. subj. of πιστεύω (LN 31.85) (BAGD 2.a.α. p. 661): 'to believe' [AB, BAGD, HNTC, LN, Lns, WBC; all versions except REB], 'to give allegiance to' [REB]. The aorist tense is used to indicate the initial act of believing [Alf, Br, Brd, NIC, NTC, TNTC, WBC, Ws], or it is used to indicate that the action is seen as a unified whole [ICC, TH].

b. ὄνομα (LN 9.19) (BAGD I.4.b. p. 572): 'name' [AB, BAGD, HNTC, Lns, WBC; all versions except REB], 'the person of' [LN], not explicit [REB].

QUESTION—What relationship is indicated by ἵνα 'that'?

It indicates the contents of 'this' and explains what the command consists of [AB, Brd, Herm, ICC, Lns, My, NCBC, TH, WBC]. It is equivalent to ὅτι 'that' [Brd].

QUESTION—What is the significance of using the dative case for the object of 'believe' rather than the common prepositional phrase with εἰς 'in' with the accusative object?

1. There is no significant difference between the two forms: it indicates a trust and confidence in the person of Christ [AB, Br, Herm, Lns, NCBC, WBC].

1 JOHN 3:23

2. The use of the dative case indicates a conviction about the truth of a fact rather than a relationship to a person: the conviction that Jesus is the Christ, the Son of God [ICC, NIC, TH, Ws]. It is a conviction that Christ is really what his name implies that he is [ICC].

QUESTION—What is the difference between 'believing in the name of the Son' and 'believing in the Son'?
 1. There is no difference, since the name stands for the person [Br, EGT, Herm, My, NIC, TNTC, WBC; REB]: we should believe in the person, Jesus Christ.
 2. Believing in the name of a person signifies believing in the person and in all that he is [AB, Alf, BAGD, Brd, ICC, Lns, NCBC, TH, Ws], including his standing and authority [NCBC]. It means to believe in the Son and to accept all that this name proclaims him to be [BAGD].

QUESTION—What is meant by the title χριστοῦ 'Christ'?
 1. It is used as a proper name, Christ [TH].
 2. It refers to his office as Messiah [Brd, ICC, NTC, TNTC, Ws].

and we-should-love[a] one-another, as[b] he-gave[c] us (the) commandment.

LEXICON—a. pres. act. subj. of ἀγαπάω: 'to love'. See this word at 2:10; 3:10, 11, 14, 18. The present tense indicates that this love is continuous [AB, Alf, Brd, Lns, NTC, TH, TNTC, WBC].
 b. καθώς (LN 64.14): 'as' [KJV, NAB, NIV, NJB, REB], 'just as' [AB, HNTC, LN, WBC; NASB, NRSV, TEV, TNT], 'even as' [Lns].
 c. aorist act. indic. of δίδωμι (LN 57.71) (BAGD 1.b.α. p. 193): 'to give' [AB, LN, Lns; KJV]. The phrase ἔδωκεν ἐντολήν 'to give commandment' is translated 'to command' [BAGD, HNTC; all versions except KJV], 'to direct' [WBC].

QUESTION—What relationship is indicated by the use of the conjunction καί?
It conjoins the two parts of the commandment [Brd, EGT, Herm, HNTC, ICC, Lns, My, NIC, TNTC, Ws]. Love is not the sum total of being a Christian; belief and love go together and each needs the other [NIC].

QUESTION—To whom does ἀλλήλους 'one another' refer?
It refers to fellow believers [Brd, EGT, Lns].

QUESTION—Who is the implied subject of the verb ἔδωκεν 'he gave'?
 1. It refers to Christ [Alf, Br, Brd, EGT, ICC, My, TNTC, Ws; REB, TEV]. Christ gave the command to love one another in John 13:34 and 15:12, 17 [Alf, Br, Brd, TNTC]. In this case, the phrase goes with just the second part of the command [Alf, Br, Brd, My].
 2. It refers to God [AB, Lns, TH, WBC]. In this case, the phrase goes with both parts of the command [Lns].
 3. The author does not intend to distinguish between the two [EBC, EGT]. The deeds of the one are the deeds of the other [EBC].

3:24 **And the-(one) keeping[a] his commandments[b] remains[c] in[d] him and he in him;**

LEXICON—a. pres. act. participle of τηρέω: 'to keep'. See this word at 3:22. The present tense indicates that the keeping is continuous [Brd].
   b. ἐντολή: 'commandment'. See this word at 3:22, 23.
   c. pres. act. indic. of μένω: 'to remain'. See this word at 2:6, 27, 28; 3:6. The present tense indicates that the remaining continues [Brd, WBC].
   d. ἐν with dative object: 'in'. See this word at 2:6, 27, 28; 3:6.

QUESTION—How is this verse related to its context?
   This verse ties in the theme of keeping the commandments with abiding in God [Alf]. It also introduces a new theme, the Spirit [HNTC]. This takes up 'keeping God's commandments' from 3:22, thus making 3:23 a parenthetical comment about the contents of the commandments [Brd, My, WBC, Ws].

QUESTION—What is the relationship between 'keeping his commandments' and 'remaining in him'?
   Keeping his commandments is a proof of 'remaining in him' [Br, Brd, EGT], not the cause [Br].

QUESTION—To whom does αὐτοῦ 'his' in the phrase 'his commandments' refer?
   It refers to God [AB, Alf, Br, Brd, EGT, Herm, HNTC, ICC, Lns, My, NIC, TH, WBC, Ws; NJB, TEV, TNT].

QUESTION—What is the significance of the change in the number of the noun 'commandment' from singular in 3:23 back to plural here?
   1. The switch is stylistic [AB]. The verb 'to keep' is always used with the plural form [AB].
   2. The switch stresses the many subordinate commands implied by the one great command to love and believe [NIC, WBC].

QUESTION—What is the significance of the believer's remaining in God and God's remaining in the believer?
   The reciprocal relationship stresses the closeness of the spiritual union [Brd, NIC], a continuous fellowship [TH].

and by[a] this we-know[b] that he-remains in us,

LEXICON—a. ἐν with dative object (LN 89.76) (BAGD I.5.d. p. 259): 'by' [LN; NASB, NRSV]. The phrase ἐν τούτῳ 'by this' is translated 'this is how' [AB, WBC; NAB, NIV], 'hereby' [KJV], 'in connection with' [Lns], not explicit [HNTC; NJB, REB, TEV, TNT]. See this phrase at 3:19.
   b. pres. act. indic. of γινώσκω: 'to know'. See this word at 3:16, 19.

QUESTION—To what does the pronoun τοῦτο 'this' refer?
   1. It refers to the following clause [AB, Alf, BAGD, Herm, HNTC, ICC, My, NCBC, NIC, TH, WBC]: we know that he remains in us by this, namely, by the Spirit that he gave us.

2. It refers to the preceding clause [Brd]: by our keeping of the commandments, we know that he remains in us. The Spirit uses the fact of obedience to produce assurance [Brd].

by[a] the Spirit[b] whom he gave[c] us.
LEXICON—a. ἐκ with genitive object (LN 89.77) (BAGD 3.g.β. p. 235): 'by' [LN, WBC; KJV, NASB, NIV, NRSV], 'from' [AB, HNTC, Lns; NAB, REB], 'through' [TNT], not explicit [NJB], 'because of' [TEV].
- b. πνεῦμα (LN 12.18) (BAGD 5.d.α. p. 677): 'Spirit' [AB, BAGD, HNTC, LN, Lns, WBC; all versions].
- c. aorist act. indic. of δίδωμι (LN 57.71): 'to give' [AB, HNTC, LN, Lns, WBC; all versions]. The aorist tense indicates that this occurred at a definite time in the past [Alf, Brd].

QUESTION—What is the relationship between knowing that we remain in him and 'from the Spirit'?
1. The fact of the presence of the indwelling Holy Spirit is a proof that we remain in him [AB, Alf, ICC, TNTC, WBC]. The Spirit's presence is manifested by enabling us to believe [TNTC], to obey the commandments and to love one another [TNTC, WBC].
2. The Holy Spirit causes us to know with assurance that God remains in us [Brd, EGT, Lns, My, NIC, TH]. Since obedience is imperfect, the Spirit brings assurance to the knowledge [NIC].

QUESTION—Who is the implied subject of the verb ἔδωκεν 'he gave'?
1. It is God [AB, Alf, Br, Brd, HNTC, ICC, NTC, WBC, Ws].
2. It is Christ [TNTC].

QUESTION—When was the Spirit given to them?
1. The Spirit was given to the Church at Pentecost [Alf, EBC, Herm].
2. The Spirit was given to believers at the beginning of their individual Christian lives [EGT, Lns, TNTC, WBC, Ws].

DISCOURSE UNIT: 4:1–6 [AB, Alf, Br, Brd, EBC, EGT, Herm, HNTC, ICC, Lns, NCBC, NIC, TH, TNTC, WBC, Ws; NAB, NASB, NIV, NJB, TEV]. The topic is truth and deceit [AB], the two spirits [Br, HNTC], the spirit of truth and spirit of error [EGT, Lns, NCBC, NIC, TH, Ws; NAB, NASB, NIV, TEV], a warning against false spirits [EBC], a warning against false teaching [Alf, Herm; NJB], sonship tested by faith in Christ [Brd, TNTC], guarding against worldliness [WBC; NJB].

4:1 Beloved,[a] (do) not believe[b] every spirit,[c] but test[d] the spirits if[e] they-are from[f] God,
LEXICON—a. ἀγαπητός: 'beloved'. See this word at 2:7; 3:2, 21; 4:7, 11.
- b. pres. act. impera. of πιστεύω (LN 31.35) (BAGD 1.b. p. 661): 'to believe' [AB, BAGD, LN, Lns, WBC; all versions except NAB, NJB, REB], 'to trust' [HNTC; NAB, NJB, REB]. It means to accept their statements as true [Brd, ICC, TH, WBC].

c. πνεῦμα (LN 12.33, 12.18) (BAGD 7. p. 678): 'spirit' [AB, BAGD, HNTC, LN, Lns, WBC; all versions except TEV]. The phrase 'every spirit' is translated 'all who claim to have the Spirit' [TEV].
d. pres. act. impera. of δοκιμάζω (LN 27.45) (BAGD 1. p. 202): 'to test' [HNTC, LN; all versions except KJV, NAB], 'to put to a test' [AB, BAGD, WBC; NAB], 'to test out' [Lns], 'to examine' [BAGD, LN], 'to try' [KJV]. The present tense indicates that they were to make a practice of testing each one who spoke as a prophet [AB, Brd, Lns].
e. εἰ (LN 90.26) (BAGD V.2.a. p. 219): 'if' [HNTC, LN; NAB, TEV], 'whether' [BAGD, LN, Lns, WBC; all versions except NAB, TEV], not explicit [AB].
f. ἐκ with genitive object (LN 89.3): 'from' [LN, Lns, WBC; NASB, NIV, NJB, REB, TNT], 'of' [KJV, NRSV]. The phrase 'to be from' is translated 'to belong to' [AB; NAB], 'to come from' [HNTC; TEV]. See this word at 3:10.

QUESTION—How is this verse related to its context?

It resumes the warnings against false teachers of 3:1–10 [EBC, Herm, My, NIC, NTC, Ws] and introduces a Christological test [Brd, EBC, Ws]. It ties into the preceding phrase which speaks of the Spirit he has given by giving the criterion of determining the nature of spirits [AB, Alf, ICC, My, NCBC, NIC, TNTC, WBC].

QUESTION—What verb is implied for introducing the conditional clause?

The implied verb is 'to see' [AB, HNTC; all versions except KJV, TEV], 'to discern' [WBC], 'to find out' [TEV]: test the spirits to see/discern/find out if they are from God.

QUESTION—What is meant by 'every spirit' and 'the spirits'?

1. 'Spirit' refers to an incorporeal being who inspires the person [AB, EBC, ICC, My]: do not believe every spirit (who speaks through a person). The spirit is either the Holy Spirit or an evil spirit that dwells within the antichrists [AB].
2. 'Spirit' refers to a person who is inspired by a spirit [Brd, NIC, TNTC, WBC]: do not believe every spirit-inspired person. A prophet is so closely identified with the spirit who inspires him, that the term 'spirit' may be used for the person himself [Brd]. The plural form 'spirits' means that there are many people who are inspired by either the Spirit of God or by Satan [NIC]. A person is either inspired by the spirit of truth of the spirit of error [WBC].
3. 'Spirit' refers to the person's own spirit [Alf, Lns, TH]: do not believe every person. The spirit of a person is the representative part of the inner life [TH], the person as such with his inner, spiritual character [Lns]. Human spirits are to be tested to see if they are spokesmen for the Spirit of truth or the spirit of error [Alf].
4. 'Spirit' refers to the utterances inspired by a spirit [NCBC, NTC]: do not believe every utterance inspired by a spirit. 'Spirit' is a metonymy for 'teaching' [NTC].

because^a many false-prophets^b have-gone-out^c into^d the world.^e

LEXICON—a. ὅτι (LN 89.33): 'because' [AB, LN, Lns; KJV, NAB, NASB, NIV], 'for' [HNTC, WBC; NJB, NRSV, REB, TEV, TNT].
- b. ψευδοπροφήτης (LN 53.81) (BAGD p. 892): 'false prophet' [AB, BAGD, HNTC, LN, WBC; all versions], 'pseudo prophet' [Lns].
- c. perf. act. indic. of ἐξέρχομαι (LN 15.40) (BAGD 1.a.ε. p. 274): 'to go out' [AB, BAGD, HNTC, LN, Lns; all versions except NAB, NJB], 'to defect' [WBC]. The phrase ἐξέρχομαι εἰς 'to go out into' is translated 'to appear in' [NAB], 'to be at large in' [NJB]. The perfect tense indicates that the results from a past act continue on [Brd, HNTC, TH, Ws] so that they are now present in the world [Brd].
- d. εἰς with accusative object (LN 84.22): 'into' [AB, HNTC, LN, Lns, WBC; all versions except NAB, NJB]. For NAB, NJB, see above. The phrase εἰς τὸν κόσμον 'into the world' is translated 'everywhere' [TEV].
- e. κόσμος (LN 9.23) (BAGD 5.a. p. 446): 'world' [AB, HNTC, Lns, WBC; all versions]. For TEV, see above.

QUESTION—What relationship is indicated by ὅτι 'because'?
It indicates the grounds for the preceding command [AB, Alf, ICC, Lns, My, TH, TNTC, Ws; KJV, NAB, NASB, NIV]: test the teaching of the one claiming to speak God's message (because they may not truly be speaking for God), since many false prophets have gone out into the world.

QUESTION—To whom does ψευδοπροφήται 'false prophets' refer?
It refers to teachers of false doctrine who are the mouthpieces of the evil spirits [AB, Alf, Br, Herm, HNTC, Lns, My, WBC, Ws]. They are false because they teach false doctrine [AB, Alf, Br, EBC, Herm, HNTC, My, WBC], or they pretend to have the Holy Spirit when in fact they have only an evil spirit [Lns].

QUESTION—What is being implied by ἐξεληλύθασιν 'they have gone out'?
1. They were sent out as spokesmen of the evil one [Alf, ICC, My, NIC, Ws].
2. They left the church [AB, EBC, EGT, WBC]. They have defected to be part of the unbelieving world [WBC].
3. They appeared and go about in the world [Brd, Herm, Lns, NIC, TH]. The world is full of such false prophets [TH].

QUESTION—What is being implied by πολλοί 'many'?
The emphasis here is on the large number. It does not imply that some remain in the fellowship [AB].

QUESTION—Which component of meaning is in focus in κόσμον 'world'?
1. It refers to those outside the church [AB, EGT, WBC].
2. It refers to the world of men [BAGD, ICC] and does not contrast with the church [ICC].

4:2 By^a this you-know^b the spirit^c of God:

LEXICON—a. ἐν with dative object: 'by'. See this word at 2:3, 5; 3:10, 16, 19.

b. pres. act. indic./impera. of γινώσκω: 'to know'. See this word at 2:3a, 5, 18, 29; 3:16, 19, 24; 4:6. The present tense indicates that the coming to know is a repeated action [Lns]. It means to distinguish or recognize [Br, HNTC, Ws], and to observe [BAGD, Brd].

c. πνεῦμα (LN 12.18) (BAGD 5.a. p. 676): 'Spirit' [AB, BAGD, HNTC, Lns, WBC; all versions].

QUESTION—To what does the pronoun τοῦτο 'this' refer?

It refers to the following clause [AB, Brd, Herm, ICC, My, NIC, TH, TNTC, WBC]: you can know the Spirit of God by this, namely, the spirit who acknowledges that Jesus came in the body is from God.

QUESTION—What is the mood of the verb γινώσκετε 'you know'?

1. It is indicative, making a statement [AB, Alf, Brd, EGT, Herm, HNTC, ICC, NTC, TH, TNTC, WBC, Ws; all versions except KJV]: by this you know the Spirit of God.
2. It is imperative, making a command [Lns; KJV]: know the Spirit of God by this.

QUESTION—How are the two nouns related in the genitive construction τὸ πνεῦμα τοῦ θεοῦ 'the Spirit of God'?

1. It means 'God's Spirit', the Holy Spirit [AB, Alf, Brd, EBC, Herm, Lns, NIC, NTC, TH, WBC, Ws; all versions except NJB]: because of this you will know God's Spirit. They will know the presence of the Holy Spirit in the prophet [Brd]. They will recognize whether or not a person is inspired by the Holy Spirit [WBC].
2. It means 'the spirit from God' [WBC]: because of this you will know the spirit that is from God.

every spirit[a] who acknowledges[b] Jesus Christ having-come[c] in[d] (a) body[e] is from[f] God,

LEXICON—a. πνεῦμα (LN 12.33) (BAGD 5.a. p. 676): 'spirit' [BAGD, HNTC, LN, Lns, WBC; all versions except TEV], 'one who has the Spirit' [AB; TEV].

b. pres. act. indic. of ὁμολογέω (LN 33.274; 33.275) (BAGD 4. p. 568): 'to acknowledge' [BAGD, HNTC, WBC; NAB, NIV, NJB, REB, TEV, TNT], 'to confess' [AB, LN, Lns; KJV, NASB, NRSV]. See this word at 2:23; 4:3, 15; 2 John 7.

c. perf. act. participle of ἔρχομαι (LN 15.81) (BAGD I.1.a.η. p. 311): 'to come' [AB, BAGD, HNTC, LN, Lns; all versions], 'to come before the public' [BAGD].

d. ἐν with dative object (LN 13.8) (BAGD I.4.b. p. 259): 'in' [AB, BAGD, HNTC, LN; all versions], 'into' [Lns], 'as' [TEV]. For WBC, TEV and TNT, see below.

e. σάρξ (LN 8.4; 58.10) (BAGD 2. p. 743): 'body' [BAGD, LN], 'flesh' [AB, HNTC, Lns; all versions except NJB, TEV, TNT], 'human nature' [LN; NJB]. The phrase ἐν σαρκί 'in flesh' is translated 'as a human being' [TEV, TNT], 'incarnate' [WBC].

f. ἐκ with genitive object (LN 89.3): 'from' [HNTC, LN, Lns; NASB, NIV, NJB, REB, TNT], 'of' [KJV, NRSV]. This preposition is also translated 'belongs to' [AB; NAB], 'derives from' [WBC], 'comes from' [TEV]. See this word at 4:1.

QUESTION—What is acknowledged?

Here there are two possible meanings of ὁμολογέω 'to acknowledge': (1) to publicly express one's allegiance to a person [LN (33.274)], or (2) to publicly acknowledge a fact about a person [LN (33.275)].

1. The object of the acknowledgment is the person of Jesus Christ. Although most commentators do not clearly state what this specifically means, it is assumed that they would take the first meaning, 'to acknowledge one's allegiance to Jesus Christ'. There are different views about the phrase 'Jesus Christ having come in a body'.

1.1 The object of the acknowledgment is the whole phrase as a unit [AB, Brd, ICC, My, WBC, Ws; NAB, NJB]: acknowledge (his allegiance to) Jesus Christ, the one who has come in the flesh. This is a confession of a person about whom certain propositions are true [ICC]. The participial phrase is attributive: Jesus Christ come in the flesh is confessed [Brd].

1.2 The object of the acknowledgment is Jesus Christ and the participial phrase is the predicate [Alf, Herm, Lns, NIC, TH]: acknowledge (his allegiance to) Jesus Christ as one who has come in the flesh. Some think that there is little difference in this from the meaning 'acknowledge that Jesus Christ has come in the flesh'.

1.3 The object of acknowledgment is Jesus and the rest of the phrase is the predicate [EGT]: acknowledge (his allegiance to) Jesus as the Christ who came in the flesh.

2. The object of the acknowledgment is a statement about Jesus.

2.1 He acknowledges that Jesus Christ came in a body [Br, NTC; KJV, NASB, NIV, NRSV, REB, TEV].

2.2 He acknowledges that Jesus is the Messiah who came in a body [HNTC, TNTC; TNT].

QUESTION—What is the significance of the perfect participle ἐληλυθότα 'having come'?

The perfect voice indicates that an event in the past has continuing results [Alf, ICC, Lns, NTC, TH, TNTC, WBC, Ws]. At the time of the writing, Jesus was still incarnate and in heaven, possessing his resurrection body [Brd, NTC]. It focuses on the present human state of Jesus rather than on the past event of the incarnation [NIC, WBC]. It implies the pre-existence of Christ with God before his birth [Br, EBC, NIC].

4:3 and[a] every spirit who (does) not acknowledge[b] Jesus is not from God;

TEXT—Instead of μὴ ὁμολογεῖ 'does not acknowledge', some manuscripts have λύει 'negates'. GNT selects μὴ ὁμολογεῖ 'does not acknowledge' with a B rating, indicating some degree of doubt. The reading λύει 'negates, annuls' is selected by only AB and Herm.

TEXT—After τὸν Ἰησοῦν 'Jesus' some manuscripts have ἐν σαρκὶ ἐληλυθότα 'come in the flesh'. GNT leaves out ἐν σαρκὶ ἐληλυθότα 'come in the flesh' with a B rating, indicating some degree of doubt. It is included only by KJV.

LEXICON—a. καί (LN 89.92): 'and' [KJV, NASB, NJB, NRSV, REB, TNT], 'while' [AB; NAB], 'but' [WBC; NIV, TEV].

b. pres. act. indic. of ὁμολογέω: 'to acknowledge'. See this word at 4:2.

QUESTION—What relationship is indicated by καί 'and'?

It conjoins this statement with the previous statement as a negative-positive contrast [AB, Alf, Brd, EBC, EGT, Herm, NIC, TH, TNTC, WBC, Ws], and this gives it an adversative function 'but' [AB, TH, WBC; NIV, TEV].

QUESTION—How does 'acknowledge Jesus' correspond with 'acknowledge Jesus having come in a body' in 4:2?

1. The sense is the same as in 4:2 [Alf, Br, Brd, HNTC, TNTC, WBC]. The use of the article with 'Jesus' means that one who was previously referred to [Brd, EGT, Lns, WBC; TEV, TNT].
2. There is a difference intended [NIC, TH, Ws]. Instead of the fuller confession in 4:2, personal allegiance is intended here [NIC, TH]. It means to publicly declare one's belief in Jesus [TH], to confess Jesus as Lord [Ws].

and this is the (spirit) of-the antichrist,[a] which you-have-heard[b] that he-is-coming,[c]

LEXICON—a. ἀντίχριστος: 'antichrist'. See this word at 2:18, 22; 2 John 7.

b. perf. act. indic. of ἀκούω (LN 33.212): 'to hear' [AB, HNTC, LN, Lns, WBC; all versions except REB], 'to be warned' [REB]. The perfect tense indicates that the thing heard was a traditional saying [AB], still remembered [TH]. See this word at 2:18.

c. pres. mid. (deponent = act.) indic. of ἔρχομαι: 'to come'. See this word at 2:18. The present indicative indicates that the coming is fixed and sure [Alf].

QUESTION—To what or whom does the pronoun τοῦτο 'this' refer?

1. It refers to the preceding mention of the spirit who does not acknowledge Jesus [AB, Alf, Brd, HNTC, Lns, NIC, NTC, TH, WBC; all versions except TNT]: this spirit is the spirit of the antichrist.
2. It refers to the denial of Jesus and is the characteristic of the antichrist [ICC, My, NCBC] or the work of antichrist [TNT]: this denial of Jesus is the characteristic or work of the antichrist.

and now[a] is in[b] the world[c] already.[d]

LEXICON—a. νῦν (LN 67.38) (BAGD 1.c. p. 545): 'now' [AB, BAGD, LN, Lns; NASB, NRSV], 'even now' [WBC; KJV, NIV, TNT], 'here' [REB], 'now here' [TEV], not explicit [HNTC; NAB, NJB]. See this word at 2:18.

b. ἐν with dative object (LN 83.13): 'in' [AB, HNTC, LN, Lns, WBC; all versions except NJB], 'at large in' [NJB].

c. κόσμος: 'world'. See this word at 4:1.

d. ἤδη (LN 67.20) (BAGD 1.a. p. 344): 'already' [AB, BAGD, HNTC, Lns; all versions], not explicit [WBC]. Its position at the end of the clause makes it emphatic [AB, Brd].

QUESTION—Which component of meaning is in focus in κόσμῳ 'world'?
1. It is referring to the part of mankind that is against God and under the control of the devil [AB, HNTC, WBC].
2. It refers to that sphere in which all people live [Brd, Herm, TH].

QUESTION—In what sense is the antichrist already in the world?
This spirit of the antichrist is operating through the many antichrists [Alf, Br, EBC]; it is embodied in them [TNTC]. It is working in and through the false prophets [Brd]. 'To be in the world' here means to be active in the world [TH].

4:4 You are from[a] God, children,[b] and you-have-overcome[c] them,

LEXICON—a. ἐκ with genitive object (LN 89.3) (BAGD 3.a. p. 234): 'from' [BAGD, HNTC, Lns, WBC; NASB, NIV, NJB], 'of' [KJV, NAB, NRSV]. The phrase 'to be from' is translated 'to belong to' [AB; REB, TEV, TNT]. See this word at 4:1.
b. τεκνίον: 'child'. See this word at 2:1, 12, 28; 3:7, 18.
c. perf. act. indic. of νικάω: 'to overcome'. See this word at 2:13. The perfect tense indicates that the overcoming was in the past but its effect continues to the present [Brd, Lns, NTC, WBC].

QUESTION—What is the significance of the overt pronoun ὑμεῖς 'you' here occurring first in the clause?
This gives it prominence [AB, Alf, Brd, EGT, ICC, NTC, WBC, Ws] and points up the contrast between them and the false teachers [AB, Alf, Brd, EGT, ICC, WBC] or those who are in the world [My, NCBC, NIC, Ws].

QUESTION—To whom does αὐτούς 'them' refer?
It refers to the false prophets (4:1) [AB, Alf, Br, Brd, EBC, EGT, Herm, HNTC, My, NCBC, NIC, NTC, TH, TNTC, WBC; NAB, REB, TEV, TNT].

QUESTION—What is meant by 'overcoming' them?
They overcame them by rejecting their false teaching and by remaining faithful to the apostolic doctrine [Brd, EBC, ICC, Lns, My, NTC, TNTC, WBC], they resisted the temptation to accept the false teaching [NIC], and they refused to behave wrongly or to join those who withdrew from the congregation [WBC].

QUESTION—What is the significance of the use of the perfect tense in regard to their overcoming the false prophets?
1. The victory has already been won by the Christians by their remaining true to the apostolic doctrine [Br, Brd, EBC, ICC, My, NIC, NTC, TNTC, WBC]: you have overcome them.
2. The victory is to be accomplished in the future since the false teachers are still a threat to the congregation [NCBC]. They must claim the results of the victory won by Christ [Ws]. The perfect tense is used because the

victory is so certain [Alf], and has been won for them in principle by Christ [Ws].

because[a] the-(one) in[b] you is greater[c] than the-(one) in the world.[d]

LEXICON—a. ὅτι (LN 89.33): 'because' [HNTC, LN, Lns, WBC; all versions except NAB, NRSV], 'for' [AB; NAB, NRSV].

b. ἐν with dative object (LN 89.119): 'in' [AB, Lns, WBC; all versions except REB]. The phrase 'to be in' is translated 'to inspire' [HNTC; REB].

c. μέγας (LN 78.2) (BAGD 2.b.α. p. 498): 'greater' [AB, BAGD, HNTC, Lns; all versions], 'more powerful' [WBC].

d. κόσμος (LN 41.38) (BAGD 7. p. 446): 'world' [AB, BAGD, HNTC, LN, Lns, WBC; all versions].

QUESTION—What relationship is indicated by ὅτι 'because'?

It indicates the reason they were able to overcome the false teachers [Alf, Brd, ICC, NIC, WBC, Ws]. God working in them has overcome the enemy [AB]. The victory is the product of being enabled by the one who was in them [Brd].

QUESTION—Who is the one in them?

1. He is God [Alf, Herm, HNTC, ICC, Lns, My, NIC, TH; TNT].
2. He is the Holy Spirit [AB, Br, Brd, NTC, TNTC; TEV].
3. This refers to God as Father, Son, and Holy Spirit [WBC].

QUESTION—Who is the one who is in the world?

1. He is the devil [Alf, Herm, HNTC, ICC, Lns, My, NIC, TH, TNTC, WBC, Ws].
2. He is the spirit of the antichrist [AB, Br, Brd, NTC; TNT].

QUESTION—To whom or what does κόσμῳ 'world' refer?

It refers to all that is hostile to God [Herm, HNTC, NTC, TH, TNTC, WBC]. The word is used here in its moral sense rather than as a location [Brd]. It is the world of people who are hostile to God [NTC].

4:5 They are from[a] the world, because-of[b] this they speak[c] from[d] the world

LEXICON—a. ἐκ with genitive object (LN 89.3) (BAGD 3.b. p. 235): 'from' [Lns; NASB, NIV, NJB], 'of' [KJV]. The phrase 'to be from' is translated 'to belong to' [AB, HNTC; NAB, REB, TEV, TNT], 'to be derived from' [WBC].

b. διά with accusative object (LN 89.26): 'because of' [LN]. The phrase διὰ τοῦτο 'because of this' is translated 'therefore' [KJV, NASB, NIV, NJB, NRSV], 'that is why' [AB; NAB], 'and so' [REB, TNT], 'so' [HNTC], 'for this reason' [Lns], 'and as a result' [WBC].

c. pres. act. indic. of λαλέω (LN 33.70): 'to speak' [AB, HNTC, LN, Lns, WBC; KJV, NASB, NIV, TEV, TNT], 'to say' [NJB, NRSV], not explicit [NAB, REB]. The present tense indicates that it is customary for them to speak this way [Brd].

d. ἐκ with genitive object (LN 90.16): 'from'. The phrase 'to speak from the world' is translated 'to speak of the world' [KJV], 'to speak about matters of the world' [TEV], 'to speak from the viewpoint of the world' [NIV], 'to speak as from the world' [NASB], 'to speak as the world speaks' [TNT], 'to speak the language of the world' [AB, HNTC, WBC], 'what they say is of the world' [NRSV], 'the world inspires what they say' [NJB], 'their teaching belongs to the world' [REB], 'theirs is the language of the world' [NAB].

QUESTION—What is the significance of the use of the overt pronoun αὐτοί 'they' occurring first in the clause?

It indicates prominence [Brd, WBC] and makes a strong contrast with 'you (pl.)' in 4:4 [EBC, EGT, TH], or with 'we' (teachers of truth) in 4:6 [Brd, TNTC], or with both 'you' and 'we' [WBC].

QUESTION—What is meant by κόσμου 'world'?

It is a metonymy for the customs, culture, and philosophy of unregenerated mankind, who live in the world [Brd, Lns, Ws] and who are hostile to the concepts from God [WBC]. It is the sinful principle found in sinful mankind [NIC]. It is all that is ruled by the devil [Alf, Brd, EBC, HNTC, Lns, My, NTC].

QUESTION—What relationship is indicated by διὰ τοῦτο 'because of this'?

It indicates that this clause is the result of the previous clause [AB, Brd, HNTC, Lns, TH, WBC; all versions]: they are from the world, therefore they speak from the world. This principle is stated in John 3:31 [AB].

QUESTION—What relationship is indicated by ἐκ 'from'?

It indicates that the source of their ideas comes from the viewpoint of the culture and philosophy of the world around them [Alf, Br, Brd, EBC, ICC, Lns, NIC, NTC, WBC, Ws; NIV, REB]. Therefore they speak as the world would have them speak [HNTC, NIC; NAB, NJB].

and the world listens-to[a] them.

LEXICON—a. pres. act. indic. of ἀκούω (LN 31.56): 'to listen to' [AB, HNTC, LN; all versions except KJV], 'to pay attention to' [WBC], 'to hear' [Lns; KJV]. The present tense indicates that it is customary for them to listen in this way [Brd].

QUESTION—What is meant by κόσμος 'world' used here?

Here the metonymy is for the unbelieving people who live in the world [EBC, HNTC, NIC, TH].

QUESTION—What is implied by ἀκούει 'listens'?

It means that the listeners accept what they teach [AB, Brd, Lns, My, TH, WBC].

4:6 We are from[a] God;

LEXICON—a. ἐκ with genitive object (LN 89.3) (BAGD 3.a. p. 234): 'from' [BAGD, Lns; NASB, NIV, NJB], 'of' [KJV, NRSV]. This preposition is also translated 'to belong to' [AB, HNTC; NAB, REB, TEV, TNT], 'to be begotten by' [BAGD], 'to be derived from' [WBC]. See this word at 4:1, 4.

QUESTION—What is the significance of the use of the overt pronoun ἡμεῖς 'we' occurring first in the clause?

The pronoun 'we' is made emphatic and is contrasted with αὐτοί 'they' in 4:5 [Brd, Lns, NIC, WBC].

QUESTION—To whom does ἡμεῖς 'we' refer?

1. It is 'we inclusive' and includes the author and the readers [AB, EBC, Herm, Lns, NIC, TH, WBC]. This refers to the same people as 'we' in the last part of the verse [AB]. All believers are called upon to proclaim Jesus [WBC].
2. It is 'we exclusive' and refers to the Apostles and other true teachers, but not the readers [Alf, Brd, HNTC, ICC, My, NCBC, NTC, TNTC, Ws]. He is contrasting one set of teachers with another set [Alf, Br].

the-(one) knowing[a] God listens-to[b] us, (the one) who is not from God (does) not listen-to us.

LEXICON—a. pres. act. participle of γινώσκω: 'to know'. See this word at 2:3b, 4, 13, 14; 3:1, 6.

b. pres. act. indic. of ἀκούω: 'to listen to'. See this word at 4:5. The present tense indicates that the action of acquiring knowledge is in focus [NTC], or that the relationship with God indicated by the 'knowing' continues on [WBC].

By[a] this we-know[b] the spirit[c] of-truth[d] and the spirit[c] of-error.[e]

LEXICON—a. ἐκ with genitive object (LN 89.77) (BAGD 3.g.β. p. 235): 'by' [LN; NASB, NRSV, TNT], 'from' [Lns]. The phrase ἐκ τούτου 'by this' is translated 'hereby' [KJV], 'this is how' [AB, HNTC, WBC; NIV, NJB, TEV], 'that is how' [REB], 'thus' [NAB].

b. pres. act. indic. of γινώσκω (LN 28.1): 'to know'. See this word at 4:2.

c. πνεῦμα: 'spirit'. See this word at 4:1.

d. ἀλήθεια (LN 72.2) (BAGD 2.b. p. 36): 'truth' [AB, BAGD, HNTC, LN, WBC; all versions], 'plain and open evidence' [Lns].

e. πλάνη (LN **31.8**) (BAGD p. 666): 'error' [BAGD, HNTC; all versions except NAB, NIV, NJB], 'deceit' [AB, Lns], 'deception' [LN; NAB], 'falsehood' [WBC; NIV, NJB].

QUESTION—What relationship is indicated by ἐκ 'by'?

It indicates the source of their knowledge [BAGD, Lns, TH, WBC, Ws; NIV, TNT] or the means by which they can know [Brd, NTC].

QUESTION—To what does the pronoun τούτου 'this' refer?

It refers back to the positive and negative tests of listening [AB, Alf Brd, EGT, Herm, ICC, Lns, My, NIC, NTC, TH, WBC, Ws]: from the way one listens, we can recognize the kind of spirit.

QUESTION—Who is the implied subject of the verb γινώσκομεν 'we know'?

It is 'we inclusive' and refers to the readers as well as the writer [Alf, ICC, WBC, Ws].

QUESTION—To whom does 'the spirit of truth' refer and how are the nouns related in this genitive construction?
1. This refers to the Holy Spirit [AB, Alf, Br, EBC, ICC, My, NIC, NTC, TH, TNTC, Ws; NIV, TEV]. The phrase means the Spirit whose essential quality is truth [AB, ICC, My, TH] or the Spirit who teaches truth [Alf] or the Spirit who inspires people to say what is true [TH].
2. This refers to the human spirit [Lns, WBC]. The phrase means a person who speaks the truth [Lns, WBC], a person who belongs to the truth [Lns]. It means a person who is inspired, either by the Holy Spirit or by the antichrist [WBC].

QUESTION—To whom does 'the spirit of error' refer and how are the nouns related in this genitive construction?
1. This refers to Satan [AB, ICC] or a spirit from Satan [Alf, Br, My, TH]. The phrase means a spirit who is characterized by falsehood [ICC], who leads people astray [Br, ICC], who teaches lies and deceives people [Alf], and seduces people to error [My].
2. This refers to human spirits [Lns, WBC]. The phrase means people who deceive [Lns]. The 'spirit of falsehood' and 'false prophets' mean the same thing [WBC].

DISCOURSE UNIT: 4:7–5:21 [Ws]. The topic is the victory of faith.

DISCOURSE UNIT: 4:7–5:13 [NAB, NJB]. The topic is God's love and ours [NAB], the sources of love and faith [NJB].

DISCOURSE UNIT: 4:7–5:12 [Brd, EBC, ICC]. The topic is the ethical and Christological aspects of Christian life [Brd], the requirements for fellowship with God [EBC].

DISCOURSE UNIT: 4:7–5:5 [Brd, TNTC]. The topic is the ethical test of love [Brd, TNTC].

DISCOURSE UNIT: 4:7–5:4 [TH, WBC; NJB]. The topic is the mutual love of God's children [TH, WBC; NJB].

DISCOURSE UNIT: 4:7–5:4a [AB]. The topic is loving one another as a way of abiding in and loving God.

DISCOURSE UNIT: 4:7–5:3 [Lns]. The topic is love.

DISCOURSE UNIT: 4:7–21 [Alf, Br, EGT, HNTC, ICC, NCBC, Ws; NASB, NIV, TEV]. The topic is walking in love [Br], the blessedness of love [EGT], the meaning of love [HNTC], God's being love [Ws; NASB, TEV], God's love and ours [NIV], brotherly love [Alf], living in love [Br].

DISCOURSE UNIT: 4:7–16 [Brd]. The topic is the source of love.

DISCOURSE UNIT: 4:7–12 [Br, EBC, Herm, ICC, NIC, NTC, TNTC]. The topic is the praise of love [Br], loving each other [NCBC, NIC], brotherly love

[EBC, Herm, NTC], God's love and ours [NIC], love based on the revelation of love [ICC], the test of love [TNTC].

4:7 Beloved,[a] let-us-love/we-love[b] one-another,

LEXICON—a. ἀγαπητός: 'beloved'. See this word at 3:2, 21; 4:1, 11.
    b. pres. act. subj./indic. of ἀγαπάω: 'to love'. See this word at 2:10; 3:10, 11, 14, 18, 23. The present tense indicates that Christians should continue to love others [AB, Brd, Lns, TH, WBC].

QUESTION—What is the mood of the verb?
1. It is in the subjunctive mood and is a commandment [AB, Alf, EBC, EGT, Herm, HNTC, Lns, NIC, NTC, TH, TNTC, WBC, Ws; all versions]: let us love one another because love is from God.
2. It is in the indicative mood and is a statement [Brd]: we love one another because love is from God. Love is a characteristic of the believer because, being a child of God, he has received this quality from God [Brd].

QUESTION—To whom does ἀλλήλους 'one another' refer?
    It refers to fellow Christians [AB, Brd, Lns, My, NCBC, Ws].

because[a] the love[b] is from[c] God,

LEXICON—a. ὅτι (LN 89.33): 'because' [HNTC, LN, Lns; NAB, REB, TEV], 'for' [WBC; KJV, NASB, NIV, NRSV, TNT], 'since' [AB; NJB].
    b. ἀγάπη: 'love'. See this word at 2:5, 15; 3:1, 16, 17.
    c. ἐκ (LN 90.16): 'from' [AB, HNTC, LN, Lns, WBC; NASB, NIV, NJB, TEV, TNT], 'of' [KJV, NAB, NRSV], 'the source of' [REB].

QUESTION—What relationship is indicated by ὅτι 'because'?
1. It indicates the grounds for the exhortation to love one another [Alf, Brd, HNTC, Lns, My, NIC, NTC, TNTC, WBC, Ws]: we should love one another because love is from God.
2. It indicates the reason believers love one another [Brd]: we love one another because God gives us such love.

QUESTION—What is the significance of the use of the article before ἀγάπη 'love'?
1. It refers to the previously mentioned love, the love for one another [Brd, Herm, Lns, NCBC]: let us love one another because such love is from God.
2. It indicates that love in the abstract is being spoken of rather than a relationship between particular individuals [Alf].

QUESTION—What relationship is indicated by the use of the preposition ἐκ 'from'?
    It indicates the source of the love [AB, Alf, Br, EBC, Herm, ICC, NIC, NTC, TH, TNTC, WBC, Ws; NIV, TEV, TNT]: God causes/enables us to love one another. It also belongs to the divine sphere [NIC].

and everyone loving[a] has-been-begotten[b] by[c] God and knows[d] God.

LEXICON—a. pres. act. participle of ἀγαπάω: 'to love'. The present tense indicates that this is a continuing action [Brd].

b. perf. pass. indic. of γεννάω: 'to be begotten'. See this word at 2:29; 3:9. The perfect tense indicates that the begetting was in the past and the consequences remain [AB], and the person is now a member of God's family [Brd].
c. ἐκ with genitive object: 'by'. See this word at 2:29; 3:9.
d. pres. act. indic. of γινώσκω: 'to know'. See this word at 4:6. The present tense indicates that this is a continuing action [Alf, WBC, Ws].

QUESTION—What relationship is indicated by the beginning καί 'and'?

It is not a part of the grounds for the exhortation [AB, Brd, TH, WBC; KJV, NAB, NASB, NIV, NRSV, REB, TEV]. It is an inference from the preceding clause [My, NIC, TNTC]: love is from God, therefore he who loves must have been begotten by God and knows God.

QUESTION—Who is being loved?
1. The implied objects are fellow Christians [EBC, ICC, Lns, My, NCBC, NTC]: everyone loving his brother has been begotten by God.
2. The implied objects are all fellow humans [Herm]: everyone loving his neighbor has been begotten by God.
3. The referent is not in focus [AB, Alf, Brd, WBC] because the emphasis is on the event of loving, not on the object [AB, Brd]: everyone loving has been begotten by God.
4. The implied objects are both God and others [TH]: everyone loving God and his brother has been begotten by God.

QUESTION—What is the relationship between ἀγαπῶν 'loving' and ἐκ τοῦ θεοῦ γεγέννηται 'begotten from God'?

Being 'begotten of God' causes 'the loving of one another' [AB, Brd, ICC, My, NIC, WBC], so that love then becomes the proof of being born of God and knowing God [Br, Brd, EBC, Herm, HNTC, ICC, Lns, NTC, TNTC, Ws].

QUESTION—What relationship is indicated by καί 'and' (knows God)?
1. Love is the sign of both being begotten by God and of knowing God [HNTC, ICC, Lns, NTC].
2. Love leads to a knowledge of God [AB] or by practicing love, they get to know God more and more [EGT].

4:8 The-(one) not loving[a] (has) not known[b] God,

LEXICON—a. pres. act. participle of ἀγαπάω: 'to love'. See this word at 4:7. The phrase 'to not love' is translated 'to be unloving' [WBC; REB], 'to fail to love' [NJB]. The present tense indicates a pattern of life [Brd].
b. aorist act. indic. of γινώσκω: 'to know'. See this word at 4:6, 7.

QUESTION—How is this verse related to its context?

This argument follows from the preceding verse [My] and is the negative counterpart of it [AB, Alf, Brd, EBC, EGT, ICC, TH]. The thought of 4:7 is emphasized by stating its reverse [Brd, NIC, WBC].

because^a God is love.^b

LEXICON—a. ὅτι (LN 89.33): 'because' [HNTC, LN, Lns; NIV, NJB], 'for' [AB, WBC; all versions except NIV, NJB].

b. ἀγάπη: 'love'. See this word at 4:7.

QUESTION—What relationship is indicated by ὅτι 'because'?

It indicates the grounds for saying that the one who does not love has never known God [Alf, Brd, Lns, My]. The argument is that knowing God leads people to love one another, since God is love [NIC].

QUESTION—What is meant by saying that God 'is love'?

It means that all of God's activity is loving activity [AB, EBC, NIC, TH, TNTC, WBC]. Love is an essence of God, not just an attribute [Alf, ICC]. It is his essential quality [Brd] and nature [My]. The use of ἀγάπη 'love' without an article indicates a nonsymmetrical relationship, that is, that the relationship between God and love is not equational and is not reversible so as to say 'love is God' [AB, Alf, Br, Brd, EBC, EGT, Herm, NIC, NTC, TH, WBC].

4:9 By^a this the love^b of-God was-shown^c for/in/among^d us,

LEXICON—a. ἐν with dative object: 'by'. See this word at 2:3, 5; 3:10, 16, 19; 4:2.

b. ἀγάπη: 'love'. See this word at 4:7, 8.

c. aorist pass. indic. of φανερόω (LN 28.36) (BAGD 1.b. p. 852): 'to be shown' [NIV, REB, TEV], 'to be revealed' [AB, BAGD, HNTC, LN, WBC; NAB, TNT], 'to be made known' [BAGD, LN], 'to be made manifest' [Lns; KJV, NRSV], 'to be manifested' [NASB]. This verb is also translated as a noun: 'the revelation' [NJB]. The aorist tense indicates that there was a particular act of showing (the incarnation) [Brd, ICC, Lns, WBC]. See this word at 2:19; 3:2.

d. ἐν with dative object (LN 90.56; 83.9): 'for' [NJB, TEV], 'towards' [KJV], 'in' [AB; NASB], 'within' [TNT], 'among' [WBC; NIV, NRSV, REB], 'in the midst of' [NAB], 'in connection with' [Lns], 'to' [HNTC].

QUESTION—What does τούτῳ 'this' refer to?

It refers to the following ὅτι 'that' clause [AB, Alf, Brd, Herm, ICC, Lns, My, NCBC, TH, TNTC, WBC, Ws]: the love of God was shown in us by means of this, namely, by God sending his only Son into the world.

QUESTION—How are the two nouns related in the genitive construction ἡ ἀγάπη τοῦ θεοῦ 'the love of God'?

It means God's love for us [AB, Brd, HNTC, NIC, TH, TNTC, WBC, Ws].

QUESTION—What relationship is indicated by ἐν 'for/in/among'?

1. It is to be taken with the noun 'love' and indicates the object of God's love [My, TH; KJV, NJB, TEV]: by this God's love for us was shown. This is the evident meaning of the preposition in 4:16 [TH].

2. It is to be taken with the verb 'was shown' and indicates the external location of this action [Brd, TNTC, WBC; NAB, NIV, NRSV, REB]: by this God's love was shown among us. In this case, it was shown as an

historical manifestation among us [Brd], by the Son appearing in the world [AB]. God's love was shown in the church and also in the world by the Son's incarnation [WBC].
3. It is to be taken with the verb 'was shown' and indicates the internal location of the action [AB, EGT, ICC; NASB, TNT]: by this God's love was shown within us. Not only was God's love shown in the incarnation, it was also shown in the effects of it indwelling believers [AB]. It was shown in those who have the life God sent his Son to give us [ICC].
4. It is to be taken with the verb 'was shown' and indicates the medium in which God's love was shown [Alf, Lns, Ws]: by this God's love was shown in connection with us. The manifestation involved us as the recipients of God's love [Lns]. God showed it in our persons and our cases [Alf].
5. It is to be taken with the verb 'was shown' and indicates to whom it was shown [HNTC]: by this God's love was shown to us.

QUESTION—Who is the implied actor of the passive verb ἐφανερώθη 'was shown'?

God is the actor [Lns, TH]: God showed his love in/for us.

that God has-sent[a] his only[b] Son into[c] the world[d]

LEXICON—a. perf. act. indic. of ἀποστέλλω (LN 15.66): 'to send' [AB, HNTC, LN, Lns, WBC; all versions]. The perfect tense indicates that this happened in the past and its results remain with us into the present [Alf, Brd, EGT, Lns, TH, WBC, Ws]. Another interpretation is that it means the same as the aorist tense in 4:10 and refers only to the act of sending [AB]. It means 'to send on a mission' [Brd, Lns, NCBC, NTC, TH, WBC, Ws].
  b. μονογενής (LN **58.52**) (BAGD p. 527): 'only' [AB, BAGD, HNTC, LN, WBC; all versions except KJV, NASB, NIV], 'one and only' [NIV], 'unique' [BAGD, LN], 'only begotten' [Lns; KJV, NASB].
  c. εἰς with accusative object (LN 84.22): 'into' [AB, HNTC, LN, Lns, WBC; all versions except NAB], 'to' [NAB].
  d. κόσμος (LN 1.39) (BAGD 4.c. p. 446): 'world' [AB, BAGD, HNTC, LN, Lns, WBC; all versions], 'earth' [BAGD, LN].

QUESTION—What relationship is indicated by ὅτι 'that'?

It indicates the content of 'this' [BAGD, Brd, Lns, WBC, Ws; all versions except KJV].

QUESTION—What is meant by μονογενῆ 'only'?

It means 'one of a kind', 'unique', 'only' [AB, BAGD, Br, Brd, EBC, Herm, ICC, My, NCBC, NIC, NTC, TH, TNTC, WBC; all versions except KJV, NASB]. It includes the idea of 'beloved' [AB, Br, Brd, EBC, EGT, Herm, TNTC, WBC].

QUESTION—What is meant by κόσμον 'world'?

It means the earth, the place where he was sent, the place where mankind lives [AB, BAGD, Brd, WBC].

in-order-that[a] **we-might-live**[b] **through**[c] **him.**

LEXICON—a. ἵνα (LN 89.59): 'in order that' [HNTC], 'so that' [AB, LN, WBC; NASB, NRSV, TEV], 'that' [Lns; all versions except NASB, NRSV, TEV].
  b. aorist act. subj. of ζάω (LN 23.88) (BAGD 2.b.β. p. 336): 'to live' [BAGD, HNTC, LN, Lns, WBC; KJV, NASB, NIV, NRSV, TNT], 'to have life' [AB; NAB, NJB, REB, TEV].
  c. διά with genitive object (LN 90.4): 'through' [AB, HNTC, LN, Lns, WBC; all versions].

QUESTION—What relationship is indicated by ἵνα 'in order that'?
  1. It indicates the purpose for which God sent his Son [Br, Brd, EBC, HNTC, ICC, Lns, My, NTC, TH, WBC, Ws]: God sent his only Son in order that we might live through him.
  2. It indicates the result of sending his Son [AB]: God sent his only Son, therefore we can live through him. The purpose was to save the world and that everyone who believes might have life. As a result, 'we' are selected from the world to have this life [AB].

QUESTION—What is meant by ζήσωμεν 'we might live'?
  It refers to eternal life [EGT, NTC, TH] and means the living out of salvation in the individual [WBC, Ws].

QUESTION—What relationship is indicated by διά 'through'?
  It indicates the intermediate agent [AB, Brd, Herm, HNTC, Lns, TH, WBC, Ws; all versions]. He is the channel for giving eternal life [Lns]. Being the intermediary, he is the direct cause of life, the ultimate cause being God [TH, Ws]. Through his life, death, and exaltation we have life [WBC].

4:10 In[a] this is the love,[b] not that we have-loved[c] God, but[d] that he loved[e] us

TEXT—Instead of ἠγαπήκαμεν 'we have loved (perfect tense)', some manuscripts have ἠγαπήσαμεν 'we loved (aorist tense)'. GNT selects the perfect tense and does not mention the other reading. The aorist tense is translated by Alf, My, KJV, NASB, NIV, NJB, NRSV, and TNT.

LEXICON—a. ἐν with dative object (LN 89.141): 'in' [AB, Lns; NAB, NASB, NJB, NRSV, TNT], 'herein' [KJV], not explicit [HNTC, WBC; NIV, REB, TEV].
  b. ἀγάπη: 'love'. See this word at 4:7, 8, 9.
  c. perf. act. indic. of ἀγαπάω: 'to love'. See this word at 4:7, 8.
  d. ἀλλά (LN 89.125): 'but' [AB, HNTC, LN, Lns, WBC; all versions].
  e. aorist act. indic. of ἀγαπάω: 'to love'. The aorist tense indicates that the loving is considered as a single act [AB, Alf, Brd, My, TH, WBC, Ws] which is then specified to be the sending of his Son [AB, Alf, Brd].

QUESTION—How is this verse related to its context?
  It is a further development of the idea that God is the only source of love [TH, WBC, Ws]. God acts in love toward us without our having done anything [TNTC]. Our love is merely a response to his love [TNTC, Ws],

contrary to what the false teachers may have taught [NCBC, NIC, WBC]. It explains 'through him' (4:9) [Herm].

QUESTION—To what does the pronoun τούτῳ 'this' refer?

It refers to the following ὅτι 'that' clause [AB, Alf, Brd, EBC, Herm, ICC, TH, WBC, Ws]: love is this, namely, that God loved us.

QUESTION—What is the significance of the use of the article before ἀγάπη 'love'?

It indicates that love is being spoken of in the abstract and no reference is implied for either agent or subject [Alf, Brd, Lns, My, Ws].

QUESTION—What is meant by saying that love is 'in this'?

It means that love consists in this demonstration [AB, Brd, TNTC; NAB, NJB], or 'this is what love is' [Brd, TH; REB, TEV]. God's love defines what true love is [EBC, WBC].

and^a sent^b his Son (as) an-expiation/propitiation^c for^d our sins.^{e}

LEXICON—a. καί (LN 89.93): 'and' [AB, HNTC, Lns, WBC; all versions].
- b. aorist act. indic. of ἀποστέλλω (LN 15.66) (BAGD 1.b.γ. p. 98): 'to send' [AB, BAGD, HNTC, LN, Lns, WBC; all versions]. The aorist tense points to a past historical fact [EGT, My, NIC]. See this word at 4:9.
- c. ἱλασμός (LN 40.12) (BAGD 1., 2. p. 375): 'expiation' [BAGD, LN, Lns; NRSV], 'propitiation' [KJV, NASB], 'atonement' [AB], 'atoning sacrifice' [WBC; NIV], 'the means of forgiving' [TEV], 'the means of taking away' [TNT], 'sacrifice to atone' [REB], 'sacrificial offering' [HNTC], 'offering' [NAB], 'sin offering' [BAGD]. See this word at 2:2.
- d. περί with genitive object: 'for'. See this word at 2:2.
- e. ἁμαρτία (LN 88.289; 88.310): 'sin'. See this word at 1:8; 2:12. The plural form indicates that specific acts of sins by individuals are in focus [WBC]. See this word at 2:2.

QUESTION—What is meant by ἱλασμός 'expiation/propitiation'?

1. It means 'expiation' and refers to the effect that Christ's atonement had on removing sin [AB, BAGD, Herm, Lns, NCBC, TH; NJB, NRSV, TEV, TNT].
2. It means 'propitiation' and refers to the effect that Christ's atonement had on the anger of God, fulfilling the requirements of his justice [Alf, Br, Brd, NIC, Ws; KJV, NASB].

4:11 Beloved,^{a} if^b God so^c loved^d us,

LEXICON—a. ἀγαπητός: 'beloved'. See this word at 2:7; 3:2, 21; 4:1, 7.
- b. εἰ (LN 89.30) (BAGD III. p. 219): 'if' [AB, HNTC, Lns, WBC; all versions except NIV], 'since' [BAGD, LN; NIV].
- c. οὕτως (LN 78.4) (BAGD 3. p. 598): 'so' [AB, HNTC, LN; all versions except REB, TEV, TNT], 'so intensely' [BAGD], 'so much' [LN], 'how' [TEV], 'thus' [Lns; REB], 'in this way' [WBC; TNT].
- d. aorist act. indic. of ἀγαπάω: 'to love'. See this word at 4:7, 8, 10. The aorist tense points to the historical event that demonstrated God's love, the life and death of Christ [NTC].

QUESTION—How is this verse related to its context?
 The theme of 3:16, 4:7 and 4:10 is repeated here [Herm, Lns, My, NTC, WBC]. What was commanded in 4:7 is now repeated after the grounds for it have been given in 4:8–10 [Herm, My].
QUESTION—What relationship is indicated by εἰ 'if'?
 It indicates the grounds for the following exhortation [AB, Alf, BAGD, Brd, Lns, NCBC, TH, WBC; NIV]: since God loved us, we ought to love one another. The particle εἰ 'if' with the indicative assumes the reality of the assumption [AB, Alf, Brd, Lns].
QUESTION—What relationship is indicated by οὕτως 'so'?
 1. It indicates the manner in which God loved us [ICC, Lns, NIC, TH, TNTC, WBC; REB, TEV, TNT]: if God loved us like that. The way he showed us his love was by sending his Son to die for us [ICC]. It means in like manner and like degree of sacrifice [TNTC].
 2. It indicates the extent of God's love [Brd, NTC]: if God loved us so much. God loved us to the extent that he sent his Son to die for us [NTC].

we also[a] ought[b] to love[c] one-another.
LEXICON—a. καί (LN 89.93): 'also' [LN, WBC; all versions except NAB, NJB, TEV], 'too' [HNTC, Lns; NJB], 'in turn' [AB], not explicit [NAB, TEV].
 b. pres. act. indic. of ὀφείλω: 'ought'. See this word at 2:6; 3:16. The present tense indicates that the obligation of loving is continuing [Brd].
 c. pres. act. infin. of ἀγαπάω: 'to love'. See this word at 4:7, 8, 10. The present tense indicates that the action of loving is continuous [Brd].
QUESTION—What relationship is indicated by καὶ ἡμεῖς 'we also'?
 The pronoun is emphatic, comparing what we should do with what God has done [AB, Alf, Brd]: God loves us: we also ought to love one another.
QUESTION—On what grounds does the author say we ought to love one another?
 It is a moral obligation [Brd, NTC, WBC], and inward constraint [Br, EBC]. God's children must be loving because God is loving [Br, EBC, EGT, My]. Those who experience love should show love [NIC, NTC, Ws]. Our love for God will cause us to be like him and love those whom he loves [Alf].

4:12 God no-one ever[a] has-seen.[b]
LEXICON—a. πώποτε (LN 67.9) (BAGD p. 732): 'ever' [AB, BAGD, HNTC, LN, Lns, WBC; all versions except KJV, NASB, REB], 'at any time' [LN; KJV, NASB]. With 'no one' translated as 'anyone', it is translated 'never' [REB].
 b. perf. mid. (deponent = act.) indic. of θεάομαι (LN 24.14) (BAGD 1.a. p. 353): 'to see' [AB, BAGD, HNTC, WBC; all versions except NASB], 'to look at' [BAGD, LN], 'to behold' [BAGD, Lns; NASB].
QUESTION—How is this clause related to the context?
 This explains why the statement in 4:11 is that we are to love *others* instead of saying that we are to love God [Alf, HNTC, NTC, WBC]. It tells how

God can be perceived, not by physical eyes, but by the evidence of his indwelling when we love others [Br, Brd, EBC, EGT, Herm, ICC, My, NIC, TH, TNTC, WBC, Ws].

QUESTION—What is the significance of θεόν 'God' occurring without an article?
1. It indicates God in his essence and deity [Brd, ICC, NCBC, TNTC, WBC, Ws].
2. It has no significance for the meaning but is left out for stylistic reasons [AB].

If[a] we-love[b] one-another, God remains[c] in[d] us

LEXICON—a. ἐάν (LN 89.67): 'if' [AB, HNTC, Lns, WBC; all versions except NJB], 'as long as' [NJB].
  b. pres. act. subj. of ἀγαπάω: 'to love'. See this word at 4:7, 8, 10, 11. The present tense indicates that this is a continuing action [Brd, Lns].
  c. pres. act. indic. of μένω: 'to remain'. See this word at 2:6, 27, 28; 3:6, 24. The present tense indicates that this is a continuing action [Brd].
  d. ἐν with dative object: 'in'. See this word at 2:6, 27, 28; 3:6, 24.

QUESTION—What relationship is indicated by ἐάν 'if'?
It indicates the condition for knowing that God remains in us [AB, Brd, TNTC, WBC]. It makes no presupposition as to whether or not they are loving [AB]. The fact of their love for others is not the condition for God's remaining in them; it is the evidence that he does [Brd, WBC].

and love[a] of him has-been-perfected[b] in[c] us.

LEXICON—a. ἀγάπη: 'love'. See this word at 4:7, 8, 9, 10.
  b. perf. pass. participle of τελειόω (LN 88.38) (BAGD 2.e.β. p. 810): 'to be perfected' [BAGD, HNTC, LN; KJV, NASB, NRSV], 'to come to perfection' [NJB], 'to be made perfect' [LN; TEV, TNT], 'to reach perfection' [AB], 'to be brought to perfection' [NAB, REB], 'to be brought to its goal' [Lns], 'to be brought to completion' [WBC], 'to be made complete' [NIV]. See this word at 2:5.
  c. ἐν with dative object (LN 83.13): 'in' [AB, HNTC, Lns, WBC; all versions except REB], 'within' [REB].

QUESTION—How are the event noun and the personal pronoun related in the genitive construction ἡ ἀγάπη αὐτοῦ 'the love of him' and what is meant by τετελειωμένη 'to have been perfected'?
1. It means that God loves us [EBC, Herm, ICC, Lns, NIC, NTC, TH, TNTC]: God's love for us has been perfected. When we love others, God's love for us has reached its goal [Herm, Lns], it has reached its full effect of creating the same kind of love he has [NIC, TNTC]. Another view is that God's love for us is most fully accomplished in his condescending to dwell in us [ICC].
2. It means the love that God has produced in us [AB, Br, Brd, My, Ws]: our love for others that God has produced in us has been perfected. That love

reaches perfection when we love others [AB], both people and God [Br]. That love is in us in its completed form [Ws].
3. It means our love for God [Alf, BAGD, HNTC], our love for God has been perfected. Loving each other is the way of expressing our love for God [HNTC]. Our love for God has reached full maturity [Alf].
4. It means the love we have for others, the kind of love that God has [NCBC]: our God-like love for others has been perfected.

DISCOURSE UNIT: 4:13–5:4 [NIC]. The topic is assurance and Christian love.

DISCOURSE UNIT: 4:13–21 [Br, TNTC]. The topic is perfect love and sound doctrine [Br, TNTC].

DISCOURSE UNIT: 4:13–16 [EBC, Herm, ICC]. The topic is living in God and in love [EBC], faith in God's salvation [Herm, NCBC].

4:13 By^a this we-know^b that we-remain^c in him and he in us,
LEXICON—a. ἐν with dative object: 'by'. See this word at 2:3, 5; 3:10, 16, 19; 4:2, 9.
  b. pres. act. indic. of γινώσκω: 'to know'. See this word at 2:3a, 5, 18, 29; 3:16, 19, 24; 4:2, 6, 8.
  c. pres. act. indic. of μένω: 'to remain'. See this word at 4:12. The present tense indicates that this is a continuing action [Brd, WBC].
QUESTION—How does this verse advance the author's theme?
  It gives grounds of reassurance that God would not have given us his Holy Spirit if he didn't have a vital relationship with us [EGT, ICC]. So even though God is invisible we can know that he abides in us by his Spirit [Alf]. In addition to the practical test of showing love, is this psychological test of receiving the Spirit [NIC].
QUESTION—To what does τούτῳ 'this' refer?
  1. It refers to the following ὅτι 'that' clause [AB, Brd, EBC, Lns, My, NIC, TNTC, WBC; NAB, NIV, NJB, REB, TEV, TNT]: we know that we remain in him because of this, namely, that he has given us his Spirit.
  2. It refers to the preceding clause [NTC, Ws]: because we love one another, we know that we remain in him and he remains in us.
QUESTION—To whom does αὐτῷ 'him' refer?
  It refers to God [AB, Alf, Brd, EBC, EGT, Lns, NTC, TNTC, WBC].

that/because^a he-has-given^b us from^c his Spirit.^d
LEXICON—a. ὅτι (LN 89.33) (BAGD 1.a. p. 588): 'that' [BAGD, Lns; NAB, NJB], 'in that' [AB], 'by the fact that' [HNTC], 'because' [WBC; all versions except NAB, NJB, REB], not explicit [REB].
  b. perf. act. indic. of δίδωμι (LN 57.71) (BAGD 1.b.β. p. 193): 'to give' [AB, BAGD, LN, Lns, WBC; all versions except REB], 'to impart' [HNTC; REB].

c. ἐκ with genitive object (LN 63.20) (BAGD 4.a.ε. p. 236): 'of' [AB; KJV, NAB, NASB, NIV, NRSV], 'from' [BAGD, Lns], 'a share of' [WBC; TNT], 'a share in' [NJB], 'a part of' [LN], not explicit [HNTC; REB, TEV].

d. πνεῦμα (LN 12.18) (BAGD 5.a. p. 676): 'spirit' [AB, HNTC, Lns, WBC; all versions], 'Spirit of God' [BAGD].

QUESTION—What relationship is indicated by ὅτι 'because'?

It explains the contents of 'this' [AB, BAGD, Brd, HNTC, Lns, NIC, TNTC]: we know that we remain in him because of this, namely, *that* he has given us his Spirit. Many translate the word as 'because' to indicate the grounds for knowing [Herm, ICC, WBC; all versions except NAB, NJB, REB]: we know that we remain in him because of this, namely, *because* he has given us his Spirit. There is little difference between the two ways of expressing this [AB].

QUESTION—What is the significance of the use of the perfect tense δέδωκεν 'he has given' here instead of aorist ἔδωκεν 'he gave' used in 3:24?

1. There is no significant difference. The perfect tense indicates that the action was completed in the past [AB, NIC, TH, WBC].
2. The perfect tense is in contrast with the aorist tense. It has in view the continuing possession of the Spirit after having received him [Brd].

QUESTION—What relationship is indicated by ἐκ 'from'?

1. It indicates that they have a share of the Spirit [AB, Alf, BAGD, Brd, My, NIC, WBC; NJB]: he has given us from his Spirit. The Spirit has been given to the church in fullness, each individual member having a share of that fullness [My, WBC]. All have the indwelling Spirit, but each according to the measure given him [Alf]. Only Christ had the Spirit without measure (John 3:34) [Alf, Brd].
2. It carries no special significance but is a stylistic variant of 3:24 'he gave us his spirit' [Br, EBC, TH; REB, TEV]: he has given us his Spirit.
3. It indicates that the Spirit is the source of the gift [Lns]: he has given us gifts from the Spirit. The gifts are those listed in the fruit of the Spirit (Gal. 5:22), especially love [Lns].

4:14 And[a] we have-seen[b] and we-testify[c] that the Father has-sent[d] the Son (as) savior[e] of-the world.[f]

LEXICON—a. καί (LN 89.93): 'and' [HNTC, Lns, WBC; KJV, NASB, NIV, NRSV, TEV], 'moreover' [REB], 'as for us' [AB], not explicit [NAB, NJB, TNT].

b. perf. mid. (deponent = act.) indic. of θεάομαι (LN 24.14) (BAGD 2. p. 353): 'to see' [AB, BAGD, HNTC, WBC; all versions except NASB], 'to observe' [LN], 'to behold' [BAGD, Lns; NASB]. The perfect tense indicates that they not only saw but still remember [Brd]. See this word at 1:1.

c. pres. act. indic. of μαρτυρέω (LN 33.262) (BAGD 1.a. p. 492): 'to testify' [AB, BAGD, HNTC, Lns; all versions except NASB, TEV, TNT],

'to bear witness' [BAGD, WBC; NASB, TNT], 'to witness' [LN], 'to tell others' [TEV]. The present tense indicates that the testifying is still going on [Brd, Lns, WBC, Ws].
d. perf. act. indic. of ἀποστέλλω: 'to send'. See this word at 4:9, 10. The perfect tense indicates that this happened in the past but still has its effect in the present saving of the world [Alf, TNTC, WBC].
e. σωτήρ (LN 21.31) (BAGD 2. p. 801): 'savior' [AB, BAGD, HNTC, Lns, WBC; all versions].
f. κόσμος: 'world'. See this word at 2:2. The noun phrase 'the whole world' is translated 'everyone' [TEV].

QUESTION—What relationship is indicated by the use of the initial conjunction καί 'and'?

It joins the following statement as an additional reason for knowing that we remain in him [Brd ICC, Lns, NIC, TNTC]: we know that we remain in him and he in us because he gave us the Holy Spirit and because we have seen and testify that the Father sent the Son into the world. Besides the internal witness of the Spirit, they have the external witness of those who saw the working out of God's love [Brd, ICC]. The emphatic 'and we' contrasts this statement with the statement in 4:12 that no one has seen God [AB, Herm, NCBC, WBC, Ws].

QUESTION—To whom does ἡμεῖς 'we' refer?
1. The pronoun ἡμεῖς 'we' is 'we exclusive' and speaks of the author and fellow eye-witnesses, the apostolic band, but not the readers [Alf, Brd, EGT, ICC, Lns, My, NTC, TNTC]. They have seen with their physical eyes Christ's life on earth [Lns, TNTC].
2. The pronoun ἡμεῖς 'we' is 'we inclusive' and refers to all true believers, including the readers [AB, Br, EBC, NIC, WBC, Ws]. They can 'perceive' [AB, Ws] by faith [EBC, Herm, HNTC, WBC] even though they did not physically see God sending his Son. They have contemplated the life of Jesus and they testify about the meaning of that life [WBC, Ws].

QUESTION—What is meant by σωτῆρα 'savior'?

It indicates one who delivers from harm [TH], spiritual death [Brd, TH], and sin [WBC]. Positively it means to bring spiritual life [TH, WBC].

QUESTION—How are the two nouns related in the genitive construction σωτῆρα τοῦ κόσμου 'savior of the world'?

It means the one who saves the people of the world [Alf, Brd, Herm, ICC, NTC, TH]. 'World' refers to all the people who live in the world [Alf, BAGD, Br, Brd, NCBC, NIC, NTC, TH], all being sinners and separated from God [TNTC, WBC]. Salvation is not limited in its sufficiency or availability, but unbelief prevents its application to individuals [Brd]. Those actually saved are those described in the following verse [NTC, WBC].

4:15 Whoever acknowledges[a] that Jesus is the Son of God, God remains[b] in[c] him and he in God.

LEXICON—a. aorist act. subj. of ὁμολογέω (LN 33.274): 'to acknowledge'. See this word at 4:2, 3.
- b. pres. act. indic. of μένω: 'to remain'. See this word at 4:12, 13.
- c. ἐν with dative object: 'in'. See this word at 4:12, 13.

QUESTION—What is meant by acknowledging that Jesus is the Son of God?

It is agreeing that God sent his Son as a Savior of the world (4:14) [Alf, EBC, Herm, NIC, WBC] and equating the Son of God with the historical Jesus [AB, Brd, EBC, ICC, Lns, NIC, NTC, TH]. The aorist tense refers to the specific confession made at the time of conversion [AB, Alf, Brd, EGT, TNTC, WBC].

4:16 And[a] we have-known[b] and have-believed[c] the love[d] which God has[e] for/in[f] us.

LEXICON—a. καί (LN 89.93): 'and' [Lns, WBC; KJV, NASB, NIV, TEV], 'so' [NRSV], 'thus' [REB], not explicit [AB, HNTC; NAB, NJB, TNT].
- b. perf. act. indic. of γινώσκω (LN 27.2): 'to know' [AB, Lns; KJV, NIV, NRSV, TEV, TNT], 'to come to know' [HNTC, WBC; NAB, NASB, REB], 'to learn' [LN], 'to recognize' [NJB]. The perfect tense indicates that they came to know this in the past, with the result that they now possess that knowledge [Brd, Herm, NIC, TH, WBC].
- c. perf. act. indic. of πιστεύω (LN 31.35) (BAGD 1.a.α. p. 660): 'to believe' [AB, HNTC, LN, Lns; KJV, NASB, NRSV, REB, TEV], 'to be convinced of' [BAGD; NAB], 'to trust' [WBC], 'to rely on' [NIV], 'to put our faith in' [NJB, TNT]. See this word at 4:1. The perfect tense refers to a past act of belief with a continuing confidence [Brd].
- d. ἀγάπη: 'love'. See this word at 4:7, 8, 9, 10, 12.
- e. pres. act. indic. of ἔχω (LN 90.65) (BAGD I.2.e.β. p. 332): 'to have' [AB, BAGD, HNTC, LN, Lns, WBC; all versions]. The present tense expresses the continuance of this love [TH].
- f. ἐν with dative object (LN 90.56): 'for' [HNTC, WBC; all versions except KJV], 'to' [KJV], 'in' [AB], 'in connection with' [Lns].

QUESTION—To whom does ἡμεῖς 'we' refer?
1. 'We' is inclusive and speaks of the whole Christian community [AB, Alf, Brd, EGT, Herm, Lns, My, NTC, WBC, Ws].
2. 'We' is exclusive, as it is in 4:15, and refers to the author and other eyewitnesses of Jesus' ministry [ICC].

QUESTION—What is the significance of the order in which ἐγνώκαμεν 'we have known' and πεπιστεύκαμεν 'we have believed' occur?
1. There is no significant difference of meaning [AB, ICC, Lns, NTC, Ws]. The knowing and the believing both occurred at the time of entering the Christian life and the word order is not significant [AB]. The inner realization is accompanied by a corresponding confidence [Lns].

Knowledge and growth of faith involve each other and as one occurs, so does the other [ICC, NTC, Ws].

2. Knowledge comes first because it precedes faith [Brd, EBC, EGT, My].

QUESTION—What relationship is indicated by ἐν 'for/in' in the phrase 'love for/in us'?

1. It means 'for' and indicates that we are the object of God's love [EBC, Herm, HNTC, ICC, My, NTC, WBC; all versions]: the love which God has for us.
2. It means 'in' and refers to the love from God in us towards others [Br, Brd, Ws]: the love which God has put in us for others.
3. It means 'in' and refers to a personal experience of God's love for us made real by the Spirit [NIC].

DISCOURSE UNIT: 4:16b–21 [ICC, Ws]. The topic is the activity of love [Ws], love and faith in relation to judgment [ICC].

4:16b **God is love,**[a]

LEXICON—a. ἀγάπη: 'love'. See this phrase at 4:8.

and the-(one) remaining[a] **in**[b] **the love remains**[c] **in God and God in him.**

LEXICON—a. pres. act. participle of μένω (LN 68.11): 'to remain' [Lns; NJB], 'to abide' [AB; NAB, NASB, NRSV], 'to dwell' [HNTC; KJV, REB], 'to live' [WBC; NIV, TEV, TNT]. The present tense indicates that this is a continuous state [Brd, TH].

b. ἐν with dative object (LN 89.119): 'in' [AB, HNTC, Lns, WBC; all versions except TEV], 'in union with' [LN; TEV].

c. pres. act. indic. of μένω: 'to remain'. See this word at 4:12, 13, 15.

QUESTION—What relationship is indicated by καί 'and' at the beginning of the clause?

It indicates the conclusion of the preceding grounds [AB, Brd, Lns, NIC, TNTC, Ws]: God is love; therefore, those who abide in love abide in God and he in them.

QUESTION—What does μένων ἐν τῇ ἀγάπῃ 'remaining in love' mean?

The love is active and continuing [WBC]. It is the basis for one's attitude and actions [Brd]. The article indicates the preceding love from God [Brd] and this probably affects how the object of this love is to be taken. It means love for God [Herm], love for others [My], love for both God and others [Alf, WBC].

DISCOURSE UNIT: 4:17–21 [TNTC]. The topic is perfect love.

DISCOURSE UNIT: 4:17–19 [Brd]. The topic is the fruit of love.

DISCOURSE UNIT: 4:17–18 [EBC, Herm]. The topic is the displacement of fear by love [EBC], confidence from love [Herm].

4:17 By[a] this love[b] has-been-perfected[c] with/among[d] us,

LEXICON—a. ἐν with dative object (LN 89.76): 'by' [NASB], 'in' [AB, Lns; NAB, NRSV], not explicit [HNTC; NJB, TEV, TNT]. The phrase ἐν τούτῳ 'by this' is translated 'this is how' [WBC; REB], 'in this way' [NIV], 'herein' [KJV]. See this word at 4:2, 9, 13.
   b. ἀγάπη: 'love'. See this word at 4:8, 9, 10, 12, 16.
   c. perf. pass. indic. of τελειόω (LN 88.38) (BAGD 2.e.β. p. 810): 'to be perfected' [BAGD, LN; NASB, NRSV], 'to be made perfect' [KJV, TEV, TNT], 'to become perfect' [BAGD], 'to come to its perfection' [NJB], 'to reach perfection' [AB; REB], 'to be brought to perfection' [NAB], 'to be completed' [WBC], 'to be made complete' [NIV] 'to be brought to its goal' [Lns]. This phase is translated 'this is the perfection of love' [HNTC]. See this word at 2:5; 4:12.
   d. μετά with genitive object (LN 83.9; 90.60): 'with' [AB, Lns; NASB, NRSV], 'in' [NJB, TEV, TNT], 'among' [HNTC, WBC; NIV, REB], not explicit [KJV, NAB].

QUESTION—To what does the pronoun τούτῳ 'this' refer?
   1. It refers to the following ἵνα 'that' clause [Alf, Br, Herm, HNTC, ICC, Lns, My, NCBC, TH, TNTC, WBC; TEV]: love has been perfected with us by this, namely, having confidence on the day of judgment.
   2. It refers to the following ὅτι 'that' clause [EGT]: love has been perfected with us by this, namely, our being like him in this world.
   3. It refers to the preceding clause [AB, Brd, NIC, NTC, Ws]: by remaining in God and he is us, love has been perfected with us.

QUESTION—Who are the participants of the event word 'love'?
   1. It means our love for others [Br, EBC, ICC, My, NCBC, NTC; KJV, NAB].
   2. It means love in the abstract [Alf, Brd] or mutual love between God and us [NIC, WBC].
   3. It means God's love for us [AB, Herm, Lns, TH].

QUESTION—What is meant by τετελείωται 'it has been perfected'?
   1. It means love has reached God's goal for it [Herm, Lns, NTC, WBC].
   2. It means love has reached its full maturity or has come to its full expression [Br, ICC, NIC, NTC, TH, TNTC].
   3. It means both reaching its goal and coming to its full development [Brd, NTC].

QUESTION—What relationship is indicated by μετά 'with/among'?
   1. It means 'in our case' or 'with regard to us' [Alf, Herm].
   2. It means 'with us' and is referring to God's cooperation with us in perfecting love [AB, Brd, Ws]. God's love has reached perfection with what we do [AB].
   3. It means 'among us' and is referring to God's work in our midst [NCBC, NTC].
   4. It is a literal translation from Hebrew and means 'in us' and refers to God's love in our lives [NCBC, TH, TNTC].

that/so-that[a] we-may-have confidence[b] on[c] the day of-judgment,[d]
LEXICON—a. ἵνα (LN 90.22; 89.33) (BAGD II.1.e. p. 378): 'that' [BAGD, Lns; KJV, NAB, NASB, NRSV], 'so that' [NIV, REB], 'in order that' [TEV], 'with the result that' [AB], 'so that' [NIV, REB], 'in order that' [TEV], 'to' [HNTC], 'when' [WBC; NJB], not explicit [TNT].
  b. παρρησία (LN 25.158) (BAGD 3.b. p. 631): 'confidence' [AB, BAGD, HNTC, WBC; all versions except KJV, NJB, TEV], 'boldness' [BAGD, LN, Lns; KJV], 'courage' [LN; TEV]. The phrase παρρησίαν ἔχωμεν ἐν 'to have confidence in' is translated 'to face fearlessly' [NJB]. See this word at 2:28; 3:21.
  c. ἐν with dative object (LN 67.33): 'on' [AB, WBC; NAB, NIV, REB, TEV, TNT], 'in' [HNTC; KJV, NASB], 'at the time of' [LN], 'for' [NRSV], 'in connection with' [Lns], not explicit [NJB].
  d. κρίσις (LN 30.110) (BAGD 1.a.α. p. 452): 'judgment' [AB, BAGD, HNTC, LN, Lns, WBC; all versions].
QUESTION—What relationship is indicated by ἵνα 'that/so that'?
  1. It explains the preceding τούτῳ 'this' [Alf, Br, Herm, HNTC, ICC, Lns, My, NCBC, TH, TNTC, WBC; NAB, NJB]: love has been perfected with us by this, namely, having confidence on the day of judgment.
  2. It indicates the result of love's being perfected [AB, My, NIC, TH, Ws]: love has been perfected with us, with the result that we can have confidence on the day of judgment.
  3. It gives the purpose for love's being perfected [Brd]: by remaining in God and he is us, love has been perfected with us, in order that we may have confidence on the day of judgment. There are other purposes, but this is singled out to show the value of love [Brd].
QUESTION—What is meant by having confidence on the day of judgment?
  The day of judgment is the final judgment at the end of the world [AB, Alf, Br, Brd, EBC, Herm, HNTC, ICC, My, NCBC, TH, TNTC, Ws]. The confidence is in knowing that the verdict will be in our favor [AB, Brd, Lns, NTC, TH, TNTC, WBC] and knowing that love has been made perfect [Alf].

because[a] as[b] that-one is also[c] are we in[d] this world.[e]
LEXICON—a. ὅτι (LN 89.33): 'because' [AB, HNTC, LN, Lns; all versions except NAB], 'since' [WBC], 'for' [NAB].
  b. καθώς (LN 64.14) (BAGD 1. p. 391): 'as' [KJV, NASB, NJB, NRSV, REB], 'even as' [HNTC, Lns, WBC], 'just as' [BAGD, LN], 'the same as' [TEV, TNT], 'just the same as' [AB], 'just like' [NAB], 'like' [NIV].
  c. καί (LN 89.93): 'also' [Lns], 'so' [KJV, NASB, NRSV], 'even' [NJB], not explicit [AB, HNTC, WBC; NAB, NIV, TEV, TNT].
  d. ἐν with dative object (LN 83.13): 'in' [AB, HNTC, Lns, WBC; all versions except NAB, TNT], 'relationship to' [NAB, TNT].
  e. κόσμος (LN 41.38) (BAGD 7. p. 446): 'world' [AB, BAGD, HNTC, LN, Lns, WBC; all versions]. It refers to the earth as a place of residence [AB, Brd, EBC, ICC, WBC].

QUESTION—What relationship is indicated by ὅτι 'because'?
  It indicates the reason we can have confidence [AB, Alf, Brd, HNTC, ICC, Lns, My, NIC, NTC, TH, TNTC, WBC, Ws; all versions except NAB]: we may have confidence because we are like that one.
QUESTION—To whom does ἐκεῖνος 'that one' refer?
  It refers to Christ [AB, Alf, Br, Brd, EGT, Herm, HNTC, ICC, Lns, My, NCBC, NIC, TH, TNTC, WBC, Ws; TEV, TNT].
QUESTION—In what way are we like Christ?
  As Christ dwells in God, so we dwell in God [AB, ICC], as Christ is related to God in love and fellowship, so we are related to God [NIC, TH], as Christ is the Son of God, so we are sons of God [TNTC], as Christ is righteous, so we are righteous [Alf], as Christ is loving, so we are loving [Brd, Lns, My, NCBC, NTC], as Christ was the expression of God on earth, so we should be the expression of Christ on earth [EGT, NIC, Ws], as Christ is confident, so we are confident [HNTC], as Christ is loved by God, so we are loved by God [Herm, WBC].
QUESTION—Who is in the world?
  We are 'on this earth' in contrast to Christ who is not on this earth at present [AB, Brd, HNTC, ICC, Lns, My, NCBC, NTC, TH, WBC, Ws]. Jesus is in the world unseen, and we are to make him visible in the world [EGT].

4:18 **Fear**[a] **is not in**[b] **love,**[c] **but**[d] **perfect**[e] **love drives**[f] **out**[g] **fear,**
LEXICON—a. φόβος (LN 25.251) (BAGD 2.a.β. p. 863): 'fear' [AB, BAGD, HNTC, LN, Lns, WBC; all versions].
  b. ἐν with dative object (LN 89.80): 'in' [HNTC, WBC; all versions except NAB], 'in connection with' [Lns]. The phrase 'is not in' is translated 'has no room for' [AB; NAB].
  c. ἀγάπη: 'love'. See this word at 4:8, 9, 10, 12, 16, 17.
  d. ἀλλά (LN 89.125): 'but' [all versions except NAB, REB, TEV], 'rather' [AB, WBC; NAB], 'on the contrary' [HNTC, Lns], 'indeed' [REB], not explicit [TEV].
  e. τέλειος (LN **73.6**) (BAGD 1.a.α. p. 809): 'perfect' [AB, BAGD, HNTC; all versions], 'complete' [BAGD, WBC], 'genuine' [LN], 'goal attaining' [Lns].
  f. pres. act. indic. of βάλλω (LN **13.45**) (BAGD 1.b. p. 130): 'to drive out' [AB, BAGD, LN, WBC; NIV, NJB, TEV, TNT], 'to cast' [KJV, NAB, NASB, NRSV], 'to throw' [Lns], 'to do away with' [LN], 'to cause to cease' [LN]. The phrase 'to drive out' is translated 'to banish' [HNTC; REB]. The present tense indicates that the driving out is a general rule and always true [Brd, EBC].
  g. ἔξω (LN 84.27) (BAGD 1.b. p. 279): 'out' [AB, BAGD, LN, Lns; all versions except REB], 'away' [LN, WBC]. For HNTC, REB see above.
QUESTION—How is this verse related to its context?
  This is the negative of the preceding verse [Brd] and speaks about the opposite of confidence, fear [Brd, EBC, EGT, HNTC, Lns, NCBC, Ws].

QUESTION—What is meant by φόβος 'fear'?

It refers to servile fear [Brd, TNTC, WBC, Ws] of a guilty person [Ws], concern for oneself [Brd, WBC] and apprehension of impending harm [Brd]. Punishment on the day of judgment is what is specifically feared [AB, Br, Brd, Lns, NCBC, NIC, NTC, TH, WBC] and being afraid of God as judge [TH].

QUESTION—Who loves and what is the relationship between ἀγάπη 'love' and φόβος 'fear'?

1. This refers to God's love for Christians [Br, Lns, NCBC, TH]. Knowing that God loves us [EBC, TH] and that Christ has paid the penalty for our sins [Br, Lns, NTC] makes it impossible for us to fear him [EBC, Lns, TH].
2. This refers to a mutual love between God and the Christian [NIC, TNTC, WBC]. Because we love, we do not fear and because we are loved, we have nothing to fear [NIC, WBC].
3. This is a general statement. 'Love' refers to the love of Christians for others [AB, Brd, Ws] and for God [AB]. 'Love' and 'fear' are mutually exclusive because love is other-centered; fear is self-centered [Brd, ICC].

QUESTION—What is meant by τελεία 'perfect'?

It refers to love that has been made complete, mature, fully developed [Brd, Herm, Lns, NCBC, NTC, TH, WBC, Ws]. It is real love [WBC]. This means the same as the verb forms in 4:17 [AB] and 2:15 [TH].

because[a] fear has[b] punishment,[c]

LEXICON—a. ὅτι (LN 89.33): 'because' [Lns; all versions except NAB, NRSV, TNT], 'for' [AB, HNTC, WBC; NRSV], 'and since' [NAB], not explicit [TNT].

b. pres. act. indic. of ἔχω (LN 90.51) (BAGD I.4. p. 333): 'to have' [KJV], 'to have to do with' [NAB, NIV, NRSV, REB, TEV], 'to imply' [NJB], 'to involve' [NASB], 'to be a part of' [TNT], 'to bring about' [BAGD, LN], 'to carry with it' [AB].

c. κόλασις (LN 38.2) (BAGD 2. p. 441): 'punishment' [AB, BAGD, Lns, WBC; all versions except KJV], 'torment' [HNTC; KJV].

QUESTION—What relationship is indicated by ὅτι 'because'?

1. It indicates the reason why perfect love casts out fear [Brd, Herm, My, NTC].
2. It introduces an expansion of the argument [TH].

QUESTION—What is meant by ὁ φόβος κόλασιν ἔχει 'fear has punishment'?

This is translated in a general way 'fear has to do with punishment' [WBC; NAB, NIV, NRSV, REB, TEV], 'fear involves punishment' [NASB], 'fear implies punishment' [NJB]. Some commentators explain that this can be taken in two ways: fear both anticipates final punishment and that fear is a punishment in itself [NIC, NTC, TH]. Some think that both meanings are involved [Alf, TNTC, WBC, Ws]. Fear in itself is a form of punishment [Brd, Herm, ICC] and this is translated 'fear is itself a part of punishment'

[TNT], 'fear has its own agony' [Herm]. Another approach is to take this to mean that fear, since it results from unbelief, is deserving of punishment [My].

and the-(one) fearing[a] has-not-been-perfected[b] in[c] love.

LEXICON—a. pres. pass. (deponent = act.) participle of φοβέω (LN 25.252): 'to fear' [HNTC, LN, Lns; KJV, NASB, NIV, NRSV], 'to be afraid' [AB, WBC; NAB, NJB, REB, TEV, TNT].
  b. perfect pass. indic. of τελειόω (LN 88.38) (BAGD 2.e.α. p. 810): 'to be perfected' [LN; NASB, NRSV], 'to be perfect' [NAB], 'to be made perfect' [BAGD, LN; KJV, NIV, TEV, TNT], 'to come to perfection' [NJB], 'to reach perfection' [AB, HNTC], 'to be brought to the goal' [Lns], 'to attain to in perfection' [REB]. The phrase οὐ τετελείωται 'to not be perfected' is translated 'to be incomplete' [WBC]. See this word at 4:17.
  c. ἐν with dative object (LN 89.5): 'in' [WBC; all versions except REB], 'in connection with' [Lns], 'of' [HNTC], not explicit [AB; REB].

QUESTION—How is love still not perfected in the one fearing?

The goal of love is to make the Christian confident [Lns, WBC]. So when he is fearful, he has not yet reached his goal [Herm, Lns, TH, WBC], and love has not fully matured [Br, Brd].

DISCOURSE UNIT: 4:19–5:4 [Herm]. The topic is brotherly love as the essence of the commandments.

DISCOURSE UNIT: 4:19–21 [EBC]. The topic is a summary of love.

4:19 **We love,[a] because[b] he first[c] loved[d] us.**

TEXT—Instead of ἀγαπῶμεν 'we love', some manuscripts have ἀγαπῶμεν αὐτόν 'we love him'. GNT selects ἀγαπῶμεν 'we love' with a B rating, indicating some degree of doubt. The reading ἀγαπῶμεν αὐτόν 'we love him' is selected only by KJV.

LEXICON—a. pres. act. indic. of ἀγαπάω: 'to love'. See this word at 4:7, 8, 10, 11, 12. The present tense indicates that love is a continuing action [Brd, Lns].
  b. ὅτι (LN 89.33): 'because' [AB, HNTC, Lns, WBC; all versions].
  c. πρῶτος (LN 60.46) (BAGD 1.a. p. 725): 'first' [AB, BAGD, HNTC, LN, WBC; all versions], 'as first one' [Lns].
  d. aorist act. indic. of ἀγαπάω (LN **25.43**) (BAGD 1.b.α. p. 4): 'to love' [AB, BAGD, HNTC, LN, Lns, WBC; all versions]. The aorist tense indicates that a single act of love is in focus [Brd]. That act of love was the sending his Son to earth [Alf] or the giving of his Son to die for us [Brd, Lns].

QUESTION—To whom does ἡμεῖς 'we' refer?

It is 'we inclusive' and means all Christians, as in 4:17 [ICC].

QUESTION—What is the significance of the order in which ἡμεῖς 'we' occurs?
It is made prominent by coming first in the sentence, thus pointing out the contrast with 'he' in the second clause [AB, Alf, Brd, Lns, TH, WBC].

QUESTION—What is the mood of the verb ἀγαπῶμεν 'we love'?
1. It is in the indicative mood to make a statement [AB, Alf, Brd, EBC, EGT, HNTC, ICC, Lns, My, NIC, NTC, TH, TNTC, WBC, Ws; all versions except NJB]: we love.
2. It is in the subjunctive mood and has an imperative sense [Herm; NJB]: let us love.

QUESTION—Who is being loved?
1. Love is used in an absolute sense [AB, Brd, EGT, Lns, My, TNTC, WBC, Ws] and both God and others are included [AB, Brd, EBC, TH, WBC]: we love.
2. It refers to love for God [Herm, HNTC, NIC]: we love God. God's love for us causes us to respond with a love for him [HNTC].

QUESTION—What relationship is indicated by ὅτι 'because'?
It indicates the reason we love [Brd, HNTC, ICC, Lns, My, NIC, TH, TNTC, WBC, Ws]. Our love is a grateful response to God's love [EBC, EGT, Herm, HNTC, ICC, NIC, NTC, TNTC]. He provided the power to love through his love [Brd, EBC, TNTC].

QUESTION—To whom does αὐτός 'he' refer?
It refers to God [Alf, Brd, EGT, Herm, ICC, NCBC, NIC, WBC; TEV]: God first loved us.

DISCOURSE UNIT: 4:20–5:1 [Brd]. The topic is the necessary association of love for God with love for Christians.

4:20 **If[a] anyone says[b] "I love[c] God" and hates[d] his brother,[e] he is a-liar;[f]**

LEXICON—a. ἐάν (LN 89.67): 'if' [AB, HNTC, LN, Lns; all versions], not explicit [WBC].
b. aorist act. subj. of εἶπον (LN 33.69): 'to say' [HNTC, LN, Lns, WBC; all versions], 'to boast' [AB]. The aorist tense indicates that the saying is a single declaration [Alf, Lns, Ws].
c. pres. act. indic. of ἀγαπάω: 'to love'. See this word at 4:19. The present tense indicates that the loving continues as part of a life pattern [Brd].
d. pres. act. subj. of μισέω (LN 88.198) (BAGD 1. p. 522): 'to hate' [AB, BAGD, HNTC, LN, Lns, WBC; all versions], 'to detest' [BAGD], 'to abhor' [BAGD]. The present tense indicates that hating continues as part of a life pattern [AB, Alf, Brd, TH, WBC].
e. ἀδελφός (LN 11.23): 'brother' [AB, HNTC, Lns, WBC; all versions except REB], 'fellow Christian' [REB], 'fellow believer' [LN].
f. ψεύστης (LN 33.255) (BAGD p. 892): 'liar' [AB, BAGD, HNTC, LN, Lns, WBC; all versions]. See this word at 1:10; 2:4, 22.

1 JOHN 4:20

QUESTION—How does this verse relate to the context?
   It is a return to the direct attack on the false teachers [AB, NCBC, NTC, TH, WBC]. It reasserts that love must express itself in action [ICC, Ws] because love for others is the proof of love for God [WBC].
QUESTION—What relationship is indicated by the use of the conjunction ἐάν 'if'?
   It indicates a hypothetical condition [Brd], but one that was, in fact, found among them in the claims of the false teachers [Brd, NCBC, TH, WBC].
QUESTION—What is meant by μισῇ 'he hates'?
   The author speaks in extremes; one either loves or hates [AB, My, WBC, Ws]. 'To hate' here means anything less than pure love [AB, Herm, My, NCBC, WBC].
QUESTION—To whom does ἀδελφός 'brother' refer?
   It refers to other Christians [Alf, Brd, HNTC; REB]. Although its primary reference is to fellow believers, it does not exclude all other human beings [WBC].
QUESTION—What is meant by ψεύστης 'liar'?
   It refers to a person whose actions contradict his words [EBC, Herm, TNTC]. His claims are not backed up by his actions [EBC, Lns, Ws], he attempts to deceive [Brd, EBC, Herm]. The falseness of his character is in view [ICC].

for[a] the-(one) not loving[b] his brother whom he-has-seen,[c] can[d] not love God whom he has not seen.

TEXT—Instead of οὐ δύναται ἀγαπᾶν 'he cannot love', some manuscripts have πῶς δύναται ἀγαπᾶν 'how can he love?'. GNT selects οὐ δύναται ἀγαπᾶν 'he cannot love' with a B rating, indicating some degree of doubt. Only KJV and My follow the reading πῶς δύναται ἀγαπᾶν 'how can he love?'. There is little semantic difference between the two readings since the declarative has a negative and the rhetorical question requires a negative answer [AB, TH].
LEXICON—a. γάρ (LN 89.23): 'for' [AB, HNTC, Lns, WBC; all versions except NAB, NJB, REB], 'since' [NJB], 'if' [REB], not explicit [NAB].
   b. pres. act. participle of ἀγαπάω: 'to love'.
   c. perfect act. indic. of ὁράω (LN 24.1) (BAGD 1.a.α. p. 577): 'to see' [AB, BAGD, HNTC, LN, Lns, WBC; all versions]. The perfect tense indicates that the seeing was in the past but the effect still continues [Alf, Brd, TH, TNTC, WBC, Ws]. Combined with the negative, it gives the idea of never having seen [My].
   d. pres. pass. (deponent = act.) indic. of δύναμαι (LN 74.5): 'can' [LN], 'to be able' [AB, HNTC, Lns, WBC; all versions except REB]. The phrase οὐ δύναται 'can not' is translated 'to be incapable of' [REB].
QUESTION—What relationship is indicated by γάρ 'for'?
   It indicates the grounds for the preceding statement [Brd, Lns, My, TNTC].

1. The argument is that it is easier to love someone who can be seen than it is to love someone who has not been seen [ICC, My, TH, TNTC, Ws]: he is a liar who claims to be doing what is more difficult when he fails to do what is easier.
2. The argument focuses on the persons involved, the brother whom one has seen and God who cannot be seen [Alf, Lns, NIC, WBC]. Since a Christian brother is a child of God, it is necessary to love him if one loves the Father [NIC]. Involved in love for God is love for the brothers [NIC].

QUESTION—What is meant by οὐ δύναται 'can not'?
It doesn't mean that he is incapable of loving God, but that it is proven that he does not do so [Brd, EBC, TNTC, Ws].

4:21 And^a this command^b we-have^c from^d him,
LEXICON—a. καί (LN 89.93): 'and' [AB, Lns, WBC; KJV, NASB, NIV, NRSV], 'indeed' [NJB], not explicit [HNTC; NAB, REB, TEV, TNT].
  b. ἐντολή (LN 33.330): 'command' [TEV], 'commandment' [AB, HNTC, LN, Lns, WBC; all versions except TEV].
  c. pres. act. indic. of ἔχω (BAGD I.2.i. p. 333): 'to have' [AB, BAGD, HNTC, Lns, WBC; all versions except NIV, NJB], 'to receive' [NJB]. The phrase 'we have from him' is translated 'he has given to us' [NIV, TEV].
  d. ἀπό with genitive object (LN 90.15) (BAGD V.4. p. 88): 'from' [AB, BAGD, HNTC, Lns, WBC; all versions except NIV, TEV].

QUESTION—What relationship is indicated by καί 'and'?
It expands the previous thought [My] and reinforces it [NIC]. It gives another reason why Christians will love their brothers [Alf, Brd, EBC, ICC, NTC, WBC].

QUESTION—To what does ταύτην ἐντολήν 'this command' refer?
It refers to the following clause [AB, BAGD, Brd, HNTC, Lns, My, WBC; all versions].

QUESTION—To whom does αὐτοῦ 'him' refer?
1. It refers to God [AB, Alf, Brd, ICC, Lns, My, NIC, TH, WBC, Ws].
2. It refers to Christ [EBC, TNTC; REB, TEV].

that/in-order-that^a the-one loving^b God should-love^c also^d his brother.
LEXICON—a. ἵνα (LN 90.22; 89.33) (BAGD II.1.e. p. 378): 'that' [BAGD, Lns, WBC; all versions except NAB, NIV, REB], not explicit [AB, HNTC; NAB, NIV, REB].
  b. pres. act. participle of ἀγαπάω: 'to love'. See this word at 4:20. The present tense indicates that the need to love is continual [WBC] or that this is a general truth [TH].
  c. pres. act. subj. of ἀγαπάω (LN 25.43): 'to love' [AB, HNTC, Lns, WBC; all versions].
  d. καί (LN 89.93): 'also' [HNTC, Lns, WBC; all versions except REB], 'too' [REB], 'as well' [AB].

1 JOHN 4:21

QUESTION—What relationship is indicated by ἵνα 'that/in order that'?
It indicates the content of the preceding command [AB, BAGD, Brd, HNTC, Lns, My, WBC; all versions]. There is also a measure of purpose in the word [AB, WBC, Ws] to indicate that the command has a particular aim [WBC].

QUESTION—What relationship is indicated by the use of the conjunction καί 'also'?
It indicates that the two loves are inseparable. To love God one must also love one's brother [WBC].

DISCOURSE UNIT: 5:1–21 [ICC]. The topic is faith as the ground of love.

DISCOURSE UNIT: 5:1–13 [NCBC]. The topic is the testimony of the Spirit and faith in the Son.

DISCOURSE UNIT: 5:1–12 [HNTC, ICC, NTC, Ws; NASB, NIV]. The topic is witness and faith [HNTC, Ws], faith in the Son of God [NIV], faith as the ground of love [ICC], loving God [NTC], overcoming the world [NASB].

DISCOURSE UNIT: 5:1–5 [Br, EBC, EGT, TNTC; TEV]. The topic is the victory of faith [Br], victory over the world [TEV], love for the Father and faith in the Son [EBC], the commands of God being easy [EGT].

5:1 Everyone believing[a] that Jesus is the Christ[b] has-been-begotten[c] by[d] God,

LEXICON—a. pres. act. participle of πιστεύω: 'to believe'. See this word at 4:16. The present tense indicates that this is a continuing state [Brd, TNTC, WBC].
  b. χριστός (LN 53.82) (BAGD 1. p. 887): 'Christ' [AB, BAGD, LN, Lns, WBC; all versions except TEV], 'Messiah' [BAGD, HNTC, LN; TEV], 'Anointed One' [BAGD].
  c. perf. pass. indic. of γεννάω: 'to be begotten'. See this word at 2:29; 3:9; 4:7. The perfect tense indicates that the effect of the birth still continues [Brd, NTC, WBC]. It indicates the present state of the believer [NIC].
  d. ἐκ with genitive object: 'by'. See this word at 2:29; 3:9; 4:7.

QUESTION—How is this verse related to its context?
It comments on the connection between love for God and love for the brethren mentioned in 4:20–21 [Br, Brd, EGT, TH, WBC]. It identifies the brother and explains why he should be loved [Alf]. It also introduces the idea of faith which will become central later in the passage [NIC, TH, WBC].

QUESTION—What is involved in believing that Jesus is the Christ?
It means an affirmation that the historical Jesus is the Christ [AB, EGT, Herm, HNTC, Lns, TNTC, WBC]. The man Jesus is all that is contained in the term Christ [Lns]. Some commentators think that this includes a personal commitment to him as well as an intellectual belief [Br, Brd, EBC, ICC, Ws]. It is a submission to the person who possesses the character which is implied by his title [ICC].

QUESTION—What is the relationship between believing and being begotten by God?

Belief is a sign of regeneration [Brd, HNTC, NIC, NTC, TH, TNTC, WBC, Ws]. Some commentators explain that faith is the sign of regeneration because faith is the result of regeneration [EBC, ICC, NIC, TNTC]. Others say that faith is the condition for the new birth [Brd, NIC, WBC]. However, the logical order between faith and regeneration is not in focus here; for the true believer, each is present with the other [Brd, ICC, NIC, Ws].

and[a] everyone loving[b] the-(one) having-begotten[c] loves also the-(one) having-been-begotten[d] by him.

TEXT—The second καί 'also' does not occur in some manuscripts. It is included in GNT with a C rating, indicating a considerable degree of doubt. It is either not included or not translated by AB, HNTC, NAB, NASB, NJB, NRSV, REB, and TNT.

LEXICON—a. καί (LN 89.93): 'and' [AB, HNTC, Lns, WBC; all versions except NAB, REB], 'now' [NAB], not explicit [REB].
- b. pres. act. participle of ἀγαπάω: 'to love'. See this word at 2:10; 3:10, 11, 14, 18, 23; 4:7, 8, 10, 11, 12, 19, 20, 21. The present tense in both occurrences here indicates a continuing action [Brd].
- c. aorist act. participle of γεννάω: 'to beget'. See this word in the preceding clause.
- d. perf. pass. participle of γεννάω: 'to be begotten'. The perfect tense indicates a past event with a lasting significance [NTC].

QUESTION—How is this statement used?
1. It is a general statement that applies to any parent and child [AB, NIC, WBC] or to one's own parent and brothers and sisters [EBC, Herm, ICC, TH, TNTC]. A child naturally loves his own father [TNTC]. Because he loves his father, he will also love the rest of his father's children [EBC, Herm]. It is human nature to love the children of those whom you love [ICC, NIC, TH, TNTC, Ws].
2. It is a statement that develops from the preceding clause and applies directly to God the Father and to his children [Brd, Lns, My, Ws]. Everyone who loves God the Father loves the rest of God's children [Brd].

5:2 By[a] this we-know[b] that we-love[c] the children of God,

LEXICON—a. ἐν with dative object: 'by'. See this word at 2:3, 5; 3:10, 16, 19; 4:2, 13.
- b. pres. act. indic. of γινώσκω: 'to know'. See this word at 2:3a, 5, 18, 29; 3:16, 19, 24; 4:2, 6, 13.
- c. pres. act. indic. of ἀγαπάω: 'to love'. See this word at 5:1. The present tense indicates that this is a continuing action [Brd].

QUESTION—To what does the pronoun τούτῳ 'this' refer?
1. It refers to the following clause [AB, Alf, Br, Brd, Herm, HNTC, ICC, Lns, My, NTC, TNTC, WBC]: we know that we love God's children by

this, namely, when we love God and do what he commands. Implicit in love for God is love for his children and therefore if one truly loves God, he will love God's children [Brd]. Love for God and love for God's children mutually prove one another [My, WBC]. If a person says that he loves his brothers and yet does not love God, he cannot show his brother the true love that comes only from God [EBC]. When we love God and show this by obeying him, we then know that our love for God's children is real love [ICC].

2. It refers to the preceding verse (5:1) [NCBC, NIC, TH]. If we act in accordance with the principle that everyone who loves the parent also loves the parent's child, then we know that we love God's children when we love God and carry out his commands [NCBC]. Another way of taking this is that when we act in accordance with the preceding principle, we know how we *ought to* love God's children when we love God and keep his commandments [NIC].

when[a] we-love God and do[b] his-commandments.[c]

TEXT—Instead of ποιῶμεν 'we do,' some manuscripts have τηρῶμεν 'we keep'. GNT selects ποιῶμεν 'we do' with a C rating, indicating a considerable degree of doubt. 'We keep' is selected only by KJV and NJB.

LEXICON—a. ὅταν (LN 67.31): 'when' [WBC; all versions except NIV, TEV], 'whenever' [AB, Lns], 'if' [HNTC], 'by' [NIV, TEV]. It means 'every time that' [Alf, Brd, ICC, TH, Ws].

b. pres. act. subj. of ποιέω (LN 42.7): 'to do' [AB, LN, Lns; NAB, TNT], 'to obey' [NRSV, REB, TEV], 'to keep' [KJV, NJB], 'to carry out' [HNTC, WBC; NIV], 'to observe' [NASB]. The present tense indicates that this is a continuing action [Brd].

c. ἐντολή: 'commandment'. See this word at 2:3; 3:22, 23, 24.

QUESTION—What is meant by 'doing God's commandments'?

Some commentators think that this means the same as 'keeping his commandments' (3:22) [AB]. Others see an emphasis here in the active character of obeying the commandments [ICC]. The foremost of all the commandments is love [Br] and the commandments all amount to loving the Christian brethren [HNTC].

5:3 For[a] this is the love[b] of God,

LEXICON—a. γάρ (LN 91.1): 'for' [AB, HNTC, Lns, WBC; all versions except NAB, NIV, NJB], not explicit [NAB, NIV, NJB].

b. ἀγάπη: 'love'. See this word at 2:5, 15; 3:1, 16, 17; 4:7, 8, 9, 10, 12, 16, 17, 18. This noun is also translated by a verb 'to love' [HNTC; REB, TNT].

QUESTION—What relationship is indicated by γάρ 'for'?

It indicates the grounds for adding the last clause of 5:2 [Alf, ICC, Lns, My, Ws]: we love God and keep his commandments, since love for God is this: that we keep his commandments.

QUESTION—To what does αὕτη 'this' refer?

It refers to the following clause 'that we keep his commandments' [AB, Alf, Brd, HNTC, My, NCBC, TH, WBC]: love for God is this, namely, that we keep his commandments. Our love for God is expressed by our obedience [NIC, TH, WBC]. The test of love is obedience [Brd]. Obedience is a necessary outcome of love for God [ICC, WBC] and a part of such love [WBC].

QUESTION—How are the event noun and the personal noun related in the genitive construction ἡ ἀγάπη τοῦ θεοῦ 'the love of God'?

It means love for God [BAGD, Brd, EBC, EGT, HNTC, Lns, NCBC, NIC, NTC, TH, TNTC, WBC; TEV]: this is our love for God.

that[a] we-keep[b] his commandments;[c]

LEXICON—a. ἵνα (LN 90.22) (BAGD II.1.e. p. 378): 'that' [AB, BAGD, Lns, WBC; KJV, NAB, NASB, NRSV, TEV], not explicit [HNTC; NIV, NJB, REB, TNT].

b. pres. act. subj. of τηρέω: 'to keep'. See this word at 2:3, 4, 5; 3:22, 24. The present tense indicates that the obeying is a continuous action [Brd, Ws].

c. ἐντολή: 'commandment'. See this word at 5:2.

QUESTION—What relationship is indicated by the conjunction ἵνα 'that'?

It explains what is meant by 'this' in the preceding clause [AB, Alf, Brd, ICC, My, NCBC, NTC, TH, WBC].

QUESTION—What is meant by keeping his commandments?

It means to accept them as principles on which to base one's life [ICC] and to obey them [AB, Brd, WBC]. The word 'commandments' refers particularly to the command to love one another (5:2) [AB, NIC, WBC] or to the two commands to love God and to love one another [EGT, NCBC, TNTC].

and[a] his commandments are not burdensome,[b]

LEXICON—a. καί (LN 89.93): 'and' [AB, HNTC, Lns, WBC; all versions except NJB, TNT], 'nor' [NJB], not explicit [TNT].

b. βαρύς (LN **22.30**) (BAGD 2.a. p. 134): 'burdensome' [AB, BAGD, HNTC, LN, Lns, WBC; all versions except KJV, TEV], 'too hard (for us)' [TEV], 'difficult to fulfill' [BAGD], 'grievous' [KJV].

QUESTION—What is meant by βαρύς 'burdensome'?

It refers to the effect on the person; they are burdensome [AB, Br, EBC, Herm, HNTC, Lns, My, NIC; all versions except TEV], oppressive [ICC, WBC, Ws], a source of irritation [NTC], that crushes the spontaneity of love [WBC]. They would be burdensome if the person felt that they were too difficult to accomplish [AB, TH], and beyond one's ability to keep [ICC, NIC]. This is not much different from saying that they are 'not difficult' [AB, TH] and this is translated 'not too hard' [TEV].

QUESTION—Why are God's commandments not burdensome?

They are not burdensome because God enables us to do them [AB, Br, Brd, ICC, NIC, TH, TNTC, WBC, Ws] and gives us the desire to do them [Brd, EBC]. The Christian delights to do God's will [Br, Lns, NTC]. Although they are not easy to obey, they are not burdensome because of the new birth (5:4) [Brd].

5:4a because[a] all that has-been-begotten[b] by God overcomes[c] the world;[d]

LEXICON—a. ὅτι (LN 89.33): 'because' [AB, HNTC, Lns; NJB, REB, TEV, TNT], 'for' [WBC; KJV, NASB, NIV, NRSV], not explicit [NAB].
  b. perf. pass. participle of γεννάω: 'to be begotten'. See this word at 2:29; 3:9; 4:7; 5:1. The perfect tense stresses the continuing new life that results from the new birth [Brd].
  c. pres. act. indic. of νικάω (LN **39.57**) (BAGD 2.a. p. 539): 'to overcome' [AB, BAGD, HNTC; all versions except NAB, TEV, TNT], 'to be victorious over' [Lns], 'to win the victory over' [LN], 'to conquer' [NAB, TNT], 'to defeat' [WBC; TEV]. See this word at 2:13; 4:4.
  d. κόσμος (LN 41.38) (BAGD 7. p. 447): 'world' [AB, HNTC, Lns, WBC; all versions].

QUESTION—What relationship is indicated by ὅτι 'because'?

It indicates the reason why God's commandments are not burdensome [AB, Alf, Br, Brd, EGT, Herm, Lns, My, NCBC, TH, TNTC, WBC, Ws]: God's commandments are not burdensome to God's children because all his children overcome the world by their faith. God's children overcome the temptations from the world that would prevent obedience to God [NIC].

QUESTION—To what does the neuter pronoun πᾶν 'all' refer?

1. The neuter form refers to all children of God as a unit or category [AB, Alf, HNTC, My, NCBC, NIC, NTC, Ws]: because all those who are begotten of God overcome the world.
2. The neuter form refers to the birth from God [EBC, ICC, TNTC, WBC]: because the birth from God overcomes the world. It focuses on the power in the new birth, rather than on the power possessed by each person [ICC].

QUESTION—In what way do they overcome the world?

They overcome the world by resisting Satan who rules the world [Lns]; they resist his temptations to unbelief and disobedience [My, NIC]. Since the false teachers belong to the world, the rejection of their teaching is a specific example of overcoming the world [AB, HNTC].

QUESTION—What does the use of the present tense of the verb νικάω 'to overcome' indicate?

1. The present tense indicates that the conquest is continuous and habitual [Alf, HNTC, Lns, My, NCBC, TH, WBC].
2. The present tense indicates that overcoming is a general rule that is always true [Brd, Herm].
3. The present tense indicates that the fighting is still in progress but the victory is assured [EGT, NTC].

DISCOURSE UNIT: 5:4b–12 [AB]. The topic is faith as conqueror of the world.

5:4b **and this is the victory,[a] the-(one) having-overcome[b] the world, our faith.[c]**

LEXICON—a. νίκη (LN 39.57) (BAGD p. 539): 'victory' [LN, Lns, WBC; all versions except NAB], 'conquering power' [AB], 'power' [NAB], 'the means for winning a victory' [BAGD], not explicit [HNTC; TNT].
  b. aorist act. participle of νικάω: 'to overcome'. See this word in the previous clause.
  c. πίστις (LN 31.85; 31.102) (BAGD 2.d.α. p. 663): 'faith' [AB, HNTC, LN, Lns, WBC; all versions], 'true piety' [BAGD].

QUESTION—To what does the pronoun αὕτη 'this' refer?
  It refers to the following appositive, 'our faith' [Brd, HNTC, Lns, My, NTC, TH]: our faith is the victory.

QUESTION—What is meant by νίκη 'victory'?
  It is a metonymy for the means of bringing about the victory [AB, NCBC, NIC, TNTC, WBC; NAB]: the means of victory over the world is our faith. The believer is victorious over the world because of his faith [NTC].

QUESTION—What does the use of the aorist tense of the participle νικήσασα 'having overcome' indicate?
  1. The aorist tense indicates that the overcoming happened at some point in the past [AB, Br, Brd, EBC, Herm, HNTC, Lns, My, NIC, TH, WBC, Ws]. It refers to Jesus' victory in which they share by faith [Br, NIC, TH, WBC, Ws]. Or it refers to the time of conversion [ICC]. Or it refers to the time they rejected the false teaching of the heretics and the heretics withdrew from their fellowship [HNTC, ICC, TNTC].
  2. The aorist tense indicates that, although overcoming is still in progress, it is assured [EGT].
  3. The aorist tense is timeless and indicates that the overcoming is a fact that is always true [NTC].

QUESTION—What is meant by πίστις 'faith'?
  'Faith' is belief in the facts of the Christian doctrine [TH, WBC]. It is belief in the incarnation [Brd]. It is belief that Jesus is the Christ (5:1) [TH, TNTC], that Jesus is the Son of God (5:5) [AB, Brd, TNTC], that Jesus has been victorious [NIC].

DISCOURSE UNIT: 5:5–13 [Herm, WBC; NJB]. The topic is faith in the Son of God and witnessing for him [Herm], keeping the faith [WBC; NJB].

DISCOURSE UNIT: 5:5–12 [NIC, NTC]. The topic is the confirmation of true faith [NIC], accepting God's testimony [NTC].

5:5 And who is the-(one) overcoming[a] the world if not[b] the-(one) believing[c] that Jesus is the Son of God?
LEXICON—a. pres. act. participle of νικάω: 'to overcome'. See this word at 5:4. The present tense indicates that this is a continuing action [Brd, NTC, TNTC, WBC, Ws] or that it is a general rule [TH].
  b. εἰ μή (LN 89.131): 'if not', 'none other than' [AB], 'but' [HNTC, Lns, WBC; all versions except NAB, NIV, TEV], 'only' [NIV, TEV], not explicit [NAB].
  c. pres. act. participle of πιστεύω (LN 31.35) (BAGD 1.a.β. p. 660): 'to believe' [AB, BAGD, HNTC, Lns, WBC; all versions]. The present tense states a general truth [TH]. See this word at 4:1, 16; 5:1.
QUESTION—What is the implied answer to the rhetorical question?
  It implies that no one but a believer overcomes the world [AB, BAGD, Brd, Lns, TH].
QUESTION—What is the significance of believing that Jesus is the Son of God?
  It is identifying the historical Jesus with the divine Son of God [AB, Brd, EBC, Herm, ICC, NIC, TNTC]. Compare this with the clause 'whoever acknowledges that Jesus is the Son of God' (4:15).
QUESTION—What is the significance of the use of 'Son of God' here instead of 'Christ' used in 5:1?
  They are shown to be equivalent [Alf, Brd, EGT, Herm, ICC, NIC, TH, TNTC, WBC]. Both 'Christ' and 'the Son of God' indicate the exalted state of Jesus and there is little difference in meaning [WBC].

DISCOURSE UNIT: 5:6–17 [TNTC]. The topic is the three witnesses and our consequent assurance.

DISCOURSE UNIT: 5:6–12 [Br, Brd, EBC, TNTC, Ws; TEV]. The topic is the ground of assurance [Br], the divine test [Ws], the Christological test for being a child of God [Brd], the three witnesses [TNTC], the witness about Jesus Christ [TEV], the Spirit, water, and blood [EBC].

DISCOURSE UNIT: 5:6–9 [Brd]. The topic is the agreement of the Holy Spirit and historical facts [Brd].

DISCOURSE UNIT: 5:6–8 [EGT]. The topic is the three-fold testimony to the incarnation [EGT].

5:6 This is the-(one) having-come[a] through[b] water[c] and blood,[d] Jesus Christ,
LEXICON—a. aorist act. participle of ἔρχομαι (LN 15.18) (BAGD I.1.a. p. 311): 'to come' [AB, BAGD, HNTC, Lns, WBC; all versions]. The aorist tense refers to the historical events [AB, Brd, HNTC, ICC, Lns, NTC, TH, TNTC, WBC, Ws].

b. διά with genitive object (LN 90.8) (BAGD A.I.1. p. 179): 'through' [BAGD; NAB, TNT], 'by' [AB, HNTC, WBC; KJV, NASB, NIV, NJB, NRSV], 'by means of' [Lns], 'with' [REB, TEV].
c. ὕδωρ (LN 2.7) (BAGD 1. p. 833): 'water' [AB, BAGD, HNTC, LN, Lns, WBC; all versions except TEV], 'water of his baptism' [TEV].
d. αἷμα (LN 23.107) (BAGD 2.b. 23): 'blood' [AB, BAGD, HNTC, Lns, WBC; all versions except TEV], 'blood of his death' [TEV].

QUESTION—To whom does οὗτος 'this' refer?

'This' refers to the person spoken of in 5:5, Jesus [Alf, Brd, EGT, ICC, Lns, NIC, TH, TNTC, WBC, Ws].

QUESTION—What is meant by Jesus 'coming through water and blood'?

1. The terms 'water' and 'blood' refer to Jesus' baptism and death [Alf, Br, Brd, EBC, EGT, Herm, HNTC, ICC, Lns, My, NIC, NTC, TH, TNTC, WBC; TEV]. These terms bracket Jesus' earthly ministry as Messiah: by his baptism he began his ministry and by his death he finished it [Alf, Brd, ICC, My, NTC, WBC]. Blood refers to Jesus' death on the cross [Alf, Brd], specifically, his death as a sacrificial offering [HNTC, Lns] to bring about atonement for sin [My]. He came from the Father [ICC, Lns] into the world [NIC] to manifest himself to those in the world [Alf] as the Messiah [ICC, Lns]. The use of 'water' and 'blood' was already familiar to the original readers [Brd, HNTC, TNTC, WBC].

2. The terms refer to the water and the blood that came from the pierced side of Jesus after his death [AB]. Jesus came to be Savior by his death, when water and blood flowed from his side [AB].

QUESTION—What is the significance of placing the name 'Jesus Christ' at the end of this clause?

This position gives prominence to it [AB, TH]. The name 'Jesus Christ' is equivalent to saying 'Jesus, the Christ' and focuses on his office as Messiah [Alf, HNTC, NIC, TNTC, WBC, Ws]. Jesus Christ is one person, in contrast with the heretical teaching that a heavenly Christ came on the human Jesus at his baptism [EGT].

not by[a] the water only,[b] but[c] by the water and by the blood;

LEXICON—a. ἐν with dative object (LN 89.76) (BAGD I.4.c.β. p. 259): 'by' [KJV, NIV, REB, TNT], 'with' [BAGD; NASB, NJB, NRSV, TEV], 'in' [AB, WBC; NAB], 'in connection with' [Lns], not explicit [HNTC].
b. μόνος (LN 58.51) (BAGD 2.c.α. p. 528): 'only' [AB, BAGD, WBC; all versions except REB], 'alone' [HNTC, LN, Lns; REB].
c. ἀλλά (LN 89.125): 'but' [AB, HNTC, Lns, WBC; all versions].

QUESTION—Why is this clause added?

This emphasizes the fact that Jesus came by blood [AB, Alf, Br, ICC, My, NIC]. Many commentators think that this was emphasized to refute the heretics who taught that the heavenly Christ came down on the man Jesus at his baptism but left him before he died on the cross [Br, Brd, EBC, Herm, HNTC, ICC, Lns, My, NIC, NTC, TH, TNTC]. The true identity of Jesus is discovered by looking at the whole of his ministry, right up to its end on the cross [WBC].

QUESTION—What is the significance of the change of prepositions from διά 'through' in the preceding clause and ἐν 'by' here?

Many think that there is no significant difference of meaning [Brd, EGT, Herm, ICC, NCBC, NIC, TH, WBC]. Both prepositions express the manner of Jesus' coming [Herm, NIC, WBC], or the accompanying circumstances [NCBC, TH]. Some think that there is a difference: the mediums through which he came versus the elements in which he came [Alf], the elements by which the coming was characterized versus what accompanied it [My], the means of his coming versus what was connected with it [Lns], the means versus the accompanying circumstances [NTC].

QUESTION—What is the significance of the use of the article before the nouns 'water' and 'blood'?

It indicates that 'water' and 'blood' are those already referred to in the preceding clause [AB, Brd, ICC, Lns, My]. It also indicates well-known ideas [Alf].

and[a] the Spirit[b] is the-(one) testifying,[c]

LEXICON—a. καί (LN 89.87): 'and' [AB, Lns, WBC; all versions except NAB, TNT], not explicit [HNTC; NAB, TNT].

b. πνεῦμα (LN 12.18) (BAGD 5.d.α. p. 677): 'Spirit' [AB, HNTC, Lns, WBC; all versions].

c. pres. act. participle of μαρτυρέω: 'to testify'. See this word at 1:2; 4:14. The present tense indicates that this is a continuing testimony [AB, EBC, Lns, NIC, Ws] through what the author has written [AB], through the Scriptures [Lns, NIC] and the gospel [Brd], and also through inwardly causing people to realize the truth about Jesus [NIC, TNTC, WBC].

QUESTION—How does this clause relate to the preceding context?

Besides the historical testimony implied by the water and blood, the Spirit is an additional witness [Alf, Br, ICC, NIC, TNTC, WBC] The water and blood testify to the character of Christ's ministry, but there is an even more important witness, the Spirit [ICC]. The three witnesses are explained in the next verse [Alf]. The 'Spirit' refers to the Holy Spirit [Alf, Brd, Br, EBC, Herm, HNTC, ICC, Lns, My, NIC, NTC, TH, TNTC, WBC, Ws; all versions] and he testifies in the hearts of believers [Br, NIC, WBC] and in the sacraments and preaching of the church [NIC, WBC]. In the latter case, 'Spirit' can be taken as a metonymy for the prophetic utterances which were inspired by the Holy Spirit as in 4:1 [NCBC].

QUESTION—To what does the Spirit testify?

The Spirit testifies to the truth of the preceding statement that Jesus came through water and blood [AB, HNTC, My, TH, WBC] and testifies that Jesus' baptism and death point to his being the Christ (5:1) and the Son of God (5:10) [NIC]. He testifies to the facts about Jesus [Br], concerning the person and work of Christ Jesus [NTC, TNTC]. He testifies that Jesus is the

Christ [Alf, Brd], the gospel is true [Br], and that eternal life comes through him [Alf].

because[a] the Spirit is the truth.[b]

LEXICON—a. ὅτι (LN 89.33): 'because' [Lns; all versions except NAB, NJB], 'for' [AB, HNTC, WBC; NJB], 'and' [NAB].

b. ἀλήθεια (LN 72.2) (BAGD 2.b. p. 36): 'truth' [AB, BAGD, HNTC, LN, Lns, WBC; all versions]. See this word at 4:6.

QUESTION—What relationship is indicated by ὅτι 'because'?

It indicates the reason that the testimony of the Spirit is valid and can be trusted [Alf, Br, Brd, Herm, HNTC, ICC, My, NIC, TH, TNTC, WBC, Ws]. In addition, this might also indicate that the Spirit testifies because his essential nature of truth constrains him to do so [ICC, TNTC, WBC, Ws].

QUESTION—What is meant by the Spirit 'being the truth'?

The Spirit is truth personified, the very source of truth [Brd]. His essential nature is truth [ICC, Ws].

5:7 Because[a] three are the-(ones) testifying,[b]

TEXT—After μαρτυροῦντες 'the ones testifying', some manuscripts have ἐν τῷ οὐρανῷ, ὁ πατὴρ, ὁ λόγος, καὶ τὸ ἅγιον πνεῦμα. καὶ οὗτοι οἱ τρεῖς ἕν εἰσιν. (5:8) καὶ τρεῖς εἰσιν οἱ μαρτυροῦντες ἐν τῇ γῇ 'in heaven, the Father, the Word, and the Holy Spirit. And these three are in the one. (5:8) And the ones testifying are three on earth'. It is omitted by GNT with an A rating, indicating virtual certainty. It is included only by KJV.

LEXICON—a. ὅτι (LN 89.33): 'because' [Lns], 'for' [KJV, NASB, NIV], 'so' [NJB], 'indeed' [AB, WBC], 'in fact' [HNTC; REB], 'thus' [NAB], not explicit [NRSV, TEV, TNT].

b. pres. act. participle of μαρτυρέω : 'to testify'. See this word at 5:6. The present tense indicates that this is a continuing action [AB, Brd, TH, WBC, Ws].

QUESTION—What relationship is indicated by ὅτι 'because'?

1. It indicates an additional comment concerning the testimony of the Spirit [AB, Brd, NCBC, NIC, TH, WBC]. This is a further specification, not another reason [AB, TH]. With the sense of 'indeed', ὅτι is used for emphasis here [WBC].
2. It indicates the grounds for saying that Jesus is the Son of God (5:5) [Ws].
3. This is a second reason for trusting the testimony of the Spirit [My]: the testimony of the Spirit can be trusted because the Spirit is truth and because his testimony is backed up by two other witnesses.

QUESTION—What is the significance of there being three witnesses?

The Greek word order emphasizes the word 'three' [AB]. It indicates that the witnesses are reliable [Brd, ICC, TH, WBC, Ws], and meet the requirement of the Mosaic law for two or three witnesses (Deut. 19:15) [AB, Alf, Brd, HNTC, ICC, Lns, NCBC, NTC, TH, TNTC, WBC, Ws].

QUESTION—What is the significance of the use of the masculine participle οἱ μαρτυροῦντες 'the ones witnessing' in spite of the three antecedents, πνεῦμα 'Spirit', ὕδωρ 'water', and αἷμα 'blood', being neuter nouns?

The writer views all three witnesses as persons giving their testimony: the Holy Spirit being an actual person and the water and the blood being personified [Alf, Brd, My, NIC, TH, WBC].

5:8 the Spirit and the water and the blood, and the three are in[a] the one.

LEXICON—a. εἰς with accusative object: 'in'. The phrase εἰς τὸ ἕν εἰσιν 'are in the one' is translated 'are one' [HNTC], 'are for one thing' [Lns], 'are at one' [WBC], 'are one in purpose' [TNT], 'agree in one' [KJV], 'agree' [NRSV], 'coincide' [NJB], 'are of one accord' [AB; NAB], 'are in agreement' [NASB, NIV, REB], 'give the same testimony' [TEV].

QUESTION—What is the significance of the order in which the three witnesses are listed?

The Spirit is listed first because he is the primary witness. The Spirit testifies and the other two substantiate his testimony in accordance with the law [Lns]. The Spirit is the only one who is actually alive; the other two are witnesses only in the sense that the Spirit interprets what they mean [Alf, TNTC, Ws].

QUESTION—What is meant by the present continuing testimony of the three witnesses?

1. 'Water' and 'blood' refer to the historical events of Christ's baptism and death as in 5:6 [Brd, EBC, ICC, Lns, My, NCBC, NIC, NTC, WBC]. Past events continue to bear witness [NIC]. The historical accounts still continue to give their testimony to whoever hears or reads them [Brd]. The Spirit still witnesses through the NT in which Jesus' baptism and death are written [EBC]. By means of the Spirit, the redemptive life of Christ constantly proves him to be the Messiah [My]. The Spirit gave his testimony by coming on Jesus at his baptism, thus proving him to be the Son of God, and there was also God's voice from heaven [Brd]. The testimony of Jesus' death was to show that Jesus was truly human [Brd].
2. 'Water' and 'blood' have different meanings than they did in 5:6 [Herm, HNTC, TH]. 'Water' is now the sacrament of baptism and 'blood' now refers to the Lord's Supper. These sacraments are a continuous witness in the church to the ministry of Christ and they join the Spirit's inward witness [TH]. The sacraments bear witness to Jesus since they mediate the salvation imparted through him. The Spirit gives them their power [Herm].

QUESTION—What is meant by the prepositional phrase εἰς τὸ ἕν 'in the one'?

The three witnesses contribute to the same result [Alf, ICC, WBC]. Their testimonies are in agreement [AB, Brd, EGT, My, NIC, TH, TNTC], being identical [Lns, NTC].

DISCOURSE UNIT: 5:9–12 [EGT]. The topic is our attitude to the testimony.

5:9 If[a] we-receive[b] the testimony[c] of men,[d] the testimony of God is greater;[e]

LEXICON—a. εἰ (LN 89.30): 'if' [AB, HNTC, Lns, WBC; KJV, NASB, NJB, NRSV], not explicit [NAB, NIV, REB, TEV, TNT].
  b. pres. act. indic. of λαμβάνω (LN 31.50): 'to receive' [HNTC, LN, Lns; KJV, NASB, NRSV], 'to accept' [AB, LN, WBC; NAB, NIV, NJB, REB, TNT], 'to believe' [LN; TEV]. It means to accept a testimony as valid [AB, Alf, Brd, ICC, NCBC, NIC, TH]. The present tense indicates that this is a general rule that is always true [Brd, NTC].
  c. μαρτυρία (LN 33.264) (BAGD 2.c. p. 493): 'testimony' [AB, HNTC, LN, Lns, WBC; all versions except KJV, NASB, TNT], 'witness' [LN; KJV, NASB, TNT].
  d. ἄνθρωπος (LN 9.1): 'man' [Lns; KJV, NASB, NIV, NRSV, TEV, TNT], 'human being' [LN]. This noun is also translated as an adjective: 'human' [AB, HNTC, WBC; NAB, NJB, REB].
  e. μέγας (LN 78.2) (BAGD 2.b.β. p. 498): 'greater' [AB, Lns; all versions except REB, TEV], 'stronger' [HNTC; REB, TEV], 'superior' [WBC].

QUESTION—What relationship is indicated by εἰ 'if'?
  It indicates an agreed-on premise [AB, Alf, Brd, ICC, Lns, My, NTC, TH, TNTC, WBC, Ws]: since we receive the witness of men.

QUESTION—What is meant by the testimony of men?
  It refers to human testimony in general [AB, Alf, Brd, EBC, HNTC, ICC, Lns, My, NCBC, NIC, NTC, TH, TNTC, WBC; NAB, NJB, REB]. The implied subject of the verb λαμβάνομεν 'we receive' is indefinite [Alf, Brd, EBC, ICC, Lns, My, NCBC, NIC, TH, TNTC, WBC, Ws]: the testimony of people is generally accepted by all. There is no specific instance in mind [Alf]. Some think that, in this context, the argument points to John the Baptist's testimony concerning Jesus (John 1:37) [AB, NTC].

QUESTION—Why isn't the condition followed by the conclusion, 'how much more should we accept the testimony of God'?
  The writer speaks of the quality of God's testimony [AB] and argues from the lesser to the greater [Brd]. God's testimony, in comparison to man's testimony, is more trustworthy [Brd, EBC, ICC, My, NIC, WBC], more significant [Lns, TH, WBC], and more authoritative [WBC, Ws]. It is implied that God's greater testimony should be accepted [AB, Alf, Brd, EBC, ICC, My, NCBC, NIC, NTC, TNTC, WBC, Ws].

for[a] this is the testimony of God that/because[b] he-testified[c] concerning[d] his Son.

LEXICON—a. ὅτι (LN 89.33): 'for' [AB, HNTC; KJV, NASB, NJB, NRSV], 'because' [Lns; NIV], 'and' [WBC; REB, TEV], not explicit [NAB, TNT].
  b. ὅτι (LN 90.21): 'that' [AB, HNTC, Lns, WBC; NASB, NRSV], 'which' [KJV, NIV, NJB], not explicit [NAB, REB, TEV, TNT].

c. perf. act. indic. of μαρτυρέω: 'to testify'. See this word at 5:6, 7. The perfect tense indicates that the testimony was given in the past but the effect remains [AB, Brd, Lns, My, NTC, TH, TNTC].

d. περί with genitive object (LN 90.24): 'concerning' [NASB], 'about' [NIV, NJB, TEV, TNT], 'on behalf of' [AB; NAB], 'in regard to' [Lns], 'to' [HNTC, WBC; NRSV, REB], 'of' [KJV].

QUESTION—What relationship is indicated by the first use of ὅτι 'for'?

1. It indicates the grounds for saying that God's testimony is greater than man's testimony [Alf, Brd, ICC, Lns, NIC, TH, TNTC] and justifies the appeal to God's greater authority [Ws]. The value of God's witness consists in the fact that he has testified concerning his Son [ICC]. This testimony is greater because it is not mere man's, but God's own testimony [Brd, ICC, NIC, TNTC]. The preceding statement applies in the case under discussion because God has testified concerning his Son [Alf]. God does not testify about unimportant things, but about the greatest thing of all, about his Son [Lns].

2. It indicates the grounds for appealing to God's testimony [My, WBC, Ws]: we may appeal to God's testimony because he has actually testified concerning his Son.

QUESTION—What relationship is indicated by the next use of the conjunction ὅτι 'that/because'?

1. It explains that God's testimony concerns his own Son [AB, Alf, Brd, Herm, ICC, Lns, My, NIC, TH, WBC, Ws]: this is God's testimony that he testified about his Son. This does not tell the contents of the testimony [TH].

2. Instead of ὅτι 'because', the word should be read as ὅ τι 'that which', making this an adjectival clause modifying 'testimony' [EGT, NTC]: this is God's testimony which he testified about his Son. The meaning is essentially the same as the first interpretation [AB].

QUESTION—How did God testify?

It is connected with the testimony of the Spirit, water, and blood. The three-fold witness is now defined as being God's witness concerning his Son [Brd, EBC, Lns, NIC, TNTC, WBC, Ws]. God is behind the witness of the three, so that they are a single testimony from God: in the past God bore witness through the water and the blood, and in the present he bears witness through the Spirit in our hearts [TNTC]. The Spirit is God's instrument of revelation, so the Spirit's testimony is God's testimony [NIC]. It is God's voice at the baptism, transfiguration, and triumphal entry, and God still speaks through his Word and the Spirit [NTC]. God testified through the descent of the Spirit, the baptism, and through Jesus' death of the cross [Brd]. He testified through his miracles and the resurrection [EGT].

DISCOURSE UNIT: 5:10–12 [Brd]. The topic is the experiential witness of eternal life.

1 JOHN 5:10

5:10 The-(one) believing[a] in[b] the Son of God has the testimony[c] in himself,

TEXT—Instead of ἑαυτῷ 'himself', some manuscripts have αὐτῷ 'him'. GNT has ἑαυτῷ 'himself' with a B rating, indicating some degree of doubt. 'Himself', referring to the believer, is also accepted by Brd and WBC. The reading αὐτῷ 'him' is accepted by AB, Alf, Herm, ICC, and NIC and these think that it is equivalent to 'himself', referring to the believer. All the translations translate as 'himself'. The reading αὐτῷ 'him' is taken by NCBC to refer to God's Son, meaning here 'the one believing in the Son of God has [God's] testimony concerning him'.

   b. εἰς with accusative object (LN 90.23): 'in' [AB, HNTC, Lns, WBC; all versions].

   c. μαρτυρία (LN 33.264) (BAGD 2.d.β. p. 493): 'testimony' [AB, BAGD, HNTC, Lns; all versions except KJV, NASB, TNT], 'witness' [WBC; KJV, NASB], 'evidence of that belief' [TNT]. See this word at 5:9.

QUESTION—What is the significance of πιστεύων εἰς 'believing in' here and πιστεύων with the dative 'believing' in the following clause, which gives the negative counterpart of this positive clause?

   1. There is no difference in meaning [AB, Herm, TH, WBC]. Both mean 'to give credence to' [TH, WBC]. Here the specific content is to believe that Jesus is God's Son [AB]. The difference between the believer and the unbeliever is not commitment, but acceptance or rejection of the fact that Jesus is the Son of God [AB].

   2. The use of the preposition εἰς 'in' stresses personal commitment while the verb without the preposition means to give credence to a statement [Brd, EGT, ICC, NIC, NTC, Ws].

QUESTION—What is meant by having the testimony in oneself?

   1. It refers to the Spirit's inner witness to the believer [Brd, EBC, ICC, TNTC, WBC]. There is an inner conviction of the truth of the testimony [Brd]. It is a Spirit-given assurance that he was right to believe in Christ [EBC, TNTC, WBC].

   2. It refers to a continuing belief in the testimony [AB, NIC, NTC, TH]. The phrase means to hold the testimony fast in the heart [NIC, TH], to ponder it [TH], and make it part of one's way of life [AB]. Faith is a lasting, active force in the heart [NTC].

the-(one) not believing God has-made[a] him a liar,[b]

LEXICON—a. perf. act. indic. of ποιέω: 'to make'. See this word at 1:10.

   b. ψεύστης: 'liar'. See this word at 1:10; 2:4, 22; 4:20.

QUESTION—Why does this not parallel the preceding clause by saying, 'the one not believing in the Son of God has made God a liar'?

   It is assumed that the one not believing in God's Son does not believe in God himself [Alf, Herm] or does not believe what God said about his Son [Brd, EBC, EGT, WBC].

QUESTION—What is meant by 'making God a liar'?
In unbelief he regards God's testimony as a lie [ICC, My] and attributes falsehood to God [TNTC]. He treats God as a deceiver [NCBC]. It is the same as considering God to be a liar [Br, Brd, HNTC, My, WBC] and implies an active rejection of belief in God and Christ [AB, Alf, EBC, Lns, NTC, Ws; REB].

QUESTION—What does the use of the perfect tense of the verb indicate?
1. The perfect tense indicates that considering God to be a liar was in the past but the rejection and its effect continue [Alf, Brd, ICC, NTC, TH, Ws].
2. This describes the general character of unbelief and the perfect tense indicates that a future action is so certain that it is spoken of as if past [AB].

because[a] **he has-not-believed**[b] **in**[c] **the testimony**[d] **which God has-testified**[e] **concerning**[f] **his Son.**

LEXICON—a. ὅτι (LN 89.33): 'because' [HNTC, Lns; all versions except NAB, REB], 'by' [AB; NAB, REB], 'for' [WBC].
b. perf. act. indic. of πιστεύω (LN 31.35) (BAGD 1.a.ε. p. 660): 'to believe' [AB, BAGD, Lns, WBC; all versions except REB], 'to give credence to' [BAGD], 'to accept' [HNTC; REB]. The perfect tense indicates that the believing was in the past but the effect continues [NTC, Ws] or it implies deliberate refusal to believe [AB]. See this word at 5:1, 5.
c. εἰς with accusative object (LN 90.23): 'in' [AB, Lns; NAB, NASB, NRSV, TNT], not explicit [HNTC, WBC; KJV, NIV, NJB, REB, TEV].
d. μαρτυρία: 'testimony'. See this word at 5:9.
e. perf. act. indic. of μαρτυρέω: 'to testify'. See this word at 5:6, 7, 9. The perfect tense indicates that the witnessing was in the past but the effect continues [Alf].
f. περί with genitive object (LN 90.24): 'concerning' [HNTC, Lns; NASB], 'about' [NIV, NJB, TEV, TNT], 'on behalf of' [AB; NAB], 'to' [WBC; NRSV, REB], 'of' [KJV].

QUESTION—What relationship is indicated by ὅτι 'because'?
It indicates the grounds for saying that the person who does not believe God has made him a liar [Brd, Herm, My]. Not believing what God has said is the same as saying that God's testimony is a lie [Brd].

5:11 **And**[a] **this is the testimony,**[b] **that God gave**[c] **us eternal**[d] **life,**[e]
LEXICON—a. καί (LN 89.87): 'and' [Lns, WBC; KJV, NASB, NIV, NRSV], 'now' [AB], not explicit [HNTC; NAB, NJB, REB, TEV, TNT].
b. μαρτυρία: 'testimony'. See this word at 5:9, 10.
c. aorist act. indic. of δίδωμι (LN 90.90): 'to give' [AB, HNTC, Lns, WBC; all versions].
d. αἰώνιος: 'eternal'. See this word at 1:2; 2:25; 3:15.
e. ζωή: 'life'. See this word at 2:25; 3:14, 15.

QUESTION—How is this verse related to its context?
   The testimony referred to in 5:9 and 10 is now described [AB, Alf, Brd, Herm, ICC]. It gives the way God's testimony shows itself in the believer [My]. Now the writer turns to the blessing given to those who respond to God's testimony [TNTC].
QUESTION—To what does the pronoun αὕτη 'this' refer?
   It refers to the following ὅτι 'that' clause [AB, Brd, Herm, HNTC, ICC, My, TH, WBC, Ws; all versions].
QUESTION—What relationship is indicated by ὅτι 'that'?
   1. Many commentators seem to state that it indicates the content of the testimony [AB, Alf, Brd, EBC, Herm, ICC, Lns, NTC]. The explanations are varied. God's testimony about his Son was that God gave us eternal life in connection with his Son [Lns]. Eternal life can be a testimony in that it was made manifest in Jesus' life and is now in Jesus for the believer [Herm]. The testimony that the believer has in himself (5:10) is the gift of eternal life [Brd]. The testimony is that eternal life is present in God's Son [EBC]. God testified to the nature and character of Jesus by sending him on a mission characterized by water and blood in order to implant new life into men [ICC].
   2. It indicates the effect or meaning of God's testimony, not the content [HNTC, My, NIC, TH, WBC]. The sending of his Son leads to eternal life [NIC]. Eternal life shows in what way God's testimony affects the heart of the believer, who experiences it as power given by God [My].
QUESTION—What time is indicated by the aorist tense in the statement 'he *gave* us eternal life'?
   1. This refers to the coming of Christ at the incarnation [EGT, ICC, TH, Ws]. The purpose of sending his Son was to give eternal life to men [ICC].
   2. This refers to the occasion on which each person became a believer and received eternal life [AB, Brd, Lns]. John has the reception of eternal life in mind, not the availability of it [Brd].
   3. It refers to both Christ's coming and our appropriation of that life through the new birth [TNTC, WBC]. It was made available by Christ's earthly ministry and it was appropriated in the experiences of those who believed [WBC].
QUESTION—To whom does ἡμῖν 'us' refer?
   It refers to all believers [Herm, ICC, My, NTC, TH, WBC, Ws].
QUESTION—What is the significance of the Greek word order in which ζωὴν αἰώνιον 'eternal life' occurs first in the clause?
   It makes eternal life the prominent thought of the clause [AB, Brd, My, TH]. The absence of the article stresses the quality of this life [Brd, ICC].

and[a] this life is in[b] his Son.
LEXICON—a. καί (LN 89.87): 'and' [AB, HNTC, Lns, WBC; all versions].

b. ἐν with genitive object (LN 90.6): 'in' [AB, HNTC, WBC; all versions except REB, TEV], 'in connection with' [Lns]. This preposition is also translated by a verb and preposition 'to be found in' [REB] and a clause 'to have its source in' [TEV].

QUESTION—What relationship is indicated by the conjunction καί 'and'?
1. This is still governed by ὅτι 'that' and so is part of the explanation of the testimony [AB, Brd, ICC, WBC]. The testimony is the gift of a life which is in the Son [ICC].
2. This clause is not dependent on ὅτι 'that' and it gives a further explanation of eternal life [Alf, My].

QUESTION—What is meant by the life being 'in' God's Son?
The means of obtaining eternal life is by faith in God's Son [NTC, WBC]. Jesus is the basis for eternal life and that life is obtained only in relationship to him [HNTC]. The eternal life of the believer is one with the life that dwells in the Son [My].

5:12 The-(one) having[a] the Son has[b] the life;[c]

LEXICON—a. pres. act. participle of ἔχω (LN 90.65): 'to have' [HNTC, Lns; all versions except NAB, REB], 'to possess' [AB, WBC; NAB, REB]. The present tense here and in the following verb indicate that the situation existed then and would continue to exist [TH]. See this word at 2:23.

b. pres. act. indic. of ἔχω (LN 90.65): 'to have' [HNTC, Lns, WBC; all versions except NAB, REB], 'to possess' [AB; NAB, REB]. The present tense indicates a continuous possession of life [Brd].

c. ζωή: 'life'. See this word at 5:11.

QUESTION—How does this verse relate to its context?
It is the logical conclusion to the last clause in 5:10: if eternal life is 'in the Son', then those and only those who have the Son have life [Brd, My, NIC, NTC, TH].

QUESTION—What is meant by ἔχων τὸν υἱόν 'having the Son'?
It means to be in a vital spiritual relationship with the Son [Brd, NIC, WBC], having fellowship with him [NTC, TH, WBC].

QUESTION—What is the significance of the use of the article with ζωήν 'life'?
It refers to the mention of 'eternal life' in 5:10 [Brd, Lns].

the-(one) not having the Son of God does not have the life.

QUESTION—How is this clause related to the clause before it?
It is a negative parallel of the preceding clause [AB, Brd, Herm, ICC, NTC, TH, WBC, Ws].

QUESTION—What is the significance of υἱὸν τοῦ θεοῦ 'Son of God' here instead of the single word υἱόν 'Son' in the preceding clause?
The longer form emphasizes the fact that God is the ultimate source of life [AB, ICC, WBC, Ws], and it is ultimately God who is being rejected by those who do not have life [Brd, NIC]. This longer form makes the negative clause more prominent than the preceding positive clause [TH].

184   1 JOHN 5:13

DISCOURSE UNIT: 5:13–21 [AB, Br, Brd, EBC, EGT, HNTC, ICC, NIC, NTC, TH, Ws; NASB, NIV, TEV]. The topic is the conclusion [AB, Br, Brd, EBC, EGT, ICC, NTC, Ws; NIV], final remarks [TH], eternal life [TEV], assurance of life [HNTC, Ws], Christian certainties [Brd, NIC; NASB], activity of a Christian life [Ws].

DISCOURSE UNIT: 5:13–17 [TNTC]. The topic is assurance.

5:13 These (things) I-wrote[a] to you in-order-that[b] you-may-know[c] that you-have[d] eternal[e] life,[f]

TEXT—After ὑμῖν 'to you', some manuscripts have τοῖς πιστεύουσιν εἰς τὸ ὄνομα τοῦ υἱοῦ τοῦ θεοῦ 'the ones believing in the name of the Son of God'. GNT does not include or note this addition. It is included only by KJV.

LEXICON—a. aorist act. indic. of γράφω: 'to write'. See this word in the aorist tense at 2:21, 26. The aorist tense is an epistolary aorist [AB, EGT, WBC] regarding the present letter as a finished product or it looks back on what has been written to this point [Brd, Ws].

b. ἵνα (LN 89.59): 'in order that' [Lns; NASB], 'so that' [AB, WBC; NIV, NJB, TEV], 'that' [KJV, NRSV, TNT], not explicit [NAB, REB]. This conjunction is also translated 'the purpose (of my writing) is that' [HNTC].

c. perf. (with present meaning) act. subj. of οἶδα (LN 28.1): 'to know' [AB, HNTC, LN, Lns; all versions except NAB, REB], 'to be sure' [WBC], 'to assure' [REB], 'to make one realize' [NAB].

d. pres. act. indic. of ἔχω: 'to have'. See this word at 5:12. The present tense indicates that the possessing is a continuous state [TNTC, WBC], and a present reality [Brd, TH].

e. αἰώνιος: 'eternal'. See this word at 5:11.

f. ζωή: 'life'. See this word at 5:11, 12.

QUESTION—How does this verse relate to its context?

This verse is transitional [EBC, WBC]. It is a conclusion to the preceding section about the three witnesses and having life through the Son of God [TNTC, WBC] and some commentators make a section break after this verse [Herm, My, NCBC, TNTC, WBC]. It also introduces concluding remarks for the entire letter [EBC, EGT], here giving an explanation of the purpose for writing it [Brd]. Many begin a new section here [AB, Br, Brd, EBC, EGT, HNTC, ICC, NIC, NTC, TH, Ws; NASB, NIV, TEV]. It also begins a series of six 'we know' statements in opposition to the false teachers who claimed superior knowledge [EBC, WBC].

QUESTION—To what does the pronoun ταῦτα 'these things' refer?

1. It is referring to the whole letter [AB, Brd, Herm, HNTC, Lns, NCBC, NIC, NTC, TH, TNTC, WBC, Ws].
2. It refers only to 5:1–12 [ICC] or to 5:6–12 [My] about the teaching that Jesus is the Christ, the Son of God [ICC, My].

QUESTION—What relationship is indicated by ἵνα 'in order that'?
It indicates the purpose for writing [Herm, My, NIC, TH, TNTC, WBC]: I wrote this in order that you may know that you have eternal life. They need to have assurance [Brd, HNTC, ICC, Lns, My, NTC, TH, TNTC, WBC, Ws].
QUESTION—What is the significance of the Greek word order ὅτι ζωὴν ἔχετε αἰώνιον 'that life you have eternal'?
'Eternal' comes at the end of the clause and is separated by the verb from the noun it modifies to make the eternal quality of the life prominent [AB, NIC, TH, WBC, Ws].

to-the-(ones) believing[a] in[b] the name[c] of-the Son of-God.
LEXICON—a. pres. act. participle of πιστεύω: 'to believe'. See this word at 3:23; 5:10. The present tense indicates that the believing is a continuous action [TH, WBC, Ws].
b. εἰς with accusative object (LN 90.23): 'in' [AB, HNTC, Lns, WBC; all versions except KJV, REB], 'on' [KJV], 'to' [REB].
c. ὄνομα (LN 9.19) (BAGD I.4.c.β. p. 572): 'name'. See this word at 2:12; 3:23.
QUESTION—What is the significance of this clause occurring at the end of the verse?
This clause identifies 'you' in the preceding clause [WBC, Ws]. By occurring separately at the end of the sentence, it is made prominent [Brd, NIC, TH, TNTC, WBC].
QUESTION—What is the significance of ὄνομα 'name' here instead of just 'the Son of God'?
It means 'the person' [Br] and is in contrast to the seceders who deny the reality of the incarnation and therefore of Christ [Br, Herm, Lns]. It stresses the qualities denoted by the name of the person [ICC, NTC] and also the ability to do what is expressed by the name [NIC].

DISCOURSE UNIT: 5:14–21 [Alf, Herm, NCBC, WBC; NAB, NJB]. The topic is the appendix [Herm, NCBC; NJB], the conclusion [Alf, WBC], Christian confidence [WBC], a prayer for sinners [NAB].

DISCOURSE UNIT: 5:14–17 [Ws; NJB]. The topic is a prayer for sinners [NJB], the certainty of answered prayer [Brd], the confidence of spiritual action [Ws].

5:14 And[a] this is the confidence[b] which we-have towards[c] him,
LEXICON—a. καί (LN 89.92): 'and' [Lns; KJV, NASB, NRSV], 'now' [AB], not explicit [HNTC, WBC; all versions except KJV, NASB, NRSV].
b. παρρησία: 'confidence'. See this word at 2:28; 3:21; 4:17.
c. πρός with accusative object (LN 89.7) (BAGD III.4.b. p. 710): 'towards' [BAGD; NJB], 'in' [HNTC, WBC; KJV, NAB, NRSV, TNT], 'with' [BAGD], 'before' [BAGD; NASB], 'in the presence of' [AB; TEV], 'in approaching' [NIV], 'regarding' [Lns], not explicit [REB].

QUESTION—How does this verse relate to its context?
This is an inference from the preceding fact of possessing eternal life [Alf, Brd, My, NIC, NTC, Ws]. Besides the assurance of eternal life, there is a second assurance, that of answered prayer [TNTC]. Since the believer can be confident that he possesses eternal life, he can also be confident in prayer [Brd].

QUESTION—To what does the pronoun αὕτη 'this' refer?
It refers to the following ὅτι 'that' clause [AB, Alf, Brd, Herm, ICC, TH, WBC, Ws]: this is the confidence we have, namely, that we are confident that God hears us when we ask for anything according to his will.

QUESTION—To whom does αὐτόν 'him' refer?
It refers to God [AB, Brd, EBC, ICC, Lns, My, NCBC, NIC, NTC, TH, TNTC, WBC, Ws; NAB, NIV, REB, TEV].

QUESTION—What is meant by having confidence before God?
It means to feel free to come to God in prayer [Alf, Br, Brd, EBC, Herm, ICC, Lns, NCBC, NTC, TNTC, WBC, Ws]. It is to be confident that God will hear and answer [EGT, My].

that[a] if[b] we-ask-for[c] anything according-to[d] his will[e] he-hears[f] us.

LEXICON—a. ὅτι (LN 91.15): 'that' [HNTC, Lns, WBC; all versions except REB, TEV], 'namely that' [AB], 'because' [TEV], not explicit [REB].
  b. ἐάν (LN 67.32): 'if' [HNTC, Lns; all versions except NAB], 'whenever' [AB, TH, WBC; NAB].
  c. pres. mid. subj. of αἰτέω (LN 33.163) (BAGD p. 26): 'to ask for' [LN, WBC; NAB, TEV], 'to ask' [AB, Lns; all versions except NAB, REB, TEV], 'to ask in prayer' [BAGD], 'to make requests' [HNTC; REB].
  d. κατά with accusative object (LN 89.8): 'according to' [AB; all versions except NJB, REB], 'in accordance with' [HNTC, WBC; NJB], 'in accord with' [Lns], 'which accord with' [REB].
  e. θέλημα (LN 30.59) (BAGD 2.b. p. 354): 'will' [AB, BAGD, HNTC, LN, Lns, WBC; all versions].
  f. pres. act indic. of ἀκούω (LN 31.56) (BAGD 5. p. 32): 'to hear' [AB, HNTC, Lns; all versions except REB, TNT], 'to listen to' [BAGD, LN, WBC; REB, TNT].

QUESTION—What relationship is indicated by ἐάν 'if'?
It indicates a condition for prayer to be heard by God [AB, Alf, EBC, Herm, ICC, NCBC, NIC, NTC, TNTC]. There is no doubt that the request will be made [AB] and some translate as 'whenever' [AB, TH, WBC; REB]. This is a self-evident condition, but it is mentioned because of the following case for which God does not want anyone to pray [Lns].

QUESTION—What is signified by the use of the middle voice instead of the active voice in the verb αἰτώμεθα 'we ask'?
  1. The middle voice is used here as a stylistic variant of the active voice and does not change the meaning of the verb [AB, BAGD, Brd, EGT, HNTC,

ICC, NTC, WBC]. In classical Greek the middle voice would mean to ask for oneself, but here there is no distinctive meaning [AB].
2. The middle voice includes a personal interest that is lacking in the active voice [Ws].
3. The middle voice is used to indicate that the requester has a right to ask [Lns].

QUESTION—What is meant by ἀκούει 'he hears'?
It means to hear and to be favorably inclined [Brd, EBC, ICC, Lns, My, NIC, TNTC, WBC, Ws]. It means that God will respond [TH]. To hear is to grant the request [HNTC, My], although this thought is not expanded until the following verse [My]. It is possible that God will not grant the request, but he will listen and answer in his own way [EGT].

5:15 And[a] if[b] we-know[c] that he-hears[d] us, whatever we-ask-for,[e]
LEXICON—a. καί (LN 89.92): 'and' [AB, Lns, WBC; all versions], not explicit [HNTC].
b. ἐάν (LN 67.32) (BAGD I.3.a. p. 211): 'if' [BAGD, HNTC, Lns, WBC; all versions except NAB, TEV], 'since' [AB; NAB, TEV].
c. perf. act. indic. of οἶδα: 'to know'.
d. pres. act. indic. of ἀκούω: 'to hear'. See this word at 5:14. The present tense indicates that this is an habitual action [TNT].
e. pres. mid. subj. of αἰτέω: 'to ask for'. See this word at 5:14.

QUESTION—What relationship is indicated by καί 'and'?
It indicates a continuation of the discussion about the certainty that God will answer prayer [Brd, WBC]. It amplifies what he meant by 'hearing us' [EGT, Herm, NIC].

QUESTION—How do we know that God hears us?
The assurance is based on the fact that the request is in accordance with God's will (5:14) [Brd, EBC, ICC, TH].

we-know that we-have[a] the requests[b] which we-have-asked-for from[c] him.
LEXICON—a. pres. act. indic. of ἔχω (LN 90.65) (BAGD I.2.g. p. 333): 'to have' [AB, Lns; KJV, NASB, NIV], 'to be granted' [HNTC, WBC], 'to possess' [NJB, TNT], 'to obtain' [NRSV], 'to be ours' [NAB, REB], 'to give' [TEV]. The present tense indicates that the possessing is an immediate certainty [AB, Brd, EBC, EGT, ICC, NIC, NTC, TNTC; NJB].
b. αἴτημα (LN 33.164) (BAGD p. 26): 'request' [BAGD, HNTC, WBC; NASB, NRSV], 'petition' [KJV], 'what (we asked for)' [AB; NAB, NIV, TEV, TNT], 'whatever (we asked for)' [NJB], 'all (we asked for)' [REB], 'asking' [Lns].
c. ἀπό with genitive object (LN 90.15) (BAGD p. 25): 'from' [BAGD, Lns; NASB, TEV], 'of' [KJV, NIV, NJB, NRSV, REB], 'to' [HNTC, WBC], not explicit [AB; NAB, TNT].

QUESTION—What is meant by ἔχομεν τὰ αἰτήματα we 'have the requests'?
It means that our assurance of the possession is so great that through anticipation we possess the answer even though there may be a delay in the

answer [AB, HNTC, NIC, WBC]. There is a sense that at the time of the request, what is requested is already granted [Brd, ICC, NTC, TH, TNTC]. The spiritual gifts we ask for are immediately available [NIC, WBC].

QUESTION—What does the use of the perfect tense ᾐτήκαμεν 'we have asked for' indicate?

The perfect tense indicates that the author is thinking of all prayers that have been offered to the present time [Alf, ICC, TH, WBC]. It indicates that continued prayer has been offered [NTC].

5:16 If[a] anyone sees[b] his brother sinning[c] a-sin[d] not to[e] death,[f]

LEXICON—a. ἐάν (LN 67.32): 'if' [AB, HNTC, Lns, WBC; all versions except NAB], not explicit [NAB].
- b. aorist act. subj. of ὁράω (LN 24.1): 'to see' [AB, HNTC, LN, Lns, WBC; all versions]. The aorist tense refers to any specific instance of the sin [Alf, NTC]. It means that the sin is observable [Brd, NIC, TH, TNTC, WBC, Ws] or known [AB].
- c. pres. act. participle of ἁμαρτάνω (LN 88.289) (BAGD 3. p. 42): 'to sin'. See this word at 1:10; 2:1; 3:6. The present tense indicates a continuing action [Br, Brd, Lns, NTC].
- d. ἁμαρτία (LN 88.290) (BAGD 1. p. 43): 'sin'. See this word at 1:8, 9; 2:2, 12; 3:4, 5, 8, 9; 4:10.
- e. πρός with accusative object (LN 89.44) (BAGD III.3.b. p. 710): 'to', 'unto' [Lns; KJV], 'to lead to' [HNTC, WBC; NASB, NIV, TEV], 'to result in' [BAGD], not explicit [AB; NAB, NJB, NRSV, REB, TNT].
- f. θάνατος (LN 23.99) (BAGD 2.b. p. 351): 'death' [HNTC, Lns, WBC; KJV, NASB, NIV, TEV], 'eternal death' [BAGD]. The phrase πρὸς θάνατον 'to death' is translated as 'to be deadly' [AB; NAB, NJB, REB, TNT], 'to be mortal' [NRSV]. See this word at 3:14.

QUESTION—What relationship is indicated by ἐάν 'if'?

It indicates a condition which has the possibility or expectation of occurring [AB, Brd, ICC, My, TH, WBC] and could be translated with a temporal 'when' [TH, WBC].

QUESTION—To whom does ἀδελφόν 'brother' refer?

It refers to a fellow Christian [AB, Alf, Br, Brd, EBC, EGT, ICC, Lns, My, NIC, NTC, WBC, Ws]. Some commentators think that a sin leading to death can be committed by those who are truly God's children and that there is a possibility that such a person can fall into apostasy [NIC]. Others assume that those who can commit sin that leads to death are not real Christians and conclude that 'brother' includes nominal Christians also [TNTC].

QUESTION—What relationship is indicated by πρός 'to'?

It means 'causes' [AB, Alf, Br, Herm, TH; NAB, NJB, NRSV, REB, TNT] or 'leading towards' [Brd, HNTC, TH, WBC; NASB, NIV, TEV]. If persisted in, it results in death [ICC].

QUESTION—What is meant by ἁμαρτίαν πρὸς θάνατον 'a sin to death'?
Death and life both refer to spiritual states [AB, Alf, Brd, EBC, EGT, Herm, HNTC, ICC, Lns, My, NCBC, NIC, NTC, TH, TNTC, WBC, Ws]. The sin to death is specifically denying that Jesus is Christ, the Son of God [Alf, EGT, Lns, NCBC], it is rejecting Jesus as the Christ and refusing to love one's brothers [NIC, NTC, TH], a deliberate rejection of known truth, the blasphemy against the Holy Spirit [TNTC]. It is the settled sin of the false teachers who are disobedient and walk in darkness [Brd]. Some speak of this in more general terms: any sin involving a deliberate rejection of the claims of Christ [ICC], and wanton transgression of God's commands [Herm]. Since it is observable, it is sinful conduct which results from the internal act of falling away from Christ [My].

he-will-ask,[a] and he-will-give[b] life[c] to-him, to-the-(ones) sinning[d] not to death.

LEXICON—a. fut. act. indic. of αἰτέω: 'to ask'. See this word at 5:14, 15.
    b. fut. act. indic. of δίδωμι: 'to give'. See this word at 5:11.
    c. ζωή: 'life'. See this word at 5:11, 12, 13.
    d. pres. act. participle of ἁμαρτάνω (LN 88.289) (BAGD 5. p. 42): 'to sin'. See this word in the preceding clause. The phrase τοῖς ἁμαρτάνουσιν μὴ πρὸς θάνατον 'sinning a sin not to death' is translated 'in the case of non-deadly sin' [HNTC], 'whose sin is not mortal' [WBC], 'sin not leading to death' [NASB, NIV, TEV], 'whose sin is not mortal' [NRSV], 'who do not commit a deadly sin' [TNT], 'provided it is not a deadly sin' [NJB], 'those not guilty of deadly sin' [REB]. The present tense indicates that this is a continuing action [Brd, ICC].

QUESTION—What does the future tense of the verb αἰτήσει 'he will ask' indicate?
  1. The future tense implies a command [AB, Alf, My, NTC; NAB, NIV, REB, TEV]: he should ask.
  2. The future tense is a statement of fact which assumes that one will ask when he sees his brother sinning [Lns, TNTC, Ws; KJV, NASB, NJB, NRSV, REB, TEV]: he will ask. It is an inevitable, spontaneous reaction [TNTC, Ws].

QUESTION—Who is the implied subject of the verb δώσει 'he will give' and to whom does αὐτῷ 'to him' refer?
  1. God will give life to the sinner [AB, Lns, NCBC, NIC, NTC, WBC, Ws; NIV, NJB, NRSV, REB, TEV].
  2. God will give the person praying life for the sinner [Brd; NASB].
  3. The one praying, through his intercession, will give life to the sinner [Alf, EGT, Herm, ICC, My, TH, TNTC; TNT]. The intercessor will be the means by which God will give life to the sinner [Alf]. Because of the power of intercession, the Christian may be said to give someone life [ICC].

QUESTION—What does it mean to be given life? Why does the brother need to be given life if he is a brother and has not sinned a sin to death?

The one sinning, even though he has eternal life, needs this because all sin contains the embryo of death [My], and if persisted in will lead to apostasy [Alf, EBC, WBC, Ws]. Although the sinner has not sinned irrevocably, he has already begun losing his life [Lns, Ws] or is in imminent danger of losing it [AB]. God will forgive the sin and restore him to fellowship [NTC]. God strengthens the sinner's damaged and declining spiritual life [Lns]. God will restore him to fullness of life [Brd].

QUESTION—What is the significance of the change from singular 'brother' to plural 'the ones who have sinned'?

It broadens the application to a general rule [Alf, Brd, Lns, My, WBC, Ws]. There will be others who sin from time to time [Lns].

There-is a-sin to death; not concerning[a] that (kind) do-I-say[b] that[c] he-should-ask.[d]

LEXICON—a. περί with genitive object (LN 90.24): 'concerning' [Lns], 'about' [AB, HNTC; all versions except KJV, NASB, NRSV], 'for' [WBC; KJV, NASB, NRSV].

b. pres. act. of λέγω (LN 33.64) (BAGD II.1.c. p. 469): 'to say' [AB, HNTC, LN, Lns, WBC; all versions except REB], 'to recommend' [BAGD], 'to suggest' [REB].

c. ἵνα (LN 90.22): 'that' [AB, HNTC, Lns, WBC; all versions].

d. aorist act. subj. of ἐρωτάω (LN 33.161) (BAGD 2. p. 312): 'to ask' [BAGD, LN], 'to pray' [AB; all versions except NASB, TNT], 'to intercede' [HNTC, WBC], 'to make request' [Lns; NASB, TNT], 'to beseech' [BAGD].

QUESTION—What is meant by the statement 'I do not say that he should ask'?

1. This implies a command not to pray for such sinners [AB, Alf, EBC, TNTC].
2. This does not forbid such praying [Brd, ICC, NIC, TNTC, WBC]. Praying is not advised because John doubts that it will have results in this case [TNTC]. This kind of sin must be left up to God alone [ICC] and a positive answer is not assured [Brd].

QUESTION—What is the difference between ἐρωτήσῃ 'he should ask' used here and αἰτήσει 'he will ask' used at the beginning of the verse?

1. The Greek words are synonyms; there is no semantic importance to the change of verbs [AB, Brd, ICC, NIC, NTC; probably all the commentaries that do not mention a difference].
2. There is a difference of meaning. The verb αἰτήσει 'he will ask' refers to a request of an inferior to a superior while ἐρωτήσῃ 'he should ask' refers to a request among equals where the one who asks has a right to request and, as such, implies presumption [Alf, Ws]. The request concerning a sin not to death is in submission to God's will, while a request about a sin leading to death is an act of presumption [Alf]. The verb αἰτήσει 'he

should ask' is the stronger of the two and refers to a demand while ἐρωτήσῃ 'he should ask' refers to a request [My].

5:17 All[a] wrongdoing[b] is sin,[c] but[d] (there) is (a) sin not to[e] death.[f]

LEXICON—a. πᾶς (LN 59.24): 'all' [AB, HNTC, WBC; all versions except NJB], 'every' [Lns], 'every kind of' [NJB].
- b. ἀδικία (LN 88.21) (BAGD 2. p. 18): 'wrongdoing' [AB, HNTC, WBC; NAB, NIV, NRSV, REB, TEV], 'wrong' [Lns], 'unrighteousness' [BAGD, LN; KJV, NASB, TNT], 'wickedness' [BAGD; NJB], 'injustice' [BAGD]. See this word at 1:9.
- c. ἁμαρτία: 'sin'. See this word at 5:16.
- d. καί (LN 91.12): 'but' [AB, HNTC, WBC; NAB, NJB, NRSV, TEV, TNT], 'and' [KJV, NASB, NIV], not explicit [REB].
- e. πρός with accusative object (LN 89.44): 'to', 'unto' [KJV]. This preposition is also translated as a verb: 'to lead to' [NASB, NIV, NJB, TEV]. For AB, HNTC, WBC; NAB, NRSV, REB, TNT, see below.
- f. θάνατος: 'death'. See this word at 3:14, 5:6.

QUESTION—Why is this clause mentioned?

It indicates that all sin is serious. The writer inserts this clause over a concern that the distinction between lesser and greater sin implied in the distinction between sin to death and sin not to death might lead some to think some sin was not serious [Brd, ICC, My, NIC, TH, TNTC, WBC]. Perhaps the false teachers claimed sinlessness by defining certain deeds as wrong but not sinful [Brd, EBC, HNTC, WBC]. The assurance of forgiveness would not make wrongdoing seem less sinful [AB]. Wrongdoing is sin, as well as lawlessness (3:4) [ICC].

DISCOURSE UNIT: 5:18–21 [TNTC; NJB]. The topic is three affirmations and a conclusion [TNTC], summary [NJB].

5:18 We-know[a] that everyone having-been-begotten[b] by God (does) not sin,[c]

LEXICON—a. perf. act. indic. of οἶδα (LN 28.1) (BAGD 1.e. p. 556): 'to know' [AB, HNTC, Lns; all versions except NJB], 'to be sure' [WBC], 'to be aware' [NJB]. See this word at 3:2, 5, 15.
- b. perf. pass. participle of γεννάω: 'to be begotten'. See this word at 2:29; 3:9; 4:7; 5:1, 4. The perfect tense indicates that the effect of the begetting continues [Alf, ICC, Lns, TNTC].
- c. pres. act. indic. of ἁμαρτάνω: 'to sin'. See this word at 5:16. The present tense indicates that the sinning is a continual or habitual action [Alf, Brd, EBC, EGT, NTC, TNTC, WBC, Ws; NIV, TEV, TNT].

QUESTION—How is this verse related to its context?

It begins a series of three "we know" statements that sum up the teaching of the book [AB, Alf, Br, EBC, Herm, Lns, My, NIC, TNTC, Ws]. John reminds the readers of a basic article of faith [Br].

QUESTION—To whom does πᾶς ὁ γεγεννημένος 'every one having been begotten from God' refer?

It refers to every Christian [AB, Br, Brd, EBC, EGT, ICC, My, NCBC, NIC, NTC, TH, TNTC, WBC, Ws].

but[a] the-(one) having-been-begotten[b] by God keeps[c] him,

TEXT—Instead of αὐτόν 'him', some manuscripts have ἑαυτόν 'himself'. GNT selects αὐτόν 'him' with a C rating, indicating a considerable degree of doubt. 'Himself' is chosen by Lns, My, and KJV.

LEXICON—a. ἀλλά (LN 89.125): 'but' [KJV, NASB, NRSV, TNT], 'rather' [AB, WBC; NAB], 'for' [TEV], 'on the contrary' [HNTC, Lns], 'because' [NJB], not explicit [NIV, REB].

b. aorist pass. participle of γεννάω (LN 13.56) (BAGD 1.b. p. 155): 'to be begotten' [AB; KJV, NAB], 'to be born' [Lns; NASB, NIV, NJB, NRSV]. The phrase 'the one having been begotten by God' is translated 'the Son of God' [REB, TEV, TNT]. The aorist tense refers to a specific event in the past [Alf, NTC, TH, WBC] or is used in a timeless manner [Brd].

c. pres. act. indic. of τηρέω (LN 13.32) (BAGD 3. p. 815): 'to keep' [BAGD, LN, Lns; KJV, NASB, NRSV, TNT], 'to keep safe' [NIV, REB, TEV], 'to keep unharmed' [BAGD], 'to protect' [AB, WBC; NAB, NJB], 'to hold on to' [HNTC]. The present tense indicates that this is a continuing action [Brd, TNTC, WBC].

QUESTION—To whom does ὁ γεννηθείς 'the one who is begotten of God' refer?

1. It refers to the Son of God, Jesus Christ [Br, Brd, EBC, EGT, Herm, ICC, NCBC, NIC, NTC, TH, TNTC, WBC, Ws; NASB, REB, TEV, TNT]: but the one begotten by God (i.e., the Son of God) keeps the child of God. The expression is a play on the words in a similar phrase in the preceding clause [TH] or it is a way of identifying the Son of God with his followers [NIC, TH]. This phrase is equivalent to the more common designation 'the Son of God' [TH]. The eternal relationship with the Father is described by the gnomic or timeless aorist [Brd], or the aorist refers to the time of Jesus' birth [NTC, TH, WBC].

2. It refers to the Christian [AB, Alf, HNTC, Lns, My; KJV, NAB]. Some follow the reading ἑαυτόν 'himself' and even the reading αὐτόν 'him' can be taken as a reflexive [AB] so that it means 'the one begotten by God keeps himself'. The believer keeps himself with the strength resulting from his spiritual life [Lns]. But others would rather take it to mean that God keeps the believer and translate it 'God protects the one begotten by him' [NAB]. One commentator says that the one begotten by God is protected by that divine birth [Alf].

QUESTION—What is meant by τηρεῖ 'he keeps'?

It is defined by the next clause: to keep him safe and protect him from the evil one [AB, Alf, EBC, NCBC, NTC, TH, TNTC, Ws]. It means to keep him free from sin [NIC].

and the evil-one[a] (does) not touch[b] him.
LEXICON—a. πονηρός (LN 12.35) (BAGD 2.b. p. 691): 'the evil one' [AB, BAGD, HNTC, LN, WBC; all versions except KJV], 'the wicked one' [Lns; KJV], 'Devil' [BAGD].
  b. pres. mid. indic. of ἅπτω (LN **20.16**) (BAGD 2.d. p. 103): 'to touch' [AB, BAGD, HNTC; KJV, NAB, NASB, NRSV, REB], 'to harm' [BAGD, LN, WBC; NIV, TEV], 'to fasten himself on' [Lns], 'to have a hold on' [NJB], 'to get a hold of' [TNT].
QUESTION—To whom does ὁ πονηρός 'the evil one' refer?
  It refers to Satan [AB, Alf, BAGD, Brd, EBC, Herm, HNTC, Lns, My, NTC, TH, TNTC, WBC, Ws; all versions].
QUESTION—What is meant by ἅπτεται 'touches'?
  It means to be harmed by the evil one [AB, BAGD, Brd, EBC, Herm, ICC, My, NCBC, NIC, NTC, TH, WBC; NIV, TEV], to be controlled and led into sin by Satan [NTC, TNTC].

5:19 **We-know[a] that we-are from[b] God,**
LEXICON—a. pres. act. indic. of οἶδα (LN 28.1) (BAGD 1.e. p. 556): 'to know'. See this word at 5:18.
  b. ἐκ with genitive object (LN 89.3) (BAGD 3.a. p. 234): 'from' [BAGD, Lns; NJB], 'of' [BAGD; KJV, NASB, NRSV]. This preposition is also translated 'to belong to' [AB, HNTC; NAB, TEV, TNT], 'to derive from' [WBC], 'to be of the family' [REB] 'to be children of' [NIV]. See this word at 3:10.
QUESTION—What relationship is indicated by the preposition ἐκ 'from'?
  It indicates that God is the source of their spiritual being and existence [AB, NTC, TNTC, WBC, Ws], they are born of God [Alf, Brd, EBC, Lns, My, NCBC, NIC, TNTC; REB], they are his children [Brd, EBC, NIC], and belong to God [AB, EBC, HNTC, My, NTC; NAB, TEV, TNT].

and the whole[a] world[b] lies[c] in the evil-one/wickedness.[d]
LEXICON—a. ὅλος (LN 63.1) (BAGD 2.b. p. 564): 'whole' [AB, BAGD, LN, Lns, WBC; all versions], 'entire' [BAGD, HNTC, LN]. See this word at 2:2.
  b. κόσμος (LN 41.38) (BAGD 7. p. 446): 'world' [AB, HNTC, Lns, WBC; all versions]. See this word at 2:2.
  c. pres. mid. (deponent = act.) indic. of κεῖμαι (LN 13.73) (BAGD 2.d. p. 427): 'to lie in' [Lns; KJV]. The phrase ἐν κεῖται 'lies in' is translated 'lies in the power of' [NASB, REB, TNT], 'lies under the power of' [NRSV], 'lies in the grasp of' [AB, HNTC], 'is in the power of' [WBC; NJB], 'is under the control of' [NIV], 'is under the rule of' [TEV], 'is under' [NAB].
  d. πονηρός: 'the evil one'. See this word at 5:18.
QUESTION—What relationship is indicated by καί 'and'?
  It indicates that this clause is an independent clause and not a second object of 'know' [Alf, ICC, WBC, Ws].

QUESTION—What is meant by ὁ κόσμος 'the world'?

It is a metonymy for all who are estranged from God [Brd, ICC, Ws], everything in the world that is hostile to God [AB, Alf, BAGD, Br, EGT, My, NCBC, TH, TNTC, WBC]. Those who are 'from God' are not included [TH, WBC].

QUESTION—What gender is πονηρῷ 'evil' and to whom/what does it refer?
1. It is masculine and refers to Satan [AB, Alf, BAGD, Br, Brd, EBC, EGT, HNTC, ICC, Lns, My, NCBC, NIC, TH, TNTC, WBC, Ws; all versions except KJV].
2. It is neuter and refers to wickedness [KJV].

QUESTION—What is meant by the world lying in the evil one?

It means that the world is in the power of the evil one [Alf, EBC, My, NIC], it is under his control [Brd, Lns, My, NTC, TNTC, WBC], it is in the sphere of his influence [Ws], it is in his realm and dependent on him [AB].

5:20 And/But[a] we-know[b] that the Son of God has come,[c]

LEXICON—a. δέ (LN 89.94, 89.124): 'and' [KJV, NASB, NRSV, TNT], 'yet' [HNTC], 'finally' [AB], 'moreover' [Alf, Lns], 'nevertheless' [WBC], 'too' [NAB], 'also' [NIV], not explicit [NJB, REB, TEV].
b. perf. act. indic of οἶδα: 'to know'. See this word at 5:19.
c. pres. act. indic of ἥκω (LN 85.10) (BAGD 1.c. p. 344): 'to come' [AB, BAGD, HNTC, LN, Lns, WBC; all versions].

QUESTION—What relationship is indicated by the conjunction δέ 'and/but'?
1. It adds the last of the things we know [Lns].
2. It indicates a summary of the main themes of the epistle of the sonship of Jesus and the incarnation [AB, Alf, EBC].
3. It introduces a contrast with the preceding clause [HNTC, My, NIC, WBC, Ws]: the whole world lies in the evil one, but we ... are in the true one.

QUESTION—What is meant by ἥκει 'he has come'?

This present tense form has the force of a perfect tense and means having come in the past and still being present [AB, Alf, Brd, EGT, ICC, NCBC, TH, TNTC, WBC, Ws]. It is used for the appearance of deity [AB], and referring to coming into the world at the incarnation [Alf, Br, EBC, EGT, Herm, My, NIC, TNTC, WBC] and to the abiding presence of Christ [Alf, EGT].

and[a] has-given[b] us understanding[c] in-order-that/so that/that[d] we-might-know[e] the true[f] (one);

LEXICON—a. καί (LN 89.92): 'and' [AB, HNTC, Lns, WBC; all versions].
b. perf. act. indic of δίδωμι (LN 90.51): 'to give' [AB, HNTC, Lns, WBC; all versions], 'to cause' [LN]. The perfect tense indicates that the giving was in the past but the effect continues [Lns, TH, TNTC, WBC, Ws].
c. διάνοια (LN 30.15) (BAGD 1. p. 187): 'understanding' [BAGD, HNTC, Lns; all versions except NAB], 'insight' [AB, BAGD, WBC], 'discernment' [NAB].

1 JOHN 5:20

d. ἵνα (LN 89.59) (BAGD I.3. p. 377): 'in order that' [BAGD; NASB], 'so that' [HNTC, Lns; NIV, NJB, TEV, TNT], 'that' [KJV], not explicit [AB; NAB, NRSV, REB].
e. pres. act. subj. of γινώσκω: 'to know'. See this word at 2:3b, 4, 13, 14; 3:1, 6; 4:6, 7, 8. The present tense indicates that this is a continuing action [AB, TH, TNTC, WBC, Ws].
f. ἀληθινός (LN 73.2) (BAGD 3. p. 37): 'true'. With the masculine article, it is translated 'the true one' [HNTC], 'the real one' [Lns], 'him who is true' [KJV, NASB, NIV, NRSV], 'the one who is true' [AB; NAB, NJB], 'him who is the truth' [WBC], 'the true God' [REB, TEV], 'him who is the real God' [TNT].

QUESTION—Who is the implied subject of the verb δέδωκεν 'he has given'?
The Son of God is the implied subject [Alf, Br, Herm, ICC, Lns, My, WBC].

QUESTION—What is meant by διάνοιαν 'understanding'?
It means the ability to understand [Alf, Brd, ICC, Lns, My, NTC, TH, TNTC, WBC, Ws].

QUESTION—What relationship is indicated by the conjunction ἵνα 'in order that'?
1. It indicates the purpose for giving understanding [Alf, BAGD, Brd, HNTC, Lns; NASB, NIV, NJB, NRSV, TNT]: he has given us understanding in order that we might know him who is true.
2. It indicates the result of giving understanding [Alf, Lns; TEV]: he has given us understanding and so we know him who is true. The purpose has been accomplished or at least made secure [Alf].
3. It indicates the content of what is understood [AB, My, WBC; NAB, REB]: he has given us understanding to know him who is true.

QUESTION—What is meant by γινώσκωμεν 'we might know'?
It means come to know by experience [BAGD, NTC, TNTC, WBC].

QUESTION—Who is the 'true one'?
This refers to God, the Father [AB, Alf, Brd, Herm, ICC, Lns, My, NCBC, TH].

QUESTION—What is meant by ἀληθινόν 'true'?
It means genuine as against the counterfeit idols mentioned in the next verse [AB, Alf, BAGD, Brd, EBC, EGT, HNTC, Lns, My, NCBC, NTC, TH, TNTC, WBC, Ws; TNT].

and[a] we-are in[b] the true (one), in his Son Jesus Christ.
LEXICON—a. καί (LN 89.93): 'and' [AB, Lns, WBC; KJV, NAB, NASB, NIV, NRSV], 'indeed' [HNTC; REB], not explicit [NJB, TEV, TNT].
b. ἐν with dative object (LN 89.119): 'in' [AB, HNTC, WBC; all versions except TEV], 'in connection with' [Lns]. This preposition is also translated as 'live in union with' [TEV].

QUESTION—What relationship is indicated by καί 'and'?
It indicates that the following clause is independent of the verb to know [Herm, Lns]: and we are in the true one.

QUESTION—To whom does ἀληθινῷ 'the true one' refer?
It refers to God, the Father [Alf, Herm, ICC, Lns, NTC, TH, WBC; REB, TEV, TNT].

QUESTION—What is the relationship between the two prepositional phrases beginning with the preposition ἐν 'in'?
1. The second phrase explains the first by giving the reason why we are in the true one [AB, Alf, Brd, Herm, ICC, Lns, My, NCBC, NIC, NTC, TH, TNTC, WBC, Ws; NAB]: we are in the true one because of being in his Son, Jesus Christ.
2. The second phrase is in apposition with the first [probably KJV, NIV]: we are in the true one, even in God's Son, Jesus Christ.

This-(one) is the true God and eternal^a life.^b

LEXICON—a. αἰώνιος: 'eternal'. See this word at 1:2; 2:25; 3:15; 5:11, 13.
b. ζωή: 'life'. See this word at 5:11, 12, 13, 16.

QUESTION—To whom does οὗτος 'this one' refer?
1. It refers to Jesus Christ [AB, EBC, Herm, Lns, NIC, NTC, TH]: Jesus is the true God and eternal life. It is because Jesus is the true God that the person who is in him is also in the Father [NIC].
2. It refers to God [Alf, Brd, EGT, ICC, My, NCBC, TNTC, WBC, Ws]: God is the true God and eternal life.

5:21 Children^a guard^b yourselves from^c the idols.^d

TEXT—At the end of the book some manuscripts have ἀμήν 'amen'. GNT omits it and gives the omission an A rating, indicating virtual certainty. 'Amen' is included only by KJV.

LEXICON—a. τεκνίον: 'child'. See this word at 2:1, 12, 28; 3:7, 18; 4:4.
b. aorist act. impera. of φυλάσσω (LN 13.154) (BAGD 1.c. p. 868): 'to guard' [AB, BAGD, HNTC, Lns, WBC; NASB, TNT], 'to keep from' [LN; KJV, NIV, NRSV], 'to keep safe' [TEV]. The phrase φυλάξατε ἑαυτά 'guard yourselves' is translated 'be on your guard' [NAB, NJB, REB]. The aorist imperative indicates that the guarding requires immediate action [Brd, EGT, ICC, TH, WBC].
c. ἀπό with genitive object (LN 89.122): 'from' [HNTC, Lns; all versions except NAB, NJB, REB], 'against' [AB, WBC; NAB, NJB, REB].
d. εἴδωλον (LN **12.23**) (BAGD 2. p. 221): 'idol' [AB, BAGD, HNTC, Lns; all versions except NJB, TEV, TNT], 'false god' [BAGD, LN, WBC; NJB, TEV, TNT].

QUESTION—What is the significance of the active voice with the reflexive pronoun here instead of the middle voice without the pronoun?
1. It makes the reflexive more prominent and by that emphasizes individual responsibility [ICC, Ws].
2. It is a stylistic variant without semantic distinction [AB, and possibly all commentaries that do not mention this].

QUESTION—What is the significance of the article before εἰδώλων 'idols'?
It indicates that a specific danger is in mind [AB, TNTC, Ws].

1 JOHN 5:20

QUESTION—What is meant by εἰδώλων 'idols'?
1. This is a metaphoric expression for something that takes the place of God [AB, WBC, Ws]. Here it is a false conception of God and Christ held by the false teachers [AB, Br, EGT, Herm, HNTC, ICC, Lns, My, NCBC, NIC, TNTC, WBC]. The false teaching is condemned as being nothing but paganism [Herm].
2. This is a metaphoric expression for sin and emphasizes how horrible sin is [TH].
3. This is a literal reference to idols used in pagan worship [Brd].

EXEGETICAL SUMMARY OF 2 JOHN

Title: The Second of John
QUESTION—Who wrote this letter?
    The writer calls himself ὁ πρεσβύτερος 'the Elder'. The similarities of structures, word choices, and topics between the Gospel of John, 1 John, 2 John, and 3 John lead most commentators to assign them to a single author [AB, Alf, Br, Brd, EBC, EGT, ICC, Lns, My, NIC, NTC, TH, TNTC, Ws; NJB]. Most think that the writer was the Apostle John and assume that he was also known as "the Elder" [Alf, Br, Brd, EBC, EGT, Lns, My, NTC, TNTC, Ws; NJB]. Some think that it was not the Apostle John [AB, Herm, HNTC, ICC, NCBC, WBC], but may have been a follower of the Apostle John [AB, WBC].

DISCOURSE UNIT: 1–3 [AB, Alf, Br, EBC, EGT, Herm, Lns, NCBC, NIC, NTC, TH, TNTC, WBC, Ws]. The topic is the opening formula [AB], the address and greeting [Alf, Br, EGT, Herm, Lns, NCBC, NIC, NTC, TH, TNTC, WBC, Ws], the introduction [EBC].

1 The elder[a] to-(the)-chosen[b] lady[c] and to-her children,[d]
LEXICON—a. πρεσβύτερος (LN 53.77) (BAGD 2.b.β. p. 700): 'elder' [BAGD, HNTC, LN, Lns; all versions], 'presbyter' [AB, BAGD, WBC].
  b. ἐκλεκτός (LN 30.93) (BAGD 1.b p. 242): 'chosen' [BAGD, HNTC, LN; NASB, NIV, NJB, REB, TNT], 'elect' [AB, Lns, WBC; KJV, NAB, NRSV], 'dear' [TEV].
  c. κυρία (LN **87.54**) (BAGD 1, 2. p. 458): 'lady' [AB, BAGD, HNTC, LN, WBC; all versions], 'mistress' [BAGD, Lns].
  d. τέκνον (LN 10.36) (BAGD 2.c p. 808): 'child' [AB, BAGD, HNTC, LN, Lns; all versions], 'offspring' [WBC].
QUESTION—Why does the writer call himself ὁ πρεσβύτερος 'the elder'?
  1. The term means only that he was an elderly person [Alf, HNTC, My]. His age and experience gave him qualities valued by the church [HNTC].
  2. The term was used of older respected Christian leaders [AB, Br, Herm, ICC, Lns, NCBC, NTC, TH, TNTC, Ws]. It was an honorary title given to the surviving apostles [Br, ICC, Lns, NTC, TNTC, Ws] and to those who handed down the Christian traditions [AB, Herm, ICC, NCBC, TH].
  3. The term indicates that he was a church official [EBC, NIC, WBC]. He was equivalent to a bishop who had authority over the region in which his readers lived [EBC].
QUESTION—What is meant by ἐκλεκτῇ 'chosen'?
  It means that God chose the lady to belong to himself [BAGD, HNTC, Lns, NIC, WBC; REB, TNT] and to give her salvation [TH]. It was a standard designation for Christians [TH].

2 JOHN 1:1   199

QUESTION—To whom does κυρίᾳ 'lady' refer, and to whom does τέκνοις αὐτῆς' 'her children' refer?
1. 'Lady' is a metaphorical reference to a church, and the individual members of that congregation are called her 'children' [AB, BAGD, Br, Herm, HNTC, ICC, Lns, My, NCBC, NIC, NTC, TH, TNTC, WBC, Ws; NJB, TEV]. One commentator thinks that instead of one particular church, the letter was to be passed from church to church, each of which in turn would be the lady [Herm]. The children need not be all males [Alf], the designation 'children' includes daughters [My].
2. It refers to an individual lady and her children [Alf, Brd, EGT].
2.1 Her name is not mentioned [Brd]: to the elect lady.
2.2 The lady's name is κυρία [Alf, EGT]: to the elect Kyria.

whom I love^a in^b truth,^c

LEXICON—a. pres. act. indic. of ἀγαπάω (LN 25.43): 'to love' [AB, HNTC, LN, Lns, WBC; all versions]. See this word at 1 John 2:10; 3:10, 11, 14, 18, 23; 4:7, 8, 10, 11, 12, 19, 20, 21; 5:1, 2; 3 John 1.
b. ἐν with dative object (LN 70.4): 'in' [AB, HNTC, WBC; all versions except TEV], 'in connection with' [Lns], 'within the fellowship of' [TNT].
c. ἀλήθεια (LN 70.4) (BAGD 3. p. 36): 'truth' [AB, HNTC, Lns, WBC; all versions except TEV]. The phrase ἐν ἀληθείᾳ 'in truth' is translated as an adverb modifying 'I love': 'truly' [BAGD; TEV], 'really' [LN].

QUESTION—To whom does οὕς 'whom (masculine plural)' refer?
It refers to both the lady and her children [AB, Alf, Br, Brd, EGT, My, TH, TNTC, Ws].

QUESTION—What relationship is indicated by the preposition phrase ἐν ἀληθείᾳ 'in truth'?
1. It refers to the truth of the gospel [AB, Alf, Br, Brd, EBC, EGT, Herm, HNTC, ICC, Lns, NCBC, NIC, TNTC, WBC]: whom I love in connection with the truth. He loves them as fellow believers, all believing the truth [Br]. Love is based on fellowship in Christian knowledge and faith [EGT]. Love is regulated by the truth [ICC]. He loves in a way that is consistent with Christian revelation [AB, NIC]. Truth abiding in the writer brings about such Christian love [Alf].
2. It is adverbial, indicating the manner in which he loves [BAGD, ICC, LN, My, TH, Ws; TEV]: whom I truly love.

and not I only^a but^b also all the-(ones) having-known^c the truth,^d

LEXICON—a. μόνος (LN 58.51) (BAGD 1.a.γ. p. 527): 'only' [AB, BAGD; all versions except REB], 'alone' [BAGD, HNTC, LN, Lns, WBC; REB].
b. ἀλλά (LN 89.125): 'but' [AB, HNTC, Lns, WBC; all versions except NJB], 'for so' [NJB].
c. perf. act. participle of γινώσκω (LN 32.16) (BAGD 6.a.α p. 161): 'to know' [BAGD, HNTC, Lns, WBC; KJV, NASB, NIV, NRSV, REB, TEV], 'to come to know' [AB, BAGD; NAB, NJB, TNT], 'to come to

understand' [LN]. The perfect tense indicates that the knowledge was acquired in the past and is now a present possession [Brd, Lns, NIC, WBC]. The focus is on the present knowledge [NTC].
    d. ἀλήθεια (LN 72.2) (BAGD 2.b. p. 36): 'truth' [AB, BAGD, HNTC, LN, Lns, WBC; all versions].

QUESTION—What is meant by πάντες οἱ ἐγνωκότες τὴν ἀλήθειαν 'all who know the truth'?

'The truth' refers to the truth of the gospel [BAGD, Brd, ICC, Lns, My, NIC, TH, TNTC, WBC, Ws] and to know the truth includes accepting it and being committed to it [NIC]. Those who know the truth are all Christians [AB, Alf, Br, EBC, EGT, Herm, HNTC, ICC, Lns, My, NCBC, NTC, WBC]. There is an implied contrast with the false teachers who do not know the truth [EBC, HNTC, ICC, My, NTC, TH, TNTC, WBC].

2 because-of[a] the truth[b] remaining[c] in[d] us,

LEXICON—a. διά with accusative object (LN 89.26): 'because of' [NIV, NJB, NRSV, TNT], 'because' [TEV], 'on account of' [HNTC, WBC], 'for the sake of' [Lns; KJV, NASB, REB], 'based on' [AB; NAB].
    b. ἀλήθεια (LN 72.2): 'truth' [AB, HNTC, Lns, WBC; all versions]. See this word at v. 1.
    c. pres. act. participle of μένω (LN 68.11): 'to remain' [LN, Lns, WBC; NJB, TEV], 'to abide' [AB; NAB, NASB, NRSV], 'to dwell' [HNTC; KJV, REB], 'to live' [NIV], 'to be' [TNT]. See this word at 1 John 2:14.
    d. ἐν with dative object (LN 89.119): 'in' [AB, HNTC, Lns, WBC; all versions except REB], 'among' [REB]. See this word at 1 John 2:14.

QUESTION—What relationship is indicated by διά 'because of'?

It indicates the reason that the writer and all those who know the truth love the elect lady and her children [Alf, Brd, EBC, Herm, ICC, Lns, NIC, TH, TNTC, WBC, Ws]: we love all of you because of the truth that remains in us. The truth creates an inner compulsion to love [NIC, WBC]. They love each other because of the truth they share [TNTC, Ws]. Some consider this clause to be directly related to 'I love', and the clause 'and not only I, but also all who know the truth' is parenthetical [Brd, TH, WBC; NIV]. Others connect it directly to the clause 'all who know the truth' to show how the truth is the motivation for love [Alf, EBC]. One commentator refers to two relationships: all who know the truth know it because the truth abides in all Christians and that abiding truth causes them to love the lady and her children [AB].

QUESTION—What is meant by τὴν ἀλήθειαν 'the truth'?

It means the Christian truth as in the preceding clause [AB, Brd, EBC, Herm, Lns].

QUESTION—To whom does ἡμῶν 'us' refer?

It is inclusive and refers to the writer together with those to whom he writes [Alf, ICC, Lns, My, NIC, TH, TNTC, WBC, Ws].

and will-be with^a us to the age.^b

LEXICON—a. μετά with genitive object (LN 89.108): 'with' [AB, HNTC, Lns; all versions], not explicit [WBC].

b. αἰών (LN 67.95) (BAGD 1.b. p. 27): 'age'. The phrase εἰς τὸν αἰῶνα 'to the age' is translated 'forever' [AB, HNTC, Lns, WBC; all versions], 'to eternity' [BAGD].

QUESTION—What is the significance of the change from ἐν 'in' to μετά 'with'?

Some commentators think there is no semantic difference intended [TH, TNTC, WBC]. Others make distinctions. The truth remains in our hearts and will be with us as a companion [Lns]. 'With' emphasizes the objectivity of the truth [My].

3 Grace^a mercy^b peace^c will-be^d with^e us

TEXT—Instead of ἡμῶν 'us', some manuscripts have ὑμῶν 'you'. GNT has ἡμῶν 'us' and does not mention the other reading. Only KJV follows the reading ὑμῶν 'you'.

LEXICON—a. χάρις (LN 88.66) (BAGD 2.c. p. 877): 'grace' [AB, BAGD, HNTC, LN, Lns, WBC; all versions], 'favor' [BAGD], 'kindness' [LN].

b. ἔλεος (LN 88.76) (BAGD 2.a. p. 250): 'mercy' [AB, BAGD, HNTC, LN, Lns, WBC; all versions except NJB], 'faithful love' [NJB].

c. εἰρήνη (LN 22.42) (BAGD 2. p. 227): 'peace' [AB, HNTC, LN, Lns, WBC; all versions], 'health' [BAGD].

d. fut. mid. (deponent = act.) indic. of εἰμί (LN 13.1): 'to be' [AB, HNTC, Lns, WBC; all versions except NAB, NJB], 'to have' [NAB, NJB].

e. μετά with genitive object (LN **90.60**) (BAGD A.II.1.c.γ. p. 509): 'with' [AB, BAGD, HNTC, LN, Lns; all versions except NJB, TEV], not explicit [WBC; NJB, TEV].

QUESTION—What is meant by χάρις 'grace'?

It means undeserved favor [Alf, Brd, Lns, NCBC, NIC, TH, TNTC, WBC, Ws], desiring good for his people [WBC], and forgiveness of sin [NTC].

QUESTION—What is meant by ἔλεος 'mercy'?

It means compassion in alleviating suffering [Alf, Brd, Lns, NCBC, NTC, TH, TNTC, Ws], and forgiveness of sin [NIC, WBC]. It is much the same as grace [NIC].

QUESTION—What is meant by εἰρήνη 'peace'?

It means well-being [Brd, Lns, NCBC, TH, WBC] both in health [Alf, Herm] and spiritually [Brd, WBC]. It is a good relationship between God and man [Alf, HNTC, NIC, NTC, TH, TNTC, Ws].

QUESTION—What does the use of the future tense of the verb εἰμί 'to be' indicate?

1. The future tense makes a statement of expectation or promise [AB, Brd, EBC, EGT, ICC, Lns, NIC, NTC, TH, TNTC, WBC, Ws; NAB, NJB, REB, TNT]: we will have grace, mercy, and peace. It is a positive

assertion rather than a wish [NIC, TNTC]. The recipients of the letter were in need of such assurance [WBC].
2. This is a wish or prayer [Alf, Herm, My; KJV, TEV]: may we have grace, mercy, and peace. The future tense indicates confidence that this will happen [Alf, My].

QUESTION—To whom does ἡμῶν 'us' refer?
It is we inclusive and refers to both the writer and those to whom the letter is being sent [Ws].

from[a] God (the) Father, and from Jesus Christ the Son of-the Father,

TEXT—Before Ἰησοῦ Χριστοῦ 'Jesus Christ', some manuscripts include κυρίου 'Lord'. It is omitted by GNT with a B rating, indicating some degree of doubt. The reading κυρίου 'Lord' is included only by KJV.

LEXICON—a. παρά with genitive object (LN **90.14**) (BAGD I.3.b. p. 610): 'from' [AB, BAGD, HNTC, LN, Lns, WBC; all versions except TEV], not explicit [TEV].

QUESTION—What is the significance of repeating the preposition παρά 'from' with both 'the Father' and 'his Son'?
It indicates that the Father and Son are being treated as equals [Lns, My, NCBC, NIC, NTC, TNTC, Ws].

QUESTION—What is the significance of the phrase τοῦ υἱοῦ τοῦ πατρός 'the Son of the Father'?
It emphasizes Christ's close union with the Father [Alf, Brd, TNTC, WBC, Ws]. The emphasis on Jesus' identity as the Son of God counteracts the heresy of that time [Brd, Lns].

in[a] truth[b] and love.[c]

LEXICON—a. ἐν with dative object (LN 89.26; 89.80): 'in' [AB, HNTC, WBC; all versions], 'in connection with' [Lns].
b. ἀλήθεια (LN 72.2): 'truth' [AB, HNTC, LN, Lns, WBC; all versions].
c. ἀγάπη (LN 25.43): 'love' [AB, HNTC, LN, Lns, WBC; all versions]. See this word at 1 John 2:5, 15; 3:1, 16, 17; 4:7, 8, 9, 10, 12, 16, 17, 18; 5:3.

QUESTION—What relationship is indicated by the preposition ἐν 'in'?
Commentators find the relationship puzzling [AB, HNTC, NIC, TH, TNTC, WBC]. TNTC suggests that truth and love may be conditions, consequences, or accompaniments of receiving grace, mercy, and peace. TH suggests that truth and love may qualify how the blessings work in the people or they may indicate how God and Jesus Christ give the blessings. Truth and love in the life of the believer may be the conditions for receiving grace, mercy, and peace [Alf, EBC, NIC, NTC; NAB, NJB]. We must remain in God's truth and love to receive his blessings [EBC].

QUESTION—What is meant by ἀληθείᾳ 'truth'?
It means the truth of the gospel [Brd, ICC, TH].

DISCOURSE UNIT: 4–12 [AB]. The topic is the body of letter.

DISCOURSE UNIT: 4–11 [Alf, EBC, ICC, Lns, NTC, TH, TNTC, WBC, Ws; TEV]. The topic is truth and love [Alf, TH; TEV], exhortation and warning [EBC, ICC, Lns, NTC, Ws], instructions [NTC], the body of letter [Lns, TNTC, WBC].

DISCOURSE UNIT: 4–7 [NCBC]. The topic is a warning against false teachers.

DISCOURSE UNIT: 4–6 [EBC, Herm, NIC, NTC; NJB, TEV]. The topic is exhortation [EBC, Herm, NTC], truth and love [NIC; NJB, TEV].

DISCOURSE UNIT: 4 [Br, Brd]. The topic is the occasion for rejoicing [Br, Brd].

4 I-rejoiced[a] very-much[b] because/that[c] I-have-found[d] (some) of your children walking[e] in[f] truth,[g]

LEXICON—a. aorist pass. (deponent = act.) indic. of χαίρω (LN 25.125) (BAGD 1. p. 873): 'to rejoice' LN, [BAGD, Lns; KJV], 'to be glad' [BAGD, LN; NASB, REB], 'to be happy' [TEV, TNT], 'to give joy' [AB; NAB, NIV, NJB], 'to be delighted' [HNTC], 'to be overjoyed' [WBC; NRSV]. The passive voice is active in meaning [NTC].

    b. λίαν (LN 78.1) (BAGD 1. p. 473): 'very much' [BAGD], 'much' [AB], 'greatly' [Lns; KJV], not explicit [HNTC, WBC; NRSV, TEV]. This adverb is also translated as an adjective: 'great (joy)' [NAB, NIV, NJB], 'very (glad/happy)' [NASB, REB, TNT].

    c. ὅτι (LN 89.33): 'because' [Lns], 'that' [KJV, NJB, REB, TEV], not explicit [AB, HNTC, WBC; NAB, NASB, NIV, NRSV, TNT].

    d. perf. act. indic. of εὑρίσκω (LN 27.1): 'to find' [AB, HNTC, LN, Lns, WBC; all versions].

    e. pres. act. participle of περιπατέω (LN 41.11) (BAGD 2.a.δ. p. 649): 'to walk' [AB, BAGD, Lns; KJV, NASB, NIV, NRSV], 'to live' [BAGD, LN, WBC; REB, TEV, TNT]. The phrase περιπατοῦντας ἐν 'walking in' is translated 'to walk in the way of' [HNTC], 'walking in the path of' [NAB], 'living the life of' [NJB]. The present tense indicates a continuing activity [Brd, WBC].

    f. ἐν with dative object (LN 70.4): 'in' [AB, WBC; all versions except NAB, NJB, REB], 'by' [REB], 'in connection with' [Lns]. For HNTC; NAB, NJB see above.

    g. ἀλήθεια (LN 72.2) (BAGD 2.b. p. 36): 'truth' [AB, BAGD, HNTC, LN, Lns, WBC; all versions].

QUESTION—What is indicated by the use of the aorist tense of the verb ἐχάρην 'I rejoiced'?
    1. The aorist tense refers to the specific time in the past when he received the information [Br, Brd, ICC, Lns, My, NTC, TH, WBC, Ws]. The rejoicing continues [Br, Ws].
    2. This is an epistolary aorist: he rejoices at the time of the writing, but it is past from the viewpoint of the recipients of the letter [Alf].

3. This aorist tense is a convention used in letter writing with no reference to the past [AB].

QUESTION—How did the writer find out about the lady's children?

He had actually met some of her children in a place away from where the lady lived [Alf, Br, Brd, EGT, NIC, WBC, Ws] or news about them had been brought by traveling missionaries [EBC, ICC, Lns, NTC]. Another view is that he had visited the place where the lady and her children lived [My].

QUESTION—What is indicated by the use of the perfect tense εὕρηκα 'I have found'?

1. The perfect tense indicates that the event of finding was in the past and the writer assumes that the situation continues [AB, NIC, NTC, WBC].
2. The perfect tense indicates that the finding was repeated many times as various reports came in [Lns].
3. The perfect tense here means virtually the same as the aorist tense [TH].

QUESTION—What is implied by the statement 'some of her children'?

1. This implies that all the children he found were walking in the truth [AB, Alf, Br, Brd, EGT, NIC]. It does not imply that he had also found some of her children who were not walking in the truth [AB, Alf, Br, EGT]. He felt that what he found in them was true for the church in general [NIC].
2. This implies that some of the children walked in the truth and the others did not [EBC, ICC, Lns, My, TH, WBC]. Probably news about the church was that false teachers had caused divisions and John was rejoicing that some had remained true to the faith [EBC]. Perhaps a majority of her children had been led astray [ICC], or perhaps only a minority [Lns].

QUESTION—What is meant by περιπατοῦντας 'walking'?

It means total life pattern [AB, BAGD, Brd, EGT, HNTC, NIC, TH, WBC, Ws; NAB, NJB, REB, TEV, TNT]. It involves both faith and practice [TNTC].

QUESTION—What is meant by ἀληθείᾳ 'truth' and how did they walk in it?

1. It means the Christian truth of the gospel [AB, Alf, BAGD, Brd, EGT, Lns, My, NIC, NTC, TH, TNTC, WBC]. They lived in accordance with the instruction found in the gospel [EGT, Lns, NIC, NTC, TH]. They both believed and obeyed God's truth [TNTC, WBC]. They conducted their lives in the sphere of Christian truth [Brd]. Their way of life flowed from an internal principle of truth [AB].
2. It means sincerely, properly [Herm, ICC, NCBC]. They lived in an authentic way [Herm]. There was perfection in every sphere of being [ICC].

as[a] a-commandment[b] we-received[c] from[d] the Father.

LEXICON—a. καθώς (LN 64.14): 'as' [KJV, NJB, TNT], 'just as' [AB, HNTC, WBC; NAB, NASB, NIV, NRSV, TEV], 'even as' [Lns], 'in accordance with' [REB].

b. ἐντολή (LN 33.330): 'commandment' [AB, LN, Lns; KJV, NASB], 'command' [REB]. The phrase καθὼς ἐντολὴν ἐλάβομεν 'as we

received commandment' is translated 'as we were commanded' [WBC; NAB, NJB, NRSV, TNT], 'as (the Father) commanded us' [HNTC; NIV, TEV]. See this word at 1 John 2:7.
   c. aorist act. indic. of λαμβάνω (LN 57.125) (BAGD 2. p. 465): 'to receive' [AB, BAGD, LN, Lns; KJV, NASB, REB], 'to obtain' [BAGD]. The aorist tense refers to a specific time in the past [TH, WBC], perhaps to the time Jesus spoke about it (John 13:34) [TH].
   d. παρά with genitive object (LN 90.14) (BAGD I.3.b. p. 609): 'from' [AB, BAGD, Lns; KJV, NASB, REB], 'by' [WBC; NAB, NJB, NRSV, TNT], not explicit [HNTC; NIV, TEV].
QUESTION—To what does ἐντολήν 'commandment' refer?
   1. It refers to the command to love one another (v. 5) [AB, Herm, HNTC, NCBC].
   2. It refers to the command to walk in the truth [Alf, Brd, My, TNTC]. This is general teaching of Scripture, not recorded in any specific verse [Brd].
   3. It refers to the command to love and to believe in the Son of God (1 John 3:23) [EBC, ICC, Lns, NIC, WBC].
QUESTION—Who is the implied subject of the verb ἐλάβομεν 'we received'?
   It is 'we inclusive' and refers to the writer, those he is writing to, and all Christians [AB, Lns, TH, WBC].

DISCOURSE UNIT: 5–11 [Br, Brd]. The topic is exhortation and warning [Br, Brd].

5 And^a now^b I-request^c you, lady,

LEXICON—a. καί (LN 89.87): 'and' [HNTC, Lns, WBC; all versions except NAB], 'but' [AB; NAB].
   b. νῦν (LN 67.38) (BAGD 2. p. 546): 'now' [AB, BAGD, HNTC, Lns, WBC; all versions except TEV].
   c. pres. act. indic. of ἐρωτάω (LN 33.161) (BAGD 2. p. 312): 'to request' [BAGD, LN, Lns; NAB], 'to make a request' [AB; REB], 'to ask' [BAGD, HNTC, LN; NASB, NIV, NJB, NRSV, TEV], 'to plead' [WBC], 'to beseech' [KJV], not explicit [TNT].
QUESTION—What relationship is indicated by καὶ νῦν 'and now'?
   This indicates that the writer is coming to the point of his letter [Alf, Brd, TH, WBC]. It introduces a specific way of walking in the truth (v. 4) [AB]. The 'now' may be temporal and contrast with the past rejoicing [AB, ICC, Lns, WBC], or it may be logical and give the result of rejoicing [My].
QUESTION—What is the significance of using the verb ἐρωτῶ 'I request'?
   The word ἐρωτῶ 'I request' is the usual verb of request and has no connotation of begging [AB, ICC]. It indicates a polite command between equals [Lns, My, NTC, TNTC]. It indicates that he has authority and expects obedience [Alf, Brd].

not as[a] writing[b] you a-new[c] commandment,[d]
LEXICON—a. ὡς (LN 64.12): 'as' [Lns; NASB], 'as though' [KJV, NJB, NRSV], 'as if' [AB, WBC; NAB], 'by way of' [HNTC], not explicit [NIV, REB, TEV, TNT].
  b. pres. act. participle of γράφω (LN 33.61) (BAGD 4. p. 167): 'to write' [AB, BAGD, Lns, WBC; all versions except REB], 'to send' [REB], not explicit [HNTC]. See this word at 1 John 2:7.
  c. καινός (LN 28.33) (BAGD 2. p. 394): 'new' [AB, BAGD, HNTC, LN, Lns, WBC; all versions]. See this word at 1 John 2:7.
  d. ἐντολή (LN 33.330): 'commandment' [AB, HNTC, LN, Lns; all versions except TEV], 'command' [WBC; TEV]. See this word at 1 John 2:7.
QUESTION—What relationship is indicated by the conjunction ὡς 'as'?
This does not mean that he is requesting rather than commanding. It means that his request involves a basic commandment, not something that he has devised [AB].

but[a] (that) which we-had[b] from[c] (the) beginning,[d]
LEXICON—a. ἀλλά (LN 89.125): 'but' [HNTC, Lns; KJV, NASB, NIV, NRSV, TNT], 'but only' [NJB], 'rather' [AB; NAB], 'but rather' [WBC], not explicit [REB, TEV].
  b. imperf. act. indic. of ἔχω (LN 90.65) (BAGD I.2.i. p. 333): 'to have' [AB, BAGD, HNTC, LN, Lns; all versions], 'to have over one' [BAGD], 'to receive' [WBC]. See this word at 1 John 2:7.
  c. ἀπό with genitive object (LN 67.131): 'from' [AB, HNTC, Lns, WBC; all versions].
  d. ἀρχή (LN 67.65) (BAGD 1.b. p. 112): 'beginning' [AB, BAGD, HNTC, LN, Lns, WBC; all versions except NAB], 'start' [NAB]. See this word at 1 John 2:7.
QUESTION—What is the implied subject of the verb εἴχομεν 'we had'?
It is 'we inclusive' and refers to the writer and those to whom he is writing [ICC, NCBC, WBC, Ws].

that[a] we-should-love[b] one-another.
LEXICON—a. ἵνα (LN 90.22): 'that' [Lns; all versions except NAB, TEV], not explicit [AB, HNTC, WBC; NAB, TEV].
  b. pres. act. subj. of ἀγαπάω: 'to love'. See this word at v. 1.
QUESTION—What relationship is indicated by ὅτι 'that'?
  1. It indicates the content of the request [AB, My, NTC, TH, WBC, Ws]: I request that we should love one another. At the same time, it explains what the commandment is [AB, Ws]. Everything between is parenthetical [WBC, Ws].
  2. It explains the word ἐντολήν 'command' [ICC, Lns]: but a commandment we had from beginning, namely, the command that we should love one another.

QUESTION—What is the implied subject of the verb ἀγαπῶμεν 'we should love'?

It is 'we inclusive' and refers to both the writer and those to whom he wrote [ICC, Lns, WBC, Ws].

6 And^a this is love,^b that^c we-should-walk^d according-to^e his commandments;^f

LEXICON—a. καί (LN 89.87): 'and' [Lns; KJV, NASB, NIV, NRSV], 'now' [AB], not explicit [HNTC, WBC; NAB, NJB, REB, TEV, TNT].
- b. ἀγάπη: 'love'. See this word at v. 3.
- c. ἵνα (LN 90.22) (BAGD II.1.e. p. 378): 'that' [AB, BAGD, Lns, WBC; all versions except NAB, NJB, REB], not explicit [HNTC; NAB, NJB, REB].
- d. pres. act. subj. of περιπατέω: 'to walk'. See this word at v. 4.
- e. κατά with accusative object (LN 89.8): 'according to' [AB, HNTC, Lns, WBC; all versions except KJV, NIV], 'in obedience to' [NIV, TEV], 'after' [KJV].
- f. ἐντολή (LN 33.330): 'commandment' [AB, HNTC, Lns, WBC; all versions]. See this word at v. 5.

QUESTION—To what does αὕτη 'this' refer?

It refers to the following clause ὅτι 'that' clause [AB, Alf, Brd, Herm, My, TH, WBC, Ws; NIV]: this is love, namely, that we should walk according to his commandments.

QUESTION—Who is the implied goal of the event word ἀγάπη 'love'?
1. It is love for each other [AB, ICC, Lns, My, NIC, NTC]. Love is expressed in ways that are in accord with God's commandments [NIC]. The highest expression of love for Christian brothers is obedience to all of God's commandments that concern relations between brothers [ICC, My].
2. It is love for God [Brd, NCBC].
3. It is love for both God and our fellowman [TH, TNTC, WBC].

QUESTION—To whom does αὐτοῦ 'his' refer?

It refers to God [AB, Brd, EBC, ICC, Lns, My, NIC, NTC, WBC; REB, TEV].

this is the commandment, as^a you(pl.)-have-heard^b from the beginning,^c that^d in^e it you(pl.)-should-walk.^f

LEXICON—a. καθώς (LN 64.14): 'as' [AB, HNTC, WBC; KJV, NAB, NIV, TEV], 'even as' [Lns], 'just as' [NASB, NRSV], 'which' [NJB], not explicit [REB]. The phrase is translated 'this is the same commandment you have heard' [TNT].
- b. aorist act. indic. of ἀκούω (LN 24.52): 'to hear' [AB, HNTC, LN, Lns, WBC; all versions except REB]. This is also translated 'that was given you' [REB].
- c. ἀρχή: 'beginning'. See this word at v. 5.

d. ἵνα (LN 90.22) (BAGD II.1.e. p. 378): 'that' [BAGD, HNTC, Lns; KJV, NASB, NIV, TEV], not explicit [AB, WBC; NAB, NJB, NRSV, REB, TNT].
e. ἐν with dative object (LN 89.76): 'in' [AB, Lns; all versions except NJB, REB], not explicit [NJB, REB]. The phrase ἐν αὐτῇ 'in it' is translated 'along the path it lays down' [HNTC], 'according to which' [WBC].
f. pres. act. subj. of περιπατέω: 'to walk'. See this word at v. 4.

QUESTION—To what does αὕτη 'this' refer?
1. It refers to the following ἵνα 'that' clause [Alf, HNTC, My, WBC, Ws; KJV]: this is the commandment, namely, that you should walk in it.
2. It refers to the command to love one another (v. 5) [AB]: that is the commandment; as you heard from the beginning, so (ὅτι) you must walk in it.

QUESTION—What is the significance of the change from plural ἐντολάς 'commandments' to singular ἐντολή 'commandment'?
The plural form refers to all of God's commands, while the singular form refers to the command to love one another [Alf, Brd, NIC, NTC, WBC, Ws], a commandment that sums up all the others [Alf].

QUESTION—To what does αὐτῇ 'it' refer?
1. It refers to love [Alf, Br, Brd, EGT, My, NIC, NTC, TNTC, WBC, Ws; NIV, NJB, TEV, TNT]: that you should walk in love.
2. It refers to the commandment [AB, HNTC, ICC, Lns; NAB, REB]: that you should walk in the commandment.

DISCOURSE UNIT: 7–13 [NJB]. The topic is the enemies of Christ.

DISCOURSE UNIT: 7–11 [EBC, Herm, NIC, NTC; TEV]. The topic is a warning against false teachers [EBC, Herm, NIC, NTC; TEV].

7 For[a] many[b] deceivers[c] went-out[d] into[e] the world,[f]

LEXICON—a. ὅτι (LN 89.33): 'for' [AB, HNTC, WBC; KJV, NASB, TNT], 'because' [Lns], not explicit [all versions except KJV, NASB].
b. πολύς (LN 59.1) (BAGD I.1.a.α. p. 687): 'many' [AB, BAGD, HNTC, LN, Lns, WBC; all versions], 'numerous' [BAGD].
c. πλάνος (LN 31.9) (BAGD 2. p. 666): 'deceiver' [AB, BAGD, HNTC, WBC; all versions except NAB], 'deceitful man' [NAB], not explicit [Lns].
d. aorist act. indic. of ἐξέρχομαι (LN 15.40) (BAGD 1.a.ε. p. 274): 'to go out' [AB, BAGD, HNTC, Lns; all versions except KJV, NJB], 'to defect' [WBC], 'to be at large' [NJB], 'to enter' [KJV].
e. εἰς with accusative object (LN 84.22): 'into' [AB, HNTC, Lns, WBC; all versions except NJB, TEV], 'in' [NJB], 'over' [TEV].
f. κόσμος (LN 41.38) (BAGD 4.b. p. 446): 'world' [AB, BAGD, HNTC, Lns, WBC; all versions].

QUESTION—What relationship is indicated by ὅτι 'for'?
It indicates the grounds for the preceding exhortation to walk in love (vv. 5, 6) [Alf, Brd, EGT, ICC, Lns, My, NIC, TH, WBC]: you must love one another because many false teachers are in the world. Love is a safeguard against error [Ws]. There was danger that the church would be corrupted by false teaching which would bring about a lack of mutual love [NIC, WBC]. Only by love will they withstand the false teachers who lack Christian love [TH]. Unity produced by love would enable believers to recognize and resist false teaching [Brd].

QUESTION—Who were the deceivers?
They were the false teachers [Brd, Herm, HNTC, Lns, NIC, NTC]. These were the same false teachers referred to in 1 John 2:26 and 4:1–3 [Brd].

QUESTION—What is meant by going out into the world?
1. It means that they left the church [AB, Alf, EBC, HNTC, NTC, Ws]. They have gone into the realm of darkness ruled by Satan [AB] or they have left the Christian community to go about in the world teaching their doctrine [NTC]. It is likely that they have gone out from the community where the elder is, rather than where the lady is [EBC].
2. It means that they came from Satan as his missionaries [Herm, ICC, TNTC, WBC], or from the headquarters of their leader Cerinthus [Lns]. They were sent on their mission by the Evil One [ICC]. They have gone out into the public sphere to teach their doctrine [Herm]. They have gone into the world where Christians live to teach their false brand of Christianity [NIC].

the-(ones) not acknowledging[a] Jesus Christ coming[b] in[c] a-body;[d]

LEXICON—a. pres. act. participle of ὁμολογέω (LN 33.274) (BAGD 4. p. 568): 'to acknowledge' [BAGD, HNTC, WBC; all versions except KJV, NRSV, TNT], 'to confess' [AB, LN, Lns; KJV, NRSV], 'to accept the fact' [TNT]. The present tense indicates that this is a continuous action [AB, NTC]. See this word at 1 John 4:2, 3, 15.

b. pres. mid. (deponent = act.) participle of ἔρχομαι (LN 15.81) (BAGD I.1.a. p. 311): 'to come' [AB, BAGD, HNTC, Lns; all versions]. The phrase ἐρχόμενον ἐν σαρκί 'come in a body' is translated 'incarnate' [WBC]. See this word at 1 John 4:2, 3. The present tense is used in a timeless manner and indicates that the incarnation is a permanent state [Alf, Brd, EBC, EGT, Herm, HNTC, ICC, Lns, My, NIC, TNTC, WBC, Ws]. There was a fixed formula for the incarnation which used the present tense [NTC, TH]. See this word at 1 John 4:2.

c. ἐν with dative object (LN 13.8) (BAGD I.4.b. p. 259): 'in' [AB, BAGD, HNTC, Lns; all versions except TEV, TNT]. See this word at 1 John 4:2, 3.

d. σάρξ (LN 9.12) (BAGD 2. p. 743): 'body' [BAGD], 'flesh' [AB, HNTC, Lns; all versions except NJB, TEV, TNT], 'human nature' [NJB]. the phrase ἐν σαρκί 'in a body' is translated 'as a human being' [TEV, TNT]. See this word at 1 John 4:2, 3.

QUESTION—How is this clause related to the preceding one?

It identifies the deceivers [Alf, ICC, Lns, TH]: many deceivers went out, namely, those who did not acknowledge that Jesus Christ came in a body.

QUESTION—What is meant by 'coming in a body'?

It refers to the incarnation [AB, Br, Brd, EBC, EGT, Herm, HNTC, ICC, Lns, NIC, NTC, TH, TNTC, WBC, Ws].

this is the deceiver[a] and[b] the antichrist.[c]

LEXICON—a. πλάνος (LN 31.9) (BAGD 2. p. 666): 'deceiver' [AB, BAGD, HNTC, Lns, WBC; all versions except NAB], 'imposter' [BAGD]. This noun is also translated as an adjective: 'deceitful' [NAB].

b. καί (LN 89.92): 'and' [HNTC, Lns, WBC; all versions except NAB, NJB], not explicit [AB; NAB, NJB].

c. ἀντίχριστος (LN 53.83) (BAGD p. 76): 'antichrist' [AB, BAGD, HNTC, Lns, WBC; all versions except TEV], 'enemy of Christ' [TEV]. See this word at 1 John 2:18, 22.

QUESTION—What is the significance of the change from the plural 'many deceivers' to the singular 'this is the deceiver'?

It signifies that the many deceivers are typical of antichrist and collectively they represent the great antichrist [AB, Alf, Brd, Herm, HNTC, Lns, My, NIC, NTC, TNTC, WBC, Ws]. See the discussion at 1 John 2:18. 'This' refers to the person who rejects the truth of the incarnation [Brd]. It points to a class of people, each individual being a representative and forerunner of the one great antichrist of prophecy [Alf].

QUESTION—What is the relationship between πλάνος 'deceiver' and ἀντίχριστος 'antichrist'?

These are two characterizations of the same person or group [AB, Lns, NIC, NTC, TH, WBC; NAB, NJB].

8 Watch[a] yourselves, so-that[b] (you may) not lose[c] (the) things we-worked-(for)[d]

TEXT—Instead of μὴ ἀπολέσητε 'you may not lose' and ἀπολάβητε 'you may receive', some manuscripts have μὴ ἀπολέσωμεν 'we may not lose' and ἀπολάβωμεν 'we may receive'. GNT selects μὴ ἀπολέσητε 'you may not lose' and ἀπολάβητε 'you may receive' with a B rating, indicating some degree of doubt. Only KJV follows the reading with μὴ ἀπολέσωμεν 'we may not lose' and ἀπολάβωμεν 'we may receive'.

TEXT—Instead of εἰργασάμεθα 'we worked for', some manuscripts have εἰργάσασθε 'you (pl.) worked for'. GNT selects εἰργασάμεθα 'we worked for' with a C rating, indicating a considerable degree of doubt. AB, Alf, Brd, EBC, EGT, HNTC, ICC, NTC, WBC, Ws, and all versions except NAB, NIV and TNT also follow the reading εἰργασάμεθα 'we worked for'. Br, Herm, Lns, My, NCBC, TH, TNTC; NAB, NIV and TNT follow the reading εἰργάσασθε 'you (pl.) worked for'.

LEXICON—a. pres. act. impera. of βλέπω (LN 27.58) (BAGD 6. p. 143): 'to watch' [BAGD; NASB, NJB], 'to watch out' [LN; NIV], 'to see to' [REB], 'to look out' [AB; NAB], 'to look to' [BAGD, Lns; KJV, TNT], 'to be careful' [HNTC], 'to protect' [WBC], 'to be on guard' [NRSV, TEV]. The present tense means to be continuously on guard [Brd].
  b. ἵνα (LN 89.49): 'so that' [WBC; NRSV, TEV], 'that' [AB; all versions except NJB, NRSV, TEV], not explicit [HNTC; NJB]. The phrase ἵνα μή 'in order not' is translated 'lest' [Lns].
  c. aorist act. subj. of ἀπόλλυμι (LN 57.68) (BAGD 1.b. p. 95): 'to lose' [AB, BAGD, HNTC, LN, WBC; all versions except NJB], 'to destroy' [Lns], 'to be lost' [NJB].
  d. aorist mid. (deponent = act.) indic. of ἐργάζομαι (LN 42.41) (BAGD 2.a. p. 307): 'to work for' [AB, HNTC, WBC; all versions except NASB, NJB], 'to accomplish' [BAGD; NASB], 'to have wrought' [Lns; KJV]. The phrase ἃ εἰργασάμεθα 'the things we worked for' is translated 'our work' [NJB].
QUESTION—What is the correct reading and what does it mean?
  1. Do not lose what *we* worked for [AB, Alf, Brd, EBC, HNTC, ICC, NTC, WBC; all versions except NAB, NIV, TNT].
    1.1 'We' is exclusive, referring to the apostles [Alf, Brd, EBC, Ws] and teachers [Alf]. They should not lose their belief in the truth and their active love which was produced by the apostolic teaching [Alf]. They would lose this by rejecting the truth taught them [Brd].
    1.2 'We' is inclusive, referring to the writer and his readers [AB, WBC]. Correct belief about Christ is a work that brings a reward of eternal life [AB]. The work is believing in Jesus and loving one another [WBC].
  2. Do not lose what *you* worked for [Br, Herm, Lns, My, NCBC, NTC, TH, TNTC; NAB, NIV, TNT]. The work is that done by them in their church life and in missionary labor [TH]. He does not want them to lose the reward for faithful service [TNTC].

but[a] a-full[b] reward[c] you(pl.)-may-receive.[d]
LEXICON—a. ἀλλά (LN 89.125): 'but' [HNTC, Lns, WBC; all versions except NAB, NJB], not explicit [AB; NAB, NJB].
  b. πλήρης (LN **59.31**) (BAGD 2. p. 670): 'full' [AB, BAGD, LN, Lns, WBC; KJV, NAB, NASB, NJB, NRSV], 'in full' [HNTC; REB, TEV, TNT]. For NIV see below.
  c. μισθός (LN 38.14) (BAGD 2.a. p. 523): 'reward' [AB, BAGD, HNTC, LN, Lns, WBC; all versions]. The phrase μισθὸν πλήρη ἀπολάβητε 'to receive a full reward' is translated 'to be rewarded fully' [NIV].
  d. aorist act. subj. of ἀπολαμβάνω (LN 57.128) (BAGD 1. p. 94): 'to receive' [AB, BAGD, HNTC, LN, Lns, WBC; all versions except NIV, NJB].
QUESTION—What is meant by μισθὸν πλήρη 'a full reward'?
  1. It refers to eternal life [AB, Alf, Herm, HNTC, Lns, TH, WBC].

2. It refers to a reward for faithfulness and is not referring to salvation [EBC, NTC, TNTC]. They may lose part of this reward [EBC, NIC].

9 Everyone going-beyond/forward^a and not remaining^b in^c the teaching^d of-the Christ does not have^e God;

LEXICON—a. pres. act. participle of προάγω (LN **36.25**) (BAGD 2.a. p. 702): 'to go beyond' [LN; NJB, NRSV, REB, TEV, TNT], 'to go too far' [BAGD; NASB], 'to go ahead' [Lns], 'to run on ahead' [HNTC; NIV], 'to be progressive' [AB; NAB], 'to be advanced' [WBC], 'to transgress' [KJV].

b. pres. act. participle of μένω (LN **68.11**) (BAGD 1.a.β. p. 504): 'to remain' [AB, BAGD, **LN**, Lns, WBC; NAB, NJB], 'to abide' [BAGD; KJV, NASB, NRSV], 'to dwell' [HNTC], 'to continue' [BAGD, LN; NIV], 'to keep on' [LN]. The phrase μένων ἐν 'to remain in' is translated 'to stand by' [REB], 'to stay with' [TEV], 'to keep within' [TNT].

c. ἐν with dative object: 'in' [HNTC, Lns, WBC; KJV, NASB, NIV, NJB, NRSV], 'rooted in' [AB; NAB]. For REB, TEV, TNT, see above.

d. διδαχή (LN 33.236) (BAGD 2. p. 192): 'teaching' [AB, BAGD, HNTC, LN, WBC; all versions except KJV], 'doctrine' [LN, Lns; KJV].

e. pres. act. indic. of ἔχω (LN 90.65): 'to have' [LN, Lns; all versions except NAB, REB], 'to possess' [AB, HNTC, WBC; NAB, REB]. See this word at 1 John 5:12.

QUESTION—What is meant by προάγων 'going beyond/forward'?

1. It means going beyond the limits of the teaching [AB, BAGD, Br, Brd, EBC, EGT, Herm, HNTC, ICC, My, NCBC, NIC, NTC, TH, TNTC, WBC, Ws; NASB, NJB, NRSV, REB, TEV, TNT]. The word προάγων 'going forward' can have positive connotations and was evidently used by the secessionists about themselves, professing to having a higher and better understanding than the teaching of Christ. In this case, the writer is using the word ironically or sarcastically [AB, Br, Brd, EGT, ICC, My, NIC, TNTC, WBC, Ws; NAB]. Or the word is used in an unfavorable sense of going too far, that is, farther than one should [TH]. To 'go beyond' means that one does not remain in the true teaching [AB, Br, Brd, Herm, HNTC, ICC, Lns, My, NTC, TH, WBC].

2. It means going forward, in front of the believers, to teach them [Alf].

QUESTION—How are the two nouns related in the genitive construction τῇ διδαχῇ τοῦ χριστοῦ 'the teaching of Christ'?

1. It means 'what Christ taught' [AB, Alf, Br, ICC, Lns, My, NCBC, NTC, TH, TNTC, Ws; NJB]: the doctrine which Christ taught. This is what Christ taught concerning God and the way of life [TH], or more specifically, the command to love one another [HNTC]. The doctrine came from Christ and was proclaimed by the apostles [My]. Christ still taught through his apostles [Lns].

2. It means 'what was taught about Christ' [Brd, EGT, Herm, NIC, WBC; REB]: the doctrine about Christ. This is in view of erroneous teaching about Christ and his incarnation [Brd].

QUESTION—What is meant by not having God?

It means not having a living relationship with God [AB, Herm, TNTC, WBC], and thereby forfeiting eternal life [EBC]. See this phrase at 1 John 2:23 and 5:12.

the-(one) remaining in the teaching, this-one has both^a the Father and the Son.

TEXT—After διδαχῇ 'teaching', some manuscripts have τοῦ Χριστοῦ 'of Christ'. This phrase is omitted by GNT with a B rating, indicating some degree of doubt. Only KJV follows the reading διδαχῇ τοῦ Χριστοῦ 'teaching of Christ'.

LEXICON—a. καί (LN 89.92): 'both' [AB, HNTC, Lns, WBC; all versions except NJB], not explicit [NJB].

QUESTION—How is this clause related to the context?

It restates the idea of the first clause [Herm, My, NIC, TNTC, WBC] and indicates that knowing the Father is dependent on knowing Christ [AB, Alf, Brd, EGT, ICC, Lns, NIC, NTC, TNTC, WBC]. That person has the Father as well as the Son [TH].

10 If^a anyone comes^b to^c you (pl.) and (does) not bring^d this teaching,^e

LEXICON—a. εἴ (LN 89.65): 'if' [AB, HNTC, Lns, WBC; all versions except NRSV], not explicit [NRSV].

b. pres. mid. (deponent = act.) indic. of ἔρχομαι (LN 15.7): 'to come' [AB, HNTC, LN, Lns; all versions]. The phrase ἔρχεται πρός 'to come to' is translated 'to approach' [WBC].

c. πρός with accusative object (LN 84.18): 'to' [AB, HNTC, Lns; all versions except KJV], 'unto' [KJV]. For WBC, see above.

d. pres. act. indic. of φέρω (LN 15.166) (BAGD 4.a.β. p. 855): 'to bring' [AB, BAGD, HNTC, Lns; all versions], 'to stand by' [WBC].

e. διδαχή: 'teaching'. See this word at v. 9.

QUESTION—What is the significance of an indicative following εἴ 'if'?

The writer expects the event to happen [AB, Alf, Brd, EBC, ICC, Lns, My, NTC, TH, WBC, Ws].

QUESTION—Who does this clause refer to?

It refers to a false teacher and means to come in order to bring false teaching [AB, Alf, Br, Brd, EBC, EGT, Herm, ICC, Lns, NCBC, NIC, NTC, TH, TNTC, WBC, Ws]. Since such a one brings a false teaching, this refers to a teacher of false doctrine, not just a traveler seeking hospitality [Alf].

QUESTION—To what teaching does this refer?

It refers to the teaching of Christ mentioned in v. 9 [Br, Brd, Lns, NCBC, TH, TNTC, WBC, Ws].

(do) not receive[a] **him into (your) house**[b] **and (do) not say to-him to-rejoice;**[c]

LEXICON—a. pres. act. impera. of λαμβάνω (LN 57.125) (BAGD 1.e.α. p. 464): 'to receive' [AB, BAGD, HNTC, Lns; KJV, NAB, NASB, NJB, NRSV, TNT], 'to welcome' [WBC; TEV], 'to take' [NIV], 'to admit' [REB].

b. οἰκία (LN 7.3) (BAGD 1.a. p. 557): 'house' [AB, BAGD, LN, Lns, WBC; all versions except TEV, TNT], 'home' [HNTC, LN; TEV, TNT].

c. pres. act. infin. of χαίρω (LN 33.22) (BAGD 2.a. p. 874): 'to rejoice'. The phrase χαίρειν λέγετε 'to say to rejoice' is translated 'to greet' [AB, HNTC; NAB, TNT], 'to welcome' [NIV, NRSV], 'to give a greeting' [NASB, NJB, REB], 'to pass the time of day with him' [WBC], 'to bid him Godspeed' [KJV], 'to say Greetings' [Lns], 'to say Peace be with you' [TEV].

QUESTION—What is meant by λαμβάνετε 'receive'?

It means to welcome him as a Christian brother [AB, Alf, EBC, Herm, My, Ws] or teacher [Br], and thereby give him opportunities to propagate his heresy [WBC].

QUESTION—What is meant by οἰκίαν 'house'?

1. It means a private home [EBC, HNTC, Lns, NIC, TH]. This forbids letting a false teacher use one's home as a base for his operation [Lns, NIC].
2. It means a home used for church meetings [AB, TNTC, WBC]. This forbids receiving a false teacher at the place where the false teaching could be taught and spread [AB]. This is concerned with an official welcome by the congregation, not private hospitality [WBC].

QUESTION—What is meant by χαίρειν λέγετε 'to say to rejoice' and how is this connected with the preceding clause?

1. It means to give a greeting and both clauses are aspects of the same action [AB, BAGD, Br, Herm, HNTC, Lns, My, NIC, TH, Ws; NAB, NASB, NJB, REB, TNT]: do not receive him with a greeting. Such a reception implies recognition as a fellow believer [AB, EBC, Herm, HNTC, ICC, TH] and encourages him in his work of deception [Lns, NIC]. The repetition of 'do not' indicates emphasis, not two distinct acts [AB].
2. It means to give a farewell when he departs from a house in which he had previously been received [Brd, EGT, WBC]: do not receive him when he arrives and do not bid him farewell when he leaves. If they did bid him farewell, they would be sending a false teacher on his way with a recommendation of confidence and good will [EGT].

11 for[a] **the-(one) saying to-him to-rejoice**[b] **shares**[c] **in his evil**[d] **deeds.**[e]

LEXICON—a. γάρ (LN 89.23): 'for' [AB, Lns, WBC; all versions except NIV, NJB], not explicit [HNTC; NIV, NJB].

b. pres. act. infin. of χαίρω: 'to rejoice'. See this word at v. 10.

c. pres. act. indic. of κοινωνέω (LN 57.98) (BAGD 1.b.β. p. 438): 'to share' [AB, BAGD, HNTC, LN; NAB, NIV, NJB, TNT], 'to participate'

[BAGD; NASB, NRSV], 'to partake' [KJV], 'to become an accomplice' [REB], 'to become a partner' [TEV], 'to be a partner' [WBC], 'to fellowship' [Lns].
d. πονηρός (LN 88.110) (BAGD 1.b.β. p. 691): 'evil' [AB, BAGD, HNTC, LN, WBC; all versions except NIV, NJB], 'wicked' [BAGD, LN, Lns; NIV, NJB], 'bad' [BAGD].
e. ἔργον (LN 42.11) (BAGD 1.c.β. p. 308): 'deed' [AB, BAGD, HNTC, LN, WBC; KJV, NASB, NRSV, REB, TNT], 'work' [Lns; NIV], 'activity' [NJB]. This noun is also translated as a verb: 'to do' [NAB, TEV].

QUESTION—What relationship is indicated by γάρ 'for'?
It indicates the grounds for the prohibition [Brd, ICC, Lns, My, TNTC].

QUESTION—How does receiving and greeting such a person constitute sharing in his evil deeds?
It implies approval of the person's teaching [Alf, Br, Lns, NTC, WBC], and wishing him success in his deception [Lns], and may even lead to alignment with him [NIC].

QUESTION—What is meant by ἔργοις πονηροῖς 'evil deeds'?
1. The evil work is teaching false doctrine [Brd, EBC, NTC, TNTC].
2. The evil work includes both false teaching and wrong conduct [Herm, HNTC, My, WBC]. Besides heresy, there was a lack of love [HNTC, My, WBC] and other misdeeds [Herm, HNTC]

DISCOURSE UNIT: 12–13 [Alf, Brd, EBC, EGT, Herm, ICC, Lns, NCBC, NIC, NTC, TH, TNTC, WBC, Ws; TEV]. The topic is the conclusion of the letter [AB, Brd, EBC, EGT, Herm, ICC, Lns, NCBC, NTC, TH, TNTC, WBC, Ws; TEV], final words and greeting [NIC].

DISCOURSE UNIT: 12 [Br]. The topic is a personal note.

12 Having[a] many-things to-write[b] to-you (pl.)
LEXICON—a. pres. act. participle of ἔχω (BAGD I.6.b. p. 333): 'to have' [AB, HNTC, Lns, WBC; all versions except NAB, TNT], not explicit [NAB, TNT].
b. pres. act. infin. of γράφω (LN 33.61): 'to write' [AB, HNTC, Lns, WBC; all versions except NJB], 'to tell' [NJB]. See this word at 1 John 1:4.

QUESTION—How is this verse related to its context?
It closes the letter [AB, Alf, EBC, Herm, HNTC, ICC, NTC, TNTC, WBC] and explains why it is so brief [EGT, My].

QUESTION—What relationship is indicated by the use of the participle ἔχων 'having'?
1. It indicates a concession [AB, Brd, Herm, Lns, Ws; NAB, NIV, NJB, NRSV, REB, TEV, TNT]: although I have many things to write, yet I do not want to write them. The writer did not mean that he wanted to write with some other means than paper and ink [TH]. Although he had many things to say to them, he wants to tell them in person, not just write them

[Brd]. The verb 'write' refers not to the manner of communication, but to the fact of communication [TH].
2. It indicates reason [Brd]: because I have many things to communicate, I do not want to write them here.

QUESTION—To what does πολλά 'many things' refer?
Perhaps he wanted to deal in greater detail and refer the matters he has treated briefly in this letter to specific individuals [Br] or the many things are subjects more congenial than false teaching [NIC].

(I-did) not want[a] by-means-of[b] paper[c] and ink,[d]

LEXICON—a. aorist pass. (deponent = act.) indic. of βούλομαι (LN 25.3) (BAGD 2.a.ζ. p. 146): 'to want' [LN, Lns; NASB, NIV], 'to wish' [HNTC; TNT], 'to have desire' [WBC], 'to care' [REB], 'to will' [LN; KJV], 'to think best' [NJB], 'to intend' [NAB], 'to rather not use/do' [NRSV, TEV], 'to bother with' [AB]. The aorist tense indicates that, although this is the writer's attitude at the time of writing, he is putting himself in the time frame of the readers when they receive the letter [AB, Brd, ICC, Lns, NIC, NTC, TH, WBC, Ws].

b. διά with genitive object (LN **90.8**) (BAGD A.III.1.a. p. 180): 'by means of' [BAGD, LN, Lns], 'by' [HNTC], 'with' [AB, LN; KJV, NASB, TEV], not explicit [WBC; NAB, NIV, NJB, NRSV, REB, TNT].

c. χάρτης (LN **6.58**) (BAGD p. 879): 'paper' [AB, BAGD, LN, Lns, WBC; all versions], 'papyrus' [BAGD]. The phrase 'paper and ink' is translated 'pen and ink' [HNTC].

d. μέλας (LN 6.57) (BAGD p. 500): 'ink' [AB, BAGD, HNTC, LN, WBC; all versions except NAB, REB], not explicit [NAB, REB].

QUESTION—What is meant by διὰ χάρτου καὶ μέλανος 'through paper and ink'?
It is an idiom for writing a letter [Alf, Br, Brd, EGT, Lns, NIC, TH, TNTC, WBC].

QUESTION—What verb is implied in this clause?
The implied verb is 'to do so' [NASB, TEV], 'to write' [AB; KJV], 'to communicate' [Alf, Ws], 'to put down' [NAB, REB], 'to use' [NIV, NRSV, TNT], 'to trust to' [NJB].

but[a] I-hope[b] to-come[c] to you (pl.) to-speak[d] mouth to mouth,[e]

LEXICON—a. ἀλλά (LN 89.125): 'but' [Lns; KJV, NASB], 'instead' [AB; NAB, NIV, NJB, NRSV, TEV], 'rather' [HNTC, WBC; REB], not explicit [TNT].

b. pres. act. indic. of ἐλπίζω (LN 30.54) (BAGD 2. p. 252): 'to hope' [AB, BAGD, HNTC, LN, Lns, WBC; all versions except KJV], 'to trust' [KJV].

c. aor. mid. (deponent = act.) infin. of γίνομαι (LN 85.7) (BAGD I.4.c.ε. p. 463): 'to come' [AB, BAGD, HNTC; KJV, NASB, NRSV, TNT], 'to get' [Lns], 'to visit' [WBC; NAB, NIV, NJB, REB, TEV].

d. aor. act. infin. of λαλέω (LN 33.70) (BAGD 2.a.ε. p. 463): 'to speak' [BAGD, LN, Lns; KJV, NASB, TNT], 'to talk' [HNTC, LN, WBC; all versions except KJV, NASB, TNT]. This verb is also translated as a noun: 'talk' [AB].

e. στόμα πρὸς στόμα (LN **83.39**) (BAGD 1.a. p. 769): 'mouth to mouth' [Lns]. This phrase is translated 'face to face' [BAGD, HNTC, LN, WBC; all versions except NJB, TEV], 'person to person' [LN], 'in person' [NJB], 'personally' [TEV], 'heart to heart' [AB].

QUESTION—What relationship is indicated by ἀλλά 'but'?

It indicates a contrast with writing a letter. He prefers face-to-face talking and finds it more satisfying [NTC, TNTC] and effective [EBC, Lns, NCBC]. By his use of contrast, he gives the reason he did not want to write [My].

QUESTION—What is meant by στόμα πρὸς στόμα 'mouth to mouth'?

It means 'in person' [Alf, BAGD, Br, EBC, HNTC, TH, WBC; all versions] and implies the intimacy of personal fellowship [Brd, EBC].

so-that[a] our joy[b] might-be having-been-made-complete.[c]

TEXT—Instead of ἡμῶν 'our', some manuscripts have ὑμῶν 'your'. GNT selects ἡμῶν 'our' with a C rating, indicating a considerable degree of doubt. Only Alf, ICC, Lns and NASB follows the reading ὑμῶν 'your'.

LEXICON—a. ἵνα (LN 89.49): 'so that' [AB, WBC; all versions except KJV, NASB, TNT], 'that' [KJV, NASB, TNT], 'in order that' [Lns], not explicit [HNTC].

b. χαρά (LN 25.123) (BAGD 1. p. 875): 'joy' [AB, BAGD, HNTC, LN, Lns, WBC; all versions except TEV], 'happy' [TEV]. See this word at 1 John 1:4.

c. perf. pass. participle of πληρόω (LN 59.33) (BAGD 3. p. 671): 'to be complete' [BAGD, HNTC, LN, WBC; NIV, NJB, NRSV, REB, TNT], 'to be filled' [Lns; KJV, NAB], 'to be made full' [NASB], 'to be fulfilled' [AB]. This verb is also translated as an adverb: '(to be) completely (happy)' [TEV]. See this word at 1 John 1:4.

QUESTION—What relationship is indicated by ἵνα 'so that'?

It indicates the purpose of the visit [Brd, ICC, Lns].

QUESTION—How will speaking face to face fill up their joy?

The writer expects them to heed his warning and therefore he will be happy [NTC], or hearing the message will make them happy [Alf], or the fellowship between the writer and the people will bring joy [AB, EBC, NTC, TNTC, WBC].

QUESTION—To whom does ἡμῶν 'our' refer?

1. It is 'we inclusive' and refers to the writer and readers [AB, My, NIC, NTC, TH, WBC].
2. It is an epistolary 'we' and means 'my' [HNTC].

DISCOURSE UNIT: 13 [AB, Br]. The topic is the final greeting.

13 **The children of your (sg.) chosen[a] sister[b] greet[c] you (sg.).**

TEXT—At the end of the epistle some manuscripts have ἀμήν 'amen'. This word is omitted by GNT with a B rating, indicating some degree of doubt. Only KJV follows the reading ἀμήν 'amen'.

LEXICON—a. ἐκλεκτός: 'chosen'. See this word at v. 1.
- b. ἀδελφή (LN 10.50) (BAGD 4. p. 15): 'sister' [AB, HNTC, LN, Lns, WBC; all versions].
- c. pres. mid. (deponent = active) indic. of ἀσπάζομαι (LN 33.20) (BAGD 1.a. p. 116): 'to greet' [BAGD, LN; KJV, NASB, TNT], 'to send greetings to' [AB, HNTC, WBC; NAB, NIV, NRSV, REB, TEV], 'to remember to' [BAGD], 'to salute' [Lns]. This verb is also translated as a noun: 'greetings' [NJB].

QUESTION—How is this verse related to its context?

It is the customary way of ending a letter in Greek of this period [AB, Herm, NCBC, NIC]. It also adds the authority of the sister church to the writer's own words [HNTC, WBC].

QUESTION—To whom does ἀδελφῆς 'sister' refer and who are her children?
1. Those who see the ἐκλεκτῇ κυρίᾳ 'elect lady' of verse 1 as a church see her sister also as a church, probably in the place where the writer is, and her sister's children as the members of that church [AB, BAGD, Br, EBC, Herm, HNTC, Lns, My, NIC, NTC, TH, TNTC, WBC, Ws]. The use of the relationship term 'sister' emphasizes the close relationship of the two congregations [Herm, TNTC], and basic equality [Lns].
2. Those who see the ἐκλεκτῇ κυρίᾳ 'elect lady' of verse 1 as a woman see her sister also as a woman and her sister's children as literal children of that family [Brd, EGT]. Her sister's children were at the same location of the writer [Brd].

QUESTION—Who is the implied agent of the action word ἐκλεκτῆς 'chosen'?

God chose her [BAGD, Lns; REB, TNT].

QUESTION—What is the significance of the change from the plural form of 'you' in verses 6–12 to the singular form here?

For those who see the ἐκλεκτῇ κυρίᾳ 'elect lady' of verse 1 as a church, it signifies that the writer is addressing the church as a whole [AB, Br, ICC, NTC, TH, WBC]. For those who see the ἐκλεκτῇ κυρίᾳ 'elect lady' of verse 1 as a woman, it signifies that the writer is addressing her alone, apart from her children.

EXEGETICAL SUMMARY OF 3 JOHN

Title: The Third of John
See the discussion for the title of 2 John.

DISCOURSE UNIT: 1–8 [TNTC; NJB]. The topic is a message to Gaius [TNTC].

DISCOURSE UNIT: 1–4 [EGT, NCBC, NIC, TH; TEV]. The topic is the opening introduction [TEV], address and greeting [NIC].

DISCOURSE UNIT: 1–3 [EGT]. The topic is the address and commendation.

DISCOURSE UNIT: 1–2 [AB, Br, Brd, Lns, NTC, WBC]. The topic is the introduction [AB, Brd, NTC, WBC], salutation [Br, Lns].

DISCOURSE UNIT: 1 [Alf, EBC, Herm, Ws]. The topic is the opening salutation [Alf, EBC, Ws], introduction [Herm].

1 The elder[a] to-Gaius the beloved,[b] whom I love[c] in[d] truth.[e]

LEXICON—a. πρεσβύτερος (LN 53.77) (BAGD 2.b.β p. 700): 'elder' [BAGD, HNTC, Lns; all versions], 'presbyter' [AB, WBC]. See this word at 2 John 1.
- b. ἀγαπητός (LN 25.45) (BAGD 2. p. 6): 'beloved' [AB, BAGD, LN, Lns, WBC; NAB, NASB, NRSV], 'well beloved' [KJV], 'my dear' [TEV], 'dear friend' [NIV, NJB], 'dear' [BAGD, HNTC, LN; REB, TNT].
- c. pres. act. indic. of ἀγαπάω (LN 25.43): 'to love' [AB, HNTC, Lns, WBC; all versions]. See this word at 1 John 2:10; 3:10, 11, 14, 18, 23; 4:7, 8, 10, 11, 12, 19, 20, 21; 5:1, 2; 2 John 1, 5.
- d. ἐν (LN 70.4): 'in' [AB, HNTC, WBC; all versions except NAB, TEV, TNT], 'in connection with' [Lns], 'within the fellowship of' [TNT]. For NAB, TEV, see below. See this word at 2 John 1.
- e. ἀλήθεια (LN 70.4) (BAGD 3. p. 36): 'truth' [AB, HNTC, Lns, WBC; all versions except NAB]. The phrase ἐν ἀληθείᾳ 'in truth' is translated 'truly' [BAGD; TEV], 'really' [LN], 'indeed' [NAB]. See this word at 2 John 1.

QUESTION—To whom does πρεσβύτερος 'elder' refer and what is the significance of calling himself ὁ πρεσβύτερος 'the elder'?
See the discussion at 2 John 1.

QUESTION—Who is the implied agent of the event word ἀγαπητῷ 'beloved'?
1. Gaius is loved by all Christians in general [Alf, Brd, Herm, HNTC, TNTC, WBC].
2. Gaius is loved by the elder [EBC, My, NIC, TH; TEV].
3. Gaius is loved by God [NTC].

QUESTION—Who is Gaius?
Gaius is probably not the same man called Gaius elsewhere in the New Testament [AB, BAGD, Br, Brd, Herm, ICC, Lns, My, NIC, TH, TNTC,

WBC, Ws]. He belonged to the congregation led by Diotrephes [AB, EBC, Herm, Lns], or perhaps led another congregation in the same region [AB]. He probably was an influential person in the congregation [EBC, ICC, TNTC, WBC].

QUESTION—What is meant by the phrase ἐν ἀληθείᾳ 'in truth'?
See the discussion at 2 John 1.

DISCOURSE UNIT: 2–8 [Herm]. The topic is the treatment of itinerant teachers.

DISCOURSE UNIT: 2–4 [Alf, EBC, Ws]. The topic is a wish for the prosperity of Gaius [Alf], the elder's joy [Ws], personal words [EBC].

2 Beloved,[a] concerning[b] all-things I pray/wish[c] you(sg.) to-prosper[d] and to-be-healthy,[e]

LEXICON—a. ἀγαπητός (LN 25.45) (BAGD 2. p. 6): 'beloved' [AB, BAGD, Lns; KJV, NAB, NASB, NRSV], 'dear' [BAGD], 'my dear' [HNTC], 'my dear friend' [NJB], 'dear friend' [WBC; NIV, REB, TEV, TNT]. See this word at 1 John 3:2, 21; 4:1, 7, 11.

b. περί (LN 89.6) (BAGD 1.e p. 644): 'concerning'. The phrase περὶ πάντων 'concerning all things' is translated 'in all ways' [NAB], 'in every way' [AB, WBC], 'in all respects' [NASB, TNT], 'in regard to everything' [Lns], 'everything' [NJB, TEV], 'all' [HNTC; NRSV], 'above all' [REB], 'above all things' [KJV].

c. pres. mid. (deponent = act.) indic. of εὔχομαι (LN 25.6; 33.178) (BAGD 2. p. 329): 'to pray' [HNTC, LN, Lns, WBC; all versions except KJV, NAB, NJB], 'to wish' [BAGD, LN; KJV], 'to hope' [AB; NAB, NJB].

d. pres. pass. infin. of εὐοδόω (LN **22.47**) (BAGD p. 323): 'to prosper' [Lns, WBC; KJV, NASB], 'to thrive' [NAB], 'to be well off' [AB], 'to be well' [TNT], 'to go well' [BAGD, HNTC, LN; NIV, NRSV, REB, TEV], 'to go happily' [NJB].

e. pres. act. infin. of ὑγιαίνω (LN 23.129): 'to be healthy' [BAGD, LN], 'to be in health' [Lns; KJV], 'to be in good health' [AB, HNTC, LN; NAB, NASB, NRSV, TEV], 'to enjoy good health' [NIV, REB] 'to be well physically' [NJB], 'to be well in body' [WBC].

QUESTION—What is meant by εὔχομαι 'I pray/wish'?
1. It means to pray to God [Alf, Br, Brd, HNTC, ICC, Lns, NCBC, WBC; all versions except KJV, NAB, NJB].
2. It means to wish for something [AB, BAGD, Herm, My, NCBC, NTC, TH, TNTC; KJV, NAB, NJB]. Letters of that time commonly contained a wish for good health [AB, TH].

QUESTION—What does περὶ πάντων 'concerning all things' modify?
1. It modifies εὐοδοῦσθαι 'to prosper' and means to prosper in every way or in all respects [AB, Alf, Brd, ICC, Lns, My, NIC, TH, TNTC, WBC]: I pray that you may prosper in every way and that you may be in good health.

2. It modifies both 'to prosper' and 'to be healthy' and means in every way [EGT]: I pray that in every way you may both prosper and be in good health.
3. It modifies εὔχομαι 'I pray/wish' and means 'above all' [KJV, REB]: above all I pray that you may prosper and be in good health.

QUESTION—What is meant by εὐοδοῦσθαι 'to prosper'?
1. It means financial prosperity [Brd, EGT, Lns, TNTC]. This wish is motivated by a concern for the financial drain the visiting missionaries have been putting on Gaius [Lns].
2. It means prosperity in every aspect of material life [Br, Herm, My, NTC, TH]. He wants everything to go well [Herm, My] in all external circumstances [My]. It was a customary wish at the beginning of private letters [Herm].

QUESTION—What is meant by ὑγιαίνειν 'to be healthy'?
It means physical health [AB, Alf, BAGD, Br, Brd, HNTC, Lns, NIC, NTC, TH, WBC; all versions]. Some commentators think that perhaps Gaius was in poor health [EGT, NIC, WBC]. Others think that nothing is implied about his health [EBC, ICC, Lns, My, NIC]. It was customary in letters of that time to wish for the recipient's health [EBC, ICC, NIC, WBC].

as[a] prospers[b] your soul.[c]

LEXICON—a. καθώς (LN 78.53): 'as' [AB, HNTC, WBC; NAB, NJB, TEV], 'even as' [Lns; KJV, NIV], 'just as' [NASB, NRSV], not explicit [REB].
b. pres. pass. indic. of εὐοδόω: 'to prosper'. See this word in the preceding clause.
c. ψυχή (LN 26.4) (BAGD 1.c. p. 893): 'soul' [BAGD, HNTC, Lns; KJV, NASB, NIV, NRSV, REB], 'spirit' [WBC; NAB, TEV], 'inner self' [LN]. This noun is also translated as an adverb: 'spiritually' [AB; NJB, TNT].

QUESTION—What is being implied by this clause?
It implies that Gaius is spiritually healthy [Alf, Brd, EBC, EGT, Herm, Lns, NCBC, NIC, NTC, TNTC, WBC].

QUESTION—What is meant by ψυχή 'soul'?
It refers to spiritual life [Brd, EBC, HNTC, Lns, My, NCBC, NIC, TH, TNTC, WBC, Ws]. It is one's life in relationship to God [HNTC, WBC]. It contrasts to the body [Alf, BAGD].

QUESTION—What is being compared?
The physical aspects of his life are being compared with its spiritual aspects [NIC, TNTC]. It is a wish that his earthly prosperity will equal his spiritual prosperity [Lns]. Bodily health and general prosperity should match the prosperity of his soul [Br]. Some translations group the elements in different ways: 'I pray/wish that you may be healthy and that in every way things will go well with you, as things are well with your soul' [AB; NAB, NIV]; 'I pray/wish that you may prosper in every respect, and may you prosper in every way as you prosper in spirit' [WBC].

DISCOURSE UNIT: 3–12 [Lns]. This is the body of the letter.

DISCOURSE UNIT: 3–8 [Brd, NTC, WBC]. The topic is a commendation of Gaius [Brd, NTC, WBC].

DISCOURSE UNIT: 3–4 [AB, Br, Brd, NTC]. The topic is the occasion for rejoicing [AB, Br, NTC], a commendation for Christian conduct [Brd].

3 For[a] I-rejoiced[b] greatly[c]

LEXICON—a. γάρ (LN 89.23): 'for' [AB, Lns, WBC; KJV, NAB, NASB], not explicit [HNTC; all versions except KJV, NAB, NASB].
  b. aor. pass. (deponent = act.) indic. of χαίρω (LN 25.125) (BAGD 1. p. 873): 'to rejoice' [Lns; KJV], 'to be glad' [BAGD; NASB, REB], 'to be happy' [TEV, TNT], 'to be given joy' [AB; NAB, NIV]. The phrase ἐχάρην λίαν 'rejoice greatly' is translated 'to be delighted' [HNTC], 'to be overjoyed' [WBC; NRSV], 'it is my greatest joy' [NJB].
  c. λίαν (LN 78.1) (BAGD 1. p. 473): 'greatly' [Lns; KJV], 'great' [NAB, NIV, NJB], 'very' [BAGD; NASB, REB, TNT], 'so' [TEV], 'much' [AB].

QUESTION—What relationship is indicated by γάρ 'for'?
  It indicates the reason the author knows that Gaius is prospering spiritually [Br, Lns, My, NIC, TH, TNTC, WBC, Ws] and a reason for wishing him well [Ws].

brothers[a] coming[b] and testifying[c] of-you in-the truth,[d]

LEXICON—a. ἀδελφός (LN 11.23): 'brother' [AB, HNTC, Lns, WBC; all versions except NRSV, REB, TEV], 'Christian brother' [TEV], 'fellow Christian' [REB], 'friend' [NRSV].
  b. pres. mid. (deponent = act.) participle of ἔρχομαι (LN 15.81) (BAGD I.1.a.ζ. p. 310): 'to come' [AB, BAGD, HNTC, Lns; KJV, NASB, NIV, NJB, TNT], 'to arrive' [WBC; NRSV, REB, TEV], not explicit [NAB]. The present tense indicates a repeated action as brothers arrived at various times [AB, Brd, EBC, EGT, ICC, NIC, NTC, TH, WBC, Ws].
  c. pres. act. participle of μαρτυρέω (LN 33.263) (BAGD 1.a. p. 492): 'to testify' [AB, BAGD, HNTC, Lns, WBC; KJV, NRSV], 'to bear witness' [NAB, NASB], 'testified to your faithfulness' [HNTC; NRSV], 'to tell' [NIV, NJB, REB, TEV], 'to speak about' [TNT]. The present tense indicates that the testifying is a repeated action [Brd, EGT, ICC, NIC, WBC, Ws]. See this word at 1 John 1:2; 4:14; 5:6, 7, 9, 10.
  d. ἀλήθεια (LN 72.2) (BAGD 2.b. p. 36): 'truth' [AB, BAGD, HNTC, LN, Lns, WBC; all versions except NAB]. This noun is also translated as an adverb: 'truly' [NAB].

QUESTION—What relationship is indicated by the use of the participles ἐρχομένων 'coming' and μαρτυρούντων 'testifying'?
  They indicate the reason for rejoicing [Alf, My]: I rejoiced because the brothers came and testified about you. A temporal word conveys such a relationship [Alf, My] and 'when' is included in translations [HNTC, WBC;

KJV, NASB, NJB, NRSV, TEV, TNT]: I rejoiced when the brothers came and testified about you. Another way to show this relationship is to translate 'I rejoiced to have the brothers come and testify about you' [AB; NIV].

QUESTION—To whom does ἀδελφῶν 'brothers' refer?

It refers to fellow Christians who have returned from where Gaius lived to where the elder was living [AB, Brd, EBC, NIC, WBC; NRSV, REB, TEV]. These included traveling missionaries [AB, EBC, EGT, Herm, Lns, NIC, NTC, TH, WBC] sent out by the elder [Alf, Br, HNTC, TNTC]. They probably experienced Gaius' hospitality [AB, Br, Lns, NIC, NTC, TNTC].

QUESTION—What is meant by 'testifying of you in the truth'?

They testified to Gaius' truth [Br; NASB]. 'His truth' means that his conduct corresponded to the truth of God's revelation [Herm], the highest standard of life and conduct [ICC]. His behavior was in accordance with the will of God [TH]. The brothers testified that Gaius was faithful to the truth of the gospel [Br, Brd, EBC, HNTC, WBC; NIV, NJB, NRSV, REB, TEV]. He adhered to the truth [NIC]. It is explained in the following clause that 'his truth' means that he walked in truth [AB, Alf, Brd, Lns, My, TH; NAB, NASB, NIV, NRSV].

how/as[a] you walk[b] in-truth.

LEXICON—a. καθώς (LN 89.86) (BAGD 5. p. 391): 'how' [BAGD, LN; NAB, NASB, NIV], 'namely how' [BAGD; NRSV], 'in what manner' [LN], 'even as' [Lns; KJV], 'just as' [TEV], 'as exemplified by' [AB], 'as indeed' [WBC], 'indeed' [HNTC; REB, TNT], not explicit [NJB].

b. pres. act. indic. of περιπατέω (LN 41.11) (BAGD 2.a.δ. p. 649): 'to walk' [AB, HNTC, Lns; KJV, NAB, NASB, NIV, NRSV], 'to live' [LN, WBC; REB, TEV, TNT]. This verb is also translated as a noun: 'life' [NJB]. The present tense indicates that the walking is a continuous action [WBC; NIV].

QUESTION—What relationship is indicated by καθώς 'how/as'?

1. It introduces indirect discourse [BAGD, Brd, My, TH] and indicates the content or substance of the brothers' testimony [Alf, Brd, My, TH; NAB, NASB, NIV, NRSV]: they testified to your truth, namely, how you walk in the truth.
2. It introduces the elder's own evaluation of Gaius and intensifies the expression [Herm, HNTC, WBC, Ws; REB, TNT]: they testified to your truth, as indeed I know that you live in the truth. Their testimony corresponds to what the elder knows to be true of them [Herm].

QUESTION—What is the significance of the use of the overt pronoun σύ 'you (singular)' here?

It indicates prominence [Lns, TH, Ws] and contrasts Gaius with others, especially with Diotrephes [My, TH, Ws]: as you, unlike some others I could mention, walk in the truth.

QUESTION—What is meant by ἀληθείᾳ 'truth'?
It means the truth of the gospel and refers to orthodox doctrine [BAGD, Brd, EBC, Herm, HNTC, Lns, Ws]. To walk in the truth is to apply the truth to one's behavior [TNTC].

DISCOURSE UNIT: 4–6 [TEV]. The topic is truth and love.

4 **I-have no greater[a] joy[b] (than) these, that I-should-hear[c] my children are-walking in the truth.**

TEXT—Instead of χαράν 'joy', some manuscripts have χάριν 'grace'. GNT selects χαράν 'joy' with a B rating, indicating some degree of doubt. The reading χάριν 'grace' is selected only by Ws.

LEXICON—a. μέγας (LN 78.2) (BAGD p. 497): 'greater' [AB, BAGD, HNTC, Lns, WBC; all versions except NAB, NRSV, TEV]. The phrase μειζοτέραν τούτων οὐκ ἔχω χαράν 'I have no greater joy' is translated 'nothing delights me more' [NAB], 'nothing makes me happier' [TEV], 'I was overjoyed' [NRSV].

b. χαρά (LN 25.123) (BAGD 1. p. 875): 'joy' [AB, BAGD, HNTC, Lns, WBC; all versions except NAB, NRSV, TEV].

c. pres. act. subj. of ἀκούω (LN 33.212) (BAGD 3.f. p. 32): 'to hear' [AB, BAGD, HNTC, LN, Lns, WBC; all versions].

QUESTION—How is this verse related to its context?
This explains why he rejoiced (v. 3) [Alf, Herm, My, TH, WBC].

QUESTION—What relationship is indicated by ἵνα 'that'?
It explains 'these' in the preceding clause [AB, Alf, BAGD, Br, Brd, EBC, EGT, Herm, ICC, Lns, My, NTC, TH, WBC].

QUESTION—Why is the plural form τούτων 'these' explained by the single item of news in the explanation 'that I should hear that my children are walking in the truth'?

1. The use of the plural for the singular is acceptable Greek grammar [AB, Alf, EGT, Herm, My, NTC]: I have no greater joy than this, that my children are walking in the truth.
2. The plural is used because there were a number of times this report came to the elder, each of which brought joy [ICC, WBC, Ws]: I have no greater joy than the joy of hearing from time to time that my children are walking in the truth.
3. The plural is used to refer to the various specific activities that were reported under the generic statement that they 'walked in the truth' [Brd, Lns]: I have no greater joy than the joy of hearing these many good things you are doing by walking in the truth.

QUESTION—Who are the elder's 'children'?

1. He is referring to all those under his spiritual care [AB, Brd, ICC, Lns, My, NCBC, TH, WBC], for whom he feels a fatherly concern and affection [Br, ICC, Lns, My, NCBC, TNTC].
2. He is referring to Gaius and other Christians who have been converted under his ministry [EBC, EGT, Herm, HNTC, NTC, Ws].

DISCOURSE UNIT: 5–8 [AB, Alf, Br, Brd, EBC, EGT, NCBC, NIC, NTC, TH, Ws; TEV]. The topic is praise for the hospitality shown by Gaius [AB, Alf, Br, Brd, EBC, EGT, NIC, NTC; TEV], the duty of generosity to the brethren [Ws].

5 Beloved,[a] you-do a-faithful[b] (thing) whenever you-work[c] for[d] the brothers and[e] this (you do) for-strangers,[f]

LEXICON—a. ἀγαπητός: 'beloved'. See this word at v. 2.
    b. πιστός (LN 31.88) (BAGD 1.b. p. 665): 'faithful' [LN]. The phrase πιστὸν ποιέω 'to do a faithful thing' [Lns] is translated 'to do faithfully' [KJV, NRSV], 'to act faithfully' [NASB], 'to be faithful' [NIV, TEV, TNT], 'to be loyal' [HNTC], 'to act loyally' [BAGD, WBC], 'to do a loyal work' [NJB], 'to show a fine loyalty' [REB], 'to demonstrate fidelity' [AB; NAB], 'to be faithful in what one does' [NIV].
    c. aorist mid. (deponent = act.) subj. of ἐργάζομαι (LN 90.47; 42.41) (BAGD 2.a. p. 307): 'to work' [LN, WBC], 'to do' [BAGD, HNTC; all versions except NASB, NJB, TEV], 'to accomplish' [NASB], 'to perform' [Lns], 'to do work' [AB; TEV], 'to help' [NJB]. The aorist tense sums up the many deeds [AB, Alf, Lns, NTC] or considers each act separately [EGT].
    d. εἰς (LN 90.41) (BAGD 4.g. p. 229): 'for' [AB, BAGD, HNTC, LN, Lns, WBC; all versions except KJV, NJB], 'for the sake of' [BAGD], 'to' [KJV]. For NJB, see above.
    e. καί (LN 91.12): 'and' [Lns; KJV], 'and especially' [WBC; NASB], 'even when' [TEV, TNT], 'even though' [AB, HNTC; NAB, NIV, NJB, NRSV], 'though' [REB].
    f. ξένος (LN 11.73) (BAGD 2.a. p. 548): 'stranger' [AB, BAGD, HNTC, LN, Lns, WBC; all versions], 'alien' [BAGD].

QUESTION—Why is ἀγαπητέ 'beloved' repeated?
    It marks the beginning of a new paragraph [AB, Alf, Herm] and emphasizes the elder's love for Gaius [Brd, EBC, NTC, WBC].

QUESTION—What is meant by the phrase πιστὸν ποιεῖς 'do a faithful thing'?
    1. It means to act in a trustworthy or loyal manner [BAGD, Br, Brd, EGT, HNTC, Lns, NCBC, NIC, NTC, TH, WBC; all versions]. He is doing what a Christian should do [NCBC, TH], he is faithful to the truth [NIC].
    2. It means to do actions growing out of one's faith [AB, Alf, My, TNTC]. Hospitality corresponds to his Christian profession [My].

QUESTION—What does the use of the present tense of the verb ποιέω 'to act' indicate?
    1. The present tense indicates that doing this is habitual [AB, EGT, ICC, TH, WBC, Ws] and is already going on [AB].
    2. It is an epistolary present tense, referring to when Gaius will receive the letter brought by Demetrius, to whom he should then show hospitality [Lns].

QUESTION—In what way did Gaius work for his fellow Christians?
>He helped them [TH, WBC], and this especially refers to the hospitality that Gaius has provided [AB, Herm, NTC, WBC]. Hospitality was a Christian duty [Br, ICC].

QUESTION—What is the relationship between brothers and strangers?
>It indicates two characteristics of the same people. They are 'brothers' because they share the same faith and at the same time they are 'strangers' because they had not previously met [AB, Alf, Br, Brd, EBC, Herm, HNTC, Lns, My, NIC, NTC, TH, TNTC, WBC, Ws]. The connection is brought out in different ways: 'whenever you work for the brothers, although they are strangers' [AB, HNTC, NTC, TH, WBC; NAB, NIV, NJB, NRSV, REB], 'whenever you work for the brothers, even when they are strangers' [TEV, TNT], 'whenever you work for the brothers, especially when they are strangers' [Brd, Herm, WBC; NASB, TNT],

6 who testified^a (about) your love^b before^c (the) church,^d

LEXICON—a. aorist act. indic. of μαρτυρέω: 'to testify'. See this word at v. 3. The aorist tense looks at a series of testimonies as a whole [AB, Brd] or it refers to some definite occasion when a testimony was given [TNTC].
>b. ἀγάπη (LN 25.43): 'love' [AB, HNTC, LN, Lns, WBC; all versions except KJV, REB], 'charity' [KJV], 'kindness' [REB]. See this word at 1 John 2:5, 15; 3:1, 16, 17; 4:7, 8, 9, 10, 12, 16, 17, 18; 5:3; 2 John 3, 6.
>c. ἐνώπιον (LN 83.33) (BAGD 2.a. p. 270): 'before' [AB, LN, WBC; all versions except NIV, NJB, TEV], 'in the presence of' [BAGD, HNTC, Lns], 'to' [NIV, NJB, TEV].
>d. ἐκκλησία (LN 11.32) (BAGD 4.a. p. 241): 'church' [AB, LN, Lns, WBC; all versions except REB], 'congregation' [HNTC, LN; REB].

QUESTION—Who are the participants of the event word 'love'?
>Gaius loved others [HNTC, Lns, NIC, NTC, TH, TNTC, WBC]. Gaius showed love to the itinerant teachers by his hospitality [AB, Alf, Br, EBC, Herm, ICC, Lns, NIC, NTC, TH, WBC].

QUESTION—What is meant by the preposition ἐνώπιον 'before'?
>It indicates that the report of Gaius' action was made in public before the congregation [Alf, Br, Brd, EBC, ICC, Lns, NCBC, NIC, NTC, TH, TNTC, WBC, Ws].

QUESTION—To what does ἐκκλησίας 'church' refer?
>It refers to the congregation located where the elder was then living [AB, Alf, Brd, EBC, HNTC, Lns, My, NIC, NTC, TH, TNTC, WBC, Ws], and from which the itinerants had come [Alf, Br, HNTC, Lns, TNTC].

whom you-will-do well^a having-sent-forward^b worthily^c of-God;

LEXICON—a. καλῶς (LN 88.4) (BAGD 4.a. p. 401): 'well' [Lns, WBC; KJV, NASB, NIV, NRSV], 'a good thing' [AB, HNTC; NAB]. The phrase καλῶς ποιήσεις 'you will do well' is translated 'it would be a kindness' [NJB].

b. aorist act. participle of προπέμπω (LN 15.72) (BAGD 2. p. 709): 'to send forward' [Lns], 'to send forward on one's journey' [HNTC, Lns], 'to bring forward on one's journey' [KJV], 'to send on one's way' [BAGD, LN, WBC; NASB, NIV, NRSV], 'to help on one's journey' [AB, BAGD, LN; NAB, NJB, REB], 'to help them on their trip' [TEV], 'to help them forward on their way' [TNT].

c. ἀξίως (LN 66.6) (BAGD p. 78): 'worthily'. The phrase 'worthily of God' is translated 'in a manner worthy of God' [HNTC, Lns; NASB, NIV, NRSV, REB, TNT], 'in a way worthy of God' [AB], 'in a manner that God would approve' [WBC], 'in a way that will please God' [NAB, TEV], 'as God would approve' [NJB], 'after a godly sort' [KJV].

QUESTION—What people should be sent forward?
1. The same brothers who reported to the elder planned to return to Gaius and then continue on their missionary journey [EBC, Lns, My, WBC].
2. This is a reference of traveling brothers in general [NIC, NTC, TH, TNTC]: you will do well to send such people forward worthily of God.

QUESTION—What is the function of this clause?
It is a polite request that he help again in the present situation [AB, BAGD, Br, Brd, EBC, EGT, Herm, HNTC, Lns, My, NIC, NTC, TH, TNTC, WBC, Ws; REB, TEV, TNT].

QUESTION—What does the future tense of the ποιέω 'to do' indicate?
The future is part of the standard polite request form [AB, BAGD, Br, Brd, EBC, EGT, Herm, HNTC, My, NIC, NTC, TH, TNTC, WBC, Ws; REB, TEV, TNT]. The future is used because the 'doing' is still unrealized [Lns].

QUESTION—What is meant by προπέμψας 'send forward'?
It means supplying them with what they needed for the journey [AB, BAGD, Brd, EGT, Herm, Lns, My, NIC, NTC, TH, TNTC, WBC, Ws; all versions].
He would supply food and money for the trip [NIC, TH, TNTC].

QUESTION—What does the use of the aorist tense of the participle προπέμψας 'to send forward' indicate?
1. The aorist tense refers to a single act to be performed when Gaius receives the letter [Lns, My].
2. The aorist tense indicates that the sending forward is simultaneous with 'doing well' [NTC].
3. The aorist tense indicates that the action is being viewed by the elder in its completeness [My, WBC, Ws]. The action is considered as good as done [AB].

QUESTION—How are the adverb and noun related in the genitive construction ἀξίως τοῦ θεοῦ 'worthily of God'?
1. It means that the provision must be handled in a way that will glorify God [Brd, NIC, NTC].
2. It means that the provision must be handled in a way that it would be handled if God himself were the recipient [Alf, EBC, EGT, TNTC].
3. It means that the provision must be handled in a way that God would handle it if God himself were the provider [Br, EGT, NIC, WBC; NJB].

7 for[a] for-the-sake-of[b] the name[c] they-went-out[d]

LEXICON—a. γάρ (LN 89.23): 'for' [AB, Lns, WBC; NASB, NRSV, TEV, TNT], 'because' [KJV], not explicit [HNTC; NAB, NIV, NJB, REB].

b. ὑπέρ (LN 90.36) (BAGD 1.b. p. 838): 'for the sake of' [AB, BAGD, HNTC, LN; all versions except REB, TEV], 'in behalf of' [BAGD, LN, Lns], 'for the love of' [REB], 'in the service of' [TEV], 'in' [WBC].

c. ὄνομα (LN 9.19; 33.265) (BAGD I.4.d. p. 573): 'name' [AB, BAGD, HNTC, Lns, WBC; all versions except NRSV, TEV]. The phrase 'the name' is translated 'Christ' [NRSV, TEV]. See this word at 1 John 2:12.

d. aorist act. indic. of ἐξέρχομαι (LN 15.40): 'to go out' [HNTC, LN, Lns, WBC; NASB, NIV, REB, TNT], 'to set out' [AB; NAB, NJB, TEV], 'to go forth' [KJV], 'to begin a journey' [NRSV]. The aorist tense indicates that this was a general rule or a particular case [TH, WBC].

QUESTION—What relationship is indicated by γάρ 'for'?

This indicates the grounds for urging Gaius to support such missionaries [AB, Brd, ICC, Lns, My, TNTC, WBC]. The first ground was that they went out for the sake of Christ, the second was that they did so in a sacrificial manner [Brd].

QUESTION—Whose name is referred to?

It refers to Christ [AB, Alf, Br, Brd, EBC, EGT, Herm, ICC, Lns, My, NIC, TH, TNTC, WBC, Ws; NRSV, REB, TEV]. It is an intentional parallel to the Divine Name of the Old Testament [AB, Brd]. 'Name' means the completeness of the revelation of Christ [Lns], the revelation of his divine and human nature, and his atoning work [TNTC].

QUESTION—What is meant by ὑπὲρ τοῦ ὀνόματος 'for the sake of the name'?

It means that they went out to spread the knowledge of Christ's name [My], to proclaim Christ [Herm, WBC], and thus serve him [WBC].

QUESTION—What is meant by ἐξῆλθον 'they went out'?

It means they initiated their missionary journey [AB, Alf, Br, Brd, EBC, Herm, ICC, Lns, My, NTC, TNTC, WBC, Ws]. They went forth from a sending church into the world to evangelize it [NIC, Ws].

taking[a] nothing from[b] the Gentiles.[c]

LEXICON—a. pres. act. participle of λαμβάνω (LN 57.55): 'to take' [Lns; KJV], 'to accept' [AB, HNTC, WBC; all versions except NIV, NJB], 'to receive' [NIV]. The phrase λαμβάνοντες ἀπό 'taking from' is translated 'depending on' [NJB]. The use of the participle with the negative particle μηδέν indicates a determination to take nothing [AB, Alf, My]. The present tense indicates that this was a customary action [Alf, ICC, NTC, TH, TNTC, Ws].

b. ἀπό (LN 90.15) (BAGD IV.2.a. p. 87): 'from' [AB, BAGD, HNTC, Lns, WBC; all versions except KJV, NJB], 'of' [KJV].

c. ἐθνικός (LN 11.38) (BAGD p. 218): 'Gentile' [BAGD, LN; KJV, NASB], 'heathen' [BAGD, LN; TNT], 'pagan' [AB, HNTC, LN, Lns;

NAB, NIV], 'unbeliever' [WBC; NJB, REB, TEV], 'non-believer' [NRSV].

QUESTION—To whom does ἐθνικῶν 'Gentiles' refer?

It is not primarily used as an ethnic designation but as a moral classification and refers to individual non-Christians [AB, Br, Brd, Lns, NTC, TH, TNTC, Ws; all versions except KJV, NASB].

QUESTION—What is the significance of they fact that they took nothing from the Gentiles?

Their policy was not to seek their support from non-Christians [TNTC]. They would not accept food, money, or other help from them [TH]. Since grace was free, they would not charge for the gospel [NIC, WBC]. Taking from the Gentiles might imply that the Christians did not support their own [Br]. Pagans might consider them to be like their own itinerant priests who were greedy for money [EBC, Herm, Lns, NIC, NTC, TNTC, WBC] and thus it would be a reproach to the name of Christ [EGT, Lns].

8 Therefore[a] we ought[b] to-support[c] such,

LEXICON—a. οὖν (LN 89.50) (BAGD 1.a. p. 593): 'therefore' [AB, Lns, WBC; all versions except NJB, TEV, TNT], 'so' [HNTC], 'then' [TEV], not explicit [NJB, TNT].

b. pres. act. indic. of ὀφείλω (LN 71.25) (BAGD 2.a.β. p. 599): 'ought' [AB, BAGD, LN, Lns; all versions except NAB, NJB, TEV], 'to owe to' [NAB], 'to be a duty to' [NJB], 'must' [BAGD; TEV], 'to have an obligation' [HNTC], 'to be bound to' [WBC].

c. pres. act. infin. of ὑπολαμβάνω (LN **35.1**) (BAGD 2. p. 845): 'to support' [AB, BAGD, HNTC, WBC; NAB, NASB, NRSV, REB, TNT], 'to help' [LN; TEV], 'to undertake for' [Lns], 'to welcome' [NJB], 'to receive' [KJV], 'to receive as a guest' [BAGD], 'to show hospitality to' [NIV].

QUESTION—What relationship is indicated by οὖν 'therefore'?

It indicates a conclusion to the preceding information [AB, Alf, Br, ICC, Lns, My, NIC, TH, TNTC, WBC]: since they went out for Christ's sake and do not accept support from non-Christians, we therefore should support them. It is a moral obligation that goes with being a Christian [AB].

QUESTION—To whom does 'we' refer?

It is 'we inclusive' and refers to the elder and the readers in contrast to the unbelievers of v. 6 [AB, Alf, Br, Brd, EGT, ICC, Lns, My, NIC, NTC, TH, TNTC, WBC, Ws]. It is marked as prominent by being overt [AB, Br, Brd, EGT, My, NIC, TH, TNTC, WBC].

QUESTION—What is meant by ὑπολαμβάνω 'support'?

1. It means specifically 'to show hospitality to' [Br, Brd, EGT, NTC, Ws; KJV, NIV, NJB]. It means to provide food and lodging and protection in one's house [Brd].

2. It has the more general meaning 'to support' [AB, Alf, HNTC, ICC, Lns, My, TH, TNTC, WBC; NAB, NASB, NRSV, REB, TNT], 'to help'

[TEV], and 'to assist' [Lns]. The support would provide practical help and supplies as well as a hospitable welcome [WBC].

QUESTION—Who is meant by 'such'?

It refers to the missionaries who do not accept support from the non-Christians [AB, Brd, ICC, TH, TNTC, WBC].

so-that[a] we-may-be[b] co-workers[c] for/with-the truth.[d]

LEXICON—a. ἵνα (LN 89.49; 89.59): 'so that' [WBC; NIV, NRSV, TEV], 'that' [KJV, NASB, TNT], 'in order that' [HNTC, Lns], 'and thus' [AB; NAB], 'and so' [REB], not explicit [NJB].

b. pres. mid. (deponent = act.) subj. of γίνομαι (LN 13.3): 'to be' [HNTC, Lns; KJV, NASB], 'to show' [TNT], 'to prove oneself' [WBC], 'to become' [AB; NRSV].

c. συνεργός (LN 42.44) (BAGD p. 788): 'co-worker' [AB; NRSV], 'fellow worker' [BAGD, HNTC, LN, WBC; NASB, TNT], 'joint worker' [Lns], 'fellow helper' [KJV], 'helper' [BAGD]. The phrase 'to be a fellow worker' is translated as 'to have one's share in a work' [NAB, TEV], 'to work together' [NIV], 'to contribute one's share to the work' [NJB], 'to play a part in' [REB].

d. ἀλήθεια (LN 72.2) (BAGD 2.b. p. 36): 'truth' [AB, BAGD, HNTC, Lns, WBC; all versions].

QUESTION—What relationship is indicated by ἵνα 'in order that'?

It indicates the purpose or contemplated result of supporting the missionaries [AB, HNTC, Lns, TH, WBC, Ws; NAB, NIV, NRSV, REB, TEV].

QUESTION—Who are the co-workers?

1. They and the missionaries will be co-workers for the truth [Alf, EBC, EGT, Herm, Lns, My, NIC, NTC, WBC; NIV, NJB, REB, TEV, TNT]. By helping support the missionaries, they work with them for the cause of the truth of the gospel [Alf, Lns]. Not able to go to preach the gospel themselves, they help others do so [EGT].

2. They and truth will be co-workers [AB, Br, Brd, ICC, TH, TNTC, Ws; NAB, NASB, NRSV]: so that we may be co-workers with the truth. Truth is personified [AB, ICC, TH]. They cooperate with the truth by proclaiming it and by entertaining missionaries [TNTC]. They help the truth that is effective through the missionaries [Ws].

QUESTION—What is meant by ἀληθείᾳ 'truth'?

1. It means the content of Christianity, the gospel as absolute truth [BAGD, Br, EGT, Lns, Ws]. The truth is the substance of their teaching [Ws].

2. It means the quality possessed by God [TH], the reality of God as it has been revealed [Herm, WBC].

DISCOURSE UNIT: 9–12 [TH, WBC]. The topic is Diotrephes and Demetrius [WBC].

DISCOURSE UNIT: 9–11 [NJB] The topic is the example of Diotrephes.

DISCOURSE UNIT: 9–10 [AB, Alf, Br, Brd, EBC, EGT, Herm, NCBC, NIC, NTC, TNTC, Ws; TEV]. The topic is Diotrephes' hostile conduct [Alf, Br, EGT, Herm], a condemnation of Diotrephes [Brd, EBC, NIC, NTC, TNTC; TEV], ambition [Ws].

9 I-wrote[a] something to-the church;[b]
TEXT—The word τι 'something' does not occur in some manuscripts. It is included by GNT with a C rating, indicating a considerable degree of doubt in doing so. It is omitted by KJV, NAB, NIV, REB, and TNT.
LEXICON—a. aorist act. indic. of γράφω (LN 33.61) (BAGD 2.d. p. 167): 'to write' [AB, BAGD, HNTC, Lns, WBC; all versions]. The aorist tense refers to a particular letter written before the present letter [AB, Brd, NTC, TH, WBC]. See this word at 2 John 5.
b. ἐκκλησία: 'church'. See this word at v. 6.
QUESTION—What letter does he refer to?
1. That letter has been lost [AB, Alf, Br, EBC, EGT, Herm, ICC, My, NIC, NTC, TH, TNTC, WBC, Ws], probably destroyed by Diotrephes [AB, EBC, NIC, TNTC]. It was a letter of commendation for itinerant preachers and a request that hospitality be shown them [Br, Brd, EBC, EGT, Herm, ICC, My, NIC, TNTC, WBC].
2. He is referring to 2 John [Lns, NCBC].
QUESTION—What does τι 'something' imply?
It implies that it was a letter of modest size [NIC, Ws]. The contents of the letter is not in focus [Alf, Brd, ICC, My, NTC, TH, Ws].
QUESTION—What church is he referring to?
He is speaking of the congregation of which Diotrephes' was a member [AB, Br, Brd, EBC, ICC, My, NCBC, NIC, NTC, TNTC, WBC]. The article with 'church' indicates that it was known to Gaius [AB, Alf, Br, Brd, EBC, ICC, Lns, My, NCBC, NIC, TH, TNTC, WBC], who was a member of that church [Alf, Br, Brd, ICC, Lns, My, NCBC, TH, TNTC, Ws], although his home might have been outside the town [EBC, NIC, WBC]. The reference to 'them' in the next clause might indicate that Gaius belonged to a nearby congregation [AB].

but[a] the-(one) loving-to-be-first[b] among-them, Diotrephes, does not accept/ receive[c] us.
LEXICON—a. ἀλλά (LN 89.125): 'but' [AB, HNTC, Lns, WBC; all versions].
b. pres. act. participle of φιλοπρωτεύω (LN **25.110**) (BAGD p. 861): 'to love to be first' [NASB, NIV], 'to like to be first' [AB], 'to love the first place' [TNT], 'to wish to be first' [BAGD, LN], 'to love to put oneself first' [WBC], 'to like to put oneself first' [NRSV], 'to like to be leader' [BAGD; TEV], 'to enjoy being leader' [NAB], 'to enjoy taking the lead' [REB], 'to enjoy being in charge' [NJB], 'to want to order others' [LN], 'to love to have preeminence' [KJV], 'to love to be foremost' [Lns]. This verb is also translated 'that power hungry man' [HNTC]. The present tense indicates that this is a habitual attitude [Brd].

c. pres. mid. (deponent = act.) indic. of ἐπιδέχομαι (LN **36.14**) (BAGD 2. p. 292): 'to accept' [BAGD; NASB, NJB, TNT], 'to acknowledge' [NRSV], 'to pay attention to' [AB, LN; TEV], 'to have to do with' [WBC; NIV, REB], 'to obey' [LN], 'to receive' [HNTC, Lns; KJV]. The phrase οὐκ ἐπιδέχεται 'not to accept' is translated 'to ignore' [NAB]. The present tense indicates that the refusal to receive them was a continuing action [AB].

QUESTION—What relationship is indicated by ἀλλά 'but'?

It contrasts Diotrephes' action with the implied expected action of acceptance of the author's authority [Alf, Brd, ICC, Lns]: I wrote to the church and that should have sufficed, but Diotrephes does not acknowledge us.

QUESTION—Who was Diotrephes?

He was a leader of a church [AB, EBC, Herm, ICC, My, NCBC, NIC, NTC, TNTC, WBC], perhaps self-appointed [Br, Lns, TH, WBC].

QUESTION—What is indicated by this description of Diotrephes?

It indicates the reason he does not receive the elder [AB, TH]. It may imply personal rivalry [EBC] from an ambitious man who has an inflated ego [EBC, EGT, NTC, TNTC].

QUESTION—Who is meant by αὐτῶν 'them'?

It means the members of the church [AB, Alf, Brd, Herm, ICC, WBC, Ws].

QUESTION—What is meant by ἐπιδέχεται 'accepts/receives'?

1. It means to acknowledge their authority [AB, Alf, BAGD, Brd, EGT, ICC, NCBC, TNTC, WBC, Ws; NIV, NRSV, REB, TEV, TNT]: I wrote to the church but Diotrephes does not accept our authority.
2. It means to favorably receive the letter sent by the elder [HNTC, Lns, NIC, TH]: I wrote to the church but Diotrephes pays no attention to what we wrote.
3. It means to be hospitable to the elder and his associates [AB, EGT, My, WBC]: I wrote to the church to receive our emissaries but Diotrephes refuses to welcome us. He does not receive the elder in the person of his delegates [EGT].

QUESTION—Who is meant by ἡμᾶς 'us'?

1. It is 'we exclusive' and refers to the author and his associates [AB, Br, Brd, EGT, HNTC, ICC, Lns, NIC, NTC, WBC, Ws; probably all versions except TEV]. His associates are the other apostles [AB], his messengers [Br, EGT, WBC], or all those who agree with him [ICC, Lns].
2. It is an editorial plural and refers to the author alone [Alf, TH, TNTC; TEV]: Diotrephes doesn't accept me.

10 Because-of[a] this, if[b] I-come,[c]

LEXICON—a. διά (LN 89.26): 'because of' [LN]. The phrase διὰ τοῦτο 'because of this' [Lns] is translated 'for this reason' [NASB], 'therefore' [AB; NAB], 'wherefore' [KJV], 'then' [TEV], 'so' [HNTC, WBC; NIV, NJB, NRSV, REB, TNT].

b. ἐάν (LN 67.32/89.67): 'if' [AB, HNTC, Lns; all versions except REB, TEV, TNT], 'when' [WBC; REB, TEV, TNT].
c. aorist act. subj. of ἔρχομαι (LN 15.81): 'to come' [AB, HNTC, Lns, WBC; all versions].

QUESTION—What relationship is indicated by διὰ τοῦτο 'because of this'?

It indicates the result of Diotrephes' response of not accepting them (v. 9) [AB, Brd, ICC, My]: Diotrephes does not accept us, therefore I will bring up this matter when/if I come.

QUESTION—What does the use of ἐάν 'if' imply about the author's intentions to come?

1. It implies that the author intends to come, the only uncertainty being the time he will come [Brd, Lns, My, NIC, NTC, TH, WBC, Ws; REB, TEV, TNT]: whenever I come.
2. It implies that the author is uncertain as to whether he will come [AB, EGT, ICC, NCBC]: if I come. He is still hoping that the matter can be resolved without his coming [AB].

I-will-bring-up^a his deeds^b which he-does

LEXICON—a. fut. act. indic. of ὑπομιμνῄσκω (LN **29.10**) (BAGD 1.b. p. 846): 'to bring up' [AB, BAGD, HNTC, WBC; TEV], 'to call attention to' [NASB, NIV, NRSV], 'to draw attention to' [REB], 'to speak publicly' [NAB], 'to tell everyone' [NJB], 'to remember' [KJV], 'to remind' [LN, Lns; TNT].
b. ἔργον (LN 42.11) (BAGD 1.c.β. p. 308): 'deed' [BAGD, LN; KJV, NASB], 'work' [Lns]. The phrase τὰ ἔργα ἃ ποιεῖ 'the deeds which he does' is translated 'what he is doing' [AB, WBC; NAB, NIV, NRSV, TNT], 'the things he is doing' [HNTC; REB], 'everything he has done' [TEV], 'how he has behaved' [NJB].

QUESTION—What is meant by ὑπομνήσω 'I will bring up'?

1. He will charge Diotrephes at a meeting of the church with the wrong he has been doing [AB, Alf, Brd, EBC, EGT, ICC, Lns, My, TNTC, WBC, Ws; NAB, NJB]. He will remind the congregation of what they already know [Lns] and perhaps of the misdeeds that were not known to everyone [EBC]. He will recall the conduct of their leader and show how it is wrong [ICC].
2. He will confront Diotrephes in private [NIC].

QUESTION—To what does ἔργον 'deeds' refer?

It is explained by the following clauses [Alf, WBC], and refers to slandering them, refusing hospitality to the brothers, and expelling members who want to be hospitable [AB, Alf, Herm, Lns, TH, TNTC, WBC].

with-evil^a words talking-nonsense^b about-us,

LEXICON—a. πονηρός (LN 88.110) (BAGD 1.b.β. p. 691): 'evil' [AB, BAGD, HNTC, LN; NAB], 'wicked' [BAGD, LN, Lns; NASB, NJB, TNT], 'bad' [BAGD], 'terrible' [TEV], 'vicious' [BAGD], 'malicious' [WBC; KJV, NIV], 'spiteful' [REB], 'false' [NRSV].

b. pres. act. participle of φλυαρέω (LN **33.374**) (BAGD p. 862): 'to talk nonsense about' [BAGD, LN], 'to spread nonsense' [AB; NAB], 'to pour out nonsense against' [TNT], 'to prate against' [Lns; KJV], 'to bring unjustified charges against' [BAGD], 'to make unjustified charges against' [WBC], 'to lay nonsensical charges' [REB], 'to make accusations against' [HNTC], 'to spread charges' [NRSV], 'to circulate accusations' [NJB], 'to unjustly accuse' [NASB], 'to gossip about' [NIV], 'to tell lies' [TEV]. The present tense indicates that this is a continuing action [Brd, Herm].

QUESTION—What is meant by φλυαρῶν 'talking nonsense'?

It means to make unjustified accusations against the elder [NIC, NTC, TNTC, WBC]. The accusations were mere nonsense [Br] because they were so far from the truth [Brd]. They were irrelevant [Alf]. The hostile intent of such talk is signaled by the description 'with evil words' [AB, TH].

and not being-satisfied[a] with these

LEXICON—a. pres. mid. participle of ἀρκέω (LN 59.47) (BAGD 2. p. 107): 'to be satisfied' [BAGD, HNTC, Lns; NASB, NIV], 'to be content' [AB, BAGD, WBC; KJV, NRSV, REB, TNT]. The phrase μὴ ἀρκούμενος ἐπὶ τούτοις 'not satisfied with these' is translated 'that is not all' [NAB], 'as if that is not enough' [NJB], 'that is not enough for him' [TEV].

QUESTION—To what does τούτοις 'these' refer?

It refers to the evil words mentioned in the preceding clause [Brd, Herm, NTC, TNTC], or it refers to the whole matter [Alf].

he (does) not receive[a] the brothers

LEXICON—a. pres. mid. (deponent = act.) indic. of ἐπιδέχομαι (LN 34.53) (BAGD 1. p. 292): 'to receive' [HNTC, LN, Lns, WBC; KJV, NASB, REB, TEV], 'to receive as a guest' [BAGD], 'to welcome' [AB, LN; NAB, NIV, NJB, NRSV, TNT]. The present tense indicates that this is a continuing action [AB, Alf, Brd, Herm, ICC, Lns, TH, WBC].

QUESTION—What is meant by not receiving the brothers?

It means that Diotrephes does not himself offer hospitality to the traveling missionaries [AB, Alf, BAGD, Br, Brd, EBC, Herm, ICC, LN, Lns, My, NIC, NTC, TNTC, WBC; NAB, NIV, NJB, NRSV, TNT]. The 'brothers' were traveling missionaries (v. 5) [Alf, Br, Brd, EBC, Herm, ICC, Lns, NTC, TH, TNTC]. They came from the elder [NIC] and were rejected along with the elder [EBC].

and he-prevents[a] the-(ones) wanting-to[b] and he-puts-(them)-out-of[c] the church.[d]

LEXICON—a. pres. act. indic. of κωλύω (LN 13.146) (BAGD 1. p. 461): 'to prevent' [BAGD, LN, WBC; NJB, NRSV], 'to hinder' [AB, BAGD, HNTC, LN; NAB], 'to interfere with' [REB], 'to forbid' [BAGD, Lns; KJV, NASB], 'to stop' [NIV, TEV, TNT], 'to stand in the way of' [BAGD].

b. pres. mid. (deponent = act.) participle of βούλομαι (LN 30.56) (BAGD 2.a.ζ. p. 146): 'to want to' [HNTC, Lns, WBC; NIV, NRSV, TEV], 'to like to' [NJB], 'to intend' [LN], 'to wish to' [AB; NAB], 'to desire to' [NASB], 'to will' [KJV, REB, TNT].

c. pres. act. indic. of ἐκβάλλω (LN 15.44) (BAGD 1. p. 237): 'to throw out' [Lns], 'to expel' [AB, BAGD, HNTC, LN, WBC; NAB, NJB, NRSV, REB, TNT], 'to put out' [NASB, NIV], 'to drive out' [BAGD, LN; TEV], 'to cast out' [KJV].

d. ἐκκλησία (LN 11.32): 'church' [AB, HNTC, Lns, WBC; all versions except REB], 'congregation' [REB].

QUESTION—What is meant by ἐκβάλλει 'he expels them'?
1. It means that Diotrephes excommunicates the church members who offered hospitality to the missionaries [AB, Alf, Br, EGT, Herm, ICC, Lns, NTC, TNTC]. Diotrephes was either in a position to order their excommunication [AB, Brd, EGT, Lns] or he influenced the decision of the church [AB, Brd, EGT, NIC].
2. It means that he 'drove them out' and refers to making it so uncomfortable for them that they voluntarily withdrew [TH, WBC].

QUESTION—What does the present tense of ἐκβάλλει 'he expels' indicate?
1. The present tense indicates that the casting out is a habitual action [AB, Alf, Herm, ICC, Lns, NIC, WBC]. In most cases he succeeded [Lns].
2. The present tense is conative, indicating that he was attempting to expel the people with no implication as to his success [Brd, EBC, EGT, NTC, TH, Ws; REB, TEV]. Assuming that Gaius was a member who offered hospitality and was not expelled, his attempts did not always succeed [Brd].

DISCOURSE UNIT: 11–12 [AB, EBC, EGT, Herm, NIC, NTC, TNTC; TEV]. The topic is an appeal to do good and a commendation of Demetrius [AB, EBC, Herm, NTC], a commendation of Demetrius [EGT, NIC, TNTC, Ws; TEV].

DISCOURSE UNIT: 11 [Alf, Br, Brd, NCBC]. The topic is an exhortation to do good [Alf, Br, Brd].

11 Beloved,[a] do-not imitate[b] the bad[c] but[d] the good.[e]

LEXICON—a. ἀγαπητός: 'beloved'. See this word at vv. 2, 5.
b. pres. mid. (deponent = act.) impera. of μιμέομαι (LN 41.44) (BAGD p. 522): 'to imitate' [AB, BAGD, HNTC, LN, Lns, WBC; NAB, NASB, NIV, NRSV, TEV], 'to follow' [BAGD; KJV], 'to follow an example' [NJB, REB, TNT].
c. κακός (LN 88.106) (BAGD 1.c. p. 397): 'bad' [AB; NJB, REB, TEV, TNT], 'evil' [BAGD, HNTC, LN, WBC; KJV, NAB, NASB, NIV, NRSV], 'base' [Lns].
d. ἀλλά (LN 89.125): 'but' [AB, HNTC, Lns, WBC; all versions except REB], not explicit [REB].

e. ἀγαθός (LN 88.1): 'good' [AB, HNTC, LN, Lns, WBC; all versions except NJB, REB], 'good example' [NJB, REB, TNT].

QUESTION—What does the repetition of ἀγαπητέ 'beloved' indicate?

It indicates the beginning of another unit of discourse as the author returns to his main topic and a request for action from Gaius [AB, Brd, NTC, WBC].

QUESTION—What is indicated by the order of κακόν 'bad' then ἀγαθόν 'good'?

This order is determined by the preceding bad example of Diotrephes (v. 10) and the following good example of Demetrius (v. 12) [AB]. The order 'bad/good' is in chiastic relationship with the following 'doing good/doing bad' [AB, Herm, NCBC, NIC, WBC]. This arrangement reinforces the warning [NIC, WBC].

QUESTION—What does this exhortation imply about Gaius' character?

It does not imply that Gaius was following the evil example of Diotrephes. Gaius was commended for doing good in vv. 5–6 and the elder now encourages him to continue doing so [EBC, EGT, NIC, NTC]. The elder expects that Diotrephes and his supporters will exert pressure on Gaius to stop supporting the elder and the missionaries coming from him, [EBC, NIC] and there will be a temptation to give in [Brd, TNTC, WBC].

QUESTION—What is meant by imitating the good and not the bad?

This is a general admonition [ICC, Lns, My, NCBC], but is especially applied to the issue of hospitality [AB, Herm, HNTC, NIC, NTC]. Diotrephes is a prime example of the bad [AB, Alf, Br, EGT, Herm, ICC, Lns, NIC, NTC, TH, TNTC, WBC]. Demetrius is an example of the good [Alf, Br, EGT, Herm, My, NCBC, NIC, NTC, TH, TNTC, WBC].

The-(one) doing-good[a] is from[b] God;

LEXICON—a. pres. act. participle of ἀγαθοποιέω (LN 88.3) (BAGD 2. p. 2): 'to do good' [AB, BAGD, HNTC, LN, Lns; all versions except NJB], 'to do the right' [WBC; NJB]. This verb is also translated as a noun: 'well-doer' [REB]. The present tense indicates that doing good is an habitual action [Brd, EGT].

b. ἐκ (LN 89.3): 'from' [Lns; NIV, NJB, NRSV], 'of' [KJV, NASB]. The phrase ἐκ ἐστιν 'is from' is translated 'to belong to' [AB, WBC; NAB, TEV, TNT], 'to be born of' [HNTC], 'to be a child of' [REB]. See this word at 1 John 4:4, 6.

QUESTION—What relationship is indicated by ἐκ 'from'?

It indicates that one's origin and empowering come from God [Alf, NTC, Ws], one's nature comes from God [WBC] and also one's motives for life and work [ICC, NIC]. The phrase is a shortened form for 'begotten by God' (1 John 3:10) [Brd, Lns].

the-(one) doing-bad[a] has-not-seen[b] God.

LEXICON—a. pres. act. participle of κακοποιέω (LN 88.112) (BAGD 1. p. 397): 'to do bad' [AB; TEV, TNT], 'to do wrong' [BAGD, LN; NJB], 'to do the base' [Lns], 'to do evil' [BAGD, HNTC, LN; KJV, NAB, NASB,

NIV, NRSV]. This verb is also translated as a noun: 'wrongdoer' [WBC], 'evildoer' [REB]. The present tense indicates that doing evil is a continuing or habitual action [Brd, EGT].
- b. perf. act. indic. of ὁράω (LN 24.1) (BAGD 1.c.β. p. 578): 'to see' [AB, HNTC, Lns, WBC; all versions], 'to have spiritual perception' [BAGD]. The perfect tense indicates that the seeing happened in the past but its effects remain in the present [TH, WBC]. See this word at 1 John 3:6.

QUESTION—What is meant by 'seeing' God?
It means to have fellowship with God [TH, WBC]. The one who sees Jesus has seen the Father [AB, Br, NTC, Ws]. We see God through the eyes of faith [Lns, TNTC].

DISCOURSE UNIT: 12 [Alf, Br, Brd, NCBC; NJB]. The topic is a recommendation of Demetrius [Alf, Br, Brd; NJB].

12 Demetrius has-been-testified-to[a] by[b] all and by the truth[c] itself;

LEXICON—a. perf. pass. indic. of μαρτυρέω: 'to be testified to'. See this word at vv. 3, 6. The perfect tense indicates that the previous testimony has a continuing effect [Lns, My, NTC, TH, TNTC, WBC, Ws], and stands as a fact [Brd]. This testimony has been given over a period of time [AB].
- b. ὑπό (LN 90.1): 'by' [Lns, WBC; NIV, NJB, REB], 'from' [AB, HNTC; NAB, NASB, TNT], 'of' [KJV, TEV], not explicit [NRSV].
- c. ἀλήθεια (LN 72.2): 'truth' [AB, HNTC, Lns, WBC; all versions].

QUESTION—Who was Demetrius?
He was not the Demetrius of Acts 19:23 or the Demas of Col. 4:14, Philemon 24, and 2 Tim. 4:10 [AB, Brd, EGT, Herm, ICC, NTC, TH, TNTC, WBC]. He probably was a traveling missionary [Lns, NIC, TH]. This is a letter of recommendation for Demetrius who would bring this letter to Gaius [AB, Br, Brd, EGT, HNTC, ICC, Lns, NCBC, NIC, TH, WBC, Ws]. He is renowned for his goodness and therefore is a fitting example to Gaius [NTC].

QUESTION—In what way did the people testify about Demetrius?
They spoke well of him [BAGD, HNTC, TH, WBC; KJV, NAB, NASB, NIV, NJB, NRSV, REB, TEV, TNT]. They testified that he truly believed and practiced his Christian faith [AB].

QUESTION—To whom does πάντων 'all' refer?
It means all who knew him [Alf, Br, Brd, Herm, HNTC, ICC, NTC], that is, all the Christians who knew him [AB, EGT, Lns, My, NIC, TH, WBC, Ws]. This hyperbole emphasizes the widespread extent of the testimony [Brd].

QUESTION—What is meant by the truth testifying to him?
1. It refers to the truth of God's revelation active in Demetrius' life [AB, Alf, Brd, EBC, EGT, ICC, NTC, TH, TNTC, WBC, Ws]. This rule of life gives a good testimony to the one who follows it [Alf]. Since he lived in harmony with the truth of the gospel, the truth testified as to what kind of person he was [Brd, EBC, ICC, NTC].

2. Truth is personified and stands for the Lord Jesus [Br] or the Spirit of truth [My].

and we also[a] testify and you-know[b] that our testimony[c] is true.[d]

TEXT—Instead of the singular οἶδας 'you know', some manuscripts have οἴδατε 'you (plural) know'. GNT does not mention this alternative. The plural form is followed only by KJV.

LEXICON—a. καί (LN 89.93): 'also' [KJV, NASB, NIV, NRSV, TNT], 'too' [NJB], 'as well' [AB, WBC; NAB], 'moreover' [Lns], not explicit [HNTC; REB, TEV].

b. perf. act. indic. of οἶδα (LN 28.1): 'to know' [AB, HNTC, LN, Lns, WBC; all versions].

c. μαρτυρία (LN 33.264) (BAGD 2.c. p. 493): 'testimony' [AB, HNTC, Lns, WBC; NAB, NIV, NJB, NRSV, REB], 'witness' [NASB], 'record' [KJV], 'report' [TNT], 'what we say' [TEV]. See this word at 1 John 5:9, 10, 11.

d. ἀληθής (LN 72.1) (BAGD 2. p. 36): 'true' [AB, BAGD, HNTC, LN, Lns, WBC; all versions].

QUESTION—To whom does ἡμεῖς 'we' refer?
1. It refers to the elder and his associates [AB, EGT, Herm, ICC, Lns, My, NIC, TH, WBC, Ws]. It refers to those with apostolic authority [AB, EGT, My, WBC, Ws]. It refers to the elder and all others who know Demetrius personally [ICC]. It refers to the elder and all the missionaries traveling with Demetrius [Lns].
2. It refers to only the elder himself and means 'I' [Alf, Br, Brd, NTC, TNTC].

DISCOURSE UNIT: 13–15 [Alf, Brd, EBC, EGT, Herm, ICC, Lns, NIC, TH, TNTC, WBC, Ws; NJB, TEV]. The topic is the conclusion [Alf, Brd, EGT, Herm, ICC, Lns, Ws; TEV], personal remarks and a farewell greeting [EBC, NIC, WBC].

DISCOURSE UNIT: 13–14 [AB, Br, NCBC, NTC]. The topic is the promised visit [AB], personal notes [Br], the conclusion [Brd, Herm, NTC].

13 Many-things I-have to write to you, but I do-not want by-means-of ink and pen to write to you;

Note: For comments concerning the material in vv. 13–14, see the discussion of 2 John 12. Verb tenses and some wording are different but the gist of the two passages is the same.

QUESTION—What does the imperfect tense εἶχον 'have' indicate?
1. The imperfect tense indicates that the author had planned a longer letter but changed his mind [Alf, Brd, Lns, NTC]: I had planned to write many things to you, but I won't now.
2. The imperfect tense indicates an unfulfilled obligation [AB, Herm, NIC, TH, WBC]: I have many things that I should write to you. He was released from the obligation by the upcoming personal visit [NIC, WBC].

QUESTION—What is indicated by the use of the aorist tense of γράψαι 'to write'?
1. The verb is an epistolary aorist which regards the letter from the viewpoint of the recipient [AB, WBC].
2. The aorist indicates that the author is thinking of the letter as a whole [Brd, EGT, ICC].

14 but[a] I-hope[b] immediately[c] to-see[d] you and mouth to mouth[e] we-will-speak.[f]

LEXICON—a. δέ (LN 89.124): 'but' [KJV, NASB], 'instead' [NRSV], 'rather' [AB, HNTC; NAB], 'however' [NJB], 'moreover' [Lns], not explicit [WBC; NIV, REB, TEV, TNT].
  b. pres. act. indic. of ἐλπίζω (LN 30.54) (BAGD 2. p. 252): 'to hope' [AB, BAGD, HNTC, Lns, WBC; all versions except KJV], 'to trust' [KJV]. See this word at 2 John 12.
  c. εὐθέως (LN **67.53**) (BAGD p. 320): 'immediately' [BAGD, Lns], 'at once' [BAGD], 'soon' [AB, HNTC, WBC; all versions except KJV, NASB], 'shortly' [KJV, NASB].
  d. aorist act. infin. of ὁράω (LN 34.50): 'to see' [AB, HNTC, Lns, WBC; all versions].
  e. στόμα πρὸς στόμα (LN 83.39) (BAGD 1.a. p. 769): 'mouth to mouth' [Lns]. This phrase is translated 'face to face' [BAGD, HNTC, LN, WBC; all versions except NJB, TEV], 'person to person' [LN], 'in person' [NJB], 'personally' [TEV], 'heart to heart' [AB]. See this phrase at 2 John 12.
  f. fut. act. indic. of λαλέω (LN 33.70) (BAGD 2.a.ε. p. 463): 'to speak' [BAGD, Lns; KJV, NASB, TNT], 'to talk' [HNTC, WBC; all versions except KJV, NASB, TNT]. See this word at 2 John 12.

QUESTION—What is meant by εὐθέως 'immediately'?
It implies that the intended journey is very near [AB, Brd, ICC, Lns, NIC, NTC, TH, WBC]. It will occur very soon after the letter arrives [Br]. There is an urgent need to confront Diotrephes [Brd, ICC, WBC].

DISCOURSE UNIT: 15 [AB, Br, NCBC]. The topic is the conclusion [AB, Br, NCBC].

15 Peace[a] to-you.

TEXT—Some commentaries and translations include this material in verse 14 and have no verse 15 [Brd, NTC, TNTC; KJV, NASB, NIV, NJB, REB]. The GNT and some commentaries and translations begin verse 15 here [AB, Alf, EBC, EGT, Herm, HNTC, ICC, Lns, NCBC, TH, WBC, Ws; NAB, NRSV, TEV, TNT].

LEXICON—a. εἰρήνη (LN 22.42) (BAGD 2. p. 227): 'peace' [AB, HNTC, Lns, WBC; all versions], 'welfare' [BAGD].

QUESTION—What is meant by εἰρήνη 'peace'?

It is a standard epistolary greeting and reflects the Jewish greeting *shalom* [AB, Br, Brd, EGT, Herm, HNTC, ICC, My, NIC, NTC, TNTC, WBC, Ws]. He wishes Gaius peace because of the strife caused by Diotrephes' actions [Brd, EBC, Lns, TNTC].

The friends[a] greet[b] you.

LEXICON—a. φίλος (LN 34.11) (BAGD 2.a.α. p. 861): 'friend' [BAGD, HNTC, LN, Lns, WBC; all versions except NAB], 'beloved' [AB; NAB].

b. pres. mid. (deponent = act.) indic. of ἀσπάζομαι (LN 33.20) (BAGD 1.a. p. 116): 'to greet' [BAGD, HNTC, LN, WBC; NASB, TNT], 'to send greetings' [AB, BAGD, LN; NAB, NIV, NRSV, REB, TEV], 'to salute' [Lns; KJV]. This is also translated 'greetings from' [NJB].

QUESTION—To whom does φίλοι 'friends' refer?

1. It refers to the Christians in the church where the author is [AB, Br, Brd, EGT, Herm, NIC, NTC, TNTC, WBC]: your friends here send you their greetings. This includes some whom Gaius does not personally know [AB] and reminds him that all those with the elder consider themselves his friends [EBC].
2. It refers to the friends he actually knows in the town where the author is [Alf, Lns, My, TH].

Greet[a] the-friends by[b] name.[c]

LEXICON—a. pres. middle (deponent = act.) impera. of ἀσπάζομαι (LN 33.20) (BAGD 1.a. p. 116): 'to greet' [AB, BAGD, HNTC, WBC; all versions], 'send greetings' [BAGD], 'to salute' [Lns].

b. κατά (LN 89.90) (BAGD II.3.b. p. 406): 'by' [Lns, WBC; KJV, NASB, NIV], 'in detail' [BAGD]. The phrase 'κατ' ὄνομα 'by name' is translated 'each by name' [AB; NAB, NJB, NRSV, REB, TNT], 'every one' [HNTC], 'individually' [BAGD], 'personally' [TEV].

c. ὄνομα (LN 33.126) (BAGD I.3. p. 571): 'name' [Lns, WBC; KJV, NASB, NIV]. For AB, BAGD, HNTC; NAB, NJB, NRSV, REB, TEV, TNT, see above.

QUESTION—To whom does φίλους 'friends' refer?

'Friends' refers to those friends the elder knows in the church where Gaius is located [Alf, Lns, My], or perhaps to all the Christians there who do not side with Diotrephes [AB, Br, Herm, NIC, TH, WBC]. Some think that he means all the Christians there [Br, EBC, EGT, NTC, TNTC].

QUESTION—What is meant by greeting them 'by name'?

It means to greet each one individually when Gaius sees them [AB, BAGD, Brd, HNTC, My, TH, TNTC, WBC; all versions except KJV, NASB, NIV]. It implies that the elder knew each individual there [EGT] or that the elder might not have known all the names of the true Christians there, but Gaius would [AB]. He wants them greeted individually because corporate greetings are not possible with Diotrephes blocking them in the church meetings [Brd, NIC].

www.ingramcontent.com/pod-product-compliance
Lightning Source LLC
Chambersburg PA
CBHW051521230426
43668CB00012B/1688